D0890331

St. Louis

FAMILY HISTORY RESEARCH GUIDE

ANN CARTER FLEMING

2008

Fleming Publishing
St. Louis, Missouri

St. Louis Family History Research Guide
Fleming, Ann Carter
2008

ISBN: 978-0-9815943-0-9

Permission to use quotes and graphics from:
Missouri Historical Society
Mr. Ross Wagner
National Park Service, Jefferson National Expansion Memorial
St. Louis City Recorder of Deeds Office
St. Louis Genealogical Society

Cover design: Heather Henderson

     Old Courthouse image provided by the
     National Park Service, Jefferson National Expansion Memorial

Fleming Publishing
Post Office Box 8486
St. Louis, Missouri 63132

Dedication

To Cameron and Jackson

and

the "Puddle of People" who encouraged and supported this effort.

Table of Contents

History

Communities & Neighborhoods

Research Facilities

Records

Appendix

Index

Introduction

St. Louis research can be challenging for those unfamiliar with the history of the area. After the 1876 separation of the City of St. Louis from the County of St. Louis, researchers have two sets of local governmental records to review. The primary focus of this book is to outline repositories and records pertaining to St. Louis. While some readers live in the St. Louis area with the repositories within an easy drive, other readers live out of town. For them the book provides Family History Library (FHL) film numbers.

St. Louis was one of the earliest counties formed in Missouri. Just two years after statehood, the City of St. Louis incorporated in 1823; however, that area covered only a small part of St. Louis County. As the population grew, the City limits and the size of the City of St. Louis expanded to its current boundaries. The remainder of St. Louis County consisted of small villages and towns such as Ballwin, Chesterfield, Concord, Kirkwood, Manchester, and St. Ferdinand (Florissant).

In 1876, the City decided to separate or divorce itself from St. Louis County. St. Louis County established a new government with the records starting in 1877. St. Louis City retained the pre-1877 St. Louis County records. Therefore, for records prior to 1877, researchers should search St. Louis County records held at St. Louis City Hall.

Since 1877, both St. Louis City Hall in downtown St. Louis and St. Louis County Government Center in Clayton generate records for the area residents. Researchers should review records at both facilities. City or County residents may obtain a marriage license in either location. Birth and death records are recorded where the event takes place and area hospitals are found in both jurisdictions.

This publication uses the name St. Louis when either jurisdiction applies. The headers listed below provide guidance as to research options based on the record and the time period.

ST. LOUIS COUNTY — AFTER 1876

ST. LOUIS CITY — AFTER 1876

ST. LOUIS COUNTY — BEFORE 1877

This book does not list the location of each title as several research facilities may hold the same books and microfilms. In addition those same facilities continue to add to their collection. On the other hand, archival repositories have one-of-a-kind items that are only available at their location. A good first research stop is either St. Louis County Library, Special Collections or St. Louis Public Library. Review the catalogs to determine which resources are available at each facility.

The librarians at these facilities are keenly aware of their collection and many are familiar with the collections at other facilities. Many are also genealogists and understand your research challenges. When visiting a facility for the first time, talk to the staff about the procedures and rules. Some offer lockers, some use pencils only, most offer electrical outlets for laptops, and all have a friendly staff.

Special thanks to many people who shared their knowledge about their facility and its holdings: Ron Bolte, Carondelet Historical Society; Scott Holl, Archives at Eden Seminary; Rosemary Davidson, Historic Florissant; Dennis Northcott, Missouri Historical Society Research Library; Patricia Lubberts, Missouri State Archives; Joan Stewart, Sappington House; Marie Ceselski and Dusty Reese, St. Louis City Hall; Joyce Loving, St. Louis County Library; Jeanette Zinkgraf, St. Louis County Archives; Cynthia Millar, St. Louis Public Library; Pam Sanfillipo, Whitehaven, U.S. Parks Department; and Bob Moore, Jennifer Clark, and Thomas Dewey, Old Courthouse, U.S. Parks Department.

Every author needs help and I am blessed with a great support team. Advisors, editors, and proofreaders include Joan Beach; Mary Berthold; Pamela K. Boyer, CG, CGL; Darlene Chambers; Christine Hughes; Larry Franke; Kay Haviland Freilich CG, CGL; Ruth Ann Hager CG, CGL; Ilene Murray; retired Col. Richard Sayre, CG; and Patricia Walls Stamm CG, CGL. Heather Henderson designed the cover and the layout within this publication. Their assistance, encouragement, and support enhanced this publication. And last but not least, thank you to my husband, James Fleming, for his support and inspiration during this project.

For many years I have gathered information about research in St. Louis with new resources, new facilities, and of course the Internet emerging over that time. Change will continue. Perhaps in a few years we will need a second edition. In the meantime, follow the footprints and find the facts.

St. Louis History

I have found a situation where I intend to establish a settlement,
which may become hereafter one of the finest cities in America.

Pierre Laclede, 1763[1]

Founded by Frenchmen in 1764, St. Louis was under French or Spanish rule until 1803 when it had fewer than 1,000 residents. The early citizens, most of whom were French, preferred French or Spanish rule to that of the British. Most had previously emigrated from France via New Orleans or Detroit and then on to Kaskaskia, Illinois. Prior to the Louisiana Purchase, many of these early French citizens migrated from Kaskaskia to St. Louis.

Numerous Kaskaskia records are extant.[2] The nearby Fort de Chartres, which is from the same era, is open and considered an Illinois State Historic Site. The Fort's records and its history may be of interest as well.

Kaskaskia Under the French Regime[3] and "Kaskaskia and Its Parish Records" published in the *Magazine of American History*[4] both provide information about some early pioneers.

In 1780, St. Louis had a Spanish militia consisting of two companies. In 1972, Robert Parkin, then president of St. Louis Genealogical Society and noted local genealogist, published the roster along with very limited biographical information. He also published a list of 525 Missouri

---

1. William Hyde and Howard L. Conard, editors, *Encyclopedia of the History of St. Louis, A Compendium of History and Biography for Ready Reference,* 4 volumes (New York: Southern Historical Press, 1899), 1: 683.
2. Missouri Historical Society has manuscripts from Kaskaskia including: Nettie H. Beauregard and Leon Papin, indexers, *Kaskaskia Church Register: Registre des Batêmes Dans l'Eglise de Notre Dame de l'Immaculée Conception aux Cascakias, 1695–1815* (No place: privately printed, no date). Nettie H. Beauregard, indexer, *Registre des marriages aux Kaskaskias, 1741–1834* (No place: privately printed, no date). Nettie H. Beauregard, transcriber, *Abstracts of Kaskaskia Marriage Contracts: From 1720 to 1778, and Copy of "Repertoire Général des Papiers du Greffier des Illinois," from 1714 to 1758; With an Appendix, Giving a List of Kaskaskia Documents in Possession of the University of Illinois* (No place: privately printed, 1912).
3. Natalia Belting, *Kaskaskia Under the French Regime* (Urbana: University of Illinois, 1948).
4. Edward G. Mason, "Kaskaskia and Its Parish Records," *Magazine of American History* 6 (March 1881): 161–182.

Revolutionary War soldiers, with the names of each soldier's wife or widow, birth and death dates as known for both, state from which they moved or served, and the Missouri county in which they lived. Many St. Louis families are included.[5]

Following the Lewis and Clark expedition, fur trading was important to the early St. Louis economy. Many of the notable fur traders and western explorers came through St. Louis on their way west, some living in the area for a number of years.[6] The leading citizens of St. Louis organized and owned the Missouri Fur Trade Company. Early court records include suits with the Missouri Fur Trade Company as either the plaintiff or defendant.[7]

The early St. Louis records were created under the French or Spanish rule. The United States received this collection of records in 1805 with the transfer of the property; however, some records found their way to Havana, Cuba, and Seville, Spain. Those documents are part of a collection called the Cuban Papers. Missouri Historical Society Research Library has some finding aids and early records for the Cuban Papers including the *Descriptive Catalogue of the Documents Relating to the History of the United States in the Papeles Procedentes de Cuba Deposited in the Archivo General de Indias at Seville.*[8]

Houck's *The Spanish Regime in Missouri* outlines the Spanish history, times, and records.[9] Other publications such as *French and Spanish Records of Louisiana* provide further information.[10] Billon's two publications, *Annals of St. Louis*, provide details about life in the early years of St. Louis.[11]

The settlers requested and received land grants, married, died, and filed probate records. More than one hundred years later, the Works Progress Administration (WPA) prepared an index for the 1766–1804 transactions. At least two sets of the index cards survive in the twenty-first century. The set at Missouri Historical Society Research Library lists each resident, along with spelling variations, and some biographical information. This card set lists the instrument

---

5.   Robert Parkin, "The Revolution in the Environs of St. Louis," *Spirit of '76 St. Louis Genealogical Society Fair*, May 6, 1972 (St. Louis: The Society, 1972); FHL film, 924,689, item 1.

6.   LeRoy R. Hafen, *The Mountain Men and the Fur Trade of the Far West* (Glendale, California: A. H. Clark Company, 1965).

7.   "Circuit Court Records," *Missouri State Archives* (http://www.sos.mo.gov/archives).

8.   Roscoe R. Hill, *Descriptive Catalogue of the Documents Relating to the History of the United States in the Papeles Procedentes de Cuba Deposited in the Archivo General de Indias at Seville* (Washington, D.C.: Carnegie Institute of Washington, 1916).

9.   Louis Houck, *The Spanish Regime in Missouri: A Collection of Papers and Documents Relating to Upper Louisiana Principally within the Present Limits of Missouri During the Dominion of Spain, from the Archives of the Indies at Seville, etc., Translated from the Original Spanish into English, and Including Also Some Papers Concerning the Supposed Grant to Col. George Morgan at the Mouth of the Ohio, Found in the Congressional Library* (Chicago: R.R. Donnelley and Sons, 1909).

10.   Henry P. Beers, *French and Spanish Records of Louisiana: A Bibliographical Guide to Archive and Manuscript Sources* (Baton Rouge: Louisiana State University Press, 1989). Also, William E. Foley, *A History of Missouri: 1673 to 1820*, volume 1 (1971; reprint, Columbia: University of Missouri Press, 1986).

11.   Frederic Louis Billon, *Annals of St. Louis: The French and Spanish Period* (St. Louis: The Author, 1886). Frederic Louis Billon, *Annals of St. Louis in Its Territorial Days* (St. Louis: The Author, 1888). Charles E. Peterson, *Colonial St. Louis: Building a Creole Capital* (Tucson, Arizona: The Patrice Press, 1993).

(document) numbers and many of those documents are on file at that facility. This information is available on microfilm as well. The other set with slight variations, is housed at the Old Courthouse along with some of the other documents. If your ancestors were in St. Louis in that time period, it may be beneficial to check both sets.

The early French often used two surnames separated by the word *dit* and thus called the *dit names*. Long before statehood, the *dit* names disappeared. One brother may have dropped one name while the other made the opposite choice. For example, Charles Bienvenue *dit* DeLisle became Charles DeLisle. His brother John may have used the Bienvenue name and dropped DeLisle. When using indexes and alphabetical lists, it is important to check both surnames previously used in the *dit* names. *Collet's General Index to St. Louis County Archives*, which is available at most research facilities, has a list of citizens with *dit* names.[12]

When France ceded the property to the United States in 1803, the area citizens automatically gained U.S. citizenship and St. Louis experienced rapid growth. The former District of Louisiana became the Territory of Louisiana. In 1812, the territory divided forming the Territory of Missouri with St. Louis as the capital. In 1821, Missouri became a state with St. Charles and then the City of Jefferson, now called Jefferson City, serving as the capital.

Built in 1805, Fort Belle Fontaine played an important role during the territorial period of St. Louis. This was the first military post or fort west of the Mississippi River after the Louisiana Purchase. The fort served as a trading post, in addition to its military activities. Many expeditions, including that of Lewis and Clark on their return trip, stopped at the post. In 1826, Jefferson Barracks, located south of St. Louis along the Mississippi River, replaced Fort Belle Fontaine. Currently Fort Belle Fontaine Historical Society maintains the history of the former facility.

Some publications provide an overview of the early laws for such items as alimony, bigamy, and slaves.[13] *Citizens of Missouri Territory to 1835* provides data from the American State Papers. This publication may be easier to read than the American State Papers and summarizes the Missouri entries.[14]

The territorial and legislative leaders produced more and more records as the territory moved toward statehood.[15] Auguste Chouteau wrote *Fragment of Col. Auguste Chouteau's Narrative of the Settlement of St. Louis* providing his version of those earliest days. Chouteau's son, Gabriel, donated a portion of the French document to the St. Louis Mercantile Library in the 1850s. The Library published the document, translated into English.[16]

---

12.   Oscar W. Collet, compiler, *Collet's General Index to St. Louis County Archives* (St. Louis: Globe-Democrat, 1876).

13.   Henry S. Geyer, *A Digest of Missouri Territory, To Which Have Been Added a Variety of Forms Useful to Magistrates* (St. Louis: Joseph Charless, 1818). *Laws of the Territory of Louisiana: Comprising All Those Which Are Now Actually in Force Within the Same* (St. Louis: Joseph Charless, 1808).

14.   Francis T. Ingmire, *Citizens of Missouri Territory to 1835,* 3 volumes (Signal Mountain, Tennessee: Mountain Press, 1984).

15.   *Index to Archives Records, Deeds, Land Grants Dated, 1816–1848, and Archives Records, Deeds, Land Grants, French and Spanish, 1816–1848, St. Louis, Missouri* (Salt Lake: Genealogical Society of Utah, 1968), 68.

16.   *Fragment of Col. Auguste Chouteau's Narrative of the Settlement of St. Louis* (St. Louis: St. Louis Mercantile Library, 1989).

Territorial Supreme Court records dating from 1783 to 1820 are available on microfilm with an index on the first roll. The General Court minute books for a similar time period are also available at Missouri Historical Society Research Library.

St. Louis eventually had steamboats lining the riverfront bringing immigrants from many foreign lands, some settling in St. Louis, others moving farther west. St. Louis experienced difficult times, such as the riverfront fires and epidemics, as well as good times, such as the 1904 World's Fair. St. Louis became the home of many nationally recognized businesses, such as Anheuser-Busch, formed by two German immigrants, and the St. Louis Cardinals, who are second only to the Yankees in World Series wins.

Figure 1: St. Louis County before 1818

Numerous history books chronicle the development of the area, some multi-volume scholarly books and others are easy to carry paperback reference manuals. The following selected list of books, with annotations, references the history of St. Louis. These books cover the territorial days, early statehood, the steamboat era, the World's Fair, and beyond. All the while, individuals lived and died in St. Louis leaving their footprints in history and records.

- Billon, Frederic Louis. *Annals of St. Louis in the Early Days under the French and Spanish Dominations.* St. Louis: F. L. Billon, 1886.

- Billon, Frederic Louis. *Annals of St. Louis in the Territorial Days from 1804 to 1821: Being a Continuation of the Author's Previous Work.* St. Louis: F. L. Billon, 1888.

- Bishop, William Henry. *St. Louis in 1884.* Golden, Colorado: Outbooks, 1977.

- Bryan, William S., and Robert Rose. *A History of the Pioneer Families of Missouri, with Numerous Sketches, Anecdotes, Adventures, etc., Relating to Early Days of Missouri.* St. Louis: Bryan Brand and Company, 1876.

- Carter, Clarence Edwin, compiler. *The Territorial Papers of the United States, volumes 13–15, Louisiana–Missouri Territory [1803–1821].* Washington, D.C.: Government Printing Office, 1948–1951.

- Conard, Howard L., editor. *Encyclopedia of the History of Missouri, A Compendium of History and Biography for Ready Reference.* 6 volumes. St. Louis: Southern History Company, 1901.

- Cox, James. *Old and New St. Louis: A Concise History of the Metropolis of the West and Southwest, with a Review of Its Present Greatness and Immediate Prospects.* St. Louis: Central Biographical Publishing Company, 1894. [Index at St. Louis Public Library website; digital publication at HeritageQuest.]

- Darcus, J. A., and James W. Buel. *A Tour of St. Louis, or the Inside Life of a Great City.* St. Louis: Western Publishing Company, 1878. [Index at St. Louis Public Library website.]

- Edwards, Richard, and M. Hopewell. *Edwards's Great West and Her Commercial Metropolis, Embracing a General View of the West and a Complete History of St. Louis, from the Landing of Ligueste, in 1764, to the Present Time; With Portraits and Biographies of Some of the Old Settlers, and Many of the Most Prominent Business Men.* St. Louis: Edward's Monthly, Trubner and Company, 1860. [Digital publication at HeritageQuest.]

- Faherty, William Barnaby. *St. Louis: A Concise History.* St. Louis: Print/Graphics, 1999.

- Faherty, William Barnaby. *The St. Louis Portrait.* Tulsa, Oklahoma: Continental Heritage, 1978.

- Hagen, Harry M. *This is Our Saint Louis.* St. Louis: Knight Publishing Company, 1970. [Index at St. Louis Public Library website. This book has more than 200 photos from the late nineteenth century and early twentieth century.]

- *History of St. Louis County, Missouri: A Compendium of Useful Information Written and Compiled from the Most Authentic Official and Private Sources.* Clayton: Watchman-Advocate, 1920.

- Hodes, Frederick A. *Beyond the Frontier: A History of St. Louis to 1821.* Tucson, Arizona: Patrice Press, 2004.

- Houck, Louis. *A History of Missouri: From the Earliest Explorations and Settlements Until the Admission of the State into the Union.* 3 volumes. Chicago: R. R. Donnelley and Sons Company, 1908.

- Hyde, William, and Howard L. Conard, editors. *Encyclopedia of the History of St. Louis, A Compendium of History and Biography for Ready Reference.* 4 volumes. New York: Southern Historical Press, 1899. [Index at St. Louis Public Library website; digital publication at HeritageQuest.]

- Kinnaird, Lawrence, editor. *Spain in the Mississippi Valley, 1765–1794.* 3 volumes. Washington, D.C.: Government Printing Office, 1949.

- Lionberger, Isaac. *Annals of St. Louis: A Brief Account of Its Foundation and Progress, 1764–1928.* St. Louis: Missouri Historical Society, 1930. [Digital publication at Heritage Quest.]

- Primm, James Neal. *Lion in the Valley: Saint Louis, Missouri.* 2nd edition. Boulder, Colorado: Pruett Publishing Company, 1990.

- Sanfilippo, Pamela K. *Agriculture in Antebellum St. Louis.* St. Louis: U.S. Grant National Historic Site, 2000.

- Scharf, J. Thomas. *History of Saint Louis City and County, From the Earliest Periods to the Present Day: Including Biographical Sketches of Representative Men.* 2 volumes. Philadelphia: L. H. Everts and Company, 1883. [Index at St. Louis Public Library website.]

- Sandweiss, Eric. *St. Louis: The Evolution of an American Urban Landscape.* Philadelphia: Temple University Press, 2001.

- Shoemaker, Floyd C. *Missouri's Struggle for Statehood, 1804–1821*. Jefferson City: Hugh Stephens, 1916.

- Shepard, Elihu H. *The Early History of St. Louis and Missouri*. St. Louis: privately printed, 1870.

- Smith, Clifford Neal. *Spanish and British Land Grants in Mississippi Territory, 1750–1784*. Baltimore: Genealogical Publishing Company, 2004.

- Stadler, Frances Hurd. *St. Louis: History of the City from Its Founding to the Eve of Its 200th Anniversary*. St. Louis: KSD and Kriegshauser, 1962.

- St. Louis Planning Commission. "Physical Growth of the City of Saint Louis." City of St. Louis Community Information Network, http://stlouis.missouri.org/heritage/History69/#intro .

- Stevens, Walter B. *St. Louis, The Fourth City, 1764–1909*. 3 volumes. St. Louis: S. J. Clarke Publishing Company, 1909. [Index at St. Louis Public Library website; digital publication at HeritageQuest.]

- Thomas, William L. *History of St. Louis County, Missouri*. St. Louis: S. J. Clarke Publishing, 1911. [Index at St. Louis Public Library website.]

- Troen, Selwyn K. *A Guide to Resources on the History of St. Louis*. St. Louis: University of Missouri, 1971.

- Van Ravenswaay, Charles. *St. Louis: An Informal History of the City and Its People, 1764–1865*. St. Louis: Missouri Historical Society, 1991.

- Vexler, Robert. *Saint Louis: A Chronology and Documentary History, 1762–1970*. St. Louis: Oceana, 1974.

- Williams, Walter, and Floyd Calvin Shoemaker. *Missouri: Mother of the West*. Chicago: American Historical Society, 1930.

ST. LOUIS GOVERNMENT

St. Louis County — Before 1877

As the area developed and the population grew, the county boundaries changed. Your ancestor may have lived in one location with the county name changing around him. St. Louis was one of the original five counties in Missouri Territory in 1812. The St. Louis County boundaries were from the Mississippi River to what is now the western edge of the state of Missouri.

The Missouri legislature established the current St. Louis County boundaries in 1818 with the formation of Franklin and Jefferson Counties. By 1861, there were 114 counties in Missouri and the only county boundary change in the state after that date was the separation or divorce of St. Louis City and St. Louis County.[17]

The separation or divorce of St. Louis City and St. Louis County caused the only county level boundary change since that time. Among the cities, towns, and villages in early St. Louis County (today's City and County combined) were St. Louis City, Carondelet, Creve Coeur, and

---

17.   Robert A. Cohn, *The History and Growth of St. Louis, Missouri* (St. Louis: St. Louis County Government, 1962).

Florissant. Missouri state law allowed the City of St. Louis to incorporate in 1823 and it soon elected its first mayor, William Carr Lane.

Post offices usually indicate the population centers and growth for a community. In 1837, St. Louis County had the following post offices: [18]

- Carondelet
- Fenton
- Florissant
- Fox Creek (Wildwood)
- Jefferson Barracks
- Manchester
- Owen's Station (Bridgeton)
- St. Louis City
- Waltonham (Overland)

Prior to 1876, the majority of the citizens, maybe as many as eighty percent, lived within the current St. Louis City boundaries. History tells us that the City fathers thought the County residents were a drain on the economy and decided to separate from the County. Several publications provide more in-depth information on this event. [19]

St. Louis City was the seat for St. Louis County government until the City-County division. [20] When the City and County separated, the records remained with the City. These records are currently available at St. Louis City Hall and the Civil Courts Building.

St. Louis City — After 1876

After the separation of St. Louis City and County, St. Louis City became an independent city, with the current boundaries. By state law, the City has a City government, plus County offices such as the office of the Recorder of Deeds, just like other Missouri counties.

The City population continued to grow for many years. The political division went from six wards in 1850 to twenty-eight wards by 1910. As the population grew, some City residents moved beyond the City Limits, into the County. The largest migration to the County came after World War II, with affordable new housing often the draw plus more automobiles and highways.

Several buildings have served as the seat of government for St. Louis. Used from 1827 to 1851, the first building was located on Market and Walnut Streets. The City then rented space in the building now known as the Old Courthouse until 1872, when a "temporary building" was constructed. Constructed in the 1890s and opened in 1898, the current City Hall has served the community ever since. [21]

---

18.   Alphonso Wetmore, *Gazetteer of the State of Missouri, 1837* (1837; reprint, New York: Arno Press, 1975).

19.   E. Terrance Jones, *Fragmented by Design: Why St. Louis Has So Many Governments* (St. Louis: Palmerston and Reed Publishers, 2000). William N. Cassella, Jr., "City County Separation: The Great Divorce of 1876," *Missouri Historical Society Bulletin* 15 (January 1959): 85–104.

20.   "St. Louis Mayors," *St. Louis Public Library* (http://exhibits.slpl.org/mayors).

21.   *City Hall, St. Louis, Missouri* (St. Louis: City Hall, 1990). This pamphlet outlines the floor plan, construction, art work, and changes in City Hall.

While visiting City Hall to obtain your family documents, look at the stately building where you and your ancestors walked. The Archives office in the Recorder of Deeds office is very helpful to genealogists and will direct you to the appropriate records. City Hall has an adjoining parking lot.

St. Louis County — After 1876

The new or revised St. Louis County formed its government in 1877 with the establishment of a county seat in Clayton. The County had a fraction of the number of residents compared to the City. Various early farming communities such as Ballwin, Creve Coeur, Florissant, Kirkwood, Manchester, and Mehlville developed, along with their churches, cemeteries, and schools. Several books outline the growth of St. Louis County after 1877.[22] *History of the Old Roads, Pioneers, and Early Communities of St. Louis County* provides details of the early years in the newly reformatted county.[23]

Records for events that occurred after 1876, check both City and County. Some people lived in one jurisdiction and filed records in the other jurisdiction. It was very common for a couple to obtain their marriage license in one jurisdiction and have the ceremony performed in the other.

Before visiting the County Government Center, determine if the records you seek are available on microfilm or microfiche at St. Louis County Library, Special Collections. They have a growing St. Louis County collection.

The County buildings are easy to access with a visitor parking lot across the street.

---

22.   Robert A. Cohn, *The History and Growth of St. Louis County* (St. Louis: St. Louis County, 1974). *History of St. Louis County, Missouri* (St. Louis: Watchman-Advocate, 1920). *Our Towns: A Guide to the Cities, Neighborhoods, and Villages Where We Live* (St. Louis: St. Louis Post-Dispatch, 2006).

23.   Henry Gustav Hertich, *History of the Old Roads, Pioneers, and Early Communities of St. Louis County* (St. Louis: St. Louis County Library, Special Collections, 2004).

St. Louis City Neighborhoods

The City of St. Louis had grown from a small village in the 1700s to a large metropolitan area by the time it separated from St. Louis County in 1876. Many foreign immigrants and those migrating from points east in the United States had arrived, inflating the population. While all are part of the City of St. Louis, many individual neighborhoods have an ethnic or regional focus. As an example, the area near Missouri Botanical Garden is often called the Shaw or Garden District. The adjoining area is the Tower Grove neighborhood and nearby is The Hill, an area with good Italian restaurants and many residents with Italian ancestors.

Locally, the community uses regional terms to distinguish the City areas. North St. Louis, South St. Louis, Downtown, and the Central West End are four common general geographic terms. If someone refers to the East Side, they are speaking of the adjoining area in Illinois. Today many local citizens travel back and forth across the Mississippi River on a daily basis.

A variety of books are available on the neighborhoods and landmarks of St. Louis.[24] The South side neighborhood is home to various ethnic groups.[25] The North side was a community of Germans and other European ethnic groups; now it is the home for African Americans.[26] Some books provide photos and text about St. Louis and the surrounding communities.[27] To determine the location of St. Louis neighborhoods, refer to Figure 2, and review the alphabetical listing on "Find a Neighborhood" website, which provides a current map with the outline of the

---

24. David A. Lossos, *St. Louis* (Charleston, South Carolina: Arcadia Publishing, 2005). Joan M. Thomas, *St. Louis 1875–1940* (Chicago: Arcadia Publishing, 2003). Robert E. Hannon, compiler and editor, *St. Louis: Its Neighborhoods and Neighbors, Landmarks and Milestones* (St. Louis: Regional Commerce and Growth Association, 1986). [Index at St. Louis Public Library's website.] Kenneth D. Oestreich and Norbury L. Wayman, *St. Louis Landmarks: A Guide to the City's Landmarks and Historic Districts* (St. Louis: Community Development Agency, 1977).

25. Eileen NiNi Harris, *A Grand Heritage: A History of the St. Louis Southside Neighborhoods and Citizens* ([St. Louis]: DeSales Community Housing, 1984).

26. JoAnn Adams Smith, *Selected Neighbors and Neighborhoods of North St. Louis and Selected Related Events* (St. Louis: Friends of the Vaughn Cultural Center, 1988).

27. Hannon, *St. Louis: Its Neighborhoods and Neighbors, Landmarks, and Milestones*.

neighborhoods.[28] The same website offers a link to the publication, *History of St. Louis Neighborhoods*.[29]

Landmarks Association of St. Louis is the leader in historic preservation in the City of St. Louis. Numerous publications outline their accomplishments as well as highlight historical places of interest in the city.[30] Their publications also offer photographs of many historical buildings.[31] The City produced the publication, *History: Physical Growth of St. Louis,* which shows the changes in St. Louis from 1764 to 1968. This publication is in print format and available online.[32]

B. W. Frauenthal's *Barney's Information Guide to the City of St. Louis* is a good comparison of what was important and available in 1902 as compared to today. This guide provides information on fire and police stations, parks and statues, World's Fair plans, post offices with addresses, photos of numerous stately homes and office buildings, hospitals, colleges, universities, asylums, orphanages, public schools, clubs with the name and address of the organization, a list of the street car lines, and a list of newspapers of the day.[33] An earlier guide, *St. Louis Guide to Parks, Railroads, Depots, Cemeteries, Places of Amusement, Streets, Railway, Fair Grounds, Bridges, Drives, Stock Yards, etc.*, provides the same type of information for 1884.[34]

Originally known as the Illinois and St. Louis Bridge, the *Eads Bridge* opened in 1874 and was the first bridge to cross the Mississippi River. It enhanced accessibility and ease of westward expansion. The bridge is still open to vehicular traffic today and serves as a downtown landmark. If your ancestor lived in the era of the bridge opening, he may have participated in its construction. Terminal Railroad payroll records dated July 1874 are available at Missouri Historical Society Research Library. They list the worker's name, occupation, and pay received plus an occasional signature. A crew of approximately ninety men constructed the bridge.[35]

The development at the foot of the St. Louis side of the bridge and the near by commercial area is called Laclede's Landing. A book about the Landing presents its history and development. For example, housed adjacent to the Eads Bridge for more than 100 years was the Switzer Licorice Company, which employed many people in the community.

---

28.   "Find a Neighborhood," *St. Louis Missouri* (http://stlouis.missouri.org/neighborhoods).

29.   Norbury L. Wayman, *History of St. Louis Neighborhoods,* series (St. Louis: St. Louis Community Development Agency, various dates). "Neighborhood Histories," *St. Louis Missouri* (http://stlouis.missouri.org/neighborhoods/history).

30.   Carolyn Hewes Toft, *St. Louis Landmarks and Historic Districts* (St. Louis: Landmarks Association, 2002).

31.   Mary M. Stiritz, *St. Louis: Historic Churches and Synagogues* (St. Louis: St. Louis Public Library and Landmarks Association of St. Louis, 1995).

32.   St. Louis City Planning Commission, *History: Physical Growth of the City of St. Louis* (St. Louis: The Commission, [1969]). Web version (http://stlouis.missouri.org/heritage/History69/index.html).

33.   B. W. Frauenthal, *Barney's Information Guide to the City of St. Louis* (St. Louis: B. W. Frauenthal, 1902).

34.   *St. Louis Guide to Parks, Railroads, Depots, Cemeteries, Places of Amusement, Streets, Railway, Fair Grounds, Bridges, Drives, Stock Yards, etc.* (St. Louis: Collins Brothers Drug, 1884).

35.   Howard S. Miller and Quinta Scott, *The Eads Bridge* (St. Louis: Missouri Historical Society Press, 1999). Illinois and St. Louis Bridge Company pay roll, July 1874, Terminal Railroad Association of St. Louis Records; Missouri Historical Society.

The 1904 St. Louis World's Fair was the highlight of the St. Louis area for many years. Photographs and stories in numerous publications provide details about the well-chronicled event, including the book, *From the Palaces to the Pike*.[36]

The Community Information Network (CIN) offers extensive information on St. Louis neighborhoods on their website (http://stlouis.missouri.org/neighborhoods). The map shown in Figure 2 provides an outline of the old neighborhoods.

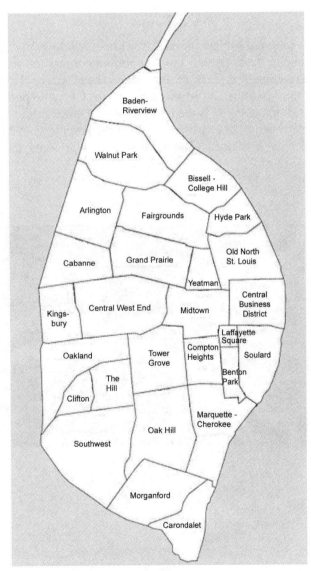

Figure 2: St. Louis Neighborhood Map,
Used with the permission of the Community Information Network

---

36. Timothy J. Fox, *From the Palaces to the Pike* (St. Louis: Missouri Historical Society, 1997).

Down by the Gravois provides photographs and stories about St. Louis between 1900 and 1930, focusing on the area south of Market Street.[37] This publication has photographs of transportation options, the inside and outside of various homes, neighborhoods, and their residents. *A Grand Heritage: A History of the St. Louis Southside Neighborhoods and Citizens* is a publication about South St. Louis with a significant name index for people, places, organizations, and events.

The City flag is a symbol of the area and it is described in the City of St. Louis Revised Code, Chapter 1.20 as follows:

> The flag with a solid red background has two broad heraldic wavy bars, colored blue and white, extending from the left top and bottom corners toward left center where they join and continue as one to the center right edge. This symbolizes the confluence of the Missouri and Mississippi rivers. Over the point of confluence a round golden disk upon which is the fleur-de-lis of France (blue) calling attention to the French background of the early city and more particularly to St. Louis of France for whom the City is named. The golden disk represents the City and/or the Louisiana Purchase.[38]

Figure 3: St. Louis City flag

---

37.   Malcom C. Drummond, *Down by the Gravois* (St. Louis: Harland Bartholomew and Associates, 1976). Harris, *A Grand Heritage: A History of the St. Louis Southside Neighborhoods and Citizens*.

38.   St. Louis City Revised Code, Chapter 1.20.010 (Ordinance 52322 § 2, 1964: 1948 C. Ch. 1 § 5: 1960 C. § 6.020). [Available at St. Louis Public Library website.]

SELECTED CITY NEIGHBORHOODS

Oral tradition, family documents, or personal memory may direct you to a particular part of St. Louis. Some neighborhoods grew due to commerce, while others were expanded from the influx of new immigrants. Each neighborhood had its own personality with special religious facilities, schools, and shops.

While these neighborhoods still exist, some have a new focus. The following information is based on the history of the neighborhood, not the current status. In many cases, there are new smaller communities within these neighborhoods.

BADEN, established by Germans in the 1850s and named after Baden, Germany, is the northern-most community within the City of St. Louis. Baden was annexed by the City of St. Louis in 1876. Bellefontaine and Calvary cemeteries are two landmarks in the Baden neighborhood as is the Chain of Rocks Bridge, now a pedestrian walkway across the Mississippi River, formerly a toll bridge that was part of old Route 66. Baden borders the Riverview neighborhood.[39]

BENTON PARK is the location of many stately homes constructed in the late nineteenth century after the Civil War. The Chatillon-DeMenil mansion still stands and represents this era. [See HISTORIC HOMES.] The City cemetery was removed in 1865 and the same area became a city park known as Benton Park. Several underground caves are located in this area.[40]

CABANNE, a neighborhood between Delmar Boulevard and Martin Luther King Drive, extends west to the City-County boundary. It connects to the Central West End neighborhood and includes much of the Skinker-DeBaliviere area. This residential area has many large homes, churches, schools, and orphanages. It was the home of several institutions, including the Girls' Home, Soldan High School, St. Luke's Hospital, and Visitation Academy in the early to mid-1900s.[41]

CARONDELET, founded in 1767, became a town in 1832, was incorporated as a city in 1851, and was annexed by St. Louis in 1870. Carondelet is located in the southernmost part of St. Louis along the Mississippi River. Des Peres School, located in Carondelet, offered the first public kindergarten in the United States. Today, Carondelet Historical Society [See REPOSITORIES.] owns Des Peres School where the Society maintains a museum and research facility for the rich history of the area.[42]

---

39.   *Baden Through the Years* (St. Louis: Lutheran Altenheim Society of Missouri, 1956). Norbury L. Wayman, *History of St. Louis Neighborhoods: Baden-Riverview* (St. Louis: St. Louis Community Development Center, 1978).

40.   Edna Campos Gravenhorst, *Benton Park West* (Charleston, South Carolina: Arcadia Publishing, 2005). Norbury L. Wayman, *History of St. Louis Neighborhoods: Benton Park* (St. Louis: St. Louis Community Development Center, 1978).

41.   Norbury L. Wayman, *History of St. Louis Neighborhoods: Cabanne* (St. Louis: St. Louis Community Development Center, 1978).

42.   NiNi Harris, *A History of Carondelet* (St. Louis: Patrice Press, 1991). Carolyn H. Toft, *Carondelet:The Ethnic Heritage of an Urban Neighborhood* (St. Louis: Washington University, 1975). Conversation with Ron Bolte at Carondelet Historical Society, October 2007. Timothy J. Fox, *Where We Live* (St. Louis: Missouri Historical Society, 1993–1994). Norbury L. Wayman, *History of St. Louis Neighborhoods: Carondelet* (St. Louis: St. Louis Community Development Center, 1978).

CENTRAL WEST END, the most affluent area in the City of St. Louis, is located near Forest Park. There are several areas with stately homes and businesses. A few books listed in the HISTORIC HOMES chapter describe some of the streets in this area.[43]

COMPTON HEIGHTS, developed in the 1860s, this formerly affluent German area, still has several hundred mansions maintained by the current residents. This was the home of the German Liederkranz Society. Harris Teachers College and Gallaudet School for the Deaf were originally part of this neighborhood.[44]

DOGTOWN, originally an Irish community, is located south of Forest Park in the Oakland area and has several other names, including Clayton-Tamm, Cheltenham, and Hi-Pointe. The railroad development in the 1850s influenced the growth of this neighborhood. The Dogtown Historical Society maintains the history of the area.

DOWNTOWN, which includes the oldest part of town and the central business district, has many historic and interesting sites including the Arch, Old Courthouse, and the Eugene Field House and St. Louis Toy Museum. The area baseball, football, and hockey venues are also in the downtown area. In addition and of interest to genealogists, are the St. Louis City Hall, Civil Courts building, Thomas Eagleton Federal Courthouse, and St. Louis Public Library. The *Walking Historic Downtown St. Louis* describes these sites and others.[45]

FAIRGROUNDS was the original site of the yearly St. Louis Fair held during part of the nineteenth century and today is a park surrounded by mostly residential neighborhoods. During the Civil War, Fairgrounds Park was the site of Benton Barracks a staging are for Union troops. In the same neighborhood in the twentieth century was Sportsman's Park, where the St. Louis Browns and St. Louis Cardinals played, including the 1944 World Series against each other.[46]

---

43.   Albert Montesi and Richard Deposki, *Central West End* (Chicago: Arcadia Publishing, 2000). Norbury L. Wayman, *History of St. Louis Neighborhoods: Central West End* (St. Louis: St. Louis Community Development Center, 1978). Norbury L. Wayman, *History of St. Louis Neighborhoods: Kingsbury* (St. Louis: St. Louis Community Development Center, 1980). Jeff Tallent, *Terrace Tales: A Contemporary History of Washington Terrace, Street of Mansions* (St. Louis: Finbar Company, 1992). Julius K. Hunter, *Westmoreland and Portland Places: The History and Architecture of America's Premier Private Streets, 1888–1988* (Columbia: University of Missouri Press, 1988). Julius K. Hunter, *Kingsbury Place: The First Two Hundred Years* (St. Louis: C. W. Mosby Company, 1982).

44.   Albert Montesi and Richard Deposki, *St. Louis Garden District* (Charleston, South Carolina: Arcadia Publising, 2004). Betty Pavlige, *Soulard Second Century* (Chicago: Arcadia Publishing, 2001). Carolyn Hewes Toft, *Compton Heights: A History and Architectural Guide* (St. Louis: Landmarks Association, 1984). Norbury L. Wayman, *History of St. Louis Neighborhoods: Compton Hill (Heights)* (St. Louis: St. Louis Community Development Center, 1980).

45.   Charles Brennan and Ben Cannon, *Walking Historic Downtown St. Louis: 250 Incredible Years in Two Hours or Less* (St. Louis: Virginia Publishing, 2000). Albert Montesi and Richard Deposki, *Downtown St. Louis* (Chicago: Arcadia Publishing, 2001). Norbury L. Wayman, *History of St. Louis Neighborhoods: Central Business Area* (St. Louis: St. Louis Community Development Center, 1978).

46.   Norbury L. Wayman, *History of St. Louis Neighborhoods: Fairgrounds* (St. Louis: St. Louis Community Development Center, 1978). Timothy J. Fox, *Where We Live, Fairgrounds* (St. Louis: Missouri Historical Society, 1993–1994). Norbury L. Wayman, *History of St. Louis Neighborhoods: Hyde Park* (St. Louis: St. Louis Community Development Center, 1978). Dan O'Neill, *Sportsman's Park: The Players, The Fans, and The Game, 1940–1965.* John Heidenry, *The Boys Who Were Left Behind: The 1944 World Series between the Hapless St. Louis Browns and the Legendary St. Louis Cardinals* (Lincoln: University of Nebraska Press, 2006).

FOREST PARK, an area larger than Central Park in New York City, was the location of the 1904 World's Fair, and currently is home to the St. Louis Zoo, The Municipal Opera (The Muny), Art Museum, Jewel Box, Missouri Historical Society Museum, golf courses, and other recreational facilities.[47] Forest Park is in the Kingsbury and Central West End neighborhoods.

GARDEN AREA was established as the country or summer home of Henry Shaw, who otherwise lived in the city near Seventh Street. Shaw purchased numerous acres and donated the property, today known as Tower Grove Park, to the City. His personal estate is the world-renowned Missouri Botanical Garden. The book *Henry Shaw His Life and Legacies* describes the development of the area.[48]

THE HILL, named after one of the highest points in the city, the Italian immigrants populated this community starting in the late nineteenth century.[49] Today the Hill is known for its fine Italian restaurants.

HYDE PARK borders the Mississippi River on the east, and thus is the home of industry along Interstate 70. The early Germans named the town Bremen, after their home area in Germany; however, in 1856 the area became part of the City of St. Louis.[50]

LAFAYETTE SQUARE, an area south of Chouteau Avenue and east of Jefferson Avenue, was a bustling community until the 1896 tornado devastated it causing many residents to move farther west.[51] Today this is a beautiful revitalized area.

MIDTOWN, now known as the theater district, is an area on or near Grand Avenue, approximately halfway between the Mississippi River on the east and the City Limits on the west. Today it is home of the Fox Theater and the St. Louis Symphony as well as other theaters. St. Louis University is a mainstay in the neighborhood.[52]

---

47.   Timothy J. Fox, *Where We Live, Forest Park* (St. Louis: Missouri Historical Society, 1993–1994). Sally J. Altman and Richard Weiss, *Forest Park: The Jewel of St. Louis* (St. Louis: St. Louis Post-Dispatch, 2007). Norbury L. Wayman, *History of St. Louis Neighborhoods: Kingsbury* (St. Louis: St. Louis Community Development Center, 1978). Caroline Loughlin and Catherine Anderson, *Forest Park* (Columbia: University of Missouri Press, 1986).

48.   William Barnaby Faherty, *Henry Shaw His Life and Legacies* (Columbia: University of Missouri Press, 1987). Albert Montesi and Richard Deposki, *St. Louis Garden District* (Charleston, South Carolina: Arcadia Publishing, 2004). Timothy J. Fox, *Where We Live, Shaw* (St. Louis: Missouri Historical Society, 1993–1994).

49.   Timothy J. Fox, *Where We Live, The Hill* (St. Louis: Missouri Historical Society, 1993–1994). Norbury L. Wayman, *History of St. Louis Neighborhoods: The Hill* (St. Louis: St. Louis Community Development Center, 1978).

50.   Norbury L. Wayman, *History of St. Louis Neighborhoods: Hyde Park and Bissell College* (St. Louis: St. Louis Community Development Center, 1978).

51.   Albert Montesi and Richard Deposki, *Lafayette Square, St. Louis* (Charleston, South Carolina: Arcadia Publishing, 1999). Timothy J. Fox, *Where We Live, Near South Side* (St. Louis: Missouri Historical Society, 1993–1994). Norbury L. Wayman, *History of St. Louis Neighborhoods: Lafayette Square* (St. Louis: St. Louis Community Development Center, 1978).

52.   Norbury L. Wayman, *History of St. Louis Neighborhoods: Midtown* (St. Louis: St. Louis Community Development Center, 1978). Jean Fahey Eberle, *Midtown: A Grand Place to Be* (St. Louis: Mercantile Commerce Trust Company, 1980).

OLD NORTH ST. LOUIS, located north of downtown St. Louis, is near the Mississippi River. This part of town contained the Irish area called "Kerry Patch" and a large German area, along with other ethnic communities.[53]

SKINKER–DeBALIVIERE is an area along the City-County boundary line, near Washington University, adjacent to Forest Park and the Central West End. This is primarily a residential area with many churches and schools. The area is convenient to St. Louis University, Downtown, and Midtown.[54]

SOULARD, established in the late eighteenth century by a Frenchman, Antoine Soulard, this community is just south of the downtown area and runs along the Mississippi River. Soulard Market is the oldest farmers' market in the country, and the Anheuser-Busch brewery and corporate headquarters are mainstays of the area today.[55]

TOWER GROVE, established in the mid-nineteenth century, became part of the City in 1876 when the City expanded westward for the last time. Tower Grove Park is the center of this mainly residential area.[56]

THE VILLE, part of the north side of the City, is known for the now-closed Homer G. Phillips Hospital and its famous Sumner High School, whose graduates include Chuck Berry and Tina Turner.[57]

Over time, neighborhoods change due to population shift, new construction, and revitalization. Some churches are the hub of the neighborhood, others have closed. The Germans that lived in North St. Louis now live in South St. Louis or the County with some moving to St. Charles County. Many African Americans still live in the City and some have migrated to the County as well. The Irish are dispersed throughout the region.

Today some south St. Louis neighborhoods have new residents from Bosnia and other European countries. The downtown area has new lofts attracting new City residents. Over time all of these neighborhoods will change again.

---

53.   Albert Montesi and Richard Deposki, *Historic North St. Louis* (Chicago: Arcadia Publishing, 2003). Norbury L. Wayman, *History of St. Louis Neighborhoods: Old North St. Louis* (St. Louis: St. Louis Community Development Center, 1978).

54.   Norbury L. Wayman, *History of St. Louis Neighborhoods: Skinker-DeBaliviere* (St. Louis: St. Louis Community Development Center, 1978). Kathleen M. Harleman, Georgiana B. Stuart, and Susan K. Tepas, *The Neighborhood: A History of Skinker-DeBaliviere* (St. Louis: Skinker-DeBaliviere Community Council, 1973).

55.   Albert Montesi and Richard Deposki, *Soulard, St. Louis* (Chicago: Arcadia Publishing, 2000). Betty Pavlige, *Soulard's Second Century* (Chicago: Arcadia Publishing, 2001). Norbury L. Wayman, *History of St. Louis Neighborhoods: Soulard* (St. Louis: St. Louis Community Development Center, 1978). Carolyn Hewes Toft, editor, *Soulard: The Ethnic Heritage of an Urban Neighborhood* (St. Louis: Washington University, 1975). Timothy J. Fox, *Where We Live, Soulard* (St. Louis: Missouri Historical Society, 1993–1994).

56.   Norbury L. Wayman, *History of St. Louis Neighborhoods: Tower Grove / Shaw* (St. Louis: St. Louis Community Development Center, 1978).

57.   John A. Wright, *The Ville* (Chicago: Arcadia Publishing, 2001). Timothy J. Fox, *Where We Live, The Ville* (St. Louis: Missouri Historical Society, 1993–1994).

St. Louis County
Municipalities & Communities

S t. Louis County has more than 500 square miles of land, as compared to about 70 square miles for the City of St. Louis. With the same boundary lines, in 1876 the City had the majority of the residents with only a sparse population in St. Louis County.

History of Old Roads, Pioneers, and Early Communities of St. Louis County provides a good overview and history of municipalities, churches, and schools of St. Louis County.[58] After the separation of St. Louis City and County, these communities and others worked together to form the St. Louis County government. In 1877, the new St. Louis County government officials considered several locations for their government center before settling on the Clayton area, which was geographically in the middle core of the County. Land was donated and Clayton was formed as the County seat.

Early St. Louis County citizens had established businesses and homes in St. Louis County prior to the City and County separation. Preservation and restoration have saved some facilities. Others are visible only through photographs, postcards, and historical places in both St. Louis County and St. Louis City on the *History's Time Portal* website.[59] St. Louis County Parks Department is gathering old County buildings and relocating them to form a historical village at Faust Park in Chesterfield. *The Past in Our Presence: Historic Buildings of St. Louis County* shows some of the original establishments.[60]

Local citizens often refer to the county in regional terms, South St. Louis County or South County, and the same for the North and West areas. They are all part of the same St. Louis County, with just a geographic distinction. Some areas in the County are incorporated into a city or town; other areas are unincorporated and just part of St. Louis County. To the east is the City of St. Louis and then the Mississippi River and Illinois.

---

58.   Henry Gustav Hertich, *History of Old Roads, Pioneers, and Early Communities of St. Louis County* (St. Louis: St. Louis County Library, Special Collections, 2004).

59.   "History's Time Portal," *USGenNet* (http://www.usgennet.org/usa/mo/county/stlouis).

60.   St. Louis County Department of Parks and Recreation. *The Past in Our Presence: Historic Buildings in St. Louis County* (St. Louis County: St. Louis County Parks Department, 1996).

Figure 4: St. Louis County Outline Map, 1909

SELECTED COUNTY MUNICIPALITIES & COMMUNITIES

AFFTON is a community southwest of the St. Louis City Limits along Gravois Road. This area, formerly called Gravois Station, is the home of Oakland House. [See HISTORIC HOMES.] Affton has a large residential community served by the Affton School District with numerous churches representing many faiths. Affton Historical Society maintains the history of the community.

ALLENTON, established in 1852 by Thomas Allen, is a small community thirty-two miles from the City of St. Louis in the far southwestern part of the County, approximately seven miles west of Valley Park along Interstate 44.

BALLWIN, settled by John Ball in 1798 and incorporated in 1837, is approximately twenty miles west of the City of St. Louis. Ballwin has an active business district along Manchester Road and is in the Parkway and Rockwood School Districts. The Ballwin Historical Society maintains the history of the community.[61]

BELLEFONTAINE NEIGHBORS is a community in North St. Louis County near Jennings Station Road and Bellefontaine Road. This is the location of the Bissell House, former home of American Revolution and War of 1812 patriot, General Daniel Bissell. Riverview Gardens School District serves the area.[62]

BEL-NOR is a small community along Natural Bridge Road. The University of Missouri–St. Louis campus is located in this area. Normandy School District serves this area.

BEL-RIDGE is a small community north of the intersection of St. Charles Rock Road and Carson Road. Normandy School District serves this area.

BERKELEY is a community near the airport along Airport Road, Lindbergh Boulevard, and Natural Bridge Road that was formerly part of the Berkeley School District. Students now attend the Ferguson-Florissant School District.

BLACK JACK is a community in the north portion of the County near the intersection of Parker and Old Halls Ferry Roads. Hazelwood School District serves the community and the Black Jack Historical Society maintains the history.[63]

BRENTWOOD is a residential and commercial area between Interstate 64 and Manchester Road along Brentwood Boulevard. Brentwood School District serves the area. The Brentwood Historical Society maintains the history of the community.[64]

---

61.   Doretha M. Loehr, *A History of Ballwin* (Ballwin: City of Ballwin, 1979). David Fiedler, *Ballwin* (Charleston, South Carolina: Arcadia Publishing, 2005). "History of Ballwin," *Ballwin, Missouri* (http://www.ballwin.mo.us/history.html).

62.   *Community Assessment of Bellefontaine Neighbors* (St. Louis: Maryville University, 1992). "The History of Our City," *City of Bellefontaine Neighbors* (http://www.cityofbn.com/ourtown/history.htm).

63.   "City Beginnings," *BlackJack, Missouri* (http://www.cityofblackjack.com).

64.   Brentwood Historical Society, *Brentwood, Missouri* (Chicago: Arcadia Publishing, 2002). Robert E. Easton and Brentwood Anniversary Committee, *The Golden Anniversary History of Brentwood, Missouri, 1919–1969; Compiled from Personal Interviews, Recollections, and City Records* (Brentwood: The Committee, 1969). *History of Brentwood, Missouri, 1919–1969* (Brentwood: Lafayette Printing, 1969).

BRIDGETON, established by Robert Owen in 1794 and incorporated in 1843, is a community about fifteen miles west of the City of St. Louis, south of Lambert St. Louis International Airport and Natural Bridge Road, along Lindbergh Boulevard. Marais des Liards and Owen's Station were previous names for this area. Pattonville School District serves the community. This is the home of the Payne-Gentry Historical House. [See HISTORIC HOMES.] The Bridgeton Historical Society and the Bridgeton Historical Commission maintain the history of the community.[65]

CASTLEWOOD is a small community in West St. Louis County south of Manchester Road extending south along the Meramec River.

CHESTERFIELD is a residential and commercial community located on each side of Interstate 64 in West St. Louis County shaped partially by the Missouri River. Faust Park, located in this community, is the location of a historic house, Thornhill, home of former governor, Frederick Bates. [See HISTORIC HOMES.] Schools are in Parkway and Rockwood School Districts. The Chesterfield Historical Commission and the Creve Coeur-Chesterfield Historical Society maintain the history of the community.[66]

CLAYTON is located in the central portion of St. Louis County and serves as the county seat. Work began on the new town and government center in 1878 on property donated by Ralph Clayton and Martin Hanley. Clayton School District serves the area and the Clayton Historical Society maintains the history of the community.[67]

CONCORD VILLAGE, established by German immigrants in the late 1830s, is a community in South St. Louis County situated near Lindbergh Boulevard and Tesson Ferry Road. Early and influential families included the Bowles, Dents, Kennerlys, Longs, Ochs, Parkes, Rotts, Sappingtons, Tessons, and Theiss. Many streets and buildings are named after these families. Lindbergh and Mehlville School Districts serve the area with the Sappington-Concord Historical Society maintaining the history of the area.[68]

CRESTWOOD is a community located between Webster Groves and Kirkwood along Watson Road, or old Route 66. Lindbergh School District serves the area. This is the home of the Sappington House. [See HISTORIC HOMES.][69]

---

65.   Bridgeton Historical Commission, *Bridgeton Since 1794* (Bridgeton: The Commission, 1968). Jane Mobley, *Home Place: A Celebration of Life in Bridgeton, Missouri* (Bridgeton: City of Bridgeton, 1993). "Bridgeton Facts," *City of Bridgeton, Missouri* (http://www.bridgetonmo.com/DesktopDefault .aspx?tabid=24).

66.   Mark W. Leach, *A Guide to Chesterfield's Ancient History* (Chesterfield: Mark Leach, 2002). Dan A. Rothwell, *A Guide to Chesterfield's Architectural Treasurers* (Chesterfield: City of Chesterfield, 1998).

67.   Clayton Public Schools, *The Story of Clayton* (Clayton: Clayton Schools, 1931). Terry Dickson, *Clayton: A History* (St. Louis: Von Hoffman Press, 1976). "The Early Years," *City of Clayton* (http://www.ci.clayton.mo.us/index.aspx?location=127).

68.   Jean Fahey Eberle, *A Starting Point: A History of Oakville-Mehlville-Concord Village Community* (Virginia Beach, Virginia: Donning Company, 1993). *Sappington-Concord: A History* (St. Louis: Sappington–Concord Historical Society, 1999).

69.   *The Crestwood Story: A Glimpse into the Origins of the Gravois Creek Settlement* (Crestwood: The City, 1976).

CREVE COEUR is an old community located on both sides of the intersection of Interstate 270 and Olive Boulevard. Parkway and Ladue School Districts serve the area. The Creve Coeur-Chesterfield Historical Society maintains the history of the community. Creve Coeur means *broken heart* in French.[70]

DES PERES, incorporated in 1934, is a community along Interstate 270 and Manchester Road about fourteen miles west of the St. Louis City Limits. Parkway and Kirkwood School Districts serve the area.[71]

ELLISVILLE, incorporated in 1932, is a community along Manchester and Clarkson Roads, between Ballwin and Wildwood. Rockwood School District serves the area and the Ellisville Historical Society maintains the history.[72]

EUREKA, established in 1858 along the Missouri Pacific Railroad line, is a community about thirty miles from the City of St. Louis in the southwest portion of St. Louis County with part bordering the Jefferson County line. Old Route 66 was located near the present Interstate 44 and cuts through this community. Rockwood School District serves the area and the Eureka Historical Society maintains the history.[73]

FENTON, established by William Long, is an old community along the Meramec River and Gravois Road, approximately fourteen miles west of St. Louis with portions over the Jefferson County boundary line. Lindbergh and Rockwood School Districts plus the Jefferson County schools serve the area. The Fenton Historical Society maintains the history of the community.[74]

FERGUSON is about six miles from the City of St. Louis along the Wabash Railroad line on land donated by William B. Ferguson. This community is in North St. Louis County along Florissant Road and is served by Ferguson–Florissant School District. Ferguson Historical Society and Ferguson Landmarks Commission maintain the history of the community.[75]

FLORISSANT, known previously as St. Ferdinand, is one of the oldest communities in St. Louis County. The first parish, *St. Ferdinand de Florissant*, was established in 1789. There are several historic buildings and homes including the Gittemeier House. [See HISTORIC HOMES.] Ferguson–Florissant School District serves the area. Historic Florissant, The Florissant

70.   Gloria Dalton, *Heritage of Creve Coeur Area* (Creve Coeur: City of Creve Coeur, 1976). *Creve Coeur and Surrounding Area* (No place: Hausman Publications, 1968). *Reflections of the Creve Coeur Lake Area* (St. Louis: Parkway School District, 1982). "Creve Coeur History," *City of Creve Coeur* (http://www.creve-coeur.org/history.htm).

71.   Carl F. Stolwyk, *A History of Des Peres, Missouri* (Des Peres: City of Des Peres, 1976).

72.   Chylene Jahn Daub, *Golden Anniversary of Ellisville, Missouri, 1931–1982* (Ellisville: The City, 1983). *The City of Ellisville* (Ellisville: P and R Printing, 1976).

73.   *Eureka, Missouri: Sesquicentennial, 1858–2008* (Eureka: Bell Books, 2007). "History," *City of Eureka* (http://www.eureka.mo.us/history.htm).

74.   Della Lang, *River City: The Story of Fenton, Missouri* (Fenton: The City, 1992).

75.   Irene Sanford Smith, *Ferguson: A City and Its People* (Ferguson: Ferguson Historical Society, 1976). Timothy J. Fox, *Where We Live, Ferguson* (St. Louis: Missouri Historical Society, 1993–1994). Jean Montgomery, Irene Smith, Ruth Brown, and Carol Rehg, *Ferguson: The First 100 Years* (St. Louis: Nutwood Publishing, 1994).

Historic Commission, Friends of Old Florissant, and the Florissant Valley Historical Society maintain the history of the community.[76]

FOX CREEK is an old community about twenty-eight miles from the City of St. Louis in far west St. Louis County, along Manchester or Route 100 and Wild Horse Creek Road, not far from Franklin County. This is the Rockwood School District.

FRONTENAC is a relatively new community, formed in 1947, in West St. Louis County located west of Lindbergh Boulevard near Clayton Road and served by the Ladue School District.

GLENDALE, established in 1912, is along Manchester and Berry Roads east of Kirkwood, approximately twelve miles west of St. Louis City along the Missouri Pacific Railroad lines. The Glendale Historical Society maintains the history of the community.

GRANTWOOD VILLAGE is located along Laclede Station, Rock Hill, and Gravois Roads on property formerly owned by President Ulysses S. Grant. White Haven and Grant's Farm are in this community. [See HISTORIC HOMES.]

GROVER is a small community in West County, approximately twenty-eight miles from the St. Louis City Limits. The community is east of Wildwood and served by the Rockwood School District.

GUMBO, between Chesterfield and the Missouri River in far West St. Louis County, is rich farmland in the river bottom area. It is served by the Rockwood School District.

HANLEY HILLS is a small community north of Hanley Road and Page Boulevard, named after Martin Hanley who, in 1837, owned a farm in this area.

HAZELWOOD, a large community named after Henry Clay's estate in Kentucky, is in North St. Louis County situated between the communities of Florissant and Bridgeton and served by the Hazelwood School District. The Hazelwood Historic Preservation Commission maintains the history of the community.[77]

JENNINGS, established in 1839 and incorporated in 1946, is a community adjacent to the St. Louis City Limits along Florissant Road. Jennings School District serves this area. The Jennings Historical Society maintains the history of the community.[78]

---

76.   Rosemary S. Davidson, *Florissant, Missouri* (Virginia Beach, Virginia: Donning Company Publishers, 2002). John Wright, *Florissant* (Charleston, South Carolina: Arcadia Publishing, 2004). Gilbert J. Garraghan, *Saint Ferdinand de Florissant: The Story of an Ancient Parish* (Chicago: Loyola University, 1923). *Florissant Valley Historical Society Quarterly* (Florissant: The Society, 1959–). Mary Lilliana Owens, *The Florissant Heroines* (Florissant: King Publication, 1960). Louis E. Pondrom, *Historical Records of St. Ferdinand of Florissant and St. Charles with Notes on Other Settlements of North St. Louis County* (No place: privately printed, 1898). Gretchen Crank, *Reflections of the Florissant Valley* (St. Louis: Curtis Media, 1990). John Wright, *Images of America: Florissant* (St. Louis: Arcadia Publishing, 2004). Timothy J. Fox, *Where We Live, Florissant* (St. Louis: Missouri Historical Society, 1993–1994).

77.   *The City of Hazelwood: The Past Forms the Future* (Hazelwood: Jostens Printing, 1992). "Welcome to the City of Hazelwood," *City of Hazelwood* (http://www.ci.hazelwood.mo.us).

78.   McCune Gill, *Jennings* (St. Louis: Title Insurance Corporation of St. Louis, 1945). "Brief History of Jennings," *Jennings Historical Society* (http://www.ci.hazelwood.mo.us).

KINLOCH is a small city with an African American population located near Ferguson. The community lost much of its land to the expansion of Lambert St. Louis International Airport property.[79]

KIRKWOOD, established in 1853, is an active community in southwest St. Louis County along Kirkwood Road (Lindbergh) between Manchester and Watson Roads. The community is about thirteen miles from the City of St. Louis along the Missouri Pacific Railroad line, and took its name from the railroad engineer James P. Kirkwood. Kirkwood School District serves the area. The Kirkwood Historical Society and the Kirkwood Landmarks Commission maintain the history of the community and Mudd's Grove. [See HISTORIC HOMES.] The Kirkwood Railroad Station is on the National Register of Historic Places.[80]

LADUE is an affluent residential community in the middle of the County located along Interstate 64, east of Lindbergh Boulevard. Ladue School District serves the area.

LEMAY is located south of the St. Louis City Limits along Lemay Ferry Road, between the Mississippi River and Union Road. This community includes Jefferson Barracks and it is served by the Hancock and Mehlville School Districts.[81]

MANCHESTER, originally called Hoardstown until an 1825 name change, is located along Manchester Road near Woods Mill Road in West St. Louis County approximately eighteen miles west of the St. Louis City Limits. Parkway School District serves the area and the Old Trails Historical Society maintains the history.[82]

MAPLEWOOD is located along Manchester Road and adjacent to the St. Louis City Limits. This was part of Charles Gratiot's 1785 land grant. Maplewood-Richmond Heights School District serves the area. The Historical Society of Maplewood maintains the history of the community.[83]

---

79.   John A. Wright, *Images of America, Kinloch, Missouri, First Black City* (St. Louis: Arcadia Publishing, 2004). John A. Wright, *Kinloch: Missouri's First Black City* (Chicago: Arcadia Publishing, 2000). *Kinloch: Yesterday and Tomorrow* (St. Louis: Kinloch Historical Committee, 1983). [Index at St. Louis Public Library website.]

80.   June Wilkinson Dahl, *The History of Kirkwood, Missouri, 1851–1965* (Kirkwood: Kirkwood Historical Society, 2003). *A Pictorial Glimpse of Early Kirkwood* (Kirkwood: Kirkwood Chamber of Commerce, 1974). *Kirkwood: A Pictorial History* (St. Louis: G. Bradley Publishing, 2002). *The Wonderful City of Kirkwood, 100 Years Young 1865–1965 Centennial Edition* (Kirkwood: City of Kirkwood, 1965). Kirkwood Historical Society, *Kirkwood Historical Review* (Kirkwood: The Society, 1961–). Barbara J. Byerly and J. B. Lester, editors, *Kirkwood, Missouri: The Greentree City* (Kirkwood: Webster-Kirkwood Times, 1994). [Index at St. Louis Public Library website.] *City of Kirkwood* (http://www .ci.kirkwood.mo.us/history.htm). Timothy J. Fox, *Where We Live, Kirkwood* (St. Louis: Missouri Historical Society, 1993–1994).

81.   Vernon G. Schertel, *Historic Lemay, 1700–1945: A Collection of Historic Beginnings, Historic Places, Historic Events, Historic Buildings, Historic Persons* (Lemay: Nabor News Print, 1995). William Alden, *It Happened in Lemay*, 2 volumes (St. Louis: Naborhood Link News, no date).

82.   R. Miriam Andre, *The Moving Forces in the History of Old Bon Homme: The Manchester, Missouri, Area* (Manchester: C. E. Biggs and R. M. Andre, 1982). Timothy J. Fox, *Where We Live, Manchester* (St. Louis: Missouri Historical Society, 1993–1994).

83.   "History," *City of Maplewood* (http://www.cityofmaplewood.com/History.aspx). Maplewood Business Men's Association, *Directory of the City of Maplewood, Missouri* (Maplewood: J. Lethem, 1912, 1915).

MARYLAND HEIGHTS is a relatively new community near Dorsett and Fee Fee Roads and Interstate 270. Parkway and Pattonville School Districts serve the community. The Maryland Heights Historical Society maintains the history of the community.[84]

MATTESE is a small old community established by Germans in South St. Louis County, located along Mattis and Lemay Ferry Roads, in the Lindbergh School District.

MEHLVILLE was established by German immigrants, carries the name of Charles Mehl who owned a farm along Lemay Ferry Road in South St. Louis County. The community is approximately four miles from the St. Louis City Limits. Jefferson Barracks Historical Park and National Cemetery are near this community. [See HISTORIC HOMES.] Mehlville School District serves this area.[85]

NORMANDY is a community west of Wellston along St. Charles Rock Road and Lucas and Hunt Road. Normandy School District serves the area. The Normandy Historical Society maintains the history of the community.[86]

OAKVILLE is located five miles south of the St. Louis City Limits in South St. Louis County, near Telegraph and Baumgartner Roads. The community was founded in 1859 by German immigrants who established farms, schools, and churches. This area is part of the Mehlville School District.[87]

OLIVETTE, formerly called Central, is along Olive Boulevard, approximately four miles west of the St. Louis City Limits. Ladue School District serves this community.

OVERLAND, established in the late eighteenth century and incorporated in 1939, is a community along St. Charles Rock Road between Midland and Ashby Roads. Ritenour School District serves the community. The Overland Historical Society maintains the history of the community.[88]

PACIFIC, named after the Missouri Pacific Railroad, is in the western portion of St. Louis County and partially in Franklin County along old Route 66, now Interstate 44, approximately thirty-six miles west of the St. Louis City Limits.[89]

---

84.   "Maryland Heights History Project," *City of Maryland Heights* (http://www.cityofmaplewood.com/History.aspx).

85.   Eberle, *A Starting Point: A History of Oakville-Mehlville-Concord Village Community*, previously cited.

86.   Doris Benz, *Normandy, Missouri: History of Normandy* (Normandy: privately printed, 1973). *Heritage of the Normandy Area in the Twentieth Century* (Normandy: Normandy Area Historical Association, 1987). *The Fred Small Collection of Historic Normandy* [video recording] (Normandy: Normandy Area Historical Association, 2005). "Brief History of Normandy," *City of Normandy* (http://www.cityofnormandy.gov).

87.   Barbara Messmer Waddock, *Foundation of a Community: Oakville Before the Turn of the Century* (St. Louis: Lemay Bank and Trust Company, 1977). Eberle, *A Starting Point: A History of Oakville-Mehlville-Concord Village Community*, previously cited. *Oakville, Missouri: One Hundred Years of Progress, 1859–1959* (Oakville: Oakville Centennial Fair Committee, 1959).

88.   Robert E. Parkin, *Overland Trails and Trials and Your Community Today* (Overland: Krawll Printing Company, 1956).

89.   "Welcome to Pacific," *Pacific, Missouri* (http://www.pacificmissouri.com/about_history.php).

PATTONVILLE is located along St. Charles Rock Road and Fee Fee Road, near Fee Fee Creek, today adjacent to Lambert St. Louis International Airport. The location was originally part of the Patton family property. Pattonville School District serves this community.

PINE LAWN is a community near the St. Louis City Limits along Natural Bridge Road. Normandy School District serves this area.

RICHMOND HEIGHTS is west of the St. Louis City Limits along Clayton Road and Interstate 64 and Innerbelt 170. The Maplewood-Richmond Heights School District serves this area. The Richmond Heights Historical Society maintains the history of the community.[90]

RIVERVIEW, situated along the St. Louis City Limits, Chambers Road, and the Mississippi River, is in North County along the old Route 66 as it crossed the Mississippi River via the Chain of Rocks Bridge. Riverview Gardens School District serves this area.

ROCK HILL is an old but small community along Manchester Road near Rock Hill Road, approximately ten miles west of St. Louis. Webster Groves School District serves the area. The Rock Hill Historical Society maintains the history of the community.[91]

SAINT ANN is a community incorporated in 1948 and is located between Overland and Bridgeton along St. Charles Rock Road and borders Lambert St. Louis International Airport. Pattonville and Ritenour School Districts serve the area.[92]

SAPPINGTON is an area with the Sappington Post Office located near the triangle of Sappington Road, Gravois Road, and Lindbergh Boulevard, approximately ten miles from St. Louis. Lindbergh School District serves this area and the Sappington-Concord Historical Society maintains the history.[93]

SHREWSBURY, established in 1889 and incorporated in 1913, is adjacent to the St. Louis City Limits, south of Maplewood, along Interstate 44. The Shrewsbury Historical Society maintains the history of the community.[94]

SPANISH LAKE is in the northeastern part of the County with some areas bordering the Missouri River. In the early 1800s, Fort Belle Fontaine was located on a bluff overlooking the river in what is now Spanish Lake. Most explorers and fur traders visited the fort, including Lewis and Clark on their return trip. This is in the Hazelwood School District. The Fort Belle Fontaine Historical Society maintains the history of the fort. The Spanish Lake Historical Society maintains the history of the community.

SUNSET HILLS is a small community in southwest St. Louis County near the intersection of Lindbergh Boulevard and Watson Road. Watson Road was apart of the old Route 66 before the Interstate highway system was established. Laumeier Sculpture Park is located in this

---

90.   Joellen Gamp McDonald and Ruth Nickolas Keenoy, *Richmond Heights* (Charleston, South Carolina: Arcadia Publishing, 2006).

91.   Celeste Wagner Blann, *A History of Rock Hill* (Rock Hill: C. W. Blann, 1976). "History," *City of Rock Hill* (http://www.rockhillmo.net/history.asp).

92.   Sue Smith, *City of St. Ann: 1948–1983* (St. Ann: City of St. Ann, 1983).

93.   *Sappington-Concord: A History*, previously cited. *History of Sappington, Missouri* (Sappington: Sappington School, 1937).

94.   Helen G. McMahon, *No Knots in Our Thread: Shrewsbury, 1913–1993, Our 80th Year* (Shrewsbury: The Author, 1993).

community. Lindbergh School District, named after Charles Lindbergh, serves the area. The Sunset Hills Historical Society maintains the history of the area.[95]

TOWN AND COUNTRY is primarily a residential community in the western part of St. Louis County which was incorporated in 1950. It is located near the intersection of Interstate 270 and Interstate 64. Parkway School District serves the area and the Town and Country Historical Society maintains its history.

UNIVERSITY CITY, established in 1906, is adjacent to the St. Louis City Limits near Washington University in the central part of the County. The Loop area is the community hub and the home of the St. Louis Walk of Fame. University City School District serves the area. The Historical Society of University City and University City Historic Preservation Commission maintain the history. Several books chronicle the area.[96]

VALLEY PARK is a small community established in the late 1800s in southwest St. Louis County along the Meramec River and the Missouri Pacific Railroad. Originally called Valley, it served as a summer destination via the train for family outings. Valley Park School District serves this suburb. Meramec Station Historical Society maintains the history of Valley Park.

WEBSTER GROVES, established in the mid-nineteenth century and incorporated in 1896, is in the southwest portion of the County approximately ten miles from the City of St. Louis, along Big Bend Road and Lockwood Avenue. Webster Groves School District serves this area. The Webster Groves Historical Society and the Webster Groves Historic Preservation Commission maintain the history of their community.[97]

WELLSTON is adjacent to the St. Louis City Limits along Martin Luther King Boulevard, formerly Easton Avenue. In the day of streetcars, the Wellston Loop was the transportation hub for the

---

95.   *The History of Sunset Hills: Sunset Hills, 50 Years, 1957–2007* (St. Louis: Sunset Hills Historical Society, 50th Anniversary Committee, 2006). *The History of Sunset Hills* (Sunset Hills: Sunset Hills Bicentennial Commission, 1976–1982).

96.   John A. Wright, *University City, Missouri* (Chicago: Arcadia Publishing, 2002). Judy Little, *University City: Landmarks and Historic Places* (University City: Historic Commission of University City, 1997). NiNi Harris, *Legacy of Lions* (University City: Historical Society of University City, 1981). *Urban Oasis: 75 Years in Parkview, A St. Louis Private Place* (St. Louis: Boar's Head Press, 1979). "Edward Gardner Lewis and University City," *University City Library* (http://history.ucpl.lib.mo.us). Timothy J. Fox, *Where We Live, University City* (St. Louis: Missouri Historical Society, 1993–1994). Helen Elliott Roche, *Brief History of University City* (St. Louis: privately printed, 1971).

97.   Clarissa Start, *Webster Groves* (Webster Groves: The City, 1975). Velma Benner, *Webster Groves* (Webster Groves: privately printed, 1950). Marilynn Bradley, *Arpens and Acres: A Brief History of Webster Groves, Missouri* (Webster Groves: M. Bradley, 1975). *Pictorial History of Webster Groves, Missouri* (Webster Groves: Webster-Kirkwood Times, 1991). Wilda H. Swift and Cynthia S. Easterling, *Webster Park: 1892–1992* (Webster Groves: Scholin Brothers Company, 1993). *In Retrospect: Webster Groves, Missouri* (Webster Groves: Webster Groves Local History Project, No date). Mary Jo Mahley, *The Rock Beneath: 100 Years Ago in Webster Groves* (St. Louis: Century Registry, 1996). Ann Morris and Henrietta Ambrose, *North Webster: A Photographic History of a Black Community* (Bloomington, Indiana: Indiana University Press, 1993). Timothy J. Fox, *Where We Live, Webster Groves* (St. Louis: Missouri Historical Society, 1993–1994).

area. Wellston School District serves the area. Early photographs and memorabilia about Wellston are available online.[98]

WILDWOOD, incorporated in 1995, is located in far west St. Louis County and borders Franklin County. This rural and wooded suburb covers more square miles than the City of St. Louis and includes Babler State Park, Greensfelder County Park, and Rockwoods Reservation, maintained by Missouri Department of Conservation. Rockwood School District serves the area. The Wildwood Historical Society and the Wildwood Historic Commission maintain the community history and have identified the location of numerous cemeteries and historical buildings in Wildwood.[99]

Contact the local historical society for information about that area. Many societies focus on the structures and landmarks in their community, others have some genealogical background. The State Historical Society of Missouri in Columbia offers an online listing of these societies and their contact information (http://shs.umsystem.edu/directory). The local city hall or government center can provide contact information as well.

Today St. Louis County consists of ninety-one incorporated cities or towns listed in Figure 5. The St. Louis County government website (http://www.stlouisco.com/scripts/communities) offers information, statistics, and contact information for each community. Did your ancestors live in one or more of these areas? Perhaps their local history may assist in your research.

---

98.   "History-Memories-Stories of Wellston, St. Louis County, Missouri," *RootsWeb* (http:// freepages.history.rootsweb.com). *Built St. Louis: Vanished Buildings* (http://www.builtstlouis .net/wellstonloop01.html).

99.   Wildwood Historical Society, *At Rest in Wildwood: Burial Sites, History of Cemetery Traditions and Stories of Our Passing* (Wildwood: Wildwood Historical Society, 2005). "City History," *City of Wildwood, Missouri* (http://www.cityofwildwood.com).

St. Louis County Municipalities

Ballwin	Ladue
Bella Villa	Lakeshire
Bellefontaine Neighbors	Mackenzie
Bellerive	Manchester
Bel-Nor	Maplewood
Bel-Ridge	Marlborough
Berkeley	Maryland Heights
Beverly Hills	Moline Acres
Black Jack	Normandy
Breckenridge Hills	Northwoods
Brentwood	Norwood Court
Bridgeton	Oakland
Calverton Park	Olivette
Champ	Overland
Charlack	Pacific
Chesterfield	Pagedale
Clarkson Valley	Pasadena Hills
Clayton	Pasadena Park
Cool Valley	Pine Lawn
Country Club Hills	Richmond Heights
Country Life Acres	Riverview
Crestwood	Rock Hill
Creve Coeur	Saint Ann
Crystal Lake Park	Saint George
Dellwood	Saint John
Des Peres	Shrewsbury
Edmundson	Sunset Hills
Ellisville	Sycamore Hills
Eureka	Town and Country
Fenton	Twin Oaks
Ferguson	University City
Flordell Hills	Uplands Park
Florissant	Valley Park
Frontenac	Velda City
Glendale	Velda Village Hills
Glen Echo Park	Vinita Park
Grantwood Village	Vinita Terrace
Greendale	Warson Woods
Green Park	Webster Groves
Hanley Hills	Wellston
Hazelwood	Westwood
Hillsdale	Wilbur Park
Huntleigh	Wildwood
Jennings	Winchester
Kinloch	Woodson Terrace
Kirkwood	

Figure 5: Table of St. Louis County Municipalities

St. Louis Area Repositories

Government repositories hold original records dating from the formation of St. Louis to the current day. St. Louis City Hall and the Civil Courts Building hold County records up to 1877 and City records from 1823 to the current day. St. Louis County Government Center includes the Administration Building and the Courts Building, each holding records from 1877 forward.

Missouri State Archives, in Jefferson City, maintains the history of the state, and some of their records relate to St. Louis and its citizens. Another state supported facility, the State Historical Society of Missouri, in Columbia, houses a reference room, manuscript collection, and the largest newspaper collection in the state.

Federal repositories include the Thomas Eagleton Federal Courthouse, NARA Military Personnel Records Center, and NARA Civilian Personnel Records Center, all located in St. Louis. The National Archives–Central Plains regional facility in Kansas City holds St. Louis federal records.

There are several archival facilities in St. Louis, including Missouri Historical Society Research Library and Mercantile Library. Each facility has unique collections important to genealogists.

Educational facilities such as University of Missouri–St. Louis, St. Louis University, and Washington University house publications and records pertinent to St. Louis. Each campus has a government documents department. St. Louis University and Washington University have law libraries.

The National Park Service, with two locations in St. Louis, maintains the Jefferson National Expansion Memorial (the Arch and Old Courthouse), and White Haven, all important areas in the history of the area.

St. Louis Genealogical Society collects records and volunteers index the data. Historic houses and museums offer insight into their community. The Association of St. Louis Area Archivists provides a directory of research facilities on their website, including archival facilities, business, and libraries.[100]

---

100. *Association of St. Louis Area Archivists* (http://www.stlarchivists.org/index.php?pr=Directory).

The options for families who crossed county or even state boundaries to live or work are just as extensive. Some of your ancestors may have lived in an adjoining county as a child or perhaps married there. It is common to find St. Louis direct and collateral families living or working in the surrounding St. Louis counties, often referred to today as the St. Louis metropolitan area. Madison, St. Clair, and Monroe Counties in Illinois have great connections to St. Louis. Likewise, St. Charles, Franklin, and Jefferson Counties in Missouri are important locations for St. Louis residents. While not specifically covered in this publication, all of the previously mentioned counties have very good research facilities.

In addition, the Illinois State Archives in Springfield, Illinois, may hold a missing document. Or, a document may be located at an Illinois Regional Archives Depository (IRAD). The IRAD website provides information on their locations and holdings.[101]

ST. LOUIS GOVERNMENT CENTERS

St. Louis City Hall

Completed about 1898, St. Louis City Hall (1200 Market Street, St. Louis 63103) is located at the corner of Market Street and Tucker (12th) Boulevard. This facility is the repository for the original deed records dating back to 1804 and some dated even earlier. It also holds all St. Louis County records before 1877 and all City records to date.

RECORDER OF DEEDS OFFICE (City Hall, Archives Department, Room 127; phone 314-622-4610; http://stlouis.missouri.org/citygov/recorder) maintains and houses the deed, birth, death, and marriage records. You may visit City Hall or send requests by mail.

COMPTROLLER'S ARCHIVES OFFICE (City Hall, Microfilm Archives, Room 1; phone 314-622-4274) has an assortment of records, including topics such as employment, taxes, and voting, available via microfilm in the lower level comptroller's office.

ASSESSOR'S OFFICE (City Hall, Room 114; phone 314-622-3212) is the best place to trace the history of a house or property by following the trail of ownership.

St. Louis Civil Courts Building

The Civil Courts Building (10 North Tucker Street, St. Louis 63101), across the street from City Hall, houses the Probate Court office and the Circuit Court office. The Probate Court houses wills, guardianships, and estate files.

PROBATE COURT OFFICE (Civil Courts Building, 10th floor; phone 314-622-4301) houses original probate packets—including wills, guardianships, and estate files—after 1900 to the present. Missouri State Archives is microfilming earlier records, so their availability varies. Records starting in 1802 are available on microfilm (ending date varies) and records from 1802 to 1900 are online at the Missouri State Archives website.

CIRCUIT COURT OFFICE (Civil Courts Building, 1st floor; phone 314-622-4405) maintains civil and criminal court records including divorce records. Since the office stores some

---

101. "Illinois Regional Archives Depository System," *Illinois State Archives* (http://www .cyberdriveillinois.com/departments/archives/irad/iradhome.html).

records offsite, contacting the clerk to order records prior to a visit provides the most efficient use of your time.

Law Library Association of St. Louis

The Law Library Association of St. Louis (Civil Courts Building, 10 North Tucker Boulevard, St. Louis 63101; phone 314-622-4386; http://tlc.library.net/lla/default.asp), established in 1838, brought a law library to the courthouse. Today it is available to attorneys and is open to the public.

St. Louis County Government Center

St. Louis County Government Center (41 South Central, Clayton 63105; phone 314-615-5000; http://www.co.st-louis.mo.us) is the repository for County records starting in 1877. In the twenty-first century, St. Louis government records are available in three buildings within the center. Some of the offices within these buildings are pertinent to family historians. A St. Louis County Government Center campus map is available online (http://www.stlouisco.com/ Clayton_Campus.pdf).

- The Administration building holds the Recorder of Deeds office, County Planning (maps), and the County Clerk's office.

  RECORDER OF DEEDS OFFICE (Administration Building; phone 314-615-3747; http://revenue .stlouisco.com/RecorderOfDeeds) houses marriage and deed records. They will copy and mail most marriage records, eliminating the need for an onsite visit.

- The Courts Building (7900 Carondelet Avenue, Clayton 63105; phone 314-615-5000; http://www.co.st-louis.mo.us) contains Probate Court (probate and wills), plus general court records including Civil (divorce) and Criminal Court records.[102]

  PROBATE OFFICE (Courts Building; phone 314-615-2629; http://www.stlouisco.com/circuit court/probate.html) houses St. Louis County wills and probate documents starting in 1877. Their website offers a search option which provides the probate case numbers. Many of these records are available at St. Louis County Library, Special Collections, on microfilm or microfiche.

  COURT RECORDS (Courts Building; phone 314-615-8015; http://stlouisco.com/circuitcourt/ circlerk.html) includes an online searchable database for court cases.

  ST. LOUIS COUNTY LAW LIBRARY (Courts Building, 5th floor; phone 314-615-4726).

- Vital Records Department (111 South Meramec Avenue, Clayton 63105), which includes birth and death certificates, is in a building across the street from the other two buildings.

  BIRTH AND DEATH RECORDS (Vital Records Building; phone 314-615-0376; http://www .stlouisco.com/doh/vitals/vitals.html) are available for St. Louis County and other Missouri counties.

---

102. Bernard L. Lewandowski and Mary C. Dahm, *Mount Olive to Carondelet: 125 Years of Justice in the St. Louis County Circuit Court* (Clayton: St. Louis County Law Library, 2006).

RESEARCH REPOSITORIES

Carondelet Historical Society and Museum

Carondelet Historical Society and Museum (6303 Michigan Avenue, St. Louis 63111; phone 314-481-6303) is perhaps a hidden treasure for many genealogists. Their scope and collections include an area far beyond the original village of Carondelet. They cover the area approximately from the Mississippi River on the east and Gravois Road on the west, Morganford Road on the north to an area south of Forder Road, including Jefferson Barracks and part of South St. Louis County.

The holdings include books, photographs, newspapers, and memorabilia. The subject files contain organized material on cemeteries, churches, histories, parks, and schools. Books line many shelves and they have a great map collection. The library houses three area newspaper collections: the *Carondelet News*, 1900–1935; *Naborhood Link News,* 1930–1998; both on microfilm, and the *Bugle*, 1945–1994, available in paper format.

Special collections include the original papers from Clement Delore, the founder of Carondelet. The Cleveland High School Collection features donated yearbooks and other school memorabilia. The Military collection offers more than 1,000 photographs and a family fact sheet on each veteran. A donated art collection is often on display, as are artifacts from years past. Tony Fusco, an unofficial volunteer historian at Jefferson Barracks, donated his collection of some park artifacts. Other donated collections are the Golden Eagle River Museum Collection, the Carondelet Sunday Morning Club Collection, and the Carondelet Women's Club, all old established social organizations.

Mercantile Library

Mercantile Library (University of Missouri–St. Louis, Thomas Jefferson Library, One University Boulevard, St. Louis 63121-4400; phone 314-516-7240; http://www.umsl.edu/mercantile), established in 1847, is one of the oldest private libraries west of the Mississippi River. This formerly private library, now open to the public, is located on the campus of the University of Missouri–St. Louis. Their website offers various St. Louis resources including some unique items listed under Special Collections.

This facility is the repository for the *St. Louis Globe-Democrat* newspaper morgue. Published from 1849 to 1989, this newspaper served as the conservative voice for the community. An online surname index, dating from approximately 1930 to 1989, offers the date and title of articles. Starting about 1920, the *Globe* staff clipped and filed articles in envelopes for easy retrieval and research. Upon request, genealogists can view these articles in the research room.

Herman T. Pott National Inland Waterways Library is located within the Mercantile Library. This collection includes more than 15,000 volumes covering river history, vessel information, river transportation, navigation practices, and other topics on the inland waterways dating from the 1820s to the present. Photographs and manuscript collections are also part of the Pott

Collection. Refer to the Mercantile Library catalog or the WorldCat catalog for further collection information.[103]

John W. Barriger III, National Railroad Library is also located within the Mercantile Library. The extensive collection consists of more than 15,000 books, photographs, and corporate papers. Another collection, Association of American Railroads—Bureau of Railway Economics Historical Collection, has more than 30,000 volumes of printed material. All of this material is open to the public.[104]

Missouri Historical Society Research Library

The Missouri Historical Society Research Library (225 South Skinker Boulevard; MAILING ADDRESS Post Office Box 11940, St. Louis 63112-0040; phone 314-746-4500; http://www .mohistory.org), dates to 1866, when forty-seven founding individuals met at the courthouse to organize a historical society "for the purpose of saving from oblivion the early history of the city and state." The society rented space prior to establishing their first permanent home located at 1600 Locust Street from 1887 to 1913. Today their museum is located in Forest Park on Lindell Boulevard.[105]

The library and archives specialize in territorial, early statehood, and St. Louis records. Missouri Fur Trade records, city directories, fire insurance maps, newspapers, and numerous manuscript collections are just a sample of their holdings. They also have family histories, county histories, and a collection of printed resources from every state.

The library card catalog and archives catalog index people, places, and events in the history of St. Louis. The *Guide to the Civil War Manuscripts* is a helpful online finding aid.[106]

The online *Guide to Archival Collections* provides an alphabetical list of the collections and their contents. Detailed information about some of these collections is online with more being added regularly. Among the notable collections is the Swekosky Collection, which includes photographs of St. Louis and its citizens from the first half of the twentieth century. The favorite school, church, or building of your ancestor may be in this collection and copies may be ordered. Other collections, such as the Dexter Tiffany Collection, contain original documents that are of interest and available to genealogists.

The *Genealogy and Local History Index* contains several hundred thousand names, continues to grow and will soon be available online. This index includes names from unique publications and many manuscript collections that are available in the library or archives. The staff and many volunteers have spent countless hours preparing this valuable index. Researchers may find their

---

103. "Herman T. Pott National Inland Waterways Library Collection," *St. Louis Mercantile Library* (http:// www.umsl.edu/pott).

104. "John W. Barriger III National Railroad Library," *St. Louis Mercantile Library* (http://www .umsl.edu/barriger).

105. "Missouri Historical Society 140th Anniversary," *Missouri Historical Society 140th Anniversary Magazine Special Edition* (July/August 2006).

106. "Civil War Manuscript Guide," *Missouri Historical Society* (http://www.mohistory.org/ content/LibraryAndResearch/lrccollectionguide.html).

ancestors listed in publications and records otherwise often overlooked, then order a copy of the publication or manuscript from the index. The publications or images are not available online.

Special articles and features about St. Louis history appear on the *Voices* section of their website (http://www.mhsvoices.org). Check it out!

Missouri State Archives — St. Louis Branch

Missouri State Archives has a St. Louis branch (710 North Tucker, Globe Building, St. Louis 63101; phone 314-588-1746; http://www.sos.mo.gov/archives), which houses St. Louis-related records. The staff works directly with St. Louis City Circuit Court records, some of which are online with more to follow. While working with the documents, the staff has uncovered many records important to the area including those dealing with fur trading and emancipation.[107]

St. Louis Genealogical Society

St. Louis Genealogical Society (4 Sunnen Drive, Suite 140, St. Louis 63143; phone 314-547-8547; http://www.stlgs.org) is an all-volunteer organization founded in 1968. The Society has two publications: a monthly newsletter *News 'N Notes* and the *St. Louis Genealogical Society Quarterly*. The Society's research collection is housed at St. Louis County Library, Special Collections Department, but there are some reference materials at the office to assist volunteers with indexing and microfilming projects and to aid in the genealogical educational opportunities available at the office. The society is proud of their more than 2,100 national and international members who support and assist the Society's mission.

The St. Louis Genealogical Society promotes family history research by providing educational and research opportunities, offering community services, and collecting, preserving, and publishing genealogical and historical records.

St. Louis County Library

St. Louis County Library, Special Collections Department (1640 South Lindbergh Boulevard, St. Louis 63131; phone 314-994-3300; http://www.slcl.org) has extensive genealogical holdings. It houses the St. Louis Genealogical Society Collection, the National Genealogical Society Book Loan Collection, the Julius K. Hunter and Friends African American Research Collection, and the Mary F. Berthold Collection. The St. Louis Catholic Archdiocesan Parish records are available on microfilm as are many Lutheran and United Church of Christ church records. They also hold the library collection from the former Jewish Genealogical Society of St. Louis and a rich collection of Yizkor books.

The website contains many indexes and finding aids. While this facility has numerous records and maps on St. Louis, it also holds publications on all states east of the Mississippi River and most states west of the River.

St. Louis Public Library

St. Louis Public Library (1301 Olive Boulevard, St. Louis 63103; phone 314-241-2288; http://www.slpl.org) was established in 1865 and expanded in 1901. It has an extensive book

107. "St. Louis Circuit Court Historical Records Project," *Missouri State Archives* (http://www.stlcourtrecords.wustl.edu/index.php).

collection and an excellent microfilm collection. This collection specializes in the states that were part of the migration path to St. Louis. They also have a good collection on immigration related resources. The library website offers an index of the family histories (http://www.slpl.org/slpl/gateways.asp). The staff-developed online information continues to expand and now includes obituary indexes, book indexes, and various lists. To easily locate the online databases, select the site map, move to the bottom of the list, and click on *Other Databases*. In addition to the Local History and Genealogy department, the library has an extensive European map collection and a great government documents collection.

St. Louis University Library, Pius XII Memorial Library

St. Louis University Pius XII Memorial Library (3650 Lindell Boulevard, St. Louis 63108; phone 314-977-3580; http://www.slu.edulibraries/pius) is on the campus in midtown St. Louis. The University, established in 1818, includes a law library and federal depository library, which offers an extensive government documents collection.

University of Missouri–St. Louis, Thomas Jefferson Library

The Thomas Jefferson Library (University of Missouri–St. Louis Campus, One University Boulevard, St. Louis 63121; phone 314-516-5060; http://www.umsl.edu/services/tjl) is the home of the University of Missouri–St. Louis Library, Mercantile Library, and the St. Louis branch of the Western Historical Manuscript Collection. Numerous online databases are available while you are visiting the campus. This facility is a federal depository library and has a government documents collection.

Washington University Library

Washington University Library (Olin Library, One Brookings Drive, St. Louis 63130; phone 314-935-5444; http://www.library.wustl.edu/unitsspec/archives) has more than 200 collections that document St. Louis communities. An online finding aid details the holdings (http://library.wustl.edu/units/spec/archives/guides).

The Washington University West Campus Library (7425 Forsyth Boulevard, Lower Level, St. Louis 63105; phone 314-935-9889; http://library.wust.edu/unitswestcampus) houses the government documents collection of the library, including the U.S. Serial Set. The facility has original local Sanborn Fire Insurance maps and other St. Louis information. Visitors have access to the university's computer databases while onsite.

Western Historical Manuscript Collection — St. Louis Branch

The Western Historical Manuscript Collection (Thomas Jefferson Library, University of Missouri–St. Louis, One University Boulevard, St. Louis 63121; phone 314-516-5143; http://www.umsl.edu/~whmc) is part of the State Historical Society of Missouri. Though based in Columbia, branches operate at University facilities in Kansas City, Rolla, and St. Louis. The material from any repository is available via the St. Louis site. Online finding aids address businesses, individuals, locations, and an assortment of other topics. The St. Louis facility has a special African American collection and a St. Louis vertical file with the folder index online (http://www.umsl.edu/~whmc/guides/whm0694/htm).

FAMILY HISTORY CENTERS

The Church of Jesus Christ of Latter-day Saints provides access to the Family History Centers microfiche, microfilm, and databases. The Family History Library website includes the library catalog and many research guides (http://www.familysearch.org). Two centers operate in St. Louis.

- Frontenac Family History Center (10445 Clayton Road, Frontenac 63131; phone 314-993-2328).

- Hazelwood Family History Center (6386 Howdershell Road, Hazelwood 63042; phone 314-731-5373).

REPOSITORIES OUTSIDE ST. LOUIS

Family History Library — Salt Lake City, Utah

The Family History Library (FHL) (35 North West Temple Street, Salt Lake City, Utah 84150–3440; http://www.familysearch.org) is the premier genealogical library in the world and includes a good collection of St. Louis records. St. Louis City and St. Louis County records are available under both the City and County heading; therefore, it is necessary to look under each heading to locate all St. Louis-related records. Microfilmed copies of the St. Louis Catholic Archdiocesan Parish records are available at the Family History Library. This facility has the most complete set of St. Louis deed and marriage records on microfilm outside of St. Louis City Hall. The Family History Library continues to expand their online records, with the catalog now indicating when a book or record is available online.

Missouri State Archives — Jefferson City

Missouri State Archives (600 West Main Street, Post Office Box 1747, Jefferson City 65102; phone 573-751-3280; http://www.sos.mo.gov/archives) maintains the memory of the state. The Archives has an extensive amount of information in manuscript format, on microfilm, and online, including documents from all 114 counties. *Guide to Civil War Resources at the Missouri State Archives* and *Guide to African American History at the Missouri State Archives* are two helpful finding aids available online at the Archives website.

The Archives has an online listing of microfilmed St. Louis City and County records. Copies of some of these films are available at St. Louis repositories. For assistance with copies, researchers may use the Archives email request form.[108]

State Historical Society of Missouri — Columbia

State Historical Society of Missouri (1020 Lowry Street, Columbia 65201; phone 573-882-7083; http://www.umsystem.edu/shs) is located in the Ellis Library building on the campus of the University of Missouri. Established in 1898 and state supported, this facility has an excellent

---

108. Email policy and procedures, *Missouri State Archives* (http://www.sos.mo.gov/archives resources/email.asp).

reference room with an extensive amount of St. Louis references. The Missouri chapter of the Daughters of the American Revolution houses their collection in the reference room.

Missouri has one of the largest newspaper collections in the country. Indexes are available for some of the earlier newspapers, with a few available online. Another online listing identifies newspaper titles divided by location, cities, and counties.[109] The Society's website describes the process for requesting copies for articles found in the index with a nominal fee discounted for society members.

RELIGIOUS REPOSITORIES

Archdiocese of St. Louis Archives

The Roman Catholic Archdiocese of St. Louis Archives (Archdiocesan Archives, 20 Archbishop May Drive, St. Louis 63119; phone 314-792-7020; http://www.archstl.org/archives) preserves general church records and closed parish records including baptismal, confirmation, and marriage documents. Most open churches maintain their own records. Historical parish records are available at the Archives; however, researchers need a signed release from the individual for those records dated after 1930. The Archdiocese allowed filming of many records in the 1990s and those are available on microfilm only at St. Louis County Library, Special Collections and the Family History Library. The Archives maintains a file on all Archdiocesan priests. The biographical information contained in this file may be very helpful if a member of your family became a priest.

Brodsky Jewish Community Library

The Saul Brodsky Jewish Community Library (12 Millstone Campus Drive, St. Louis 63146; phone 314-442-3720; http://brodskylibrary.org/aboutus.php), established in 1983, combined the collections of several smaller Jewish facilities. There are numerous items of interest to genealogists including photographs and journals, including the newspaper, *St. Louis Jewish Light*.

Concordia Historical Institute

Concordia Historical Institute (804 Seminary Place, St. Louis 63105; phone 314-505-7935; http://chi.lcms.org) is located on the campus of Concordia Seminary and operated by the Lutheran Church–Missouri Synod.

The research facility has records from Lutheran congregations in the Missouri Synod. Among them are files on many Lutheran pastors and publications from the churches, such as anniversary editions. The guide, *Researching at Concordia Historical Institute,* is available at the website. The limited staff conducts research as time permits. Current hours and fees are available online or in a printed brochure.

---

109. *State Historical Society of Missouri* (http://www.umsystem.edu/shs/mhr.shtml).

Eden Theological Seminary, Luhr Library

The Archives at Eden Seminary (Luhr Library, 475 E. Lockwood Avenue, Webster Groves 63119; phone 314-252-3140; http://www.eden.edu/index.php/archives) holds information about the Evangelical Synod before it merged in 1934.

An online publication by Archivist, Scott Holl, *Guide to United Church of Christ Congregations in St. Louis City and County,* provides historical information about the churches.[110] The Archives has original church records, most of which have been microfilmed. Genealogists can use the microfilmed records at St. Louis County Library, Special Collections, checking with the Archives if the document is hard to read or flawed.

The Archives has newspapers and journals, which contain articles and obituaries about the pastors and news of congregations. The Archives has a complete (1850–1975) original set of the newspaper *Der Friedensbote.* This publication was printed in German until 1902, when the English version began.

A card index identifies clergy ordained before 1934. It provides the name, date and place of birth, date of immigration, name of seminary and when the pastor attended, plus date of graduation, marriage, date and place of death, and the obituary citation. The card also identifies the location and date of each congregation served by that pastor. The Archives has an in-house database that includes all of the graduating students from Eden Seminary. If this is of interest, email your ancestor's name and the Archivist will check the list for you.

NATIONAL ARCHIVES & RECORDS ADMINISTRATION (NARA)

National Archives and Records Administration — Kansas City

National Archives–Central Plains Region (2312 East Bannister Road, Kansas City 64131; phone 816-268-8000; http://www.archives.gov/central-plains/kansas-city) holds many federal files relating to St. Louis. As an example, they have the original post-1906 naturalization ledgers and the related card index for naturalizations in St. Louis. [This facility is scheduled to move to the Kansas City Union Station in late 2008.]

National Archives and Records Administration — St. Louis

Military Personnel Records Center

Military Personnel Records Center (9700 Page Avenue, St. Louis 63132; phone 314-801-0800; http://www.archives.gov/st-louis/military-personnel/public/archival-programs.html) is the repository of military personnel records for various years. Some of the records have been "archived" sixty-two years after the veteran separated from the service. These archived records are open and available to all researchers. More recent records are still considered "Official Military Personnel Files" and only available to the veteran or next-of-kin. Check their website for the most recent information. Record requests can be mailed to the address listed above. Some material is stored at an offsite facility.

---

110. "Guide to United Church of Christ Congregations in St. Louis City and County," *The Archives at Eden Theological Seminary* (http://library.webster.edu/luhr_library/guides/stl_guide_intro.html).

Civilian Personnel Records Center

Civilian Personnel Records Center (111 Winnebago Street, St. Louis 63118; phone 314-801-9250; http://www.archives.gov/st-louis/civilian-personnel/index.html) holds personnel records for civilian employees of the U.S. government after approximately 1880. This includes personnel records for those in the federal Works Progress Administration (WPA) and Civilian Conservation Corps (CCC).

Several CCC projects took place in St. Louis County in the 1930s. The men who participated in these projects may or may not have been St. Louisans. Assignments varied; some men stayed in their local area; others traveled to other counties and states. If an ancestor served in the CCC as a federal employee, contact the Civilian Personnel Records Center requesting your ancestor's COMPLETE file. Most files are very informative. The easiest way to obtain a record is via mail stating the request is made based on the Freedom of Information Act.

NATIONAL PARK SERVICE

National Park Service — Jefferson National Expansion Memorial

Named in honor of President Thomas Jefferson who was responsible for the Louisiana Purchase, the Jefferson National Expansion Memorial (Old Courthouse, 11 North Fourth Street, St. Louis 63102; phone 314-655-1700; http://www.nps.gov/jeff) consists of the Old Courthouse and the Arch grounds. The Louisiana Purchase opened the St. Louis area and points west to new migration and westward expansion. The Old Courthouse and surrounding area was the site of the Dred Scott case in which a slave sued for his freedom.

The Arch has a wonderful museum showing the path and hardships of Lewis and Clark. The museum has a sod house, life-size mounted plains animals, and Native American artifacts. The Arch bookstore specializes in publications on the fur traders, westward expansion, and meaning of the Gateway to the West.

The Courthouse library and archival facility are open to the public, with appointments suggested. Online finding aids provide information on the Jefferson National Expansion Park, St. Louis, and westward expansion.[111] The facility has an outstanding bookstore focusing on the events at the courthouse and St. Louis in general.

National Park Service — White Haven

Frederick Dent, the future father-in-law of President Ulysses S. Grant, owned a two-hundred-acre plantation named White Haven, located in St. Louis County approximately between Watson and Gravois Roads. His daughter, Julia, married Ulysses S. Grant in St. Louis while he was in the military service before the Civil War.

Eventually the property was subdivided into residential, commercial, and cemetery property. The present day Grant's Farm, owned by Anheuser-Busch Corporation and the Busch family, was

---

111. "Collections," *National Park Service, Jefferson National Expansion Memorial* (http://www.nps.gov/jeff/historyculture/collections.htm).

part of the southwest portion of the property. Grant's original cabin, *Hardscrabble*, is located on Grant's Farm property. The property is open for free tours from April through October.

Located across the road from Grant's Farm, the remaining White Haven (Visitor's Center, 7400 Grant Road, St. Louis 63123; phone 314-842-3298; http://www.nps.gov/ulsg) property and the restored home are open for tours daily. The National Park site has a bookstore, which focuses on President Grant, the Dent family, and St. Louis. Park rangers will help with limited research questions.[112]

ADJOINING COUNTIES

Libraries, historical, and genealogical societies, and government repositories are available in all adjoining counties. Listed below is one site for each county and that organization or their website will lead you to other facilities and records.

Missouri

FRANKLIN COUNTY: Washington Historical Society (4th and Market Streets, Washington 63090; phone 636-239-0280; http://www.washmohistorical.org/index.htm) in Franklin County is the home of the Four Rivers Genealogical Society. Other Franklin County links are available at (http://www.rootsweb.com/~mofrankl/historicalsoc.htm).

JEFFERSON COUNTY: Jefferson County Historical Society (c/o DeSoto Public Library, 71 Main Street, DeSoto 63020; http://www.rootsweb.com/~mojchs/about.html) has a great collection of Jefferson County records, including a cemetery index.

ST. CHARLES COUNTY: St. Charles County Historical Society (101 South Main Street, St. Charles 63301; phone 636-946-9828; http://www.youranswerplace.org/other/historical_society) preserves the history and the historical documents in St. Charles, Missouri's first capital, and provides links to other St. Charles research facilities and organizations.

Illinois

MADISON COUNTY: Madison County Genealogical Society (Post Office Box 631, Edwardsville, Illinois 62025; http://www.rootsweb.com/~ilmadcgs) and the Edwardsville Public Library provide assistance for the area.

MONROE COUNTY: Monroe County Genealogical Society (Post Office Box 381, Columbia, Illinois 62236; http://www.rootsweb.com/~ilmcghs) collection is housed at the Morrison-Talbot Public Library in Waterloo (http://www.waterloolibrary.org/main.shtml).

ST. CLAIR COUNTY: St. Clair County Genealogical Society (Post Office Box 431, Belleville, Illinois 62222-0431; http://www.stclair-ilgs.org/stchome.htm) maintains its genealogical collection at Belleville Public Library (http://www.stclair-ilgs.org/BPL.htm).

---

112. "Whitehaven," *National Park Service* (http://www.nps.gov/ulsg/). "Grant's Farm," *Anheuser–Busch Corporation* (http://www.grantsfarm.com/GrantsCabin.htm).

Academia in St. Louis

Educational opportunities provide insight into the life and times of our ancestors. Some ancestors could neither read nor write, while others attended school for several years. Some people had numerous books in their homes, and provided advanced education for their children.

St. Louis has a strong educational community with public and private schools, ranging from kindergarten to graduate school. The table in Figure 6 lists the names and websites for the area school districts along with a few private schools. Missouri Historical Society Research Library has eight bound volumes, *St. Louis Schools*, which include newspaper clippings dating from 1922 to 1977.[113]

Susan Blow started the first public kindergarten in the United States in the Carondelet neighborhood. Blow's kindergarten class met in the same building that today houses the Carondelet Historical Society, mentioned previously.

St. Louis Public School District (Student Record Room, 801 North 11th Street, St. Louis 63101; phone 314-231-3720; http://www.slps.org/slps_history/index.htm) for example, provides records directly to former students with proper identification. School records of a deceased family member are available if a death certificate is provided.

In 1856, St. Louis Public Schools opened the first coeducational public school west of the Mississippi, located at 15th and Olive Streets. Their website provides a brief history of the St. Louis Public School system and *The Public and the Schools: Shaping the St. Louis School System, 1838–1920* provides a more complete history of the district.[114] Harris Stowe State University, formerly part of the St. Louis Public School system, houses the history of this institution, as well as some of the history of the St. Louis Public Schools.

A *School Directory: School Addresses and Boundaries, Superintendents, Attendance Officers, Directors, Hygiene Inspectors, Nurses and Supervisors, Teachers' Names and Addresses* provides a list of teachers and other school employees, school name, and the

---

113. *St. Louis Schools*, 8 volumes (St. Louis: Missouri Historical Society, no date).

114. Selwyn K. Troen, *The Public and the Schools: Shaping the St. Louis School System, 1838–1920* (Columbia: University of Missouri Press, 1975).

employee's home address. This 1942–1943 school yearbook also lists all teachers and others employed at each school.[115]

Early St. Louis Public Schools' payroll manuals, 1874–1875 and 1885–1886, provide clues to life as a teacher in the late nineteenth century. These records provide a list of the school officials and teachers divided by school, then grade. They give the name of the teacher, subject, and salary. As an example, one teacher may have taught German, and another worked as the First German Assistant. The *semi-quarterly* pay listed for pay period of September 7 to October 9, 1874 showed salaries ranging from $2.50 to $7.50 for the teachers and principals.[116]

A publication about St. Louis County schools provides the name of each teacher and his or her home address, grade, and name of school in some school districts in 1916–1917. The St. Louis County schools consolidated or organized in 1928. The 1937–1938 report provides the school district, schools, then a list of the teachers within each school. The schools listed (in order of publication) are as follows:[117]

University City	Kirkwood	Bayless	Mehlville
Webster Groves	Wellston	Brentwood	Berkeley
Normandy	Hancock	Riverview Gardens	Pattonville
Maplewood	Ferguson	Affton	Kinloch
Ritenour	West Walnut Manor	Eureka	
Clayton	Jennings	Valley Park	

The County schools reported to a county school superintendent, who made reports to the state school superintendent. The annual reports, housed at the Missouri State Archives, provide great information about the handful of county schools at that time. *The First Published Report of the Public Schools of St. Louis County, Missouri, for the School Year Ending June 30, 1902 …* provides information about the St. Louis County schools including the name of the teachers, cities where they lived, and the names of their schools.[118]

The Missouri State Archives has a manuscript collection, *Department of Elementary and Secondary Education*, which includes information on St. Louis schools. School superintendents submitted various reports to the state superintendent. This set of records could be helpful for ancestors involved in education. Some reports date back to 1907. They usually do not list students by name.[119] The Archives also has microfilm of deeds, leases, and supporting documents for the

115.   *A School Directory: School Addresses and Boundaries, Superintendents, Attendance Officers, Directors, Hygiene Inspectors, Nurses and Supervisors, Teachers' Names and Addresses* (St. Louis: St. Louis Public Schools, 1942–1943).

116.   City of St. Louis Public Schools Board of Education Payroll Manuals, 1874–1875, 1885–1886; Missouri State Archives film C13115.

117.   R. G. Russell, *List of Teachers, Names of Districts, Clerks in St. Louis County, Missouri by Towns, Consolidated Districts and Rural Schools for 1916–1917* (Clayton: R. G. Russell County Superintendent, 1916). Rufus G. Russell, *Public Schools of St. Louis County, Missouri, 1937–1938* (Clayton: Cooperating City Schools of St. Louis County, 1937).

118.   *The First Published Report of the Public Schools of St. Louis County, Missouri, for the School Year Ending June 30, 1902, Including Institution's Reports and List of Teachers for School Year Ending June 30, 1903* (Clayton: St. Louis County Schools, 1903).

119.   "Department of Elementary and Secondary Education," Missouri State Archives manuscript collection.

St. Louis Public Schools. This film could be helpful when tracing the history of a school building.[120]

Educational catalogs provide lists of the alumni, histories of the facilities, and they usually are indexed. As an example, *Washington University General Alumni Catalogue, 1917* lists the name of the alumni, the year they graduated, and business information since graduation.[121] Directories for other years and other schools are available at various locations.

St. Louis was the home of numerous nursing schools. The website, *Early History of Nursing Schools in St. Louis,* describes the schools and provides a few photographs.[122]

The availability of school records, especially those for students, varies from location to location. Some are available on microfilm and others are considered private; therefore, not accessible. You can contact the school of interest to determine their policy for releasing historical student records. All open school districts have websites that can assist you.

If the student records are not available, look for yearbooks for that era. Yearbooks, photographs, descriptions, and class lists may provide new clues for further research. Yearbook collections for St. Louis schools, usually obtained by donations from patrons, are available at local repositories as well as the State Historical Society of Missouri in Columbia.

SELECTED COLLEGES AND UNIVERSITIES

Listed below is a selected list of colleges and universities, the known years of operation, the name of the yearbook, and the school location as known and any notes. Addresses, unless otherwise noted, are St. Louis. Some facilities publish yearbooks, some no longer publish, a few used multiple names for the yearbook, and some never published a yearbook. Library catalogs may reveal the availability of the school yearbook for one or more years. However, some repository catalogs do not include yearbooks.

- Barnes Hospital School of Nursing, 1902–open, *Blue Band,* 306 South Kingshighway Boulevard, now called Barnes-Jewish College of Nursing.
- Cardinal Glennon College, 1842–open, *Ad Altare,* 5200 Glennon Drive, Shrewsbury.
- Concordia Seminary, 1839–open, *Seminarian* or *Alma Mater*, 801 Seminary Place, Clayton.[123]
- Covenant Theological Seminary, 1956–open, no yearbook, 12330 Conway Road, Creve Coeur.
- Eden Theological Seminary, 1850–open, yearly bulletin, 475 E. Lockwood Avenue, Webster Groves. This college was first located at Marthasville, Missouri, and then moved to Wellston.
- Fontbonne University, 1923–open, *Fontbonne,* 6800 Wydown Boulevard, Clayton.[124]

---

120.   Deeds, Leases, and Supporting Documents, 1788–1956; Missouri State Archives film C13987.

121.   *Washington University General Alumni Catalog* (St. Louis: The School, 1917).

122.   "Early History of Nursing Schools in St. Louis," *Washington University of St. Louis, School of Medicine* (http://beckerexhibits.wustl.edu/mowihsp/health/stlnursingschools.htm).

123.   John W. Klotz, *Light for our World* (St. Louis: Concordia Seminary, 1989). Theodore Graebner, *Concordia Seminary: Its History, Architecture, and Symbolism* (St. Louis: Concordia Publishing House, 1926).

124.   Jane Kehoe Hassett, *As Strong As the Granite: Vitality and Vision, Fontbonne at 75* (St. Louis: The College, 2000).

- Harris-Stowe State University, 1857–open, *Torch,* 3026 Laclede Street, St. Louis.[125]
- Logan College of Chiropractic, 1935–open, *Keystone*, 1851 Schoettler Road, Chesterfield.
- Maryville University, 1872–open, no yearbook, Maryville Center, Creve Coeur.
- Missouri Baptist University, 1957–open, *Spartan*, One College Park Drive, Creve Coeur.
- Missouri Medical College, 1885–1900, 1) 9th and Cerre Streets, 2) 8th and Gratiot Streets, and 3) Jefferson and Lucas Avenues. Then merged with the Medical Department of Washington University.[126]
- Principia College, 1901–open, *Sheaf,* originally located in St. Louis, now in Elsah, Illinois.[127]
- St. Louis College of Physicians and Surgeons, 1869–ca. 1893, *Prescription,* Jefferson Avenue and Gamble Street.
- St. Louis Community College:
  ○ Florissant Valley Campus, 1965–open, *La Fleur*, discontinued in the 1970s, 3400 Pershall Road in Ferguson.
  ○ Forest Park Campus, 1965–open, *Highlander*, located on the former Highland Amusement Park grounds at 5600 Oakland Avenue.
  ○ Meramec Campus, 1965–open, no yearbook, 11333 Big Bend Boulevard in Kirkwood.
  ○ Wildwood Campus, 2007–open, no yearbook, 2645 Generations Drive in Wildwood.
- St. Louis (City) Hospital School of Nursing, 1883–1980, *Announcement*, formerly located at City Hospital.[128]
- St. Louis University, 1818–open, *Archive,* Grand Avenue and Lindell Boulevard.[129]
- St. Luke's Hospital School of Nursing, 1889–1988, *The Lamp*, formerly located at St. Luke's Hospital. This school was originally called the St. Luke's Training School. Photographs of each graduating class are available in the St. Luke's North Medical Building on Woods Mill Road, Chesterfield.
- University of Missouri– St. Louis, 1963–open, no yearbook, One University Boulevard, Normandy.
- Washington University, 1853–open, *Hatchet,* was first named Eliot Seminary, then Smith Academy, before the final change to Washington University in 1857.[130]
- Webster University, 1915–open, *Lauretanum*, 470 East Lockwood Avenue, Webster Groves.

125.   *One Hundred Years of Teacher Education in the St. Louis Public School System* (St. Louis: St. Louis Board of Education, 1958).

126.   *St. Louis Medical Society Centennial Volume* (St. Louis: The Society, 1939).

127.   Edwin S. Leonard, *As the Sowing; The First Fifty Years of the Principia* (St. Louis: The School, 1951).

128.   St. Louis Hospital School of Nursing, 1883–1980; Missouri Historical Society manuscript collection. St. Louis Public Library has their yearbook collection.

129.   William Einspanier, editor, *St. Louis University, 150 Years* (St. Louis: The University, 1968). William Faherty, *Better the Dream: Saint Louis University and Community, 1818–1968* (St. Louis: The University, 1968).

130.   Ralph E. Morrow, *Washington University in St. Louis: A History* (St. Louis: Missouri Historical Society Press, 1996).

SELECTED HIGH SCHOOLS

Native or long-time St. Louis residents often ask new acquaintances, "Where did you go to high school?" Nobody knows how, when, or why this started, but for some reason high school is an important part of St. Louisans' personal history. Dan Dillon's *So, Where Did You Go to High School?* provides background, photographs, and trivia about the major high schools in St. Louis.[131] Yearbooks may cause reflection back to those high school years.

Published monthly starting in 1947, *Prom Magazine* provided individual columns of "very important inside information" (gossip) submitted by the students about their high schools. Despite the lack of an index, the magazines are easy to search by focusing on your high school(s) of interest. Perhaps your ancestor is mentioned by name or the information provides some idea of what went on during those high school years.

The selected list of City and County high schools includes name, dates of operation, name of yearbook, location, school district, and pertinent notes.

- Academy of the Visitation, 1833–open, *Crescent*, 3020 North Ballas Road, Catholic school formerly located on Kaskaskia Island; then moved to St. Louis 1) downtown, and 2) 5448 Cabanne Avenue.
- Affton High School, 1930–open, *Tartan*, 8309 Mackenzie Road, Affton Schools.
- Bayless High School, 1928–open, *Oracle*, 4530 Weber Road, Bayless Schools.
- Beaumont High School, 1926–open, *Caduceus*, 3836 Natural Bridge Road, City Schools.[132]
- Berkeley High School, 1937–2003, *Barker*, formerly at 8710 Walter Avenue, Berkeley Schools.
- Bishop DuBourg High School, 1950–open, *Cavalier*, 5850 Eichelberger Street, Catholic Schools.
- Brentwood High School, 1927–open, *Eagle*, 2221 High School Drive, Brentwood Schools.
- Central High School, 1853–1984, *Red & Black*, formerly at 3616 North Garrison Avenue, City Schools.
- Chaminade Preparatory School, 1910–open, *Cardinal*, 425 South Lindbergh Boulevard, Catholic Schools.
- Christian Brothers College High School (CBC), 1849–open, *Guidon*, 1850 de La Salle Drive, Creve Coeur, formerly at 1) 6501 Clayton Road, and 2) Kingshighway Boulevard and Franklin Avenue, Catholic Schools.[133]
- Clayton High School, 1907–open, *CLAMO*, 1 Mark Twain Circle, Clayton Schools.[134]
- Cleveland High School, 1915–1984, *Beacon*, formerly at 4352 Louisiana Avenue, City Schools.[135]
- Cor Jesu High School, 1956–open, *Corde*, 10230 Gravois Road, Catholic Schools.
- Country Day School, 1917–open, *CODASCO*, 101 North Warson Road, Ladue, private school, now part of Mary Institute Country Day School (MICDS).[136]
- DeSmet Jesuit High School, 1967–open, *Spartan*, 233 North Ballas Road, Catholic School.

---

131. Dan Dillon, *So, Where Did You Go to High School?* (St. Louis: Virginia Publishing, 2005).

132. Ross Boehning, *Index, Caduceus Yearbook Years 1961–1964* (St. Louis: The Author, 2006).

133. Mary E. Neighbour, *Let Us Remember CBC: The First 150 Years* (St. Louis: Christian Brothers College High School, 2000).

134. *The Clayton School District: A History of Excellence* (Clayton: Clayton School District, 2000).

135. Carondelet Historic Center houses Cleveland High School memorabilia and historical artifacts.

136. Gordon M. Browne, *St. Louis Country Day School: The First 50 Years* (St. Louis: The Author, 1967).

- Eureka High School, 1908–open, *Bugle*, 829 Highway 109, Rockwood Schools.
- Ferguson High School, 1939–1962, *Crest,* formerly at 701 January Street, Ferguson Schools.
- Hadley Technical High School, 1931–1963, *Flame & Steel*, formerly at 3405 Bell Avenue, City Schools.
- Hancock High School, 1920–open, *Memento*, 229 West Ripa Avenue, Hancock Place Schools.
- Hazelwood Central High School, 1954–open, *Torch*, 15875 New Halls Ferry Road, Hazelwood Schools.[137]
- Hazelwood East High School, 1974–open, *Pegasus*, 11300 Dunn Road, Hazelwood Schools.
- Hazelwood West High School, 1974–open, *Focus*, 1 Wildcat Lane, Hazelwood Schools.
- Incarnate Word Academy, 1932–open, no yearbook, 2788 Normandy Drive, Catholic Schools.
- Jennings High School, 1936–1976, *Jenecho,* formerly at 8850 Cozens Avenue, Jennings District.
- John Burroughs High School, 1923–open, *Governor,* 755 Price Road, private school, Ladue.
- Kennedy High School, 1968–open, *Profiles,* 500 Woods Mill Road, Catholic Schools.
- Kirkwood High School, 1896–open, *Pioneer,* 801 West Essex Avenue, Kirkwood Schools.
- Ladue Horton Watkins High School, 1952–open, *Rambler,* 1201 South Warson Road, Ladue Schools. [138]
- Lafayette High School, 1960–open, *Legend,* 17050 Clayton Road, Rockwood Schools.
- Lindbergh High School, 1951–open, *Spirit,* 4900 Lindbergh Boulevard, Lindbergh Schools.
- Maplewood-Richmond Heights High School, 1907–open, *Maple Leaves,* 7539 Manchester Road, Maplewood–Richmond Heights Schools.
- Marquette High School, 1993–open, *Medallion,* 2351 Clarkson Road, Rockwood Schools.
- Mary Institute, 1850s–open, *Chronicle*, 101 North Warson Road, Ladue, formerly at 1400 Lucas Place, Lake and Waterman Avenues (1902–1930), private school, now part of MICDS.[139]
- McBride High School, 1925–1971, *Colonnade,* formerly at 1909 North Kingshighway Boulevard, Catholic Schools.
- McClure High School, 1961–open, *Crest,* 1869 South New Florissant Road, Ferguson-Florissant Schools.
- McClure North High School, 1971–open, *Polaris,* 705 Waterford Drive, Ferguson-Florissant Schools.
- McKinley High School, 1904–1988, *Carnation,* formerly at 2156 Russell Boulevard, City Schools.
- Mehlville High School, 1925–open, *Reflector,* 3200 Lemay Ferry Road, Mehlville Schools. [140]
- Mercy High School, 1948–1985, *Mercian,* formerly at 1000 Pennsylvania Avenue, Catholic Schools.
- Nerinx Hall High School, 1924–open, *Key,* 530 East Lockwood Road, Catholic Schools.
- Normandy High School, 1923–open, *Saga,* 6701 St. Charles Rock Road, Normandy Schools.[141]
- Notre Dame High School, 1934–open, *Rebellion,* 320 East Ripa Avenue, Catholic Schools.

---

137.   Gregory M. Franzwa, *History of the Hazelwood School District* (Florissant: Board of Education, 1977).

138.   "Alumni Internet Directory*,"* *Ladue Horton Watkins High School* (http://www.laduealum .com).

139.   *Mary Institute: A Country Day School for Girls, 1929–1930* (St. Louis: Simmons-Sisler Company, 1930).

140.   Tracey A. Bruce, *A History of the Mehlville School District and Its Communities* (Donning Company Publishing, 2002).

141.   *Normandy School District: The First One Hundred Years* (Normandy: The Normandy School District Centennial Committee, 1994).

- Oakville High School, 1973–open, *Tiger Paw*, 5557 Milburn Road, Mehlville Schools.
- O'Fallon Technical High School, 1956–1992, *Flame & Steel*, 5101 McRee Avenue, currently named Gateway Institute of Technology, City Schools.
- Parkway Central High School, 1957–open, *Spur*, 369 North Woods Mill Road, Parkway Schools.
- Parkway North High School, 1971–open, *Saga*, 12860 Fee Fee Road, Parkway Schools.
- Parkway South High School, 1976–open, *Declaration*, 801 Hanna Road, Parkway Schools.
- Parkway West High School, 1968–open, *PAWESEHI*, 14653 Clayton Road, Parkway Schools.
- Pattonville High School, 1935–open, *Echo*, 2497 Creve Coeur Mill Road, Pattonville Schools.[142]
- Principia High School, 1898–open, *Blade*, 13201 Clayton Road, private school, Town and Country.
- Ritenour High School, 1911–open, *Melaureus*, 9100 St. Charles Rock Road, Ritenour Schools.
- Riverview Gardens High School, 1927–open, *Echoes*, 1218 Shepley Drive, Riverview Gardens Schools.
- Rockwood Summit High School, 1993–open, *Pinnacle*, 1780 Hawkins Road, Rockwood Schools.
- Roosevelt High School, 1925–open, *Bwana*, 3230 Hartford Avenue, City Schools.
- Rosary High School, 1961–2003, *Reveille*, formerly at 1720 Redman Road, Catholic Schools.
- Rosati-Kain High School, 1912–open, *Occasional*, 4389 Lindell Boulevard, Catholic Schools.
- St. Elizabeth Academy, 1882–open, *Thuringian*, 3401 Arsenal Avenue, Catholic Schools.
- St. Francis de Sales High School, 1939–1974, *Spire*, formerly at 2647 Ohio Avenue, Catholic Schools.
- St. John the Baptist High School, 1922–open, *Lions*, 5021 Adkins Avenue, Catholic Schools.
- St. John Vianney High School, 1960–open, *Talon*, 1311 South Kirkwood Road, Catholic Schools.
- St. Joseph's Academy High School, 1840–open, *Echo*, 2307 South Lindbergh, Catholic Schools.
- St. Louis Priory School, 1956–open, *Shield*, 500 South Mason Road, Catholic Schools.[143]
- St. Louis University High School, 1818–open, *Dauphin*, 4970 Oakland Avenue, Catholic Schools.
- St. Mary's High School, 1931–open, *Dragon*, 4701 South Grand Avenue, Catholic Schools.
- St. Thomas Aquinas High School, 1958–2003, *Talon*, formerly at 845 Dunn Road, Catholic Schools.
- Soldan High School, 1909–open, *Scrip*, 918 North Union Avenue, City Schools. Now open as Soldan International Studies High School.
- Southwest High School, 1937–1992, *Roundup*, formerly at 3125 South Kingshighway Boulevard, City Schools.
- Sumner High School, 1875–open, *Maroon & White*, 4248 West Cottage Avenue, City Schools.
- University City High School, 1915–open, *Dial*, 7401 Balson Avenue, University City Schools.
- Ursuline Academy, 1848–open, *Oak Leaves*, 341 South Sappington Road, Catholic Schools.
- Vashon High School, 1927–open, *Wolverine*, 3026 Laclede Avenue, City Schools.
- Villa Duchesne, 1929–open, *Entre Nous*, 801 South Spoede Road, Catholic Schools.
- Webster Groves High School, 1889–open, *Echo*, 100 Selma Avenue, Webster Groves Schools.
- Wellston High School, 1906–open, *Welhisco*, 1200 Sutter Avenue, Wellston Schools.

---

142. *Public Education in Pattonville: 150 Years of Preparing and Caring for the Youth of the Community, 1845–1995* (St. Ann: Pattonville School District, 1995).

143. Timothy Horner, *In Good Soil: The Founding of St. Louis Priory School, 1954–1973* (St. Louis: privately printed, 2001).

St. Louis City and County School Districts

CITY SCHOOL DISTRICT	
City of St. Louis School District	(http://www.slps.org)
COUNTY SCHOOL DISTRICTS	
Affton School District	(http://www.affton.k12.mo.us)
Bayless School District	(http://www2.csd.org/schools/bayless/baylesshome.html)
Brentwood School District	(http://www.brentwood.k12.mo.us)
Clayton School District	(http://www.clayton.k12.mo.us/clayton/site/default.asp)
Ferguson-Florissant School District	(http://fergflor.schoolwires.com/fergflor/site/default.asp)
Hancock Place School District	(http://hancock.k12.mo.us)
Hazelwood School District	(http://hsdportal.hazelwood.k12.mo.us/Pages/default.aspx)
Jennings School District	(http://www.jenningsk12.net)
Kirkwood School District	(http://www.kirkwoodschools.org)
Ladue School District	(http://www.ladue.k12.mo.us)
Lindbergh School District	(http://www.lindbergh.k12.mo.us)
Maplewood-Richmond Heights School District	(http://www.mrhsd.org)
Mehlville School District	(http://www.mehlvilleschooldistrict.com/wc/default.asp_Q_info_E_856968784_1)
Normandy School District	(http://www.normandy.k12.mo.us)
Parkway School District	(http://www.pkwy.k12.mo.us)
Pattonville School District	(http://www.pattonville.k12.mo.us)
Ritenour School District	(http://www.ritenour.k12.mo.us)
Riverview Gardens School District	(http://www.rgsd.org/rgsd/site/default.asp)
Rockwood School District	(http://www.rockwood.k12.mo.us)
University City School District	(http://ucityschools.org)
Valley Park School District	(http://www.vp.k12.mo.us)
Webster Groves School District	(http://www.webster.k12.mo.us/education/district/district.php?sectionid=1)
Wellston School District	(http://www.wellston.k12.mo.us)
SELECTED PRIVATE SCHOOLS	
St. Louis Catholic Schools	(http://www.archstl.org/education)
John Burroughs School	(http://www.jburroughs.org)
MICDS	(http://www.micds.org)

Figure 6: Table of St. Louis School Districts.

Atlases, Gazetteers, & Maps

Atlases and maps provide the visual history of an area. While a map is usually on one sheet of paper of varying size, an atlas is generally a bound publication and includes a compilation of facts and maps. Atlases and maps show the physical progress and growth of any area. They show when the streets developed and how some streets disappeared due to urban development. They also indicate changes in street names. A gazetteer is a publication that textually describes and defines locations.

The first surveying maps of St. Louis show a city consisting of a few blocks west of the Mississippi River and extending only a few blocks north and south. The entire area was smaller than the current Arch grounds.

Missouri land, and thus St. Louis, is part of the township and range grid system established by Thomas Jefferson. Since the Louisiana Purchase in 1803, land sales have followed this system allowing for property lots, usually either square or rectangular. However, early French and Spanish land grants used the metes and bounds system making the often unusual shaped or skewed property lines visible on maps even today.

Maps can be very useful genealogical research tools. Ancestors may appear on maps of their time period if they were land owners. If they were renters within the City, maps show the property address. If they lived within the County, maps can help determine the municipality and hence the location of records. In all cases maps illustrate the neighborhood and help determine which churches, school, and parks were nearby.

Some maps and atlases are available online, others are on CD-ROM, and some are in book format at repositories in St. Louis and other locations. The University of Alabama has a great online map collection, which includes some St. Louis maps.[144] Gazetteers are usually found in book form.

---

144. "Missouri Maps," *University of Alabama* (http://alabamamaps.ua.edu/historicalmaps/us_states/missouri/index.html).

ATLASES

The *Atlas of the City and County of St. Louis, by Congressional Townships; Showing all the Surveys of the Public Lands, and of the Confirmed French and Spanish Grants, New Madrid Locations, and Entries of Public Lands, up to the 1st day of January 1838; With the Names of the Original Claimants, and Number of Acres Claimed by Each*, is known locally as the *Dupré 1838 Atlas*. Information includes a township and range map of St. Louis County, the names of the property owners, and the amount of acreage owned with a descriptions of the tracts. The atlas also shows the French and Spanish land grants indicated along with their survey numbers, thus giving a great illustration of the combination of township and range grid system with overlays of the metes and bounds land grants. Each page within the atlas states, *"The above map is in strict accordance with the Township map in the U.S. Surveyor's office."* [145]

Atlases are available in book form, others are on microfilm. There is an 1893 atlas[146] and an 1938 atlas, both of St. Louis County.[147] The *Plat Book of St. Louis County 1909* is available at research facilities in paper format and for purchase on CD-ROM from St. Louis Genealogical Society.[148]

The *Atlas of the City of St. Louis, 1905* provides the names of businesses, property owners, and streets. This atlas is large and in several volumes making it easy to pinpoint the city property owned by your ancestor, determine the neighbors, and understand the neighborhood by using this map.[149]

The 1952 *Handy Atlas of St. Louis and Missouri Suburbs: Combining the Index to Streets and Census Tracts with the Map of St. Louis and Missouri Suburbs* provides an index of the streets in the City and County in the first half of the book. The index provides a grid number that directs the reader to the map in the second half of the book. The exact location of the streets, airport, cemeteries, children's homes, country clubs, courthouses, city halls, and railroad tracks are as they appeared in 1952.[150]

---

145. *Atlas of the City and County of St. Louis, by Congressional Townships; Showing all the Surveys of the Public Lands, and of the Confirmed French and Spanish Grants, New Madrid Locations, and Entries of Public Lands, up to the 1st day of January 1838; With the Names of the Original Claimants, and Number of Acres Claimed by Each* (St. Louis: E. Dupré, 1838).

146. Berkley E. Johnson, *An Atlas of St. Louis County in the State of Missouri* (Clayton: C. R. Black, 1893).

147. *Atlas of the City and County of St. Louis, by Congressional Townships* (1838; reprint, Jefferson City: Capital City Family Research, 1985). [This atlas is a reprint of the map commonly called Dupré, previously listed.]

148. St. Louis Genealogical Society, *Plat Book of St. Louis County, Missouri, 1909,* CD-ROM (St. Louis: The Society, 2007).

149. *Atlas of the City of St. Louis,* 10 volumes (St. Louis: St. Louis Plat and Record Company, 1905).

150. *Handy Atlas of St. Louis and Missouri Suburbs: Combining the Index to Streets and Census Tracts with the Map of St. Louis and Missouri Suburbs* (St. Louis: Greater St. Louis Map Project, 1952).

Rafferty's *Historical Atlas of Missouri* published in 1981 provides historical data and maps of Missouri and St. Louis. This atlas shows many features of the state, including agricultural patterns, migration, railroads, and roads.[151]

GAZETTEERS

One of the few gazetteers that cover only St. Louis County is *A Directory of Towns, Villages, and Hamlets Past and Present of St. Louis County, Missouri,* which provides a description and location for numerous villages and towns within the boundaries of St. Louis County.[152]

Several statewide titles; however, include St. Louis references. The *Gazetteer of the State of Missouri, 1837* provides information on towns and villages in St. Louis County at that time.[153] Likewise, *Campbell's Gazetteer of Missouri, 1874* does the same for that later era.[154]

St. Louis Public Library has a collection of *Missouri Gazetteers* dating from 1860 to 1899; however, every year is not available. People and businesses are listed by town, making it easy to find your ancestors.

Robert L. Ramsay and graduate students at the University of Missouri compiled the most comprehensive Missouri gazetteer to date. The complete gazetteer, consisting of more than 32,000 locations in Missouri, is available in the reference room at the State Historical Society of Missouri. The data is included online at the Geographic Names Information System (GNIS) database (http://geonames.usgs.gov), maintained by the U.S. Geological Survey department. For an overview of the original Ramsay project, see *Our Storehouse of Missouri Place Names.*[155]

MAPS

Several St. Louis maps used by the election commissioners indicate the City wards for the census. Local libraries have copies of the same information. A comparison of your ancestors' census information with these maps can trace their migration within the City of St. Louis.

St. Louis Public Library has an online collection of St. Louis maps:

- 1804 — This line drawing of the young village of St. Louis lists the names and places of residents near the Mississippi River, all within a few-block area.[156]

---

151. Milton D. Rafferty, *Historical Atlas of Missouri* (Norman, Oklahoma: University of Oklahoma Press, 1981).

152. Arthur Paul Moser, *A Directory of Towns, Villages, and Hamlets Past and Present of St. Louis County, Missouri* (Springfield: A. P. Moser, 1982).

153. Alphonso Wetmore, *Gazetteer of State of Missouri, 1837* (1837; reprint, New York, Arno Press, 1975).

154. R. A. Campbell, *Campbell's Gazetteer of Missouri, 1874* (St. Louis: R. A. Campbell, 1874), 509–571.

155. Robert L. Ramsay, *Our Storehouse of Missouri Place Names* (Columbia: University of Missouri Press, 1973).

156. "Plat of the Town of St. Louis, with all of the Houses on March 10th, 1804," *St. Louis Public Library* (http://exhibits.slpl.org/maps/data/dm53513377.asp).

- 1820 — Another map displays the small town of St. Louis while it was the capitol of the Territory of Missouri, just one year before statehood.[157]
- 1830–1880 — Census ward maps are available on microfilm and paper format.[158] The area grew from four wards to twenty-eight wards during that half century.
- 1842 — This planning map of St. Louis shows the development of the city.[159]
- 1852 — The size and shape of St. Louis is visible on this map.[160]
- 1859 — This St. Louis street map provides an index and a good overview of the size of the city at that time.[161]
- 1862 — This St. Louis map indicates the governmental districts, townships, and city wards during the Civil War.[162]
- 1867 — St. Louis had eight wards outlined on this map.[163]
- 1884 — This map provides statistics on the population and death rate for the City in the year 1883.[164]
- 1895 — This City and County map shows the "pikes, county roads, and railroads."[165]
- 1904 — The World's Fair was a very important event in St. Louis. This map shows all of the buildings and exhibits from the Fair.[166]
- 1910 — Carondelet was a separate city south of St. Louis before they merged in 1870. This map shows the industry and businesses in Carondelet.[167]
- 1912 — The Rand McNally St. Louis County map shows the townships, sections, and roads.[168]
- 1914 — This map shows important parks and buildings and provides an index.[169]

---

157.   "Map of the Town of St. Louis [1820]," *St. Louis Public Library* (http://exhibits.slpl.org/ maps/data/dm65835425.asp).

158.   St. Louis Census Ward Maps, 1830–1880; FHL film 1,598,408, item 1.

159.   "Plan of the City of St. Louis, Missouri [1842]," *St. Louis Public Library* (http://exhibits .slpl.org/maps/data/dm65511585.asp).

160.   "Map of the City of St. Louis [1852]," *St. Louis Public Library* (http://exhibits.slpl.org/maps/ data/dm64333473.asp).

161.   "Kennedy's Sectional Map of St. Louis, with Street Directory," *St. Louis Public Library* (http://exhibits.slpl.org/maps/data/DM54370593.asp).

162.   "Map of St. Louis County: Compiled by and Reconstructed from U.S. Surveys and Other Authentic Sources," *St. Louis Public Library* (http://exhibits.slpl.org/maps/data/dm56090657.asp).

163.   "St. Louis," *St. Louis Public Library* (http://exhibits.slpl.org/maps/data/DM48608033.asp).

164.   "Map of Part of the City of St. Louis Showing the Density of Population and Death Rate per 1000 for the Year 1883; Prepared for the 12th Annual A. P. H. A., Oct. 1884," *St. Louis Public Library* (http://exhibits.slpl.org/maps/data/dm55061025.asp).

165.   "Higgins Road Map of St. Louis Vicinity, 1895," *St. Louis Public Library* (http://exhibits .slpl.org/maps/data/dm240010600.asp).

166.   "Ground Plan of the Louisiana Purchase Exposition, St. Louis, Missouri, 1904," *St. Louis Public Library* (http://exhibits.slpl.org/maps/data/dm56776990.asp).

167.   "Industrial Map of the Southern Part of St. Louis (Carondelet)," *St. Louis Public Library* (http://exhibits.slpl.org/maps/data/dm42500639.asp).

168.   "Map of St. Louis County [1912]," *St. Louis Public Library* (http://exhibits.slpl.org/maps/data/ dm74140448.asp).

169.   "Map of St. Louis and Suburbs [1914]," *St. Louis Public Library* (http://exhibits.slpl.org/ maps/data/dm48340767.asp).

- 1918 — The St. Louis City and County map dated 1918 includes municipalities such as Clayton, Creve Coeur, Ferguson, Kirkwood, and Valley Park.[170]
- 1930 — A census enumeration map for 1930 is available online and is in color.[171]

A wide variety of other maps cover the City and County. Plat maps for St. Louis in 1856 and 1857 are available at the Family History Library on microfiche. While they show land ownership for that time period, they are too big to print on regular-sized paper without piecing them together. Knowledge of the township and range where your ancestor(s) lived is necessary to utilize these maps effectively.[172]

The *Guide Book and Complete Pocket Map of St. Louis: Giving Early History, Statistics, and Being the Only Complete Pocket Map of the City* provides an overview of the community in 1867.[173]

In 1868, Julius Pitzman was the St. Louis County surveyor. He prepared the *Pitzman's 1868 Map* of St. Louis County and City based on surveys held by the U.S. Surveyor's office. This map is available online.[174]

The *Pictorial Saint Louis: The Great Metropolis of the Mississippi Valley: A Topographical Survey, 1875,* known locally as Compton and Dry, provides drawings of the buildings, businesses, industries, and streets of St. Louis in 1875. *Pictorial St. Louis, 1875* is available in book format or online at the Library of Congress, American Memory site.[175] Another publication, *Pitzman's 1878 Atlas,* provides the name of property owners at that time. St. Louis Genealogical Society has reissued this map with an added index.[176]

St. Louis Ward Maps, 1904–1952, produced by the St. Louis Board of Election Commissioners, are a great asset for twentieth-century research. The maps show the streets as they were before modern development. As an example, the streets removed by the Arch grounds, stadiums, shopping centers, and other developments are visible on these maps. The maps also provide guidance for the correct City ward and precinct for your ancestor.

---

170. "Latest and Most Complete Map of St. Louis and Suburbs [1918]," *St. Louis Public Library* (http://exhibits.slpl.org/maps/data/DM54370593.asp).

171. "1930 Enumeration Census Map," *St. Louis Public Library* (http://exhibits.slpl.org/maps/data/dm240010600.asp).

172. *St. Louis County, Missouri, Land Ownership Maps* (Washington, D.C.: Library of Congress, 1983), FHL microfiche 6,079,643 and 6,079,644.

173. *Guide Book and Complete Pocket Map of St. Louis: Giving Early History, Statistics, and Being the only Complete Pocket Map of the City* (St. Louis: J. H. Cook, 1867). [Digital publication at HeritageQuest.]

174. Julius Hutawa, *Pitzman's Map of St. Louis County Published after October 1868* (St. Louis: J. Hutawa, 1868), Web version (http://www.usgennet.org/usa/mo/county/stlouis/stlumap.htm).

175. Richard J. Compton, editor, *Pictorial St. Louis, the Great Metropolis of the Mississippi Valley; A Topographical Survey Drawn in Perspective A. D. 1875, by Camille N. Dry* (1876; reprint, Hazelwood: McGraw-Young Publishing, 1997. Images available at "American Memory Collection; Map Collections, 1500–2003," *Library of Congress* (http://memory.loc.gov/ammem/gmdhtml/gmdhome.html).

176. Julius Pitzman, *Pitzman's New Atlas of the City and County of Saint Louis, Missouri* (1878; reprint, St. Louis: St. Louis Genealogical Society, 1997). "Pitzman's Index," *St. Louis Genealogical Society* (http://www.stlgs.org). [Digial map on CD-ROM at St. Louis Genealogical Society.]

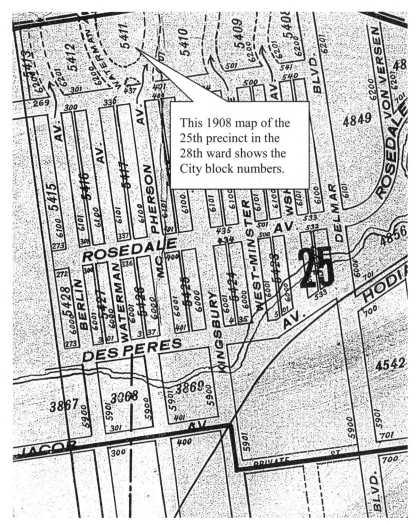

This 1908 map of the 25th precinct in the 28th ward shows the City block numbers.

Figure 7: St. Louis City Ward Map, 1908
Used with the permission of St. Louis Genealogical Society.

The map in Figure 7, shows part of the 28th Ward in 1908. The development of the area is limited, but this map does show the City block numbers and the 25th precinct.

Figure 8 shows the same area in the 28th Ward in 1946.

This map shows the City Limits just west of Skinker Boulevard, the Wabash train track, which is now the Metro Link track, and the streets in that neighborhood. The map indicates the street names and address numbers per block. It also shows the boundary lines for the precincts with the precinct numbers prominently displayed within those lines. Notice the numerous precincts within the ward indicating the growth and population shift.

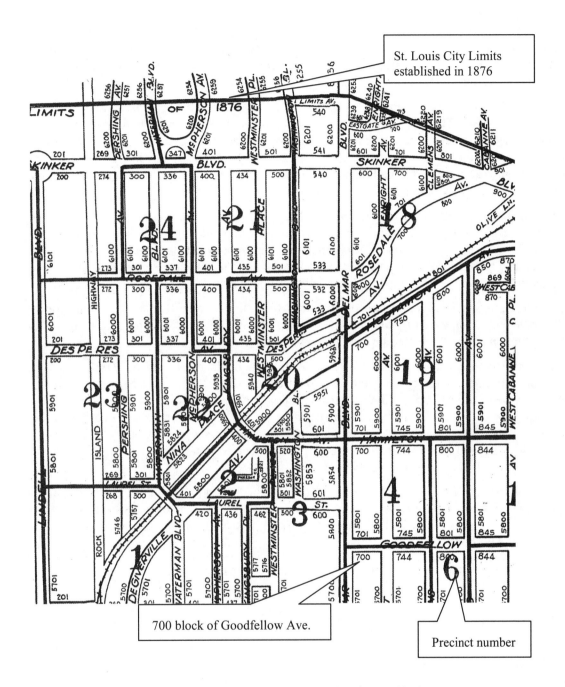

St. Louis City Limits
established in 1876

700 block of Goodfellow Ave.

Precinct number

Figure 8: St. Louis City Ward Map, 1946
Used with the permission of St. Louis Genealogical Society.

The *Street Guide of St. Louis County with a Map of St. Louis,* a 1955 pocket-size guide and map, provides a foldout street map of St. Louis City and part of the County. The map extended to the mid-County area going west only to Clayton. Municipalities farther west are not on this map. In addition to the name of the street, it provides the municipality, a description of the street, and where it starts and ends.[177] Similar maps for other years are available at various repositories.

St. Louis *Sanborn Fire Insurance Company Maps* are available for limited years ranging from 1895 to 1983. The original maps are in color, indicating each building, providing construction details, such as brick, frame, or other types of material. The maps show the number of stories, the location of the doors, windows, chimneys, and outhouses. The maps indicate street address, lot lines, and use of the buildings. They also list some city infrastructure such as street width, water pipes, and hydrants.

Sanborn maps are available for the cities of St. Louis, Kirkwood, and St. Ferdinand. Some repositories have original copies and digitized versions are available online. For a list of maps and some repositories, see the union list of Sanborn maps. The website lists the available years for the maps. Several repositories including the Missouri Historical Society Research Library and Washington University West Campus, have original Sanborn maps. [178]

In addition to Sanborn Fire Insurance maps, the Missouri Historical Society Research Library has Whipple Fire Insurance maps covering St. Louis for the 1890s. Washington University is digitizing these maps and they will be available online soon.

St. Louis streets changed names over the years. Magnan's *Streets of St. Louis* provides background information on current and former street names.[179] The St. Louis Street Index, available on the St. Louis Public Library website, offers an interactive map that allows entering a street address and then viewing the map of the area on the City of St. Louis website.[180] The St. Louis County Board of Election Commissioner's map offers current County streets as of 2004.[181] The City and County directories also provide a description and name of the streets, precincts, and wards for the year of publication.

The *St. Louis City and County Cemetery Map,* published in 2007, provides the location of all known cemeteries for the City and County. Some cemeteries are still open and visible; urban development has replaced others. The map may provide new clues about the cemeteries in your ancestor's neighborhood.[182]

---

177. Henry E. Gross, *Street Guide of St. Louis County with Map of St. Louis County* (St. Louis: H. E. Gross, 1955).

178. "Union List of Sanborn and Other Fire Insurance Maps," *University of California Berkeley* (http://www.lib.berkeley.edu/EART/sanbul.html).

179. William Magnan, *Streets of St. Louis* (Groton, Connecticut: Right Press, 1994).

180. "St. Louis Street Index," *St. Louis Public Library* (http://www.previous.slpl.lib.mo.us/libsrc/ streets.htm).

181. *St. Louis County Directory of Street Addresses: Giving Townships and Precincts and Political Districts by Precincts* (St. Louis: Board of Election Commissioners, 2004).

182. Ann Carter Fleming, *St. Louis City and County Cemetery Map* (St. Louis: A. C. Fleming, 2007).

Biographical Sources

Biographical information comes from a variety of sources: diaries, business newsletters, newspapers, obituaries, and other types of publications. Information could be on the community, county, or state level. While looking for new clues about your direct-line ancestors and collateral lines, do not overlook any possibilities. For example, Missouri Historical Society Research Library collected newspaper clippings from the 1908 to 1914 era and placed the copies in bound volumes. The articles may mention the people living during that time range as well as their ancestors.[183]

Other types of records may provide some biographical information. Club rosters, social directories, and yearbooks usually provide limited data on those included. Some of these publications provide a photograph of the subject. Compiling information from all sources creates a great ancestral biographical sketch.

Family group sheets donated by members of St. Louis Genealogical Society and information from the Society's *First Families* project document St. Louis families. The Society maintains the files and documents with the ancestors and First Family members listed on their website.[184]

WOMEN OF ST. LOUIS

For every important man, there was an important woman in the history of St. Louis. Katharine Corbett's *In Her Place: A Guide to St. Louis Women's History* describes a few women who played important roles in the development of the area.[185] An 1883 publication, *Women Prominent in the Early History of St. Louis*, provides biographical information on women in St. Louis during the first one hundred years.[186]

---

183.   *St. Louis Biographies, 1908–1914* (St. Louis: Missouri Historical Society, no date).

184.   St. Louis Genealogical Society, *The 33 Year Cumulative Alphabetical Index of the Four-Generation Pedigree Charts of the Members of St. Louis Genealogical Society, volumes 1–27, 1967–1999* (St. Louis: The Society, 2001).

185.   Katharine Corbett, *In Her Place: A Guide to St. Louis Women's History* (St. Louis: Missouri Historical Society Press, 1999).

186.   McCune B. Gill, *Women Prominent in the Early History of St. Louis* ([St. Louis]: privately printed, 1883).

Missouri Historical Society Research Library compiled an eight-volume set of newspaper clippings called *St. Louis, Missouri, Womanhood*. A 1914 publication, *Notable Women of St. Louis*, provides biographies of the early women who helped form St. Louis.[187] Two such women are Marie Chouteau and Susan Blow. The St. Louis Public Library website offers an index to this book.

Marie Chouteau was unquestionably the "first lady" of St. Louis. She was the mother of founder Auguste Chouteau and the companion of founder Pierre Laclede. Details about her life and the times she lived in are chronicled in *The First Chouteaus: River Barons of Early St. Louis*.[188]

Another prominent woman in St. Louis was Harriet Scott, who along with her husband, Dred, in 1846 filed two lawsuits seeking their freedom. Several prominent St. Louisans were involved in this action including Roswell Field and Henry Blow and his family. After many twists and turns in the case, Harriet became a free woman and lived in St. Louis until she died in 1876.[189]

As the largest metropolitan area in the state, St. Louis women are among those listed in books that cover the entire state of Missouri. Morgan's *Profiles in Silhouette: The Contributions of Black Women of Missouri* chronicles African American women.[190] *Women in Missouri History: In Search of Power and Influence* provides essays about French women and women of color, both in the colonial days, German women, farmers, domestics, and many others from the earliest times to the present day.[191] *Show-Me Missouri Women: Selected Biographies* provides information on St. Louis women as well as others in the state.[192]

MEN OF ST. LOUIS

Numerous biographical publications chronicle St. Louis businessmen and politicians, some from the 1800s, and many from the 1900s. An early important sketch is the publication, *Old and New St. Louis*.[193] In the early 1900s two editions of *The Book of St. Louisans: A Biographical Dictionary of Leading Living Men of the City of St. Louis and Vicinity* were published, one in

---

187.   Anne Andre Johnson, editor, *Notable Women of St. Louis* (St. Louis: Woodward, 1914).

188.   William E. Foley and David Rice, *The First Chouteaus: River Barons of Early St. Louis* (Urbana: University of Illinois Press, 1983). Beatrice Clark Turner, *The Chouteau Family, A Genealogy of Descendants and Collateral Branches* (St. Louis: The Author, 1934).

189.   "Missouri's Dred Scott Case, 1846–1857," *Missouri State Archives* (http://www.sos.mo.gov/archives/resources/africanamerican/scott/scott.asp). "The Dred Scott Case," *National Park Service* (http://www.nps.gov/jeff/planyourvisit/dredscott.htm).

190.   Thelma Wood Morgan, *Profiles in Silhouette: The Contributions of Black Women of Missouri* (St. Louis: St. Louis Alumnae Chapter of Delta Sigma Theta, 1980).

191.   LeeAnn Whites, Mary C. Neth, and Gary R. Kremer, editors, *Women in Missouri History: In Search of Power and Influence* (Columbia: University of Missouri Press, 2004).

192.   Mary Danis, editor, *Show-Me Missouri Women: Selected Biographies*, 2 volumes (Kirksville: Thomas Jefferson University Press, 1989).

193.   James Cox, *Old and New St. Louis: A Concise History of the Metropolis of the West and Southwest, With a Review of Its Present Greatness and Immediate Prospects, With a Biographical Appendix* (St. Louis: Central Biographical Publishing Company, 1894).

1906[194] and the second in 1912.[195] Each includes merchants and professional men living in St. Louis. The second edition has many updates and deletions. Another publication, *Men Who Make St. Louis the City of Opportunity,* is a biographical sketch for the 1927 time period.[196]

A Biographical Dictionary of Leading Men of the City of St. Louis and Vicinity provides biographical information on the leading citizens of the day. This publication, dated 1912, offers similar and additional data from the earlier version.[197] Another publication from the same era, *Men of Affairs in St. Louis: A Newspaper Reference Book* was published twice, 1913 and 1915, and provides information on prominent businessmen in St. Louis.[198] An index is available at the St. Louis Public Library website.

Who's Who in North St. Louis[199] provides biographical sketches and photographs of the men and businesses who made North St. Louis thrive before 1925. *The St. Louis Story...Library of American Lives,* is a group of biographies about contemporary civic leaders as well as some from the past.[200] *Who's Who in Saint Louis, 1928–1929,* provides lineage information, organizations, employment, and other important facts and accomplishments.[201]

Saint Louis: The Future Great City of the World; With Biographical Sketches of the Representative Men and Women of St. Louis and Missouri provides biographical information on many men and women from St. Louis.[202]

A national publication divided by states, *United States Biographical Dictionary and Portrait Gallery of Eminent and Self-Made Men, Early to 1878,* is available in microfiche, book, and online format. The Missouri portion provides extensive biographical information for some St. Louis citizens.[203]

---

194.   John W. Leonard, editor, *The Book of St. Louisans: A Biographical Dictionary of Leading Living Men of the City of St. Louis* (St. Louis: The St. Louis Republic, 1906). [This edition is available online at HeritageQuest.]

195.   Albert Nelson Marquis, *The Book of St. Louisans: A Biographical Dictionary of Leading Living Men of the City of St. Louis and Vicinity*, 2nd edition (St. Louis: St. Louis Republic 1912).

196.   Walter P. Tracy, *Men Who Make St. Louis the City of Opportunity* (St. Louis: The Author, 1927).

197.   Elizabeth B. Langley, *A Biographical Dictionary of Leading Men of the City of St. Louis and Vicinity*, 2nd edition (St. Louis: St. Louis Republic, 1912).

198.   C. C. Story, *Men of Affairs in Saint Louis: A Newspaper Reference Book* (St. Louis: Press Club of St. Louis, 1915). Also, *Newspaper Artists' Association, Men of Affairs in Saint Louis: A Newspaper Reference Book* (St. Louis: Perrin and Smith Printing Company, 1913).

199.   *Who's Who in North St. Louis* (St. Louis: North St. Louis Business Men's Association, 1925). [Available from St. Louis Genealogical Society on CD-ROM.]

200.   McCune Gill, *The St. Louis Story ... Library of American Lives* (St. Louis: privately printed, 1952).

201.   Samuel T. Larkin, *Who's Who in Saint Louis, 1928–1929* (St. Louis: Civic Union of St. Louis, 1929).

202.   L. U. Reavis, *Saint Louis: The Future Great City of the World; With Biographical Sketches of the Representative Men and Women of St. Louis and Missouri* (1876; reprint, Tucson, Arizona: W. C. Cox, 1974).

203.   *Missouri: The United States Biographical Dictionary and Portrait Gallery of Eminent and Self-made Men, Missouri Volume Early to 1878* (New York: U.S. Biographical Publishing Company, 1878). [Available online at Ancestry.com].

The *History of St. Louis County Missouri* and *St. Louis: History of the Fourth City, 1763–1909* provide interesting biographical sketches with some photographs or drawings.[204]

FAMILIES OF ST. LOUIS

Who's Who in Missouri: A Compilation of Biographical Information on Outstanding Citizens of the State of Missouri chronicles St. Louis and Missouri citizens living in the twentieth century. *Who's Who in Missouri: A Biographical Dictionary of Leading Men and Women of the Commonwealth* lists citizens born in the nineteenth century.[205] Area guides may be helpful as well. For example, *Here's Where: A Guide to Illustrious St. Louis* is a brief summary about notable St. Louisans.[206]

Robert Parkin, noted St. Louis researcher and genealogist, compiled a card index of early St. Louis families. Originally intended for his personal use only, Parkin cited his sources in a shorthand format, that is fortunately decipherable to today's researchers. He donated these cards to St. Louis Genealogical Society in the late 1990s. A publication consisting of photocopies of the cards is available at the Society office and in St. Louis County Library, Special Collections. This is a valuable research tool and finding aid for early St. Louis families. Here is an example showing the Joseph Austin James family.[207]

```
Joseph Austin James                              1807

11 Joseph Austin James,,Kentucky; Louisiana terri-          1898
   tory in 1807, St. Louis County, Florissant-m.-x
   Elizabeth Hosten
   111 John G. James (d.1834)m.-Julie Crely
   111 John G. James (d.sfcr.1834)msfcr.2/4/1812-Julie
       Crely (bsfcr.6/8/1795)(Baptiste-Elizabeth Bien-
       venue)                          town trustee, Treasurer, county judge
   1111 Samuel James, native of St. Louis County, Flor-
        issant, farmer, stock raiser (9/16/1817-1898)
        m.1838-Virginia Robertson,(1820-1901)(William
        -Sarah --- )   native of St L county Bridgeton
   11111 Jessie James-m.-John Belleville, Clayton
   11112 Jennie James       m. - Toben, St. Louis
   11113 Kate James, California
   1112 Edward James+m.-Nancy Witherington (12/2/1823
        -1/20/1881) (St. Ferdinand cemetery)(Sacred Heart cemetery (Thomas 1:82)
   11121 Charles James (1867-1915)m.- Maude --- (1870
         -1934)
   1113 (son) James
   1114 (son) JJames
```

Figure 9: Robert Parkin Card
Used with the permission of St. Louis Genealogical Society.

---

204.   Thomas, *History of St. Louis County, Missouri.* Stevens, *St. Louis: History of the Fourth City, 1763–1909,* both previously cited.

205.   *Who's Who in Missouri: A Compilation of Biographical Information on Outstanding Citizens of the State of Missouri* (Atlanta, Georgia: United States Public Relations Service, 1974). *Who's Who in Missouri: A Biographical Dictionary of Leading Men and Women of the Commonwealth* (Chicago: Larkin, Roosevelt, and Larkin, 1947).

206.   Charlie Brennan, et al., *Here's Where: A Guide to Illustrious St. Louis* (St. Louis: Missouri Historical Society Press, 2006).

207.   Robert E. Parkin, *Original Settlers of St. Louis and Out State Missouri,* 5 volumes (St. Louis: St. Louis County Library, 2003). [St. Louis Genealogical Society donated this data to the Library.]

Ross Wagner is compiling biographical information on citizens currently and previously living in the southern portion of St. Louis County. His focus area includes Concord Village, Crestwood, Mehlville, and beyond. Individual cards contain data including name, birth date and place, death date and place, spouse, parents, children, occupation, and sometimes an obituary. Mr. Wagner shared these cards with St. Louis Genealogical Society in 2007–2008 and photocopies of these cards are available at the Society office.[208] This example shows the Johann Adam Theiss family, who were early German settlers in South St. Louis County. Perhaps your family is in this index.

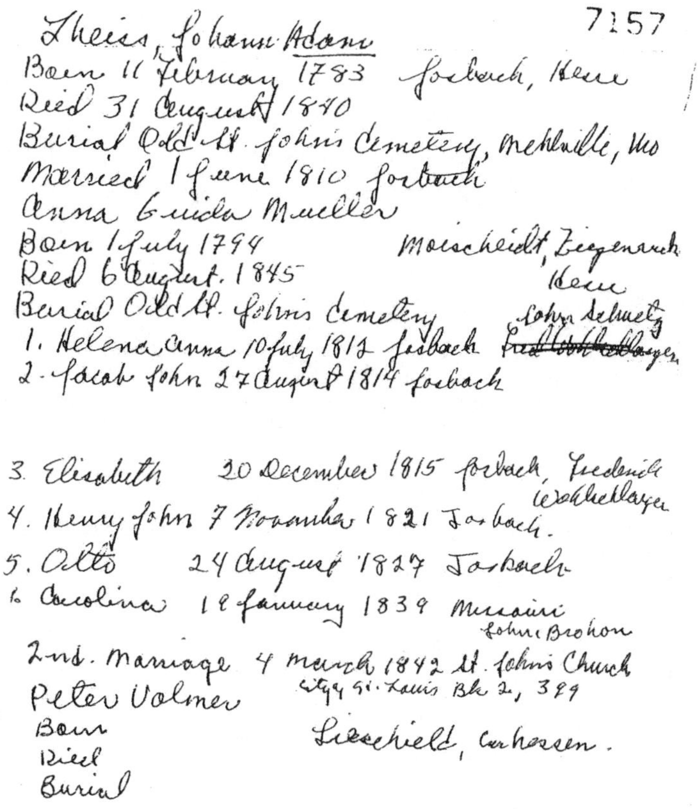
Theiss, Johann Adam 7157
Born 11 February 1783 Forbach, Hesse
Died 31 August 1840
Burial Old St. Johns Cemetery, Mehlville, Mo
Married 1 June 1810 Forbach
Anna Guida Mueller
Born 1 July 1794 Morscheidt, Ziegenrück, Hesse
Died 6 August 1845
Burial Old St. Johns Cemetery John Schuetz
1. Helena Anna 10 July 1812 Forbach ~~Friedrich Wohlschlager~~
2. Jacob John 27 August 1814 Forbach

3. Elisabeth 20 December 1815 Forbach, Frederick Wohlschlager
4. Henry John 7 November 1821 Forbach.
5. Otto 24 August 1827 Forbach
6. Carolina 18 January 1839 Missouri John Brohon
2nd. Marriage 4 March 1842 St. Johns Church
Peter Volmer City St. Louis Bk 2, 399
Born Liescheid, Curhessen.
Died
Burial

Figure 10: Ross Wagner Family Card
Used with the permission of Ross Wagner.

Family Group Sheets for Our Ancestors Who Came to South County, St. Louis, Missouri, in the 1830s is a compilation of early South County residents and their descendants including many living in the twenty-first century. This indexed three-volume set includes most early families associated with St. John Evangelical Church.[209]

---

208. Ross Wagner manuscript collection; St. Louis Genealogical Society office.

209. Marjorie Schuetz Whitney, *Family Group Sheets for Our Ancestors Who Came to South County, St. Louis, Missouri, in the 1830s,* 3 volumes (Cocoa, Florida: The Author, 2007).

St. Louis Genealogical Society

First Families of St. Louis

Application

> Check category for which you are applying:
> ☐ Founding Families (1765–1804)
> ☐ Pioneer Families (1805–1821)
> ☐ Immigrant Families (1822–1865)

Date_____   StLGS Membership Number_____

Applicant Name_____
          (First)   (Middle and/or Maiden)   (Last)

Spouse_____   Phone No. _____
     (First)   (Middle and/or Maiden)   (Last)

Address_____   E-mail _____
    Number   Street   City   State   Zip Code

Print or type ancestor's name exactly as you wish it to appear on your **First Families of St. Louis** Certificate

Founding Ancestor_____

Proof of Lineage

EACH statement of birth, marriage, and death linking the generations between the applicant and the **First Families of St. Louis** ancestor must be proven by documentation.

- Include one photocopy of each record. ***DO NOT SEND ORIGINAL RECORDS!***
- Underline or draw an arrow to area of record that proves relationship, date, or location. ***DO NOT HIGHLIGHT!***
- All documents must include source information (name and location of repository, date record was copied, certificate number, microfilm number, etc.) Published works should be cited by title, author, date of publication, volume, and page.

If a family member has been accepted into **First Families of St. Louis**, it is **NOT** necessary to duplicate his/her documentation. However, it is necessary to prove a direct-line relationship between the applicant and that person.

Example: Proof of relationship: Birth certificate, St. Louis, MO, 1950 (copy enclosed)

(Please print legibly in black ink.)

Applicant

Birth: Date_____   Place_____   Document _____
           (Day, Month, Year)   (City, County, State/Country)   (Proves Date/Place)

Marriage: Date_____   Place_____   Document _____
           (Day, Month, Year)   (City, County, State/Country)   (Proves Date/Place)

Proof of Relationship: (List which of the certificates or records submitted shows the relationship to the previous generation from which descendancy is derived): _____

Applicant's Parent

Full Name_____   (Spouse_____)

Birth: Date_____   Place_____   Document _____
           (Day, Month, Year)   (City, County, State/Country)   (Proves Date/Place)

Marriage: Date_____   Place_____   Document _____
           (Day, Month, Year)   (City, County, State/Country)   (Proves Date/Place)

Death: Date_____   Place_____   Document _____
           (Day, Month, Year)   (City, County, State/Country)   (Proves Date/Place)

Proof of Relationship: (List which of the certificates or records submitted shows the relationship to the previous generation from which descendancy is derived): _____

If you need assistance filling out this form, please call StLGS at 314.647.8547 or e-mail <firstfamilies@stlgs.org>.

1

idm: March 2005

*Figure 11: St. Louis Genealogical First Family Application
Used with the permission of St. Louis Genealogical Society.*

First Families of St. Louis provide an opportunity for you to share your lineage with the Society. They will then add the names of your ancestors to the First Families list. The original files are available at the society office. Figure 11 shows you the application form and the documents required.

The Missouri Historical Society Research Library has a great collection of forms filled out by World War I veterans or their families. These records contain biographical information about the veteran. For more information on this collection, see the MILITARY RECORDS chapter.

Pageant & Masque of St. Louis

A *St. Louis Globe-Democrat* advertisement dated May 1914 requested "native" citizens to register for the upcoming "Pageant and Masque," a historical drama about St. Louis history. The registration fee was twenty-five cents and the play was presented in front of 500,000 people on Art Hill in Forest Park.

Some residents filled out registration cards for every member of their family and other families ignored the process, or perhaps could not afford the registration fee. The cards provide name, present address, place and date of birth, occupation, and the name of their parents and their country of birth. The back of the card provided space for *Interesting Incidents in Family History*. Some people left the back blank; others wrote more than space allowed and continued on other paper. The donor could include any information in this portion.

Many of the cards list the subject's mother with her married name, sometimes her maiden name. The parents' country of birth was requested, not the city of birth. Therefore, limited new genealogical information is forthcoming from these two parts of the registration cards.

Missouri Historical Society Research Library has the original cards and photocopies of the same cards in bound volumes, *Pageant & Masque Registration Cards*.[210] Their St. Louis *Genealogical and Local History Index*, available online soon, includes the name of the person who filled out the card. The names of the parents, maiden names, spouse, or others included on the cards are not in the index. Figure 12 shows an example of the Pageant & Masque cards.

---

210.   *Pageant & Masque Registration Cards* (St. Louis: Missouri Historical Society, 1986).

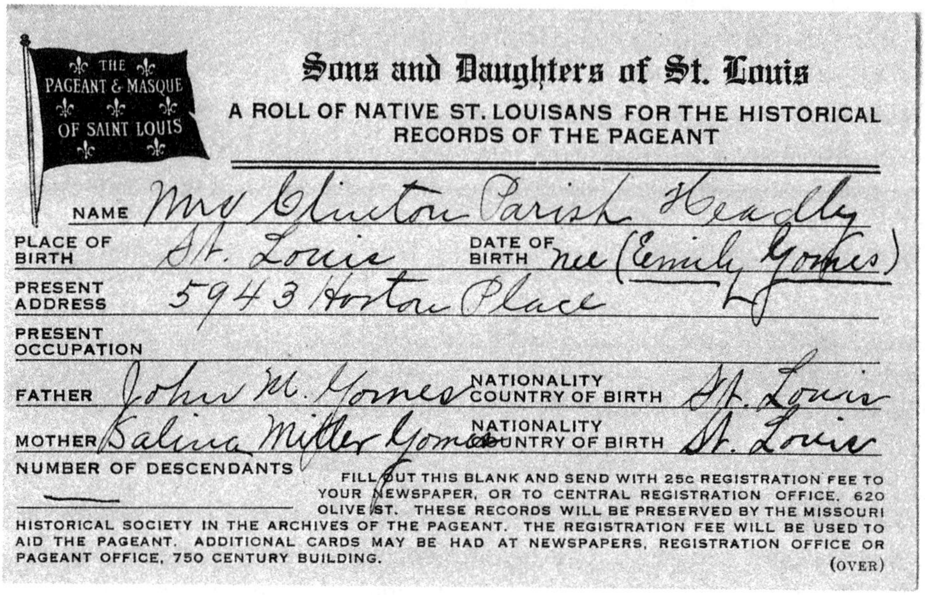

THE PAGEANT & MASQUE OF SAINT LOUIS

Sons and Daughters of St. Louis

A ROLL OF NATIVE ST. LOUISANS FOR THE HISTORICAL RECORDS OF THE PAGEANT

NAME Mrs Clinton Parish Headley

PLACE OF BIRTH St. Louis DATE OF BIRTH nee (Emily Gomes)

PRESENT ADDRESS 5943 Hoston Place

PRESENT OCCUPATION

FATHER John M. Gomes NATIONALITY COUNTRY OF BIRTH St. Louis

MOTHER Salina Miller Gomes NATIONALITY COUNTRY OF BIRTH St. Louis

NUMBER OF DESCENDANTS —

FILL OUT THIS BLANK AND SEND WITH 25c REGISTRATION FEE TO YOUR NEWSPAPER, OR TO CENTRAL REGISTRATION OFFICE, 620 OLIVE ST. THESE RECORDS WILL BE PRESERVED BY THE MISSOURI HISTORICAL SOCIETY IN THE ARCHIVES OF THE PAGEANT. THE REGISTRATION FEE WILL BE USED TO AID THE PAGEANT. ADDITIONAL CARDS MAY BE HAD AT NEWSPAPERS, REGISTRATION OFFICE OR PAGEANT OFFICE, 750 CENTURY BUILDING.

(OVER)

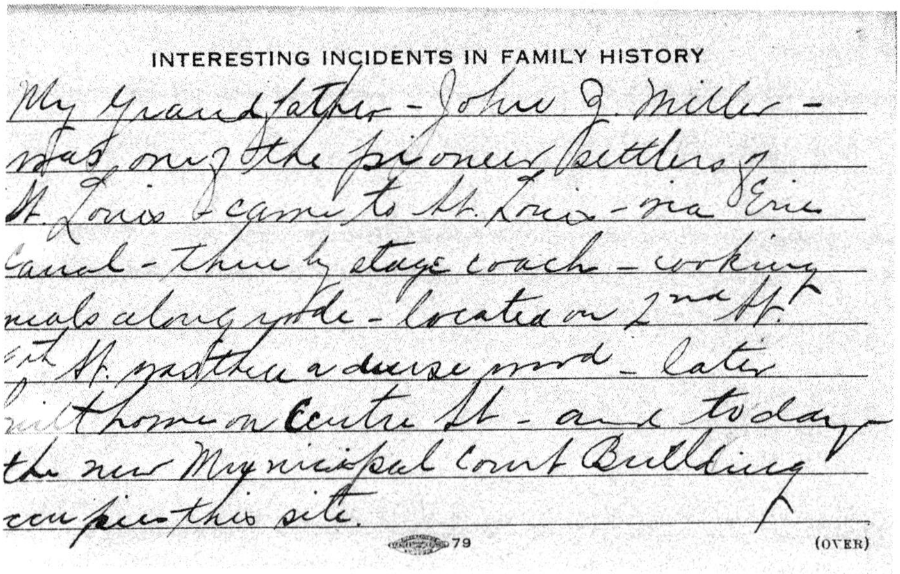

INTERESTING INCIDENTS IN FAMILY HISTORY

My Grandfather - John G. Miller - was one of the pioneer settlers of St. Louis & came to St. Louis - via Erie Canal - then by stage coach - cooking meals along route - located on 2nd St. [illegible] St. [illegible] - later built home on Centre St - and today the new Municipal Court Building occupies this site.

79

(OVER)

Figure 12: Pageant & Masque of St. Louis Cards
Used with the permission of Missouri Historical Society.

Birth & Adoption Records

The Missouri General Assembly provided legislation establishing the Board of Health and statewide registration of births and deaths in 1883. In 1893, the legislature repealed the law because compliance was low since the registration was not mandatory. The Missouri State Archives provides a database of the births that were recorded between 1883 and 1893; however, it is a work in progress. Missouri adopted its current birth registration procedures in 1910.[211]

City or County facilities can issue a document sufficient for identification purposes. The state has a database that provides basic information for the certificate, including the name of the child, date and place of birth, and a few other facts. A long form provides the name of the father and mother, their ages, place of residence, occupation, and all of the information used by genealogists. Only the Jefferson City address can issue the *LONG* form with the genealogical information.

Missouri Department of Health and Senior Services (930 Wildwood, Post Office Box 570, Jefferson City, 65102-0570; phone 573-751-6378; http://www.dhss.mo.gov/index.html).

St. Louis City Vital Records (City Hall, Recorder of Deeds Office, 1200 Market Street, St. Louis 63103; phone 314-613-3016; http://stlouis.missouri.org/citygov/recorder/vital records.html) provides the short form for Missouri birth records.

St. Louis County Vital Records (111 South Meramec Avenue, 1st Floor, Clayton 63105; phone 314-615-0376; http://www.stlouisco.com/doh/vitals/vitals.html) provides the short form for Missouri birth records.

BIRTH RECORDS

A limited number of birth records exist prior to 1910 when the state started keeping these records. State law requires that births be recorded within ten days in the district in which the birth occurs.[212] Post-1910 birth records are available at the state and county levels. Church baptismal records are the most reliable birth information for the pre-birth certificate era.

---

211. "Missouri Birth and Death Record Database, pre-1910," *Missouri State Archives* (http://www.sos.mo.gov/archives/resources/birthdeath/#search).

212. *Missouri Legislature 1909*, page 540, section 4, and page 544, section 12.

In 1939, the U.S. Census Bureau recommended forms for births and stillbirths and Missouri adopted the new forms, which include name and sex of child; date of birth; place of birth, including the name of the hospital; name, maiden name, birthplace, age, marital status, occupation, and usual residence of mother; number of months of pregnancy; name, age, birthplace, occupation, color or race of father and mother; number of other children born to mother; mother's mailing address; and the registrar's signature and date of filing.[213]

A survey conducted in the 1930s indicated that approximately thirteen percent of the population had unrecorded births. In 1931, the State Registrar in Jefferson City allowed Missouri residents born prior to 1909 to register their births. The Registrar's office requested two supporting affidavits confirming the delayed birth from two different people who knew the subject.

Documents used as proof for the delayed births included: baptismal records, family Bible, physician or hospital records, birth certificate of the registrant's child, federal or state census records, school records, insurance policy, and an assortment of other records, such as military and employment records.[214]

St. Louis County — Before 1877

St. Louis started keeping birth registers in 1850; however, the system was voluntary and therefore, incomplete. The "Register of St. Louis Births" is available on microfilm at St. Louis County Library, Special Collections and at St. Louis Genealogical Society.

St. Louis City — After 1876

The previously mentioned birth register started in 1850, but after 1876 only for those born within the City Limits. Birth records filed in St. Louis after 1910 are available at the City and State addresses listed above. The genealogical collections at St. Louis County Library and St. Louis Public Library have microfilm for the St. Louis index of births in the City, 1910–1929.

Applicants to the City or State must know the following information about the birth record requested:

> First, middle, and last name
> Place of birth
> Date of birth
> Father's name
> Mother's name
> Applicant's name and address
> Relationship of applicant to birth registrant
> Purpose of copy
> Applicant's signature and date of request

---

213.   Missouri State Board of Health, *Annual Report, 1939*, page 104. Standard Certificate of Live Birth, form Vital Statistic no. 1, revised April 20, 1939. Standard Certificate of Death, form Vital Statistic no. 2, May 17, 1939.

214.   Missouri Historical Records Survey Division of Community Service Programs WPA, *Guide to Public Vital Statistics Records in Missouri* (St. Louis: Missouri Historical Records Survey, 1941), 13.

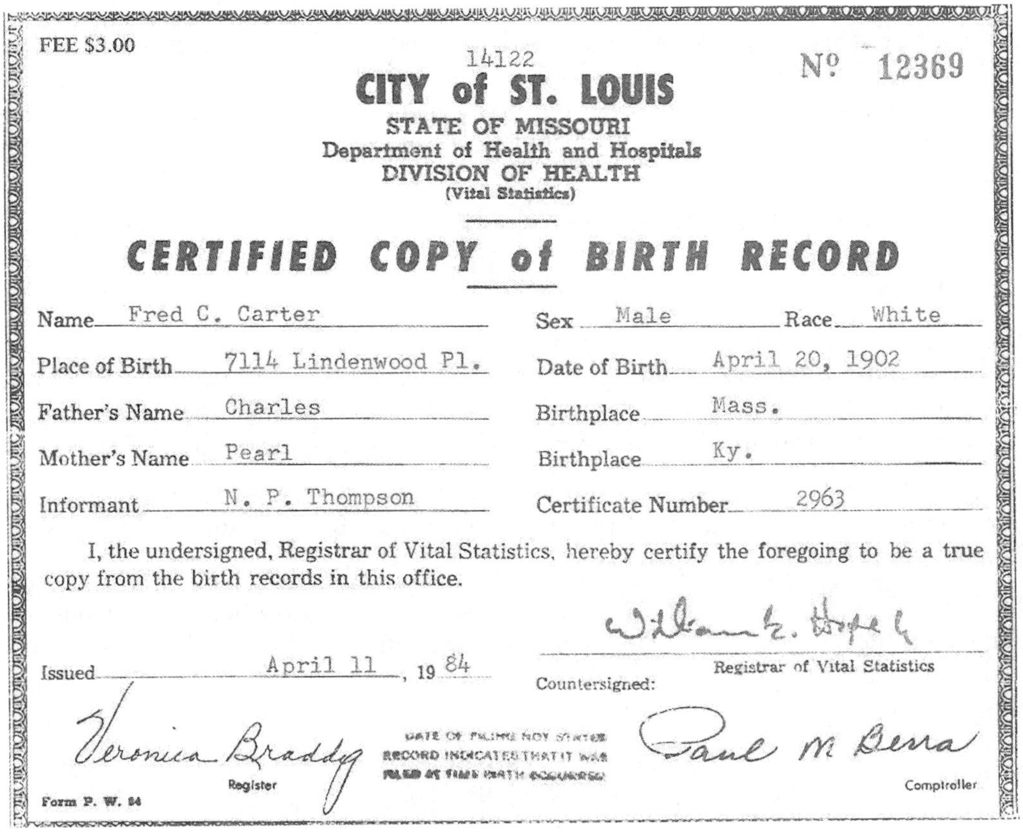
FEE $3.00

14122

No 12369

CITY of ST. LOUIS
STATE OF MISSOURI
Department of Health and Hospitals
DIVISION OF HEALTH
(Vital Statistics)

CERTIFIED COPY of BIRTH RECORD

Name Fred C. Carter Sex Male Race White
Place of Birth 7114 Lindenwood Pl. Date of Birth April 20, 1902
Father's Name Charles Birthplace Mass.
Mother's Name Pearl Birthplace Ky.
Informant N. P. Thompson Certificate Number 2963

I, the undersigned, Registrar of Vital Statistics, hereby certify the foregoing to be a true copy from the birth records in this office.

Issued April 11, 1984

Registrar of Vital Statistics

Countersigned:

Register

Comptroller

Form P. W. 84

Figure 13: Birth Certificate before 1910

Using birth records as in Figure 13 requires caution. In this record the birth occurred in 1904, but the document is dated 1984. Therefore, the record was transcribed from a register. It is advisable to check the original register to verify the information.

St. Louis County — After 1876

St. Louis County maintained a register of births starting in 1883. This register is available in print and microfilm formats. St. Louis County Library, Special Collections indexed this register and it is available online.[215] An index for St. Louis County stillbirths dating from 1883 to 1908 is available online at the St. Louis County Library website. Today Missouri born residents may obtain a copy of their birth certificate from the County office listed previously.

---

215. "Index to Register of Births, St. Louis County Missouri, 1883–1895," *St. Louis County Library* (http://www.slcl.org/sc/pdfs/stl_births_a.pdf). "St. Louis County Register of Births;" Missouri State Archives, microfilm C36954.

ADOPTION RECORDS

Although current adoption records are closed to the public, adoption records before the early 1900s are open. The pre-privacy act era provides clues to the family historian. Usually filed in the Circuit Court, adoptions are indexed under the child's name, the name of the adoption agency, or under the phrase, *In Regard*. The court sometimes uses *in regard* as an attempt to hide the name of the child.

Peggy Greenwood indexed the House of Refuge records; they were printed in the *St. Louis Genealogical Society Quarterly*,[216] and the index is available online (http://www.stlgs.org/institutionsOrphanagesHouseRefuge.htm).

Western Historical Manuscript in St. Louis holds a large collection of records for the St. Louis Protestant Orphan Asylum, see online finding aid. The Missouri Historical Society holds an abstract of a minute book, 1834–1852 of the St. Louis Protestant Orphan Asylum and an indexed record book of admissions and removals, 1882–1916, from the asylum.

St. Louis County Library, Special Collections in microfilm and book format, intake records from the German General Protestant Orphan's Home and an index to all St. Louis orphanages listed in the 1900 census.[217]

St. Louis City Hall Archives has an old card file with limited resources for adoptions and orphans in the late 1800s continuing to 1916. The information on these cards and the associated original records are only available through the City Hall Archives service.[218] An example of the adoption cards is in Figure 14.

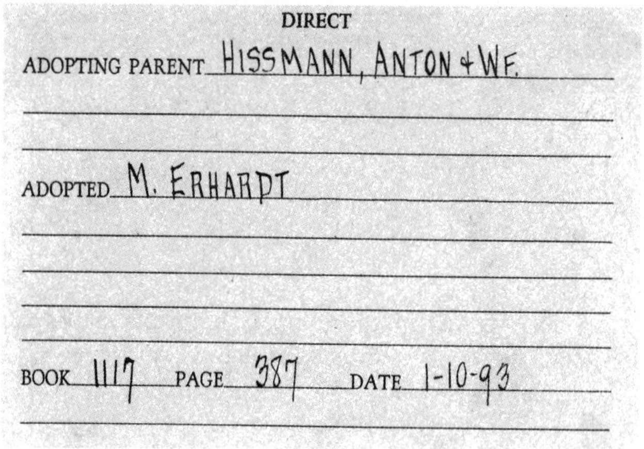

DIRECT

ADOPTING PARENT HISSMANN, ANTON & WF.

ADOPTED M. ERHARDT

BOOK 1117 PAGE 387 DATE 1-10-93

Figure 14: Adoption Card, St. Louis City Recorder of Deeds Office
Used with permission of St. Louis Recorder of Deed Office.

---

216. Peggy Greenwood, "Journal of Commitments, July 1854–January 1899," *St. Louis Genealogical Society Quarterly* 25 (1992): 46–49, and continues for five issues. The list is available on the Society website.

217. Kelly Draper, *Index to Intake Records, German General Protestant Orphan's Home, St. Louis, Missouri* (St. Louis: St. Louis County Library, 2003).

218. *Archives Services: Nearly 250 Years of St. Louis History thru Public Records* (St. Louis: Recorder of Deeds, no date).

BAPTISMAL RECORDS

Baptismal records are always an alternative for birth records and are especially important before 1910. Extant religious records for a variety of denominations provide baptismal records. Early St. Louis Catholic baptismal records listed in the St. Louis Genealogical Society publication, *Catholic Baptisms, 1765–1840,* (see Figure 16) provides proof of kinship between parent and child and often include the child's birth and baptismal dates.[219] The German Evangelical, Catholic, and German Lutheran church records from the nineteenth century are particularly helpful. Depending on the denomination and church background, the records could be in English, Latin, German, or another language, as in Figure 15.

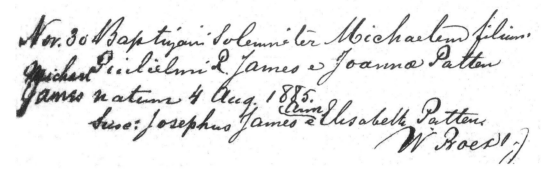

Figure 15: Religious Baptismal Record

JAMES, Jean Baptiste	John & Julie Creely	1 Jan 1811
Henry		1 Nov 1812
Cecile		May 1815
Samuel		19 Sep 1817
Edward		May 1820
Victoria		Apr 1823
Leonora (?)		Sep 1826
Louis		9 Nov 1828
Elise		30 Apr 1831
Mary		Dec 1834
Joseph		Nov 1835
John	John & Marie Musick	June 1836
Ann Elizabeth		Nov 1838
Emilia Julie	Samuel & Virginia Robertson	25 Aug 1839
Marie Francois	Joseph Jr. & Marie Burke	9 Aug 1816

Figure 16: Catholic Baptisms, St. Louis, Missouri, 1765–1840
Used with permission of St. Louis Genealogical Society.

---

219.   St. Louis Genealogical Society, *Catholic Baptisms, St. Louis, Missouri, 1765–1840* (St. Louis: The Society, 1982).

BIBLE RECORDS

Bible records offer another opportunity to locate birth information. Parents and grandparents often recorded the births, marriages, and deaths of family members in the family Bible. Some St. Louis Genealogical Society members have submitted Bible record information for publication in the *StLGS Quarterly*. Other organizations, such as the National Genealogical Society, publish Bible records in print and online.[220]

The National Union Catalog Manuscript Collection (NUCMC) provides access to manuscript records from across the country. If a St. Louis ancestor or his descendants moved to California, the Bible record may be in a California archival facility. The Library of Congress provides access to NUCMC.[221]

220.　"Bible Records," *National Genealogical Society* (http://www.ngsgenealogy.org).
221.　"National Union Catalog Manuscript Collection," *Library of Congress* (http://www.loc.gov/coll/nucmc).

Business, Occupation, & Society Sources

Many businesses and occupations are part of St. Louis history. Starting with the fur trading business in the 1700s, St. Louisans have had a wide variety of occupations extending from the shoe manufacturing and steamboat operations to the present day beer and aircraft production. Ancestral occupations might have been an attorney, civil servant, farmer, merchant, peddler, physician, or teacher. Practitioners of each occupation and many more left records.

Employment was difficult for some in St. Louis. In 1881 female teachers were informed, "Your committee would recommend that hereafter the marriage of a female teacher shall be considered an equivalent to her resignation and shall be treated as such."[222]

Some businesses are included in the *Pictorial St. Louis: The Great Metropolis of the Mississippi Valley: A Topographical Survey, 1875* previously mentioned. [See ATLASES, GAZETTEERS, & MAPS.]

If an ancestor had a business with a trademark or logo, it may be recorded. The Recorder of Deeds office at St. Louis City Hall has trademark records from 1865 to 1930. The trademark subject varies, for example: alcohol, foods, tobacco, and some organizations.

City Hall also has incorporation records from 1875 to 1920 for profit and non-profit organizations. The type of records varies from bylaws to property inventories. Charities, churches, clubs, and professional and civic groups form just a small sample of the type of organizations included.

St. Louis City Hall also has a list containing Powers of Attorney granted between 1764 and 1920. These records include the Colonial time, St. Louis County, and St. Louis City based on the document and date of the recording. While some documents are related to probate issues, many related to businesses and organizations.[223]

---

222. Rick Pierce article, *St. Louis Post-Dispatch,* October 23, 1998, Metro Section.

223. *Archives Services: Nearly 250 Years of St. Louis History thru Public Records* (St. Louis: Recorder of Deeds, no date).

BUSINESSES

Directories, newspapers, lists of incorporation, and the Better Business Bureau provide lists of local businesses. The Better Business Bureau rosters provide background information for large and small corporations.[224]

River Related Businesses

Business along the river started with fur trading and soon extensively involved transportation. The Missouri Historical Society Research Library has numerous records dealing with local fur traders, including the Missouri Fur Trade Company, St. Louis Fur Trade Company, and others. Early St. Louis families such as the Lisa, Berthold, Campbell, and Chouteau families operated fur trade companies. The Missouri Historical Society Research Library has microfilmed records for the *Papers of the St. Louis Fur Trade, 1752–1925,* in the Chouteau Collection. They also have the American Fur Company Ledger on microfilm.

The Mississippi and the Missouri Rivers provided transportation for many pioneers and immigrants who traveled from the east via the Ohio River and from the north via the Illinois River or the south from New Orleans. Many German immigrants followed the last path, traveling up the Mississippi River by steamboat landing in St. Louis. They may have sailed west to Kansas City or beyond along the Missouri River or remained in St. Louis. In either case, the rivers were a major part of daily business in St. Louis.

Steamboats arrived and departed daily from the Mississippi River levee in St. Louis. Ledgers, with an alphabetical index listed by the ships' names, aid in finding arrival and departure dates for a specific vessel. Some ships arrived often, others only occasionally. The ledgers indicate *port for* (destination city) and *port from* (departure city). Arrival ledgers provide the date of arrival, name of the ship, port from, assessed tons, time, and the docking fee. Departure ledgers provide the date, name of the ship, port for, time, and remarks. These records cover the years 1878–1881 and 1888–1918. The ports mentioned included Alton, Cairo, Carondelet, Cincinnati, Grafton, Illinois River, Kansas City, Keokuk, Memphis, Meridian, New Orleans, Peoria, Pittsburg, Tennessee River, Vicksburg, and occasionally dry dock.[225]

Vessels weighing more than twenty-one tons were required to have one-year licenses, like the one in Figure 18, that were available from the district of the Port of St. Louis. Based on an act of Congress, "An act for enrolling and licensing ships or vessels to be employed on the Carding Trade and Fisheries and for regulatory the same," the license lists the name of the owner of the ship and the date.[226]

---

224.   *St. Louis Better Business Bureau Roster, 1917–1946* (St. Louis: Better Business Bureau, 1946).

225.   *Steamboat arrivals and departures, 1878–1881, 1888–1918, Missouri Harbor and Wharf, St. Louis*; FHL film 981,668; City Archives film H379.

226.   Ship's registers and other records, 1835–1944; FHL film 1,695,040. Also see, *Vessel Documents Received from the Port of St. Louis, Missouri,* M1340, Record Group 41, 26 rolls (Washington, D.C.: NARA); FHL film 1,695,042.

Fifty Years on the Mississippi, also called *Gould's History of River Navigation,* includes more than 700 names of those who traveled the rivers. St. Louis County Library has an index online.[227]

St. Louis Businesses and Commerce

The *St. Louis Star-Times* publication, *The City of St. Louis and Its Resources,* also called *The Star-Sayings' Souvenir of St. Louis*, placed its emphasis on the business of the day, 1893, and St. Louis's leading citizens. It also displays advertisements from that era.[228]

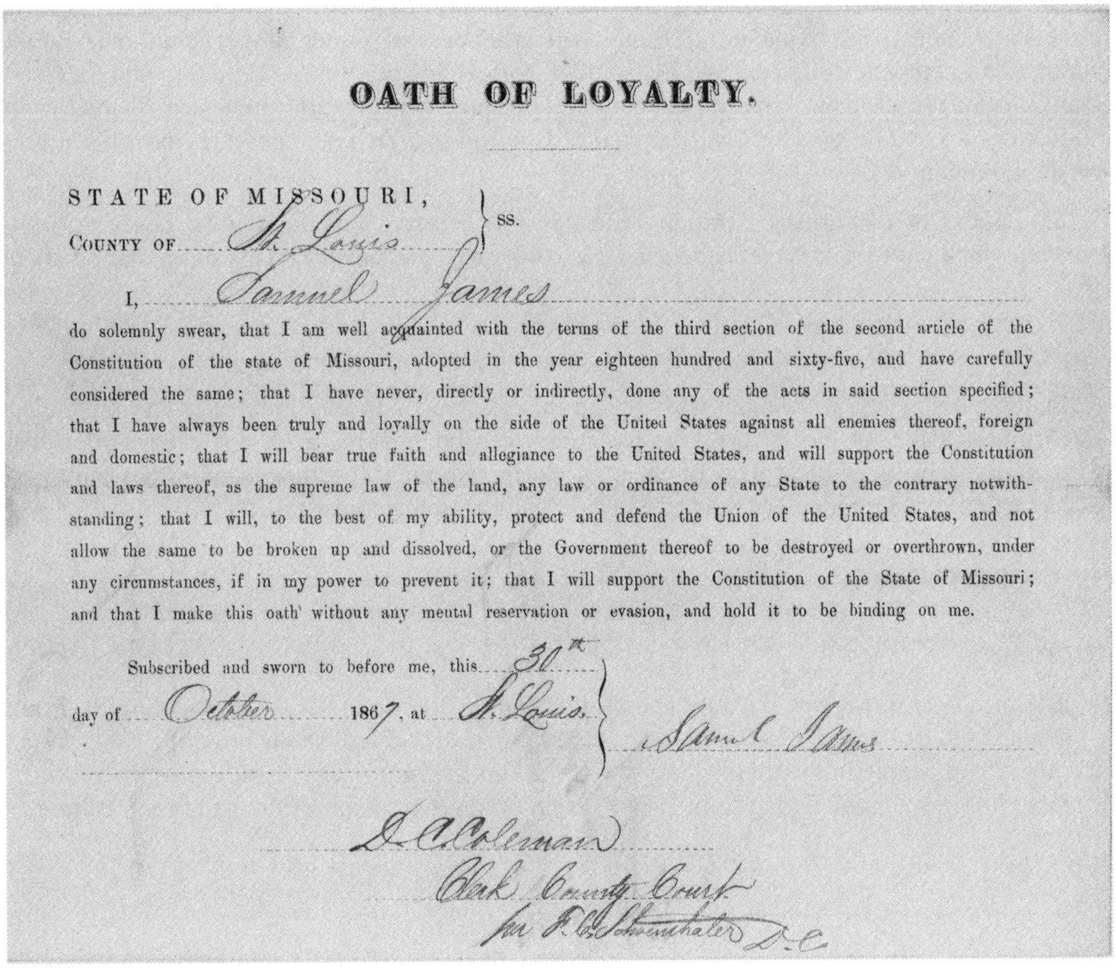

OATH OF LOYALTY.

STATE OF MISSOURI, }
COUNTY OF St. Louis } SS.

I, Samuel James

do solemnly swear, that I am well acquainted with the terms of the third section of the second article of the Constitution of the state of Missouri, adopted in the year eighteen hundred and sixty-five, and have carefully considered the same; that I have never, directly or indirectly, done any of the acts in said section specified; that I have always been truly and loyally on the side of the United States against all enemies thereof, foreign and domestic; that I will bear true faith and allegiance to the United States, and will support the Constitution and laws thereof, as the supreme law of the land, any law or ordinance of any State to the contrary notwithstanding; that I will, to the best of my ability, protect and defend the Union of the United States, and not allow the same to be broken up and dissolved, or the Government thereof to be destroyed or overthrown, under any circumstances, if in my power to prevent it; that I will support the Constitution of the State of Missouri; and that I make this oath without any mental reservation or evasion, and hold it to be binding on me.

Subscribed and sworn to before me, this 30th day of October 1867, at St. Louis.

Saml James

Clerk County Court

Figure 17: Oath of Loyalty, 1867

227. Emerson W. Gould, *Fifty Years on the Mississippi* (1889, reprint; Columbus, Ohio: Long's College Book Company, 1951). [This book is also known as *Gould's History of River Navigation.*]

228. St. Louis Star-Sayings, *The City of St. Louis and Its Resources* (St. Louis: Continental Printing Company, 1893). [Index at St. Louis Public Library website, available on CD-ROM from St. Louis Genealogical Society.]

A Century of Enterprise: St. Louis, 1894–1994 is another title that provides background information on businesses, such as automobile manufacturers, breweries, grocery stores, restaurants, shoe companies, shopping areas, theaters, and many more business establishments frequented by you or your ancestors in the St. Louis area. The index is available on the St. Louis Public Library website.[229]

St. Louis Today provides photographs of banks, bridges, businesses, homes, hospitals, hotels, orphan homes, parks, steamboats, and other places of business and pleasure. This publication may include a photograph of an important place of interest for your family history.[230]

St. Louis Commerce, published by the St. Louis Regional Commerce and Growth Association, dates back to about 1926 and still produces ten issues a year. St. Louis Public Library has a complete collection and Missouri Historical Society Research Library and St. Louis County Library each have a partial collection. The same organization published *St. Louis: Its Neighborhoods and Neighbors, Landmarks, and Milestones*, which includes a review of St. Louis and the community.[231]

St. Louis County Library, Special Collection has a card index for the *St. Louis Business Journal*, which consists of an alphabetical index of names and subjects. This index started about 1989.

Trades

Silversmithing was a valuable trade at the time of the Louisiana Purchase. The fur traders took trinkets made by the silversmiths to trade with the Indians. *St. Louis Silversmiths* lists silversmiths from the earliest days of St. Louis to the twentieth century. It describes the trade, lists the names of those involved, and often provides biographical information.[232]

OCCUPATIONS

Attorneys

The *St. Louis Bar Journal* is an ongoing publication started in 1950, representing St. Louis attorneys. The *History of the Bench and Bar of Missouri,* dated 1898, provides even earlier information on people in this field.[233] *Report of the Proceedings of the Annual Meeting of the ... Missouri Bar Association* dating from 1881 to 1930 provides a membership list in each edition.[234]

---

229.   Rockwell Gray, *A Century of Enterprise: St. Louis, 1894–1994* (St. Louis: Missouri Historical Society Press, 1994). [Index at St. Louis Public Library website.]

230.   *St. Louis Today* (St. Louis: Business Men's League of St. Louis, no date).

231.   Robert E. Hannon, *St. Louis: Its Neighborhoods and Neighbors, Landmarks, and Milestones* (St. Louis: St. Louis Regional Commerce and Growth Association, 1986).

232.   Ruth Hunter Roach, *St. Louis Silversmiths* (St. Louis: Eden, 1967).

233.   *St. Louis Bar Journal* (St. Louis: Bar Association of Metropolitan St. Louis, 1950–). *St. Louis Bar Association Yearbook* (St. Louis: privately printed, 1904–1909). A. Stewart, *History of the Bench and Bar of Missouri with Reminiscences of the Prominent Lawyers of the Past, and a Record of the Law's Leaders of the Present* (St. Louis: Legal Publishing Company, 1898).

234.   Missouri Bar Association, *Report of the Proceedings of the Annual Meeting of the ... Missouri Bar Association* (St. Louis: The Association, 1881–1930).

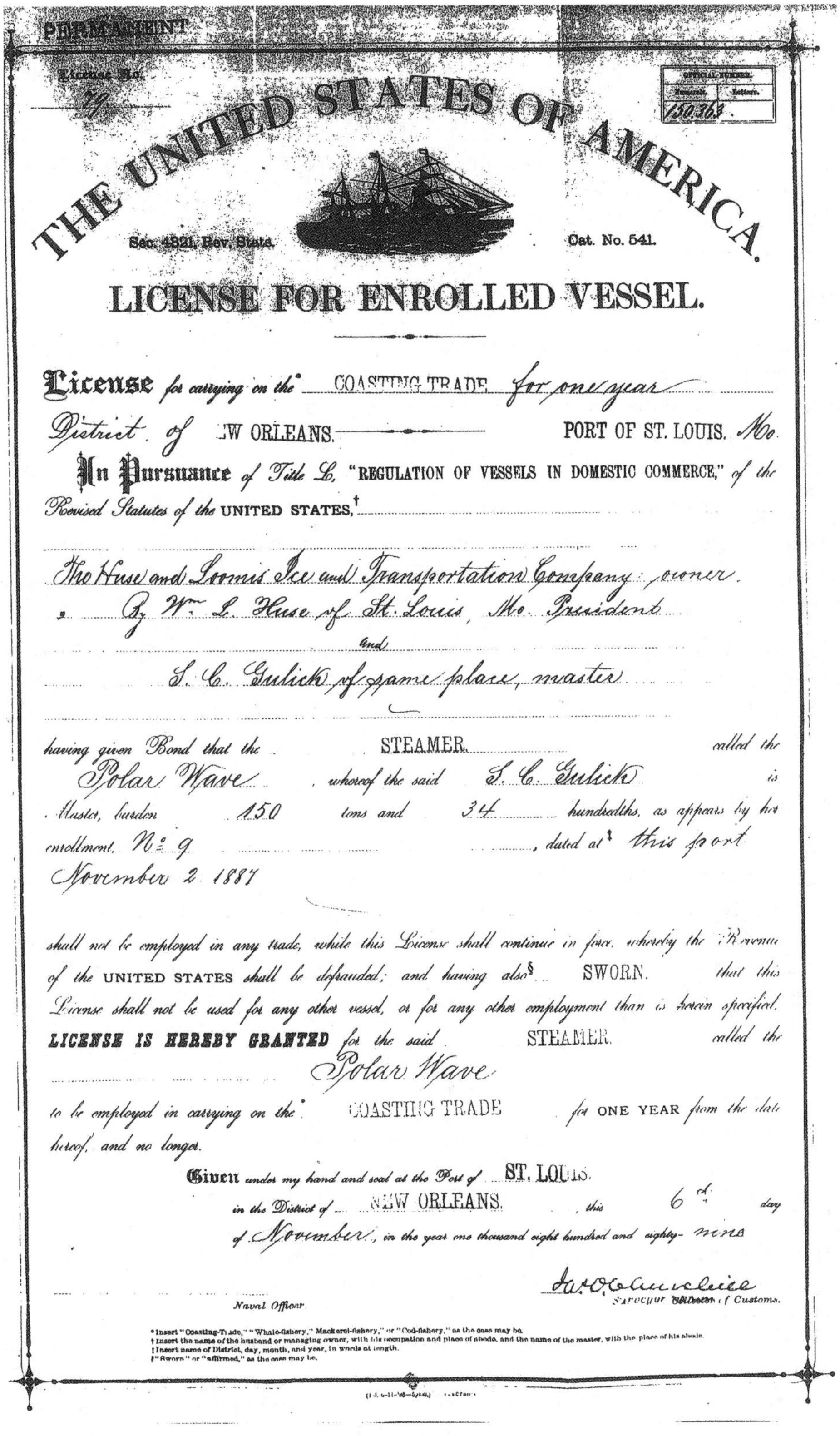

PERMANENT

License No. 79

Official Number.	
Numeral.	Letters.
150363	

THE UNITED STATES OF AMERICA.

Sec. 4321, Rev. Stats. Cat. No. 541.

LICENSE FOR ENROLLED VESSEL.

License for carrying on the COASTING TRADE for one year

District of NEW ORLEANS. PORT OF ST. LOUIS. Mo.

In Pursuance of Title L, "REGULATION OF VESSELS IN DOMESTIC COMMERCE," of the Revised Statutes of the UNITED STATES,†

The Huse and Loomis Ice and Transportation Company, owner, By Wm. L. Huse of St. Louis, Mo. President

and

S. C. Gulick, of same place, master

having given Bond that the STEAMER called the Polar Wave, whereof the said S. C. Gulick is Master, burden 150 tons and 34 hundredths, as appears by her enrollment, No. 9, dated at‡ this port November 2. 1887

shall not be employed in any trade, while this License shall continue in force, whereby the Revenue of the UNITED STATES shall be defrauded; and having also§ SWORN that this License shall not be used for any other vessel, or for any other employment than is herein specified, LICENSE IS HEREBY GRANTED for the said STEAMER called the Polar Wave to be employed in carrying on the* COASTING TRADE for ONE YEAR from the date hereof, and no longer.

Given under my hand and seal at the Port of ST. LOUIS in the District of NEW ORLEANS, this 6th day of November, in the year one thousand eight hundred and eighty-nine

Naval Officer. Surveyor Collector of Customs.

* Insert "Coasting-Trade," "Whale-fishery," "Mackerel-fishery," or "Cod-fishery," as the case may be.
† Insert the name of the husband or managing owner, with his occupation and place of abode, and the name of the master, with the place of his abode.
‡ Insert name of District, day, month, and year, in words at length.
§ "Sworn" or "affirmed," as the case may be.

Figure 18: Vessel License

Clergy

With the growing population, new religious facilities were in demand, with clergy from various denominations moving to St. Louis. The St. Louis Genealogical Society website offers a list of known St. Louis clergy along with their religious facilities and the known years they served at each location. This database is a work in progress, expanding as new information becomes available.[235] The Archives at Eden has a card file for Evangelical Synod pastors ordained before 1934 and Concordia Historical Institute has the Lutheran pastors before 1960. [See APPENDIX B for contact information.]

Engineers

The Engineers's Club of St. Louis, established in 1868, provides an annual directory of its members. Surviving volumes provide photos of most members with their street addresses and phone numbers along with their business names and locations.[236]

Firefighters

The St. Louis Public Library website offers an index for City fire fighters in 1914.[237] *St. Louis Fire Department* includes photos of the City, fire trucks, and firemen.[238] Another publication, *Volunteer Fire Department of St. Louis, 1819–1859*, is available at Missouri Historical Society's Research Library.[239]

For those with interest in early firemen, Missouri Historical Society Research Library has the constitution and by-laws of the Veteran Volunteer Firemen's Historical Society of the City of St. Louis and includes lists of firefighters.[240] They also have the St. Louis Volunteer Firemen Collection, 1826–1945.

Governmental Positions

Today and yesteryear, City officials are either elected or appointed. In the past, the mayor and others appointed citizens to official City jobs and granted a commission with a certificate filed in the City records. The certificates include the name, date issued, position, by whom appointed or the elected term ending. Many certificates state that the term ends on the first Tuesday in April of (year), which coincides with the date of the mayoral election. Other certificates indicate the term is at the pleasure of director or whoever made the appointment. Arranged by date, these

---

235.   "Clergy," *St. Louis Genealogical Society* (http://www.stlgs.org/religionsClergy.htm).

236.   *Engineers's Club of St. Louis* (St. Louis: The Club, annually).

237.   *St. Louis Volunteer Firemen Collection, 1826–1945* (St. Louis: The Department, 1945). *History of St. Louis Fire Department with a Review of Great Fires and Sidelights Upon the Methods of Fire-fighting from Ancient to Modern Times, from which the Lessons of the Vast Importance of Having Efficient Firemen May Be Drawn* (St. Louis: Central Publishing Company, 1914). [Index available at St. Louis Public Library website.]

238.   Frank C. Schaper and Betty Burnett, *Images of America, St. Louis Fire Department* (Chicago: Arcadia Publishing, 2003).

239.   *Volunteer Fire Department of St. Louis, 1819–1859* (St. Louis: privately published, 1880).

240.   *Constitution and By-laws of the Veteran Volunteer Firemen's Historical Society of the City of St. Louis, Mo. Organized Nov. 20th, 1888 with List of Members, and Names of Companies, Showing When Instituted, Incorporated, Disbanded, or Retired from Service* (St. Louis: privately published, 1893).

certificates include Justices of the Peace, constables, city surveyors, collectors of revenue, commissioners of parks, and tuberculosis controllers.[241]

The Missouri State Archives has a record series, Register of Civil Officers, which contains a list of commissioned civil officers. During the Civil War Reconstruction era, these documents served as the "oaths of loyalty," as shown in Figure 17. The listings include the name, date of appointment, county of residence, expiration of term, and remarks. The remarks may include notices of death, resignations, and political affiliation.[242]

In the mid-1800s, City employees signed an official oath on a certificate format document. The document provides the name of the employee and his signature plus the job he held. It also states who nominated him for this job; it could have been the mayor or department leaders.[243]

The City of St. Louis awarded bonds for government jobs for various tasks and equipment. These included, but were not limited to, gaslight supplies, mapping, printing, shipwrecking, steam engines, and surveys. The bonds include the name of the person awarded the job and which government official granted the bond. The City filmed these records and they are available at City Hall and at the Family History Library. Other local facilities have some of the records.[244]

BOARD OF ALDERMEN

The Board of Aldermen and formerly called the House of Delegates,[245] served as the legislature for the City. The Aldermen pass the ordinances that make the City function on a daily basis.[246] The minute books contain the text of their proceedings.[247] St. Louis Public Library has a complete printed set of the City Minutes of the Board of Aldermen.

CITY CONSTABLE

Similar to the recording of the appointment of Justices of the Peace, the City recorded the appointments of City Constables or Deputy Constables, and these records are available on microfilm. Neither publication provides an index. Some of the records are on a printed form with the name and dates inserted. Others are handwritten pages in ledger books, often difficult to read.[248]

---

241. Miscellaneous Documents filed with the City Register, 1838–1884; FHL film starting with 981,629.

242. "Register of Civil Officers," Missouri State Archives manuscript collection.

243. Official oaths, 1863–1867; oaths of loyalty, 1865–1867; FHL film 981,666, City Archives film F591.

244. Miscellaneous Documents filed with the City Register, 1838–1884; FHL film 981,629 or City Archives film F26.

245. House of Delegates' records are also available on microfilm with one example from 1877–1915; Missouri State Archives film C19441.

246. Numerous films provide the text for the ordinances. One example is Ordinances, City of St. Louis, 1839; Missouri State Archives film C13416; and City Archives film F86.

247. Board of Aldermen Minute Book, Missouri State Archives film C12789 and others; City Archives film L255. Board of Aldermen Journals, 1917–1927; Missouri State Archives film C16052.

248. Official Constable Oaths, November 1878–January 1885; Missouri State Archives film C13419; City Archives film F68. Record of Constable Bonds Appointment of Deputy Constables, November 1878–September 1894; Missouri State Archives film C13421; and City Archives film F112.

MAYOR OF ST. LOUIS

William Carr Lane was the first mayor of the City of St. Louis after incorporation in 1823. The St. Louis Public Library website provides a list of the subsequent mayors along with their biographies and photos.[249] The walls outside the Mayor's Office in City Hall have a collection of portraits of the former mayors.

Over the years, mayors have provided reports or messages to the City, similar to an annual report for corporations. The Mayor's Messages are available in print and on microfilm.[250] They sometimes provide a list of city employees divided by the area of employment. For example, they provide a complete list of the St. Louis Public Library employees along with their job title and salary. The reports also name each dairy farm in the City; the name and station house for each fireman and police officer plus injury reports. While it may seem boring to read, genealogists may find a wealth of information in the annual reports, some more than 100 years old.

JUSTICE OF THE PEACE

The local Justices of the Peace, elected by area, performed weddings and took care of small legal matters for their constituents. The Justices of the Peace took an oath allowing them to serve for four years. The oaths and statements from the governor are available on microfilm.[251]

Medical Fields

Several publications aid research in the field of medical practioners. *Medicine in St. Louis: Our Medical Ancestors, 1764–1864* is a good place to start. It provides biographical information for the earliest physicians.[252]

The City of St. Louis licensed physicians, nurses, druggists, dentists, and midwives. There are various records indicating dates of graduation, licensing, and location of their practice. The *St. Louis and St. Louis County Directory of Physicians, Druggists, Dentists, ...* provides the names of medical personnel, the types of practice, the names of their medical school, their current hospital affiliations, and their office addresses. This 1894 publication is available online at St. Louis Public Library website.[253]

If your ancestor was a physician in 1890, the *Medical and Surgical Register of the United States* may provide the municipality in which he practiced. An alphabetical list provides the name of the municipality in which each doctor practiced. The publication lists the physicians by post

---

249.   "St. Louis Mayor's QuickFacts," *St. Louis Public Library* (http://exhibits.silmslpl.org/mayors).

250.   St. Louis City Mayor's Messages, 1868–1912; Missouri State Archives film C19391. Missouri Historical Society and other facilities have the printed format.

251.   Justice of the Peace, St. Louis City, January 1825–May 1856; Missouri State Archives film C13414; City Archives film F85. Also, Records of Commissions of Justices of the Peace, November 1878–December 1888; Missouri State Archives film C13416, item 2; and City Archives film F85.

252.   Samuel D. Soule, MD, *Medicine in St. Louis: Our Medical Ancestors, 1764–1864* (St. Louis: St. Louis Medical Service Bureau, 1978).

253.   *St. Louis and St. Louis County Directory of Physicians, Druggists, Dentists, etc., Comprising a Complete and Accurate List of All Physicians, Their Correct Office and Residence Addresses, Hours of Consultation at Both Office and Residence, Telephone Number, etc.: Also a Complete and Accurate List of Dentists, Druggists, and Midwives, Arranged Alphabetically and by Streets* (St. Louis: Polk and Company, 1894).

office location; therefore, it is necessary to look under St. Louis and smaller communities in St. Louis County, such as Bridgeton, Creve Coeur, Kirkwood, Mehlville, and other municipalities by name.[254]

The St. Louis Medical Society, founded in 1837, published a yearbook of those in the medical field in 1939. This publication provides a photograph and description of each member. Other years are available at various facilities. While it does not include an index, there are only a few sections with photographs, and biographical information is listed alphabetically within each section.[255]

A more recent physicians' resource is the *St. Louis Medicine Official Bulletin of the St. Louis Medical Society, 1968.* As with the other references, it too provides photographs of the current members at the time of publication, their home and office addresses, hospital affiliations, and the medical schools with dates of graduation.[256]

The St. Louis Board of Pharmacy provides records of St. Louis druggists dating from 1893 to 1909, recording the druggist license, the certificate number, and the place of business.[257] A record for certificates issued from 1893 to 1914 in St. Louis County is available for the State Board of Pharmacy.[258]

For osteopaths a list of diplomas issued by the School of Osteopathy starts in 1893. This list includes the name of the osteopath, the school name and location, and date of the diploma.[259] St. Louis County has a record of the State Board of Osteopathy certificates issued from 1916 to 1917.[260]

An easy-to-read 1878 booklet provides the names of 481 physicians in the City of St. Louis, plus twenty-one physicians practicing outside the City Limits. This list provides the name of the doctor, date of his diploma, and the name of the medical school. The location of the medical school may provide a clue to the former place of residence or even place of birth.[261]

An alphabetical list of midwives, female practitioners, and physicians provides the name, residence, office address, date of diploma, name of school, date of registration, and signature. This registration started in 1860, with some graduation dates going back to the 1830s.[262]

The Missouri State Archives has a manuscript collection, *Board of Registration for the Healing Arts,* consisting of *Register of Midwives, 1868–1946, Physician and Surgeon Register, 1911–1945, Registers of Physicians and Accoucheurs, 1841–1894* (2 volumes). They also have rosters of physicians, surgeons, and osteopathic doctors. Exams for medical doctors, doctors of

254. *Polk's Medical and Surgical Register of the United States*; FHL film 1,598,299, item 4.

255. *St. Louis Medical Society, Centennial Volume* (St. Louis: The Society, 1939).

256. *St. Louis Medicine Official Bulletin of the St. Louis Medical Society* 62 (August 1968).

257. Record of Druggists' Licenses, 1893–1909; City Archives roll F567; FHL film 981,658.

258. St. Louis County State Board of Pharmacy Certificates, 1893–1914; Missouri State Archives film C18169, item 3.

259. Record of Osteopathy; City Archives roll F567; FHL film 981,658.

260. St. Louis County State Board of Osteopathy Certificates, 1916–1917; Missouri State Archives film C18169, item 4.

261. List of Registered Physicians in the City of St. Louis, August 20, 1878; FHL film 1,425,257.

262. Midwives and Female Practitioners; FHL film 980,607.

osteopathy, physical trainers, physical therapists, and medical examiners are also in this collection.[263]

The St. Louis County Board of Health issued certificates for doctors from 1880 to 1935. The certificate includes the name of the physician, the name of his medical school and its location, date of graduation, and a certificate number.[264] St. Louis County provided permits for doctors and druggists. Those issued from 1921 to 1933 provide the name, address, date filed, date issued, expiration date, fee, and permit number, which was good for one year.[265]

The *History of St. Louis Training School for Nurses Which Later Became the St. Louis City Hospital Training School for Nurses* provides history since the founding in 1883 and the name of many alumnae prior to 1941. Some repositories have various catalogs for this school.[266]

St. Louis City Hall has a nurses' registration book, 1921–1954. In addition to nurses, the book includes women of Catholic religious orders. It is necessary to visit City Hall to see this book.[267]

Police

St. Louis Board of Police Commissioners personnel records, 1861–1894, are available at Missouri Historical Society Research Library. Each volume provides an index. At the same location you will find the *History of the Metropolitan Police Department of St. Louis, 1810–1910.* This publication includes a photograph and biography of each policeman. A new book by Allen Wagner has a similar title, *Good Order and Safety: A History of the St. Louis Metropolitan Police Department, 1861–1906.*[268]

The *St. Louis Police Journal* started in 1911 with weekly editions. The journal provides a history of the events of the week, both about the crimes committed and about the police personnel. Crime information includes jury sentences, robberies, shootings, complaints, and new laws and the compliance expected. Employee information includes who was on sick leave or furlough, cards of thanks, Board of Police Commissioners' activities, transfers, promotions, resignations, photos (limited), roll of honor, and a few photos of the uniforms. Publications from 1918 to 1933 are available at the State Historical Society of Missouri in Columbia.[269]

---

263.   "Board of Registration for the Healing Arts," Missouri State Archives manuscript.

264.   St. Louis County Board of Health Certificates, 1880–1935; Missouri State Archives film C18168.

265.   St. Louis County Doctors and Druggists Permits, 1921–1933; Missouri State Archives film C18161, item 3.

266.   Elizabeth Green, *History of St. Louis Training School for Nurses, Which Later Became the St. Louis City Hospital Training School for Nurses* (St. Louis: St. Louis Training School for Nurses Alumnae, 1941).

267.   *Archives Services: Nearly 250 Years of St. Louis History thru Public Records* (St. Louis: Recorder of Deeds, no date).

268.   *History of the Metropolitan Police Department of St. Louis* (St. Louis: The Department, 1910). *St. Louis Police Department Illustrated, 1902* (St. Louis: The Department, 1902). Allen E. Wagner, *Good Order and Safety: A History of the St. Louis Metropolitan Police Department, 1861–1906* (St. Louis: Missouri Historical Society Press, 2008).

269.   *St. Louis Police Journals* (St. Louis: St. Louis Police Department, 1911–).

The St. Louis County Police Department, 1955–2000 provides history, photos, and interesting details about the formation and development of the St. Louis County Police department.[270]

Politicians

Campaign finance records dating from 1896 to 1972 are available at the Recorder of Deeds office at St. Louis City Hall. In addition to candidate information, the records include ballot issues, donors, and expenses. An index covers records dating from 1901 to 1945. This information is available by appointment only.[271] Similar records for those who ran for a statewide office are available at the Missouri State Archives.

SOCIETIES

In the early twentieth century St. Louis had a great number of clubs or social organizations, many with charitable and philanthropic missions. The St. Louis Public Library website has an index of fraternal and benevolent societies in St. Louis compiled from various sources.[272] Numerous publications list the local clubs, including *St. Louis Club Directories*. Most of the publications provide the names of the members and their home or business addresses and some provide biographical information.[273]

Genealogical & Historical Societies

St. Louis Genealogical Society is the largest genealogical society in the state of Missouri. The membership includes St. Louis residents and many out of state. Because St. Louis was the Gateway to the West, pioneers traveled by boat or overland to St. Louis. Some pioneers moved west, others stayed in the area. The Society publishes a monthly newsletter and the *St. Louis Genealogical Society Quarterly*.[274]

The Missouri Historical Society has a museum, library, and archival facility in St. Louis. Their collections focus on early Missouri and St. Louis resources. The society's periodic publications include *Missouri Historical Society Collections*, 1880–1931; *Glimpses of the Past*, 1933–1943; *Missouri Historical Bulletin*, 1944–1979; *Gateway Heritage*, 1980–2006; and *Gateway*, 2006–present.[275]

Likewise, many of those same ancestors left St. Louis for other parts of the state. The Missouri State Genealogical Association can assist with out-state research. The *Missouri State*

---

270.   *St. Louis County Police Department: 45th Anniversary, 1955–2000* (Paducah, Kentucky: Turner Publications, 2000).

271.   *Archives Services: Nearly 250 Years of St. Louis History thru Public Records* (St. Louis: Recorder of Deeds, no date).

272.   "Fraternal and Benevolent Societies Index," *St. Louis Public Library* (http://www.slpl.lib.mo .us/libsrc/frat1.htm).

273.   Theodore F. Childs, *St. Louis Directory of Charitable, Philanthropic and Humane Societies* (St. Louis: W. H. McClain, 1902). *St. Louis Club Directories* (St. Louis: The Club, 1886, 1916). *St. Louis Commercial Club, 1888–1889, 1890–1891* (St. Louis: The Club, 1891).

274.   St. Louis Genealogical Society (http://www.stlgs.org).

275.   *Missouri Historical Society* (http://www.mohistory.org).

Genealogical Association Journal, which started publication in 1986, provides valuable information from every county.[276]

The National Genealogical Society provides educational opportunities for genealogists, both at-home education and at their annual conferences. They publish the *NGS NewsMagazine* four times a year and the premier genealogical journal, *National Genealogical Society Quarterly.*[277]

The State Historical Society of Missouri is the keeper of many manuscript collections, newspapers, photographs, and other finding aids to assist Missouri researchers. They certainly have numerous collections pertaining to St. Louis. They publish the *Missouri Historical Review*, 1906–present.[278]

Lineage Societies

Many lineage societies are based on social standing and military participation. The organizations have local chapters and registrars. Some societies retain the records locally, others on a national basis. Most organizations publish lineage books or indexes of the patriots and some of their members. The Daughters of the American Revolution have a published patriot list as does the Sons of the American Revolution. Most local repositories have these publications.[279] Here is a list of other lineage societies. Perhaps your ancestors belonged to one of these organizations.

- Daughters of Union Veterans of the Civil War
- Descendants of Mexican War Veterans
- General Society of Mayflower Descendants
- Jamestowne Society
- Ladies of the Grand Army of the Republic
- National Society Daughters of the American Revolution (DAR)
- National Society Sons of the American Revolution (SAR)
- Society of the Cincinnati
- Society of Colonial Dames of America
- Society of Colonial Wars (Completed membership applications for the St. Louis Society of Colonial Wars are available at the Missouri Historical Society Research Library.)
- Sons of Union Veterans of the Civil War
- Sons of Confederate Veterans
- United Daughters of the Confederacy

Other societies are based on early residence in a specific area. If your family lived in St. Louis before 1865, and you can document your lineage, you are eligible to join the First Families of St. Louis and First Families of Missouri. [See BIOGRAPHIES.] For more information on the full range of lineage societies see Cyndi's List (http://www.cyndislist.com/soc-lineage.htm).

---

276. *Missouri State Genealogical Association* (http://www.mosga.org).

277. *National Genealogical Society* (http://www.ngsgenealogy.org).

278. *State Historical Society of Missouri* (http://shs.umsystem.edu/index.shtml).

279. The National Society, Daughters of the American Revolution, *DAR Patriot List* (Washington, D.C.: The Society, 2003). John St. Paul, Jr., *The History of the National Society of the Sons of the American Revolution* (New Orleans: Pelican Publications, 1962).

Missouri Athletic Club

Missouri Athletic Club opened in downtown St. Louis in 1903. Amy Norris's publication, *Missouri Athletic Club: 100 Years of Excellence*, provides insight into the organization and its members. Likewise, the same organization published a golden anniversary souvenir, *Golden Anniversary, 1903–1953, Missouri Athletic Club*. A limited number of the organization's periodical, *Ye Clubbe*, are available at repositories; the first edition was in 1906.[280]

St. Louis City Club

On 21 October 1910, downtown business men formed a men's social club, the St. Louis City Club, with their headquarters at 911 Locust Street. This organization published the *St. Louis City Club Bulletin* that provides a list of the members with their business addresses and occupations. Some issues have a "Who's Who and What's What" section, providing a glimpse into the life of members. Articles may include family facts, such as where the members vacationed, their home addresses, and the number of children. When a member took office, the journal published his or her photograph. *Bulletins* from 1910 to 1925 are available at the State Historical Society in Columbia.

St. Louis World's Fair Society

The St. Louis World's Fair was a huge event in St. Louis in 1904. Leaders and guests from around the world attended the Fair, held in Forest Park. The *World's Fair Bulletin*[281] provides some insight into the time and place. Photographs, memorabilia, and books add details about the event. The index to the *World's Fair Bulletin* is available at the St. Louis Public Library website. Among the many Fair publications are *The World Came to St. Louis: A Visit to the 1904 World's Fair* and the ten volume set, *Louisiana and the Fair: An Exposition of the World, Its People, and Their Achievements*.[282] An exhibitor's catalog, *Official Catalogue of Exhibitors, Universal Exposition, St. Louis, U.S.A., 1904*, lists all exhibitors from the Fair. Missouri Historical Society has photographs of the Fair grounds and buildings.[283]

Veiled Prophet

Starting about 1878 a group of civic leaders formed an organization called the Veiled Prophet and introduced the City's residents to an annual parade and ball. The young debutantes were introduced to the Veiled Prophet, who selected a queen and her court. This organization was modeled after the New Orleans Carnival Society.

---

280.   Amy S. Norris, *Missouri Athletic Club: 100 Years of Excellence* (St. Louis: The Club, 2002). *Golden Anniversary, 1903–1953, Missouri Athletic Club* (St. Louis: The Club, 1953). *Ye Clubbe: A Journal of the Missouri Athletic Club and its Members* (St. Louis: The Club, 1906–).

281.   *World's Fair Bulletin* (St. Louis: World's Fair Publishing Company, 1899–1904). "World's Fair Bulletin Index," *St. Louis Public Library* (http://previous.slpl.org/libsrc/lpe-wfb2.htm).

282.   J. W. Buel, editor, *Louisiana and the Fair: An Exposition of the World, Its People, and Their Achievements,* 10 volumes (St. Louis: St. Louis World's Progress Publishing Company, 1904–1905).

283.   *Official Catalogue of Exhibitors, Universal Exposition, St. Louis, U.S.A., 1904,* 4 volumes (St. Louis: Louisiana Purchase Exposition Company, 1904).

This once very secretive organization continues today in a more open manner. *The Veiled Prophet's Gifts: A Saint Louis Legacy: The Official Collector's Guide, 1878–1984* by John L. Drew III provides an inside glimpse into this society.[284]

Clubs

Sometimes business and clubs joined hands. The Mehlville Farmers' Club, the Concord Farmers' Club, the Mattese Farmers' Club, and the Gravois Farmers' Club are good examples. Many families joined country clubs, athletic organizations, fraternities, sororities, or fraternal organizations such as the Lions, and Optimists. If your ancestor belonged to any type of organization, check for records.

---

284.   John L. Drew III, *The Veiled Prophet's Gifts: A Saint Louis Legacy: The Official Collector's Guide, 1878–1984* (St. Louis: Khorassan Press, 1985).

Cemeteries in St. Louis

Cemetery research can be a very rewarding part of family research. A cemetery may provide clues about the religious affiliation of the deceased or the neighborhood where your ancestor lived. A family plot may identify other family members and provide clues to kinship. The records probably identify the lot owner(s), and list those buried, perhaps without a tombstone. Cemetery records and tombstones may reveal the exact date of death previously unknown, which may lead you to an obituary or news article. Tombstones may reveal the full name of the deceased, exact date of birth and death, place of birth, relationship to a family member, date of marriage, fraternal, military, or religious affiliation.

Due to development and expansion of City boundaries, cemeteries have come and gone. While history may indicate that a cemetery closed or moved, were all of the graves moved? Were accurate records maintained? Probably not! Auguste Chouteau, one of the founders of St. Louis, was buried three times before he really found his final resting place at Calvary Cemetery. One publication clearly lists the burial place of his mother, Madame Chouteau, in 1814 as Calvary; however, that cemetery did not open until 1849. As genealogists, we need to analyze all of the data and perhaps do a genealogy of the cemetery.

Families, religious groups, organizations, veterans, and commercial entities established cemeteries. If you study the history of the cemetery, you may discover clues to why your ancestors selected that cemetery or location for their final resting place. Did they live nearby? Did they belong to the house of worship that sponsored that cemetery? Were they eligible for burial at a veterans' cemetery? Did they belong to a social organization, such as the Odd Fellows? Or, was this a commercial cemetery on a road along the streetcar or bus route, which made it convenient for their family to visit? The answers to these questions may assist with your family history.

When visiting a cemetery, you may want to request a copy of the plot map and the lot owner card, and determine if there are any old records in a vault or hidden away. You may need to talk to the sexton or manager before feeling comfortable that you have viewed all documents.

Some cemeteries have ledger books; others have cards for each burial or each plot. A copy of each card with your surname of interest may be helpful while developing your family history. It may also save another trip in the months and years to come. Another helpful finding aid is a cemetery map that will enable you to identify the location of the graves. Cemetery photographs, both of the tombstones and an overview of the section, may be beneficial if questions arise.

Across the country, many local genealogical societies have indexed their local cemeteries. One way to do this is to create a census of the cemetery, sometimes called a neighborhood index. Neighborhood indexes list names in the order in which the tombstones are arranged in the cemetery. This list provides names of those buried nearby, as well as the section and grave numbers. This type of index provides family historians the ability to see the tombstone neighborhood without visiting the cemetery. An alphabetical index in the same book allows us to find all family names easily.

When using the neighborhood index, make a note of the section and grave number plus the names on each side of your ancestor. If your ancestor's tombstone is hard to read or has disappeared, you can locate the grave by finding the neighbors.

Cemetery maps can be helpful when trying to locate a particular section. Some larger cemeteries provide a map via their website. St. Louis County Library, Special Collections has a growing set of cemetery maps from this area.

Sometimes it is not possible to produce a neighborhood index. The indexer or society may receive the information in alphabetical order, no grave or section numbers included, or the volunteers decided alphabetical order is the best for researchers. A neighborhood index with an alphabetical index at the end is the best solution for those creating cemetery censuses.

Be aware of the date of the cemetery census that you may be using. Some tombstones disappear over time due to vandalism, weather, or age. All genealogists are most grateful to the volunteers that transcribed tombstones fifty years ago since now many of those tombstones are unreadable, broken, or have disappeared.

Cemetery indexes are very helpful; however, are all burials included? Determine the criteria for the index. Determine when and how the author obtained the information. Did your burial of interest occur outside the dates of the cemetery census? Perhaps your ancestor died in 1950 and the cemetery reading took place in 1945. If volunteers obtained the information from the tombstones, there is a very good possibility that burials occurred that are not marked with tombstones.

As with any publication, any author may make an error and omit a name or two from the index or use an alternate spelling. Any type of index is a finding aid. Always go back to the original records or cemetery office to verify that you have all of the correct information.

St. Louis Genealogical Society is actively working on an index for all St. Louis City and County cemeteries; however, some information is lost or missing. Some current cemetery owners will not allow the Society to copy their records. When necessary, society volunteers walk the cemeteries and transcribe the tombstones. Currently more than one million names are available in publications, and the number is still growing.[285]

Probably the first cemetery in St. Louis was located at the Old Cathedral, which is now part of the Arch grounds. St. Louis has more than 400 cemetery names with some cemeteries having

---

285.   St. Louis Genealogical Society, *Old Cemeteries of St. Louis,* 6 volumes (St. Louis: The Society, 1982–2002). St. Louis Genealogical Society, *St. Louis Catholic Burials,* CD-ROM 101 (St. Louis: The Society, 2002). St. Louis Genealogical Society, *St. Louis Burials,* CD-ROM 102 (St. Louis: The Society, 2003).

more than one name used over time. As an example, Bellefontaine Cemetery, the largest cemetery in St. Louis, was originally incorporated as Rural Cemetery.[286]

Picker's Cemetery has one of the most confusing histories in the St. Louis area. The original facility, named Holy Ghost Cemetery, was located near Gravois Road and Compton Avenue. The pastor of Holy Ghost Evangelical Church was Rev. Picker, thus the cemetery took on the name Picker's Cemetery. The original cemetery closed in 1917. Prior to this date, the church established a new cemetery farther west on Gravois Road situated near Sts. Peter and Paul Cemetery and the River Des Peres. Thus, the community called the cemetery at the new (second) location New Picker's Cemetery and the original site was Old Picker's. Shortly thereafter the cemetery expanded across Gravois Road and they named this site (third location) Independent Protestant Cemetery, but it was often called New Picker's. By then, the closed first cemetery was the site of Roosevelt High School, so the local residents then called the second site Old Picker's. When a new owner purchased the cemeteries on both sides of Gravois, he named the combined cemeteries Gatewood Gardens. That same owner defaulted and the City of St. Louis took over the property, cemetery, and records. The original ledger books are available on microfilm and St. Louis Genealogical Society has an index.[287] A longer, more detailed explanation is available on the St. Louis Genealogical Society website.[288]

An online database provides information for burials at St. Louis Catholic Archdiocesan cemeteries. A few Catholic cemeteries are not part of this organization. Use a variety of spellings when searching this and other databases. When you locate your family member in the alphabetical list, click on the lot number, which will show you the names of all bodies buried in the same lot.[289] An old microfiche collection with Catholic cemeteries data provides other information, including the name of the lot owner and date of purchase. Several local repositories have this helpful old resource in their microfiche collection.

Jefferson Barracks National Cemetery (101 Memorial Drive, St. Louis 63125; phone 314-263-8691; http://www.cem.va.gov/CEM/cems/nchp/jeffersonbarracks.asp#hi), established in 1826, is located in South St. Louis County nestled on the hillside overlooking the Mississippi River. President Abraham Lincoln formed the National Cemetery system with Jefferson Barracks becoming a national cemetery in 1866. This cemetery is the final resting place for veterans ranging from the American Revolution to present day conflicts, some from St. Louis, and others from afar. An online database provides daily updates for this and all other national cemeteries.[290]

There are several publications about St. Louis cemeteries. Kevin Amsler's *Final Resting Place: The Lives and Deaths of Famous St. Louisans* provides an interesting overview of

---

286. *Laws of the State of Missouri Passed at the Sessions of the Fifteenth General Assembly, March 7, 1849* (City of Jefferson: Hampton L. Boon, 1849), 276–279.

287. New Pickers Cemetery, 1877–1906, Ledger Book of Interments; Missouri State Archives film C41606. Gatewood Gardens; Missouri State Archives film C41629.

288. "Pickers Cemetery," *St. Louis Genealogical Society* (http://www.stlgs.org/researchTipPickers .htm).

289. "Catholic Cemeteries of the Archdiocese of St. Louis," database, *Catholic Cemeteries of the Archdiocese of St. Louis* (http://www.stlcathcem.com/iSearch.aspx).

290. "Historical Information for Jefferson Barracks National Cemetery," *U.S. Department of Veterans Affairs* (http://www.cem.va.gov/CEM/cems/nchp/jeffersonbarracks.asp#hi).

St. Louis cemeteries and their famous inhabitants.[291] A small pamphlet outlines the premier St. Louis cemetery, Bellefontaine, providing a "tour."[292] The Daughters of the American Revolution published the history and burials for Coldwater Cemetery in North St. Louis County. This cemetery is the final resting place for a few American Revolution patriots that moved to St. Louis after the war. An index for burials between 1877 and 1910 for Western Evangelical Lutheran Cemetery was complied by Karl and LaVerne Boehmke.[293]

Two of the largest cemeteries in St. Louis adjoin each other in North St. Louis City. Bellefontaine Cemetery (4947 West Florissant Boulevard, St. Louis 63115; phone 314-381-0750) is perhaps the most prestigious cemetery, based on the list of notable figures buried there. Calvary Cemetery (5239 West Florissant Boulevard, St. Louis 63115; phone 314-381-1313) is the largest Catholic cemetery in St. Louis. In 1970, the Landmarks Association prepared a tour of Bellefontaine and another for Calvary. These publications are available at libraries today and you may find them helpful in locating old tombstones in these cemeteries.[294]

Two other large Catholic cemeteries are Sts. Peter and Paul Cemetery located in South St. Louis City, and Resurrection Cemetery located in South St. Louis County. Burials for these cemeteries are available online (http://www.stlcathcem.com/).

Esley Hamilton published *The Cemeteries of University City,* which includes cemeteries of various ethnic backgrounds.[295] A committee, with Marcella Mertz at the helm, researched and compiled *Chesterfield, Missouri Cemeteries.*[296]

A restored small African American cemetery in Kirkwood is chronicled in a local publication, *Gone But Not Forgotten: Quinette Cemetery, A Slave Burial Ground, 1866.*[297] Father Dickson Cemetery is an African American cemetery on Sappington Road in South St. Louis County.[298] Thanks to a few dedicated volunteers, this cemetery has been restored and the records preserved. Greenwood Cemetery[299] is another African American cemetery, this one located in the Wellston area of North St. Louis County and the final resting place of Harriet Scott, wife of Dred

291.   Kevin Amsler, *Final Resting Place: The Lives and Deaths of Famous St. Louisans,* 2nd edition (St. Louis: Virginia Publishing Company, 2006).

292.   Michael W. Pierce, *A Historical Tour of Bellefontaine Cemetery* (St. Louis: privately printed, no date).

293.   Webster Groves Chapter National Society Daughters of the American Revolution, *A Stroll Through Coldwater Cemetery, Tombstone Inscriptions and Historical Information* (St. Louis: DAR, 1976). Karl and LaVerne Boehmke, *Western Evangelical Lutheran Cemetery* (St. Louis: The Authors, 1994).

294.   Landmarks Association of St. Louis, *Tombstone Talks: Landmarks Tour of Bellefontaine Cemetery, October 25, 1970* (St. Louis: The Association, 1970). Landmarks Association of St. Louis, *Tombstone Talks: Landmarks Tour of Calvary Cemetery, October 25, 1970* (St. Louis: The Association, 1970).

295.   Esley Hamilton, *The Cemeteries of University City* (St. Louis: Historical Society of University City, 1998).

296.   Marcella Stanz Mertz, *Chesterfield, Missouri, Cemeteries* (Chesterfield: Chesterfield Historical Commission, 2000).

297.   Keith Rawlings, *Gone But Not Forgotten: Quinette Cemetery, A Slave Burial Ground, 1866* (Kirkwood: Youth In Action, 2003).

298.   "Father Dickson Cemetery History," *History's Time Portal of St. Louis* (http://www.usgennet .org/usa/mo/county/stlouis/dickson/fdc.htm).

299.   "Greenwood Cemetery History," *History's Time Portal of St. Louis* (http://www.usgennet.org/ usa/mo/county/stlouis/dickson/fdc.htm).

Scott. Volunteers work diligently to restore this facility, but more help is needed. Copies of the extant records are available at some facilities. St. Louis Genealogical Society is indexing Washington Park Cemetery records from the original card file. Many bodies were moved from Washington Park to other cemeteries due to airport expansion and construction. This index will be helpful to those with ancestors at Washington Park.

Fee Fee Baptist Cemetery, one of the oldest cemeteries still in operation, opened in 1814. This cemetery was the burial ground for many pioneers who lived in the Pattonville and Bridgeton area.[300] Another old cemetery, this one in South St. Louis County, is Sappington Cemetery. This is the final resting place for many Sappington family members. This cemetery has survived many construction projects including Old Route 66 and adjacent shopping complexes.[301]

Ann Morris published *Sacred Green Space: A Survey of Cemeteries in St. Louis County.* This survey provides the history and location of existing cemeteries in St. Louis County in 2000. It does not list those buried in the cemeteries. While a valuable source, this book had limited copies printed and distributed.[302]

The *St. Louis City and County Cemetery Map,* provides a list of all St. Louis cemeteries whether open or closed, large or small, family or commercial. See Figure 19 for an example. This map provides an overview of cemeteries in each area or community. Finding the location of known family cemeteries may answer questions about property ownership or migration.[303]

The Mississippi and Missouri Rivers, the two largest rivers in the country, border the St. Louis area; therefore, it has been necessary for the Corps of Engineers to move some cemeteries. *Cemetery Relocations by the U.S. Army Corps of Engineers* outlines these relocations in St. Louis and other Midwest areas.[304]

Listed in the following table are all known St. Louis City and County cemeteries. The chart provides the name of the cemetery, known location, and a cemetery code number. Some cemeteries are open; others are closed. Some of the closed or moved cemeteries have visible signs of a former cemetery; others have structures on the site. Several cemeteries, such as family graveyards, are open but do not have an office or street address. A few cemetery names were located in death records or other documents; however, the cemetery location is unknown. The cemetery code corresponds with the indicators on the *St. Louis City and County Cemetery Map* and the codes used on the previously mentioned St. Louis Genealogical Society cemetery CD-ROMs.

St. Louis Genealogical Society has an index of known burials at most locations. If you discover new information, please share the data with St. Louis Genealogical Society. Cemeteries that were known by more than one name have an asterisk (*) in the location field followed by another, usually more predominant, name of that same cemetery.

---

300.   Erma E. Penning, *Burials in Fee Fee Cemetery, Bridgeton, Missouri* (St. Louis: Erma Penning, 1961).

301.   *Sappington Cemetery, 1811–1970: Crestwood, St. Louis County, Missouri* (Affton: John Sappington Chapter, National Society Daughters of the American Revolution, 1982).

302.   Ann Morris, *Sacred Green Space: A Survey of Cemeteries in St. Louis County* (St. Louis: privately printed, 2000).

303.   Fleming, *St. Louis City and County Cemetery Map,* previously cited.

304.   St. Louis Genealogical Society, *Cemetery Relocations by the U.S. Army Corps of Engineers,* (1977; reprint, St. Louis: The Society, 1997).

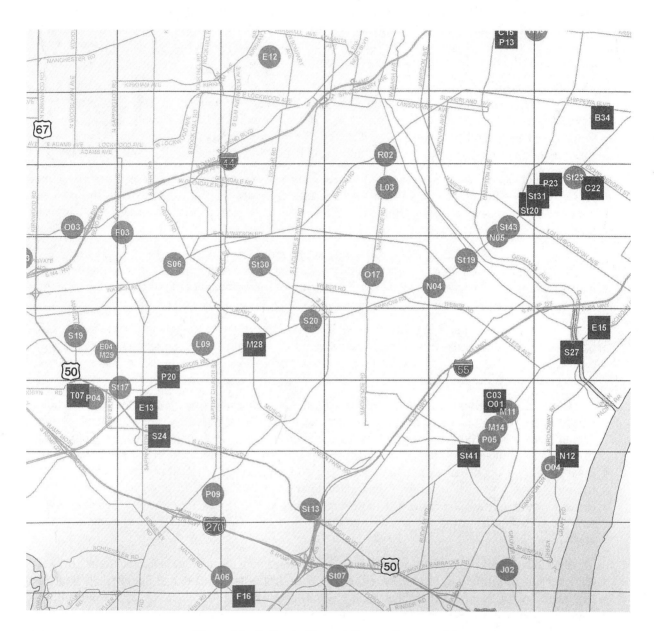

Figure 19: St. Louis City and County Cemetery Map

St. Louis City and County Cemeteries

Cemetery Name	Code	Location	City
Adas Jeshurun Cemetery	M15	* United Hebrew Cemetery	St. Louis
Allenton Cemetery	A01	18530 Old Fox Creek Road	Allenton
American-Hellenic Mem. Cemetery	St23	* St. Mathews Cemetery	St. Louis
Andrae Grave	A02	Old State Road	Ellisville
Antioch Baptist Cemetery	A03	18319 Wildhorse Creek Road	Chesterfield
Armenia Lodge Cemetery	A04	13330 Olive Boulevard	Chesterfield
Arsenal Island Cemetery	A05	Former island in Mississippi	St. Louis
Assumption Catholic Cemetery	A06	4725 Mattis School Road	Mattis
Bacon Cabin	B39	Henry Road	Manchester
Bacon Family Graveyard	B01	760 Woods Mill Road	Manchester
Bacon Family Graveyard	B02	Deer Pointe	Wildwood
Ballwin Missionary Baptist Cemetery	B03	14483 Clayton Rd. west of Schoettler	Ballwin
Baptist Cemetery	B04	Lemp near Cherokee	St. Louis
Baptist Graveyard	B05	Near Franklin & Broadway Avenues	St. Louis
Bartold Family Cemetery	B06	Hwy. 100	Wildwood
Bates Family Cemetery	B07	Babler Park	Wildwood
Bates/ Thornhill Cemetery	B08	15185 Olive Boulevard (Faust Park)	Chesterfield
Baxter's Lakes Cemetery	G12	* Gumbo Cemetery	Chesterfield
Bayer Kroenung Graveyard	B37	Chesterfield Airport Road	Chesterfield
Beinke Family Graveyard	B09	Conestoga Trail	Wildwood
Belger Cemetery	B38	14769 Olive Boulevard	Chesterfield
Bellefontaine Cemetery	B10	4947 W. Florissant Avenue	St. Louis
Bellefontaine Methodist Cemetery	B11	10600 Bellefontaine Road	Bellefontaine Neigh
Bellerive Heritage Cemetery	B12	740 N. Mason Road	Creve Coeur
Bernard Cemetery	B35	Cliff Cave Road	Oakville
Bernard Family Cemetery	B13	Rieger Road	Wildwood
Beth Hamedrosh Cemetery	B16	9125 Ladue Road	Ladue
Bethany UCC Cemetery	B14	6740 St. Charles Rock Road	Normandy
Bethel Methodist Cemetery	B15	17500 Manchester Road	Wildwood
Bethlehem Cemetery (New)	B17	9650 Bellefontaine Road	Bellefontaine Neigh
Bethlehem Lutheran Cemetery (Old)	B18	1093 Bittner Avenue	St. Louis
Bingham Family Cemetery	B34	Morganford & Osceola Avenues	St. Louis
Bissell Cemetery	B11	* Bellefontaine Methodist	Bellefontaine Neigh
Blackjack Cemetery	N03	13701 Old Halls Ferry Road	Blackjack
Blum Family Cemetery	B20	Oak Ridge Subdivision	Wildwood
B'Nai Amoona Cemetery	B21	930 North & South Boulevard	University City
B'Nai Brith Cemetery	N04	* Mt. Sinai Cemetery	Affton
B'Nai El Cemetery	B22	* Camp Springs Cemetery	St. Louis
Boisselier Cemetery	B37	* Bayer Kroenung Cemetery	Chesterfield
Bothe Glaser Family Cemetery	B23	Babler Park	Wildwood
Bouquet-Shutter Ossenfort Cemetery	B24	Bouquet Road	Wildwood
Bowles Cemetery	B25	776 Dennis Road	Fenton

Cemetery Name	Code	Location	City
Bremen Saxon Cemetery	H21	Bellefontaine & Hornsby Roads	St. Louis
Bridgeton Memorial Park	B27	4616 Long Road	Bridgeton
Brockman Cemetery	B28	Manchester Road	Wildwood
Brouster Link Family Graveyard	B29	Lindbergh Boulevard & Dorsett Road	Maryland Heights
Brown Cemetery	B31	Cliff Cave Road	Oakville
Buena Vista Cemetery	B32	Off Bellefontaine Road	St. Louis
Bukowsky Graveyard	B36	Hwy. 100 near Hollow Road	Wildwood
Burns Cemetery	B33	Off Lewis Road & I-44	Eureka
Calvary Cemetery	C01	5239 W. Florissant Road	St. Louis
Camp Spring Jewish Cemetery	B22	Pratt & Cooper Avenues	St. Louis
Carondelet Catholic Cemetery	M13	* Mt. Olive Catholic Cemetery	St. Louis
Carondelet Lutheran Cemetery	E15	* Evangelical Lutheran	St. Louis
Carondelet Protestant Cemetery	C03	* Siegerson Farm	St. Louis
Carrico Family Cemetery	C04	13115 Spanish Pond Road	North County
Cathedral Basilica of St. Louis	C02	4431 Lindell Boulevard	St. Louis
Centaur Private Cemetery	C05	Unknown	Wildwood
Centenary Methodist Cemetery	C06	13th & Olive Boulevard	St. Louis
Central Cemetery	St21	* St. Martin's Cemetery	Olivette
Chesed Shel Emeth Cemetery	C08	650 White Road	Chesterfield
Chesed Shel Emeth Cemetery	C09	7570 Olive Boulevard	University City
Chevra Kadisha Cemetery	C10	1601 North & South Road	University City
Chinese Cemetery	C11	Olive Boulevard	University City
Christ Church Episcopal Cemetery	C12	Chouteau east of California	St. Louis
Christian Brothers Cemetery	L04	* LaSalle Cemetery	Wildwood
Church of the Master Cemetery	B03	* Ballwin Cemetery	Ballwin
City Cemetery/ Benton Park	C13	Arsenal near Jefferson Boulevard	St. Louis
City Cemetery/ Rutger	C14	7th & Rutger Streets	St. Louis
City Cemetery/ Sublette	C15	* Potters Field Cemetery	St. Louis
City Cemetery/ Quarantine	Q01	Koch Hospital Grounds	Oakville
Clayton Family Cemetery	W01	* Walnut Plains Cemetery	Clayton
Clinton Hill Cemetery	C28	Unknown	Carondelet
Cold Water Cemetery	C16	15380 Old Halls Ferry Road	Blackjack
Coleman Family Graveyard	C17	Babler Park	Wildwood
Coleman Family Graveyard	C18	Spiceberry off Wild Horse Creek Rd.	Wildwood
College Farm Graveyard	C19	Unknown	Unknown
Columbarium Crematory	H13	* Hillcrest Abbey	St. Louis
Compton Hill Congregational Ch. Cem.	C21	Lafayette & Compton Avenues	St. Louis
Concordia Cemetery	C22	4209 Bates Avenue	St. Louis
Conway Cemetery	C23	14698 Conway Road	Chesterfield
Cordell Family Cemetery	C30	Unknown	Creve Coeur
Corless Cemetery	C31	Unknown	Wildwood
County Farm Cemetery	C24	Unknown	Unknown
Crescent Cemetery	C25	Allen Road	Eureka
Darby Cemetery	D11	14619 Lake Trails Road	Chesterfield
Dasher Farm Cemetery	D01	Unknown	Eureka

Cemetery Name	Code	Location	City
Daughters of Charity Cemetery	D02	7662 Natural Bridge Road	Normandy
Davis Cemetery	D08	Telegraph Road	South County
Des Peres Presbyterian Cemetery	D03	2255 N. Geyer Road	Frontenac
Dinsmore Family Burial	D04	Shepard Road	Wildwood
Doerschlen Stone	St09	* St. John Lutheran (old)	Ellisville
Dorsett Cemetery	D05	Unknown	Maryland Heights
Doss Farm Cemetery	D06	Strecker Road	Wildwood
Dreinhofer Family Cemetery	F08	1st Baptist Church Pond	Wildwood
Dunnavant Cemetery	D10	Summit Meadows Drive	Fenton
Duvall Family Cemetery	D12	Manchester Road	Ellisville
Eatherton Family Cemetery	E01	Lake Chesterfield Subdivision	Wildwood
Ebenezer Cemetery	E02	5909 Hornecker Road	Pacific
Eberwein Family Graveyard	E03	15446 Clover Ridge Drive	Chesterfield
Eddie Family Cemetery	E04	11839 Eddie & Park Road	Crestwood
Eikoetter Graveyard	E12	447 Fairview Avenue	Webster Groves
Eime Family Graveyard	E13	9907 Sappington Road	Sappington
Elert Gruben Graveyard	E05	Hwy. 109 & Bent Ridge Road	Wildwood
Elks Rest Graveyard	E06	Unknown	Unknown
Elm Lawn Cemetery	E11	* Parkway UCC	Town & Country
Emanu El Cemetery	B22	Pratt & Cooper Avenues	St. Louis
Emmanuel Episcopal Garden	E14	9 S. Bompart Avenue	Webster Groves
Episcopalian Cemetery	E09	Park & Lamotte Avenues	St. Louis
Erb Cemetery	E10	Regalway Dr.	Oakville
Essen Family Graveyard	E07	Old Eatherton Road	Wildwood
Evangelical Children's Home Cemetery	E08	8240 St. Charles Rock Road	Overland
Evangelical Lutheran Cemetery	E15	Vermont & Koeln Streets	St. Louis
Family Cemetery (Elert)	E05	* Elhert-Gruben Graveyard	Wildwood
Father Moses Dickson Cemetery	F03	845 Sappington Road	Crestwood
Fee Fee Cemetery	F04	11200 Old St.Charles Rock Road	St. Ann
Fenton Methodist Cemetery	F05	Gravois Road	Fenton
Fine Cemetery	F17	Off Sulphur Springs Road	Ballwin
Fine Family Graveyard	F06	Off Telegraph Road	Lemay
First Baptist Church Chesterfield Cem.	F07	16398 Chesterfield Airport Road	Chesterfield
First Baptist Church Wildwood Cem.	F08	2704 Pond Road	Wildwood
First Evangelical Lutheran Cemetery	E15	* Evangelical Lutheran Cemetery	St. Louis
First Missionary Church Ballwin Cem.	B03	* Ballwin Missionary Cemetery	Ballwin
First Protestant Congregation	F09	Broadway & Market Streets	St. Louis
Fohlbusch Farm Cemetery	F01	Off Kress Road	Wildwood
Forest Hill Cemetery	F10	St. Charles Rock Road	Wellston
Fort Bellefontaine Cemetery	F11	Bellefontaine Road	Spanish Lake
Fox Creek Graveyard	F15	Unknown	Wildwood
French Burial Ground	F12	7th Street	St. Louis
Friedens Cemetery	F14	8941 N. Broadway Boulevard	St. Louis
Fry Banker Cemetery	F13	Bellefontaine Road	Bellefontaine Neigh
Fuchs Cemetery	F16	Mattis Creek Road	Concord Village

Cemetery Name	Code	Location	City
Gaehle Family Cemetery	G02	Rieger Road	Wildwood
Gaehle Family Cemetery	G14	Babler Road	Wildwood
Gaertner Family Graveyard	G01	Bouquet Road	Wildwood
Gatewood Cemetery	N05	* New Picker's Cemetery	St. Louis
Georgetown Cemetery	S06	* Sappington Cemetery	Crestwood
German Evangelical Cemetery	W09	* Westerman Cemetery	St. Louis
German Protestant Cemetery	N05	* New Picker's Cemetery	St. Louis
German Protestant Orphan's Home	G04	* Evangelical Children's Home	Normandy
Gimbel Family Graveyard	G05	Hwy. T & Ossenfort Road	Wildwood
Glaser Cemetery	B23	* Boothe-Glaser Cemetery	Wildwood
Glencoe Catholic Cemetery	G06	Hwy. 109 & Old State Road	Wildwood
Grace Episcopal Cemetery	G07	11th & Warren Streets	St. Louis
Grauer Family Cemetery	G08	Melrose Road	Wildwood
Gravois Saxon Cemetery	G09	Gravois Road	St. Louis
Greb Farm Cemetery	G10	Unknown	Wildwood
Greenwood Cemetery	G11	St. Louis Avenue	Normandy
Gumbo Cemetery	G12	245 Long Road	Chesterfield
Gutman Family Graveyard	G13	Unknown	Eureka
Haag Family Graveyard	H01	Fox Run Farm	Wildwood
Halley Family Cemetery	H02	Unknown	Wildwood
Hamm Graveyard	H31	Dietrich Road	Des Peres
Hardt Family Cemetery	H03	18721 Hwy. T	Wildwood
Hartman Family Cemetery	H04	Off Puellman Road	Wildwood
Harugari Cemetery	H05	Old Meramec Station Road	Manchester
Hawkins Cemetery	H32	Unknown	Wildwood
Heimann Cemetery	H29	Tamara Trail Road	Wildwood
Heipertz-Rahm Cemetery	H06	Melrose Road	Wildwood
Hencken Family Cemetery	H07	Hwy. T & Hwy. 100	Wildwood
Hencken Family Cemetery	H08	Hencken Road	Wildwood
Hencken Family Cemetery	H09	3885 Dutch Hollow Lane	Wildwood
Hensler Family Cemetery	H10	3642 Hawks Rest Road	Wildwood
Herzig-Peterson Family Cemetery	H11	* Peterson Family	Ballwin
Herzog Cemetery	H25	Keifer Creek Road	Ellisville
Hibler Fitzgerald Cemetery	H12	Mason Road	Creve Coeur
Hilkenkamp Cemetery	H33	Unknown	Wildwood
Hillcrest Abbey Crematory	H13	3211 Sublette Avenue	St. Louis
Hiram Cemetery	B12	* Bellerive Heritage Cemetery	Creve Coeur
Hoeltge Farm Cemetery	H14	Orville Road	Wildwood
Hohmann Family Cemetery	H15	Pond Road	Wildwood
Holderrieth Family Cemetery	H16	19165 Old Manchester Road	Wildwood
Hollenbeck Graveyard	H30	Corner North & South Road	Eureka
Holy Cross Catholic Cemetery	H17	16200 Manchester Road	Wildwood
Holy Cross Lutheran Cemetery	H18	2650 Miami Avenue	St. Louis
Holy Family Fathers Cemetery	H28	Ashby & Midland Avenues	Overland
Holy Ghost Cemetery	H19	* Old Picker's Cemetery	St. Louis

Cemetery Name	Code	Location	City
Holy Ghost E&R Cemetery	H19	* Old Picker's Cemetery	St. Louis
Holy Trinity Catholic Cemetery	H21	Carrie & Florissant Roads	St. Louis
Homann Family Cemetery	H26	Manchester & Wild Horse Creek Rd.	Wildwood
Hope Cemetery	H22	5909 Hornecker Road	Pacific
Horn Cemetery	H23	Lewis Road	Eureka
Horstmann Family Cemetery	H24	Fox Creek Road	Wildwood
Hume, Lewis Cemetery	H27	Hume Road	North County
Immanual Lutheran Cemetery	I01	646 N. Warson Road	Creve Coeur
Independent Protestant Cemetery	N05	* New Picker's Cemetery	St. Louis
Inks Family Cemetery	I03	Near Legends Parkway	Eureka
Jaeger Family Cemetery	J01	Ossenfort & Hardt Roads	Wildwood
Jedburgh Sherman Cemetery	J04	Sherman off Keifer Creek Road	Ellisville
Jefferson Barracks Cemetery	J02	2900 Sheridan Drive	South County
Jesuit Cemetery	St39	Shackelford Road	Hazelwood
Kaes Cemetery	J04	Sherman off Keifer Creek Road	Castlewood
Kelpe Burial Ground	K01	Babler Park	Wildwood
Kennerly Family Graveyard	K09	Kennerly Road	Concord Village
Kesselring Sandfos Graveyard	K03	Model Realty Road	Wildwood
Kesselring Stone	K02	526 Eatherton Road	Wildwood
Kessels Family Cemetery	K04	Pond Road	Wildwood
King Family Cemetery	K05	Fishpot Creek Road	Ballwin
Klump Brundick Family Cemetery	K06	Fox Creek Road	Wildwood
Klump Cemetery	K18	Old Fox Creek Road	Wildwood
Koch Hospital Cemetery	K07	3950 Robert Koch Road	Oakville
Koewing Family Cemetery	St40	17850 Wild Horse Creek Road	Wildwood
Kopf Cemetery	F14	* Friedens Cemetery	St. Louis
Kramer Family Cemetery	K10	Joemar Street	Wildwood
Krausch Family Graveyard	K11	3743 Allenton Road	Wildwood
Kreienkamp Schmitz Family	K12	Model Realty Road	Wildwood
Kroenung Family Cemetery	K13	Babler Park	Wildwood
Krueger Family Cemetery	K14	18318 Allenton Road	Wildwood
Krueger Family Cemetery	K15	Unknown	Wildwood
Krueger Kajewicz Graveyard	K16	Old Manchester Road	Wildwood
Kuhs Graveyard	C04	Spanish Pond Road	North County
Lacy Cemetery	L01	14161 Manchester Road	Manchester
Lake Charles Burial Park	L02	St. Charles Rock Road	Normandy
Lakewood Park Cemetery	L03	7755 Harlan Road	Affton
Lamkin Carter Cemetery	L06	Unknown	Affton
Land Grant Cemetery	St03	Graham Road	Florissant
LaSalle Institute Cemetery	L04	2101 Rue De La Salle Road	Wildwood
Laurel Hill Memorial Gardens	L05	2000 Pennsylvania Avenue	Normandy
Lemp Avenue Cemetery	B04	* Baptist Cemetery	St. Louis
Lewis Cemetery	C25	* Cresent Cemetery	Wildwood
Lewis Harbison Cemetery	M30	* Morschel Cemetery	Wildwood
Lippson's Family Cemetery	L08	Unknown	Wildwood

Cemetery Name	Code	Location	City
Long Family Cemetery	L09	Pardee & Garber Roads	South County
Lucas Cemetery	L07	18th & Washington Streets	St. Louis
Mackay Mead Cemetery	M28	Musick & Gravois Roads	South Country
Manchester Methodist Cemetery	M01	129 Woods Mill Road	Manchester
Marion Cemetery	M02	Unknown	Unknown
Maryhurst Cemetery	M33	* Society of Mary Cemetery	Sunset Hills
Masonic Cemetery	M03	11th & Washington Streets	St. Louis
McClure Cemetery	A01	* Allenton Cemetery	Allenton
McCormick, Jordan Cemetery	M29	11831 Eddie & Park Road	Crestwood
McCullough Family Graveyard	M04	Unknown	Wildwood
Memorial Park Cemetery	M06	5200 Lucas & Hunt Road	Jennings
Methodist Cemetery	W06	Easton Avenue	St. Louis
Meyers Family Cemetery	M08	Bouquet Road	Wildwood
Missouri Botanical Garden	M32	4344 Shaw Avenue	St. Louis
Missouri Bottom Cemetery	G12	* Gumbo Cemetery	Chesterfield
Missouri Crematory	H13	* Hillcrest Abbey	St. Louis
Molz Family Cemetery	M09	Whipporwill Acres	Wildwood
Montana Cemetery	M35	Near Gravois Road	Unknown
Morschel Family Cemetery	M30	Sherman Road	Ellisville
Mound Cemetery	St39	* St. Stanislaus Cemetery	Hazelwood
Mount Holy Trinity Cemetery	M10	Broadway & Taylor Avenues	St. Louis
Mount Hope Cemetery	M11	1215 Lemay Ferry Road	Lemay
Mount Lebanon Cemetery	M12	11101 St. Charles Rock Road	St. Ann
Mount Olive Catholic Cemetery (New)	M14	3906 Mt. Olive Road	Lemay
Mount Olive Catholic Cemetery (Old)	M13	6304 Minnesota Avenue	St. Louis
Mount Olive Hebrew Cemetery (New)	M16	Canton & North & South Roads	University City
Mount Olive Hebrew Cemetery (Old)	M15	Spring Avenue & Olive Boulevard	St. Louis
Mount Pleasant Cemetery	B29	* Brouster-Link Cemetery	Maryland Heights
Mount Pleasant Cemetery	M18	18725 Wildhorse Creek Road	Wildwood
Mount Sheerish Cemetery	M19	Page Avenue at North & South Road	University City
Mount Zion Methodist Cemetery	M21	Olive Boulevard & Studt Road	Creve Coeur
Mueller Cemetery	M27	Unknown	Wildwood
Mueller Cemetery	M31	Mueller Road off Hwy. 100	Wildwood
Mueller Miller Graveyard	M23	Off Mueller Road & Hwy. 100	Wildwood
Mueller, Gottliebene Graveyard	M22	Bouquet Road	Wildwood
Muessemeyer Family Cemetery	M24	3940 Tamara Trail Road	Eureka
Musick Baptist Cemetery	M25	790 Fee Fee Road	Maryland Heights
Myers Ferguson Graveyard	M26	14720 Olive Boulevard	Chesterfield
Nazareth Cemetery	N10	Forder Avenue	Oakville
Neuberg Cemetery	N11	Oak Borough off Reinke Road	Ballwin
New Bremen Catholic Cemetery	H21	Broadway & Taylor Avenue	St. Louis
New Cathedral	C02	* Cathedral Basilica	St. Louis
New Coldwater Burial Gardens	N03	13701 Old Halls Ferry Road	Blackjack
New Mount Sinai Cemetery	N04	8430 Gravois Road	South County
New Picker's Cemetery	N05	7133 Gravois Road	St. Louis

Cemetery Name	Code	Location	City
New Saxon Lutheran Cemetery	C22	4209 Bates Avenue	St. Louis
New Sts. Peter & Paul Catholic Cem.	R02	* Resurrection Cemetery	Affton
Ney Family Cemetery	N07	Near Old Manchester Road	Wildwood
Niesen Family Cemetery	N08	Hencken Road	Wildwood
North St. Louis Burial Garden	G07	* Grace Cemetery	St. Louis
Notre Dame Cemetery	N12	320 East Ripa Avenue	Lemay
Oak Grove Cemetery	O02	7800 St. Charles Rock Road	Normandy
Oak Hill Cemetery	O03	10305 Big Bend Boulevard	Kirkwood
Oak Ridge Cemetery	O03	* Oak Hill Cemetery	Kirkwood
Oakdale Cemetery	O01	3900 Mt. Olive Road	Lemay
Oakland Cemetery	O06	1800 South Broadway Avenue	St. Louis
Odd Fellows Cemetery	O04	9950 South Broadway Avenue	Lemay
O'Fallon Burial Ground	O05	10th Street	St. Louis
Ohave Sholom Cemetery	O07	7410 Olive Boulevard	University City
Old Bonhomme Presbyterian Cemetery	O09	14483 Conway Road	Chesterfield
Old Bonhomme Township Cemetery	O20	* St. Martins Cemetery	Olivette
Old Bremen Saxon Cemetery	H21	* Breman Saxon Cemetery	St. Louis
Old Burial Ground	M13	* Mt. Olive Cemetery	St. Louis
Old Catholic Cathedral	O11	3rd & Walnut Streets	St. Louis
Old Cemetery	A04	Olive Boulevard at Hwy. 141	Chesterfield
Old Grace Cemetery	G07	* Grace Cemetery	St. Louis
Old Musick Burial Ground	O14	Hazelwood Avenue & Latty Road	Hazelwood
Old Picker's Cemetery	H19	Gravois Roads near Arsenal Avenue	St. Louis
Old Presbyterian Cemetery	O18	Washington & Biddle Avenues	St. Louis
One on the Curve Cemetery	O21	St. Paul Road	Castlewood
Ossenfort Bouquet Schutter Cemetery	O16	Bouquet & Ossenfort Roads	Wildwood
Our Redeemer Cemetery	O17	8300 Mackenzie Road	Affton
Paffrath Family Cemetery	P01	Booness Lane	Wildwood
Paffrath Kissing Graveyard	P02	Melrose Road	Wildwood
Papin Saxon Graveyard	W10	Papin Street	St. Louis
Park Cemetery	P18	Tesson Ferry Road	South County
Park Hill Cemetery	P04	14825 Denny Road	Sunset Hills
Park Lawn Cemetery	P05	1800 Lemay Ferry Road	Lemay
Parkway UCC Cemetery (Old)	P06	2840 N. Ballas Road	Town & Country
Patterson Piggott Graveyard	C16	* Cold Water Cemetery	Blackjack
Paxon Saxon Lutheran Cemetery	W10	Ashland & Marcus Avenues	St. Louis
Peterson Family Cemetery	H11	429 Big Bend Road	Ballwin
Piccary Cemetery	P23	4935 Ross Avenue	St. Louis
Picotte Cemetery	H19	* Old Picker's Cemetery	St. Louis
Pilgrim's Rest Cemetery	St41	* St. Trinity Cemetery	Lemay
Pillman Family Graveyard	P08	Puellman Road	Wildwood
Pipkin Burying Ground	P09	Southwick Drive	Concord Village
Pleasants Ferguson Family Cemetery	P10	Puellman Road	Wildwood
Poertner, Friedrich Family Cemetery	P11	Hwy. T & Hwy. 100	Wildwood
Poertner, Lamping Family Cemetery	P12	Hencken Road & Tamara Trail	Wildwood

Cemetery Name	Code	Location	City
Poor Man's Catholic Cemetery	H21	* Holy Trinity Catholic Cemetery	St. Louis
Poth Burial Ground	P20	Gravois Road	Affton
Potters Field Cemetery	P13	Scanlan & Fyler Avenues	St. Louis
Potts Family Cemetery	P14	Bouquet Road	Wildwood
Presbyterian Cemetery	P17	4th & Walnut Streets	St. Louis
Private Fox Creek Graveyard	P15	Unknown	Wildwood
Protestant Burial Ground	P19	4th & Market Streets	St. Louis
Puellman Family Cemetery	P16	Puellman Road	Wildwood
Puellman Family Cemetery	P21	Puellman Road	Wildwood
Quarantine Cemetery	Q01	* Koch Cemetery	Lemay
Quick Piggott Fry Cemetery	F13	* Fry Banker Cemetery	Bellefontaine Neigh
Quinette Cemetery	Q02	12166 Old Big Bend Boulevard	Kirkwood
Ranken Burns Cemetery	B33	* Burns Cemetery	Crescent
Resurrection Catholic Cemetery	R02	6901 Mackenzie Road	Affton
Rieger Family Cemetery	R03	Rieger Road at Shiloh Valley	Wildwood
Ritchey Cemetery	R10	Smitzer Mill Road	Fenton
Rock Hill Presbyterian Cemetery	R04	Rock Hill Road at Manchester Road	Rock Hill
Rock Spring Catholic Cemetery	R05	Duncan Avenue	St. Louis
Rose Hill Cemetery	St36	* St. Peter Cemetery	Kirkwood
Rosenbaum Family Cemetery	R06	3602 Allenton Road	Wildwood
Rosenzweig Family Cemetery	R07	Off St. Paul Run Road	Wildwood
Route 40 Cemetery	R11	Along Route 40	Unknown
Rural Cemetery	B10	* Bellefontaine Cemetery	St. Louis
Rutgers Cemetery	C14	7th & Rutger Streets	St. Louis
Ruwwe Graveyard	R09	Hollow Road & Manchester Road	Wildwood
Sacred Heart Catholic Cemetery	S01	5239 W. Florissant Avenue	Florissant
Sacred Heart Catholic Cemetery	S02	122 Main Street	Valley Park
Sale, Joseph Cemetery	S24	Unknown	Sunset Hills
Salem Lutheran Cemetery	S03	5825 Parker Road	Blackjack
Salem Methodist Cemetery	S04	14825 Manchester Road	Ballwin
Salem Methodist Cemetery (Old)	S05	6810 Natural Bridge Road	Normandy
San Marcos Grave	S12	2940 Thomas Avenue	St. Louis
Sappington Burial Ground	S06	9111 Watson Road	Crestwood
Schaeg Cemetery	S28	Unknown	Wildwood
Schillig Cemetery	S29	White Valley Road	Wildwood
Schmitz Family Cemetery	S07	Model Realty Road	Wildwood
Schueller Family Graveyard	S08	Starck Lane	Wildwood
Schultz Family Cemetery	S09	Unknown	Wildwood
Schwenker Family Cemetery	S10	Off Melrose Road	Wildwood
Second Catholic Graveyard	S22	Franklin Avenue	St. Louis
Sherith Israel Cemetery	S11	North & South Road	University City
Shields Cemetery	S30	Unknown	Wildwood
Shreve Burial Ground	S25	Unknown	St. Louis
Sigerson Farm Cemetery	C03	* Mt. Olive Catholic Cemetery	Lemay
Society of Mary Cemetery	M33	Vianney High School	Sunset Hills

Cemetery Name	Code	Location	City
South County Memorial Garden	O04	* Odd Fellows Cemetery	Lemay
St. Ann's Catholic Cemetery	St01	7534 Natural Bridge Road	Normandy
St. Bridget of Erin Catholic	St47	1100 N. Jefferson Boulevard	St. Louis
St. Ferdinand Catholic Cemetery (New)	St02	205 Manion Park Road	Florissant
St. Ferdinand Catholic Cemetery (Old)	St03	600 Graham Road	Florissant
St. George's Episcopal Church Cem.	St04	7th & Locust Avenue	St. Louis
St. John's Evan. UCC Cemetery (New)	St07	Lemay Ferry & Forder Roads	Mehlville
St. John's Evangelical Cemetery	St06	1293 St. Cyr Road	Bellefontaine Neigh
St. John's Lutheran Cemetery (New)	St08	15808 Manchester Road	Ellisville
St. John's Lutheran Cemetery (Old)	St09	250 Reinke Road	Ballwin
St. John's UCC Cemetery	St11	258 Sulphur Springs Road	Manchester
St. John's UCC Cemetery	St12	15370 Olive Boulevard	Chesterfield
St. John's Evan. UCC Cemetery (Old)	St13	11333 St. John's Church Road	Mehlville
St. Joseph's Catholic Cemetery	St14	11th & Biddle Streets	St. Louis
St. Joseph's Catholic Cemetery	St15	125 Creve Coeur Avenue	Manchester
St. Joseph's Catholic Cemetery	St21	* St. Martin's Cemetery	Olivette
St. Louis King of France Cemetery	St45	Old Cathedral Grounds	St. Louis
St. Louis Memorial Gardens	N05	* New Picker's Cemetery	St. Louis
St. Lucas Cemetery	St17	11735 Denny Road	Sunset Hills
St. Marcus Cemetery (New)	St19	7901 Gravois Road	Affton
St. Marcus Cemetery (Old)	St20	6638 Gravois Road	St. Louis
St. Martin Catholic Cemetery	St21	Old Bonhomme & Price Roads	Olivette
St. Mary & Joseph Catholic Cemetery	St46	* St. Louis King of France	St. Louis
St. Mary's Catholic Cemetery	St22	5200 Fee Fee Road	Bridgeton
St. Matthew's Cemetery	St23	4260 Bates Avenue	St. Louis
St. Monica's Catholic Cemetery	St25	12146 Olive Boulevard	Creve Coeur
St. Patrick's Catholic Cemetery	St27	Franklin & Broadway Boulevard	St. Louis
St. Paul's Catholic Cemetery	St28	741 Gravois Road	Fenton
St. Paul's Cemetery	St29	5508 Telegraph Road	Oakville
St. Paul' Churchyard	St30	7600 S. Rock Hill Road	Grantwood
St. Paul's Evangelical Cemetery	St31	6417 Gravois Road	St. Louis
St. Paul's Evangelical Cemetery	St32	9801 Olive Boulevard	Creve Coeur
St. Paul's Lutheran Cemetery	St33	921 N. Ballas Road	Des Peres
St. Paul's Lutheran Cemetery	St34	955 Hwy. 109	Wildwood
St. Peter Catholic Cemetery	St36	510 N. Monroe Avenue	Kirkwood
St. Peter's Cemetery	St38	Gravois Road near Hampton Avenue	St. Louis
St. Stanislaus Jesuit Cemetery	St39	700 Howdershell Road	Florissant
St. Thomas UCC Cemetery	St40	17842 Wild Horse Creek Road	Chesterfield
St. Trinity Lutheran Cemetery	St41	2160 Lemay Ferry Road	Lemay
St. Vincent's Catholic Cemetery	St42	8th & Park Avenues	St. Louis
Steines Family Cemetery	S14	Off Ossenfort Road	Wildwood
Stocke Family Graveyard	S27	Near Gravois Creek	South County
Stosberg Family Cemetery	S13	Near Pond Road	Wildwood
Strecker Family Cemetery	S15	Strecker Road	Wildwood
Stricker Family Cemetery	S16	Starck Lane	Wildwood

Cemetery Name	Code	Location	City
Sts. Peter & Paul Catholic Cemetery	St43	7030 Gravois Road	St. Louis
Stuart Family Cemetery	S17	2234 Ridgely Woods Road	Wildwood
Stump Family Cemetery	S18	Wild Horse Creek Road	Wildwood
Sturdy Family Cemetery	S19	9963 East Watson Road	Sunset Hills
Sublette Cemetery	C15	* City Cemetery/Sublette	St. Louis
Sullens Cemetery	S26	Saline Road	Fenton
Sunset Burial Park	S20	10180 Gravois Road	Affton
Sutton Family Graveyard	S21	Big Bend & Manchester Road	Maplewood
Taylor Cemetery	T01	1385 Pepperhill Drive	Florissant
Tesson Burial Ground	T07	Fox Meadows Drive	Sappington
Tholozan Family Graveyard	T02	Gravois Road	Unknown
Tribune Baptist Cemetery	T03	1753 Smizer Mill Road	Fenton
Trinity Baptist Cemetery	T03	1753 Smizer Mill Road	Fenton
Trinity Lutheran Cemetery	T04	14088 Clayton Road	Chesterfield
Trinity Lutheran Cemetery	T05	Ohio & Miami Avenues	St. Louis
Tyler Family Cemetery	T06	Laurey Lane	Wildwood
Union Baptist Church Cemetery	U01	17233 Church Road	Chesterfield
United Hebrew Cemetery	U02	23rd & Scott Avenues	St. Louis
United Hebrew Cemetery	U03	7701 Canton Avenue	University City
Valhalla Cemetery	V01	7600 St. Charles Rock Road	Normandy
Valley Cemetery	S17	* Stuart Cemetery	Wildwood
Valley Park City Cemetery	V02	Off Hwy. 141 in Valley Park	Valley Park
Villa Gesu Center Cemetery	V03	11755 Riverview Boulevard	Columbia Bottoms
Walnut Plains Cemetery	W01	Clayton Road & Brentwood Blvd.	Brentwood
Walter Cemetery	W15	Babler Forest Subdivision	Wildwood
Walton, Judge Graveyard	W02	Unknown	Unknown
Wardenburg Family Cemetery	W03	1033 Hwy. BA	Wildwood
Warfield Family Graveyard	W04	Off Manchester Road in Pond	Wildwood
Washington Park Cemetery	W05	5500 James McDonald Boulevard	Berkley
Wesleyan Cemetery (1st)	W06	19th Street & Franklin Avenue	St. Louis
Wesleyan Cemetery (2nd)	W07	Grand & Laclede Avenues	St. Louis
Wesleyan Cemetery (3rd)	W08	Olive Boulevard & Hanley Road	University City
Westerman Cemetery	W09	Lemp & Utah Avenues	St. Louis
Western Evangelical Lutheran	W10	Marcus & Lexington Avenues	St. Louis
Wetzel Farm Cemetery	W11	Unknown	Wildwood
Wickersham Family Graveyard	W12	Midland near Canton Avenues	University City
Williams Cemetery	W13	Larkin Williams Industrial Court	Fenton
Willming Farm Cemetery	W14	Melrose Road	Wildwood
Willming Cemetery	W17	Unknown	Wildwood
Wulf Cemetery	W18	Hwy. 109 & Manchester Road	Wildwood
Yates/Yeats Cemetery	Y01	Unknown	Unknown
Zion Cemetery	P06	* Parkway UCC Cemetery	Town & Country
Zion Lutheran Cemetery	Z01	12075 Dorsett Road	Maryland Heights
Zion UCC Cemetery	Z02	7401 St. Charles Rock Road	Normandy

Census: Federal, State, & Local

Census records are the border of your genealogical jigsaw puzzle. You should review EVERY federal, state, or local census that occurred during each ancestor's lifetime. While you may think you know what will be in the census record, new information often appears. Always note the neighbors, neighborhood, place of birth, age, occupation, and those living in the same household.

Analyze all of the census records for each person before planning further research. One enumerator or one informant may provide incorrect information. For example, one census record may say that a person was born in Mississippi when in fact he was born in Missouri. The enumerator may have listed the wrong state abbreviation.

Some census takers added information not officially requested. One or two census reports may say a person was born in Baden, Germany, while the others simply say Germany. In the 1860 St. Louis second ward census, the enumerator provided a city and state or country as the place of birth for all residents. In one family, the enumerator listed a city in Germany as the place of birth for the head of household, then nicely recorded Belleville, Illinois, as the place of birth for the lady of the household.

In another example from 1880, the enumerator listed the head of household and then listed the name of his wife. The name of the wife was crossed out with DEAD written in. She did appear in the 1870 census, Since this was in the era before death certificates, the present-day family now knows she died between the 1870 and 1880 census. Analyze all census data for valuable clues.

People generally moved in groups, often living close to each other in a community. When you locate one family member, you may find other family members living nearby. A search of at least ten pages, if not twenty pages, before and after your located ancestor may prove fruitful.

In a small or rural county, it is usually easy to locate family members. However, if your ancestors are *lost* in St. Louis, utilize various search strategies.

1. Prepare a list of names to search in the census. Create a timeline showing the date of birth and death for each ancestor, you can determine which census enumerations apply to that ancestor's life.

2. Search the online indexes for your ancestor. If he or she appears, record the findings and move on to the next family member. Census forms are available at St. Louis Genealogical Society and at various sites online. It may be easier to record the census data on a special form (fill in the blanks) prepared for that particular census year, or preferably, make a printout of the census page for your file.

3. If your ancestor does not appear, search by using various spellings of the surname. Enter the minimum amount of information into the search engine. You do not know what the enumerator was told or entered, or how that name might have been misinterpreted during the indexing process.

4. If the surname search is unsuccessful, enter only the given name, perhaps the place of birth, and a range for the year of birth. If the given name is unique, this will be more successful as compared to a common first name such as John or Mary.

5. City directories can help locate people that seem to be missing in the census. Check the directories for at least five years before and after the census year of interest. Determine if the person lived in St. Louis and where. On a city ward map, locate the street address.

6. Now search the census records by ward based on the street address from the city directory. HeritageQuest allows you to search by wards. Use the browse feature and enter the ward number. Then review the census page by page for the name (probably misspelled) and/or the street address. Enumerators often wrote the street name lengthwise along the left side of the census page. The same street may appear several times within the ward as the enumerator wound his way through the ward. Typically, the odd-numbered houses were recorded separately from the even-numbered houses.

7. When the online indexes do not locate your ancestor, it is time to go back to the printed indexes and soundex. The enumerator may have spelled the name incorrectly, but you will probably recognize the family group as you read each line of a county census. While this may take some time, you will probably be successful. For example, if you know this family lived in Carondelet or Florissant, read the enumeration districts for that area first, then expand the range until you locate the correct family.

Most local libraries provide free access to online census databases. FamilySearch has some census information available free with more coming soon.[305] Analyze the census data and add this information to your family history. Further census background information is available in Hinckley's *Your Guide to the Federal Census for Genealogists, Researchers, and Family Historians,*[306] which is available at genealogical libraries.

FEDERAL POPULATION SCHEDULES

The 1830–1930 federal censuses enumerate all of Missouri and thus St. Louis. Census enumerators received instructions and a set of questions to ask at each residence. Researchers may review this information online at the "Minnesota Population Center."[307]

The 1830 was the first federal census following Missouri statehood in 1821. Missouri indexes for both 1830 and 1840 include St. Louis residents. However, these census schedules only name the head of the household. Researchers can develop family groups by comparing the children's ages to later census schedules and other information. The 1830 and 1840 censuses are available online at Ancestry and are indexed in book format.[308]

---

305. *FamilySearch* (http://www.familysearch.org).

306. Kathleen W. Hinckley, *Your Guide to the Federal Census for Genealogists, Researchers, and Family Historians* (Cincinnati: Betterway Books, 2002).

307. "Minnesota Population Center," *University of Minnesota* (http://usa.ipums.org/usa/voliii/t Questions.shtml).

308. Ronald Vern Jackson, editor, *Missouri 1830 Census Index* (Salt Lake City, Utah: Accelerated Indexing Systems International, 1981). Ronald Vern Jackson, editor, *Missouri 1840 Census Index* (Bountiful, Utah: Accelerated Indexing Systems, 1980).

St. Louis Genealogical Society created and published indexes for the 1850[309] and 1860[310] federal censuses for St. Louis. Likewise, Precision Indexing published the index to the federal census of 1870, St. Louis.[311] While most people use the online census databases, these publications are very useful if you cannot locate that elusive St. Louis ancestor.

The 1880 federal census is a free database at Ancestry.com. St. Louis City had two 1880 federal census enumerations due to some inconsistencies. You should look at both versions to determine the accurate information for your family. The official census date for 1880 was June 1. On the original form June is clearly printed. November was the designated month for the second census. The enumerator crossed out June and added November. You can easily distinguish between the two enumerations. (See Figure 20.)

The 1880 and 1900 federal censuses are free online at Family Search, with more to follow. The census indexes for these years include every name in the household, not just the head of household.

The 1930 federal census also has an every-name index available on Ancestry.com. The subscription database companies are upgrading the indexes for other years. Check the description for each year to see if it is an every-name index or head-of-household index. When searching for a child or female when you do not know the name of the father or spouse, the every-name index is very helpful.

FEDERAL SPECIAL SCHEDULES

Researchers often overlook special census schedules, yet they provide a wealth of information about the family, their farm, or business. If your ancestor was a farmer, the agricultural schedule tells you what crops he grew and the quantity. It also tells you what livestock he had. Depending on the year, the agricultural schedule may ask from 45 to 100 questions for each farmer. For a detailed explanation of the special schedules, review *Your Guide to the Federal Census for Genealogists, Researchers, and Family Historians,* previously mentioned.

The mortality schedule was supposed to list the name of all of the deceased for twelve months prior to the official census date. It often provides the date, place, and cause of death, plus connects the deceased to the family on the census. This is a great resource in 1850 for those who died in the 1849 cholera epidemic in St. Louis. However, just like many other records, it may not be complete. George and Maryhelen Wilson indexed the 1850 St. Louis Mortality schedule and it is available online at the St. Louis Genealogical Society website.[312]

---

309.   St. Louis Genealogical Society, *Index to the 1850 Census of St. Louis* (St. Louis: The Society, 1971).

310.   St. Louis Genealogical Society, *St. Louis and St. Louis County Missouri, Index to 1860 Federal Census* (St. Louis: The Society, 1984).

311.   Bradley W. Steuart, editor, *St. Louis, Missouri, 1870 Census Index* (Bountiful, Utah: Precision Indexing, 1989).

312.   George F. Wilson and Maryhelen Wilson, *Index to the Mortality Schedule of St. Louis County, Missouri, 1850* (St. Louis: privately printed, 1976). "1850 Mortality Schedule," *St. Louis Genealogical Society* (http://www.stlgs.org/lifeDeaths1850Mortality.htm).

Special schedules, taken at the same time as the population schedules, survive for the St. Louis area. The Missouri Historical Society Research Library owns the originals with microfilm copies available at various repositories.

AGRICULTURAL SCHEDULES, 1850–1880, provide a list of farmers with production of more than $100 (1850–1860) and $500 (1870–1880). The schedules provide data on the production totals for crops and livestock.

DEFECTIVE, DEPENDENT, AND DELINQUENT SCHEDULES, 1880, provide the names of those who were prisoners, children in orphanages, those who were deaf, or those considered mentally retarded or disabled plus those in workhouses or poor farms. St. Louis County Library, Special Collections, has indexed this schedule.

INDUSTRIAL SCHEDULES, 1850–1880, list businesses which grossed more than $500 and the schedules provide some details about the businesses.

MORTALITY SCHEDULES, 1850–1880, list the name, date, and cause of death for those who died in the twelve months prior to the census date of June 1.

SLAVE SCHEDULES, 1850–1860, provide the slave owner's name along with the number of slaves listed by age and sex.

VETERANS' SCHEDULES, 1890, is a list of Union veterans or their widows that is available for St. Louis. Recording Union veterans was the purpose of the schedule; however, often the names of Confederate veterans appeared as well. Crossed-out entries are most likely Confederate veterans, but they are still readable.

STATE & TERRITORIAL CENSUSES

The Spanish took early enumerations of the St. Louis area. Available information appears in Houck's *Spanish Regime in Missouri*.[313]

Robert Parkin prepared a reconstructed 1776 St. Louis census as part of the 1976 bicentennial celebration. The following text, written by Parkin, appeared in the *St. Louis Genealogical Society Quarterly* and reprinted here with their permission. [314]

The first official census of St. Louis—taken by Spanish rulers in 1771 when the village was eight years old—showed a population of thirty-three white men and women and eighteen slaves. Of the seventeen males, seven were under fourteen years of age; nine were between fourteen and fifty, and one was over fifty. The entire population west of the Mississippi River did not exceed 891. This report does not name individuals.

The second Spanish census was a detailed statistical report of products of St. Louis in 1773 but does name traders and their bateaux (boats) as well as heads of farm families who produced the province's grain. The population in the whole Spanish territory had increased to 1,288 of which St. Louis now had 399 whites and 198 slaves. The third statistical report followed the same form and provided additional names of emigrants to St. Louis. The report for 1775 also was much the same. There is no extant report for 1776.

---

313.   Louis Houck, *The Spanish Regime in Missouri,* 2 volumes (Chicago: R.R. Donnelley and Sons Company, 1909).

314.   Robert Parkin, *1776 Census of St. Louis* (St. Louis: Genealogical R & P, 1983). Previously published in *St. Louis Genealogical Society Quarterly*, 9 (Spring 1976): 13–20.

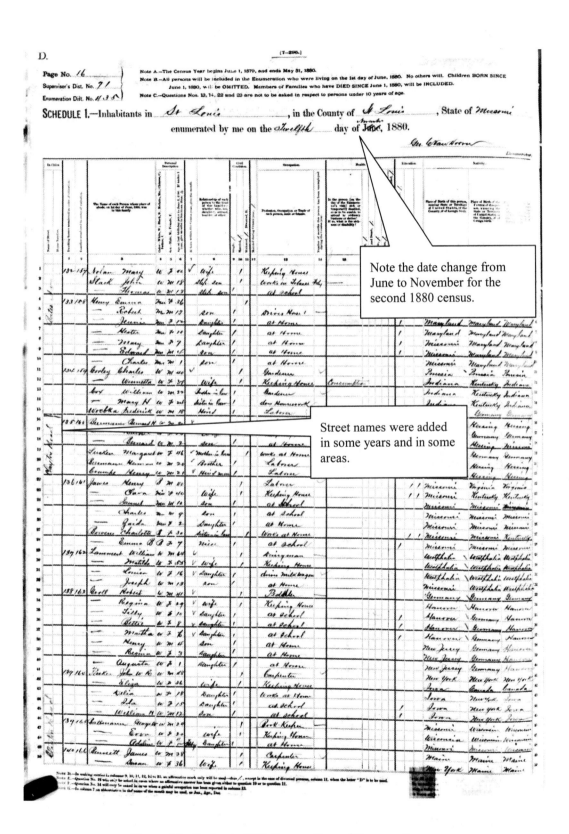

Figure 20: St. Louis 1880 Census, Second Enumeration

There was no other statistical census of St. Louis until the 1790s. However, there were substantiating records such as Catholic church registers, militia rolls of 1780, and Spanish Archives, including Livres Terriens (land books) and civil marriage contracts. All of these were used in compiling the file of original settlers as well as the "1776 Census of St. Louis."

It is conceivable the census could have been taken by village constables who—at that time—were Francois Cottin, Francois Demers, and Francois Pilet. Don Francesco Cruzat was Lieutenant Governor of the Province of Upper Louisiana.

Pierre Laclede Liguest, founder of the village as a trading post in 1764, was still its leading merchant although he, strangely, was not even mentioned in the first Spanish statistical report.

According to this reconstructed Census of 1776, the village of St. Louis had a population of 1,297 men, women, and children. There already were 115 burials in the King of France Catholic Church graveyard.

In 1787 and 1791, the village of St. Louis took a census while under Spanish control. The Archives of Havana made an exact duplicate, which is available at the Missouri Historical Society Research Library.

In 1814, 1817, and 1819, the Missouri Territory took a census in preparation for statehood. These records are available on microfilm. *Missouri Taxpayers, 1819–1826* also provides a list of the earliest households in St. Louis.[315]

The Missouri Historical Society Research Library has an easy-to-read printed copy with an index of the 1840 and 1845 census of St. Louis. Researchers can compare and analyze the 1840, 1845, and 1850 censuses to help identify their ancestors. The City of Carondelet, which is now part of the City of St. Louis, took a census in 1849 is available. A later Carondelet census covering 1857–1858 is indexed and available in print format at Missouri Historical Society and on microfilm at other facilities.[316]

Carondelet recorded their citizens again in 1866 and 1869 and these too are available on film at several facilities. The 1866 Carondelet city census provides an assortment of information for genealogists and historians. It lists the employees, city ordinances, history, minutes of meetings, court dockets, description of real estate, and the name of the owner. The actual census portion provides the name of the residence, occupation, block number, age range of the occupants, number of buildings on property, and remarks. The remarks provide a wide variety of information. One stated the name of the school for a child, another stated that the child was adopted. The 1869 Carondelet census includes school information.[317]

The state of Missouri took state censuses in years ending in five; however, none of the St. Louis schedules survived. If your ancestor moved to another part of Missouri, check the availability for the state census in that county.

---

315.   Lois Stanley, George F. Wilson, and Maryhelen Wilson, *Missouri Taxpayers, 1819–1826* (St. Louis: The Authors, 1979).

316.   *1840 Census of St. Louis* (St. Louis: Missouri Historical Society, no date). *1845 Census of St. Louis* (St. Louis: Missouri Historical Society, no date).

317.   1866 Carondelet City Census and 1869 Carondelet City Census; FHL film 981,654; and City Archives film F560. *1857–58 Carondelet Census* (St. Louis: Missouri Historical Society, no date).

CITY OF ST. LOUIS CENSUS RECORDS

Residents in the City of St. Louis took part in several local census enumerations. By using the City census, researchers can determine the neighborhood, as many list the City block number. In many cases the census only named the heads of the household. However, the age range of other residents is included with slash marks. Most libraries have these records on microfilm; some documents are easier to read than others.

The surviving portion of the 1845 census may be the easiest to use. An easy to read paper copy is available at the Missouri Historical Society Research Library and includes an index.[318]

The 1847 City census provides the full name of the head of household. The 1850–1851 census includes store keepers and head of household and gives the street address for each building. In 1853, 1856, and 1857 the census added the occupation and indicated if a license was needed for that occupation. By 1858, the census included nationality. The 1863 census listed everyone in the household and their occupation. Arranged by ward, the 1865 census includes all names, ages, and occupations.

City of St. Louis Wards

When first Missouri federal census was taken in 1830, three wards divided St. Louis geographically. The North Ward was from the Mississippi River west to Seventh Street and from Biddle Street on the north to Locust Street on the south. The Middle Ward was from the river to Seventh Street and Locust to Walnut Streets. The South Ward was the largest, running from the river to Seventh Street and Walnut Street on the north to Rutgers Street on the south.

By 1840, St. Louis had grown to four wards covering the same area overall with the north-south boundaries altered. Biddle Street was still the northernmost ward boundary for Ward Four extending south to Vine Street. Ward Three was from Vine on the north to Pine Street on the south. This small area showed the population density in that area. Ward Two extended from Pine Street on the north to Elm Street on the south. Ward One extended from Elm Street down to Rutgers Street.

The 1850 federal census indicates the expanding population, with the City divided into six wards extending west to about Taylor Avenue. The sixth ward was the north side of the city and ward one was everything south of Chouteau Avenue. The 1860 federal census consisted of ten wards, all extending from the Mississippi River to as far west as the city extended. Ward Ten consisted of the area north of Howard Street, the northernmost part of the city, and Ward One was everything south of Lafayette Street. The 1870 federal census of St. Louis consisted of twelve wards with a variety of boundaries. Wards Seven to Twelve are north of Locust. A ward map is available at the genealogical libraries.

The 1880 federal census for St. Louis City had twenty-one wards situated between the Mississippi River and the City's new western boundary, which is the same as the boundary used today. The City and County separated before this census, which may cause some problems. The Bureau of the Census duplicated some of the volume and enumerators' district numbers. When

---

318.   Dennis Northcott, *Index, St. Louis City Census, 1845* (St. Louis: Missouri Historical Society, 1995).

you use census microfilm, you need to locate the correct roll for the area in question. It is easy to mix the City and County enumeration districts.

Most genealogical libraries in St. Louis have old ward maps dating from the 1830 to 1880. Fading and dating make the documents difficult to read; therefore, they do not print well. You can make a photocopy for your use while visiting one of the libraries.

The City of St. Louis Board of Election Commissioners produced ward maps starting in 1904 and every four years afterwards, corresponding with the presidential elections. A few years are missing. The maps show the wards and precincts. Redistricting took place as the population grew and shifted from one neighborhood to another. When checking the census, use the map that applies to or is closest to that census year. These ward maps are available in paper format at St. Louis County Library, Special Collections. They are also available on a CD-ROM from St. Louis Genealogical Society.

By 1900, the City had twenty-eight wards, similar to the current wards. The 1904 City Ward map shows the political wards for that time period. Once again, the City and County had duplicate volume and enumeration numbers, requiring caution when using the census microfilm.

The 1910 City wards are the same as those displayed on the 1908 City ward maps. Once again, the Census Bureau duplicated the volume and enumerator district numbers.

The 1920 City wards are the same as those used in the 1916 ward maps. The twenty-eight World War I draft boards used the same political divisions as the twenty-eight City wards. [See MILITARY EVENTS & RECORDS.] For the last time, the census bureau used the same volume and enumerator district numbers in the City and County.

The 1930 City wards were the same as the 1928 ward maps. The enumerator district numbers changed this census year, avoiding the duplicate numbers. Local repositories have copies of the city directories and ward maps outlined above.

The 1940s and 1950s City ward maps show the political divisions during those census years, with census records will be released seventy-two years after the enumeration.

Census records are a very important part of your family research. Do not overlook any schedule that may provide genealogical clues.

Death Certificates, Funeral Homes, & Coroner Records

Death-related records provide a wealth of information for genealogists. The state of Missouri started issuing death certificates in 1910. Prior to that, St. Louis had a death register starting in 1850. Burial permits began in 1882. St. Louis coroner records are available from the 1840s and some funeral home records start in the late 1800s. In addition, death-related records in other chapters include obituaries from local newspapers (see NEWSPAPERS IN ST. LOUIS), cemetery records (see CEMETERIES IN ST. LOUIS), pension files (see MILITARY RECORDS), and religious records (see RELIGIONS IN ST. LOUIS).

The Missouri General Assembly provided legislation establishing the Board of Health and statewide registration of births and deaths in 1883. This system was not mandatory; therefore, it was unsuccessful so the legislature repealed the law in 1893. Again, in 1910, the General Assembly provided legislation for statewide registration.

Since genealogists often want an ancestral death certificate, request information presented in the REPOSITORY chapter bears repeating. If you need a death certificate for identification purposes, the documents available at the City or County government centers are sufficient. The state has a database that provides the basic information for the certificate. However, if you are looking for the genealogical information, which includes the informant, name of parents, and other interesting facts, order the *LONG* form from the Jefferson City address below.

Missouri Department of Health and Senior Services (930 Wildwood, Post Office Box 570, Jefferson City 65102-0570; phone 573-751-6385; http://www.dhss.mo.gov/index.html).

St. Louis City Vital Records (City Hall, Recorder of Deeds Office, 1200 Market Street, St. Louis 63103; phone 314-613-3018; http://stlouis.missouri.org/citygovrecorder/vital records.html) provides the short form for Missouri death records.

St. Louis County Vital Records (111 South Meramec Avenue, 1st floor, Clayton 63105; phone 314-615-0376; http://www.stlouisco.com/doh/vitals/vitals.html) provides the short form for Missouri death records.

DEATHS

Three types of records provide death information for most residents who died in St. Louis between 1850 and the present day. St. Louis death registers date from 1850 to 1909. Missouri death certificates are available online at the Missouri State Archives website (http://www.sos .mo.gov/archives/resources/deathcertificates), from 1910 to fifty years prior to the current year. The Social Security death index (http://ssdi.rootsweb.com/cgi-bin/ssdi.cgi) provides clues for deaths for many who have died since 1962. For the most complete set of information, researchers should obtain all possible records for an ancestor and then cross-reference them with cemetery records.

On 15 August 1823, the St. Louis Board of Aldermen passed an ordinance requiring physicians to report deaths to the mayor on each Monday in June, July, August, September, and October; the death reports were due monthly for the balance of the year. Unfortunately, the WPA Missouri Historical Records Survey did not locate these reports prior to 1941 and they are not thought to be extant.[319] In 1841, the Missouri legislature required physicians in the St. Louis area to register deaths and sign a certificate for each one prior to interment.[320] This law was the basis for the death registers indexed by St. Louis Genealogical Society, which are available on microfilm at various repositories.[321] Why the law passed in 1841 and the registers did not start until 1850 remains a mystery.

Newspapers often listed death information for area residents providing lists of names, each covering death-related events, and each covering a different time period. While most of these publications include all of Missouri, St. Louis was and is the largest population area in the state.[322]

When seeking a death certificate, the applicant must provide the following information:

Name of deceased	Applicant's name and address
Place of death	Relationship of applicant to deceased
Date of death	Purpose for which copy is to be used
	Applicant's signature and date of request

Several research facilities have the death registers for the years 1850–1909 on microfilm. St. Louis County deaths, 1883–1910 at St. Louis County Library, Special Collections on microfilm.[323] The information is limited because this was a voluntary registration. The same library has an index to St. Louis County deaths dating from 1910 to 1936.[324]

---

319.   Missouri Historical Records Survey, *Guide to Public Vital Statistics Records*, 32.

320.   "Bill of Mortality," *Laws of the State of Missouri, 12th General Assembly, 1843* (City of Jefferson: Allen Hammond, 1843), 161–162.

321.   *St. Louis Death Registers 1850–1908*, CD-ROM 103, previously cited.

322.   Three publications that pertain to deaths in St. Louis were all compiled by Lois Stanley, George F. Wilson, and Maryhelen Wilson, *Death Records of Pioneer Missouri Women, 1808–1853. Death Records of Missouri Men from Newspapers, 1808–1854. Death Records from Missouri Newspapers,* volume 1, 1854–1860; volume 2, 1861–1865; volume 3, 1866–1870. Publication information for all books is (Greenville, South Carolina: Southern Historical Press, 1990).

323.   St. Louis County Register of Deaths, 1883–1910; Missouri State Archives film C36953.

324.   St. Louis County Register of Deaths, 1910–1936; Missouri State Archives films C36951–C36952.

The following chart provides guidelines for a death record search in St. Louis.

If the death occurred before 1850:   ⟶

After 1850:

> • Death certificates did not exist. Check church and cemetery records, plus wills and probate records. Probate records from 1802 to 1900 are online at *Missouri State Archives* (http://www.sos.mo.gov/archives/stlprobate).

If the death occurred between 1850 and 1909: ⟶

After 1909:

> • Death certificates did not exist. The City of St. Louis had a death register between 1850 and 1909. St. Louis Genealogical Society has an index, which includes about 450,000 names. This index is available at StLGS on CD and at local libraries. Some burial permits are available after 1880. The *St. Louis Post-Dispatch* obituary index starts in 1880 with a variety of years available online. Also available is the *St. Louis Argus Obituary Index*. Check the *St. Louis Public Library's* website for available years (http://www.slpl.lib.mo.us/libsrc/obit.htm). Obituary indexes for the *Carondelet News*, *Watchman-Advocate*, and *Westliche-Post* are in process and available at the St. Louis County Library website (http://www.slcl.org).

If the death occurred between 1910 and 1957: ⟶

After 1957: (or 50 years from present year)

> • The Missouri State Archives maintains the death certificates, which are available online (http://www.sos.mo.gov/archives/resources/deathcertificates). Also check the previously mentioned obituary indexes listed above.

If the death occurred after 1957

to present day: ⟶

Also, after 1962:

> • Death certificates are available from the Missouri Vital Statistics office in Jefferson City.
> • Contact them only for death certificates within the last fifty years. When placing an order, request the long form.

If the death occurred after 1962 check: ⟶

> • The online Social Security Death Index includes most deaths that occurred after 1962. This index may provide new clues regarding your ancestor, available at *Rootsweb* (http://ssdi.rootsweb.com/cgi-bin/ssdi.cgi).

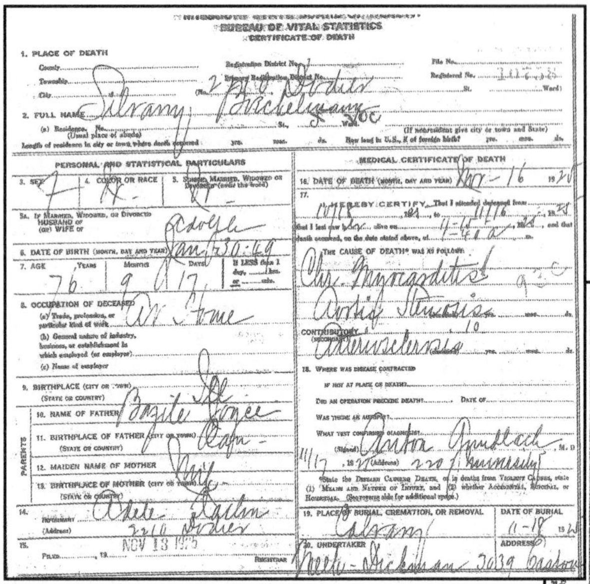
BUREAU OF VITAL STATISTICS
CERTIFICATE OF DEATH

Figure 21: St. Louis City copied death certificate

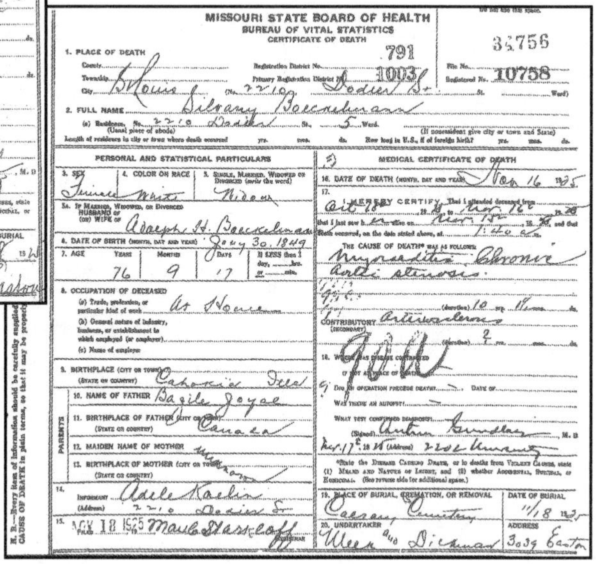
MISSOURI STATE BOARD OF HEALTH
BUREAU OF VITAL STATISTICS
CERTIFICATE OF DEATH

Figure 22: Original death certificate on file with the Missouri Archives

Clerks copied early death certificates before sending the originals to the state vital records office in Jefferson City. Some clerks occasionally used a shortcut in completing the form causing the omission of some facts. If you have a death certificate obtained from the courthouse, compare it to the online copy filed with the state. Does the information match? Perhaps it does not!

As an example, Figure 21 shows a death certificate obtained from City Hall. The copied version shows Illinois as the birthplace. In Figure 22 shows the birth place for the same person as Cahokia, Illinois. That missing word makes a huge difference to genealogists. There are a few other minor differences, not to mention the original is easier to read. Just be aware of possible differences and check the local copy against the state online copy. Remember, these omissions re not the fault of any current government employee.

Typewriters and copy machines eliminated the second handwritten copy and the entire problem. This example not only applies to death certificates, but to any transcribed record. While the recorder tries to make an exact duplicate, it does not always happen.

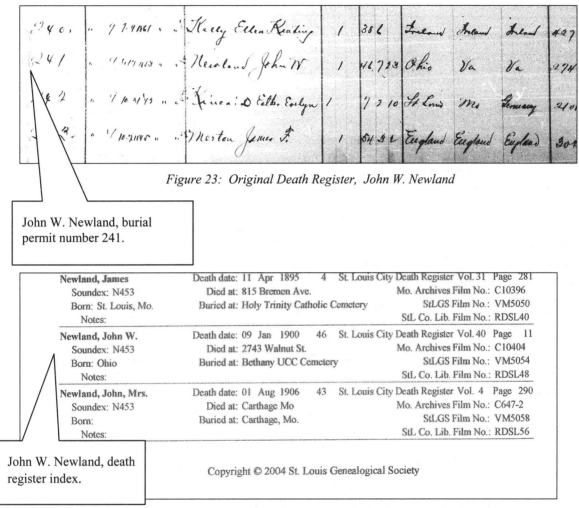

Figure 23: Original Death Register, John W. Newland

John W. Newland, burial permit number 241.

Newland, James	Death date: 11 Apr 1895 4	St. Louis City Death Register Vol. 31 Page 281
Soundex: N453	Died at: 815 Bremen Ave.	Mo. Archives Film No.: C10396
Born: St. Louis, Mo.	Buried at: Holy Trinity Catholic Cemetery	StLGS Film No.: VM5050
Notes:		StL Co. Lib. Film No.: RDSL40
Newland, John W.	Death date: 09 Jan 1900 46	St. Louis City Death Register Vol. 40 Page 11
Soundex: N453	Died at: 2743 Walnut St.	Mo. Archives Film No.: C10404
Born: Ohio	Buried at: Bethany UCC Cemetery	StLGS Film No.: VM5054
Notes:		StL Co. Lib. Film No.: RDSL48
Newland, John, Mrs.	Death date: 01 Aug 1906 43	St. Louis City Death Register Vol. 4 Page 290
Soundex: N453	Died at: Carthage Mo	Mo. Archives Film No.: C647-2
Born:	Buried at: Carthage, Mo.	StLGS Film No.: VM5058
Notes:		StL Co. Lib. Film No.: RDSL56

John W. Newland, death register index.

Figure 24: StLGS Death Register Index, John W. Newland

The death registers dating from 1850 to 1908 are very helpful. If you know the date of death, you can easily go directly to the microfilm of the original records. If you do not know the date of death, use the alphabetical index. Even if using the index, I do suggest you go back and review the actual record.

In Figure 23 you can see a portion of the John W. Newland original document and in Figure 24 you see the index prepared by St. Louis Genealogical Society. Figure 25 is the burial permit for Mr. Newland.

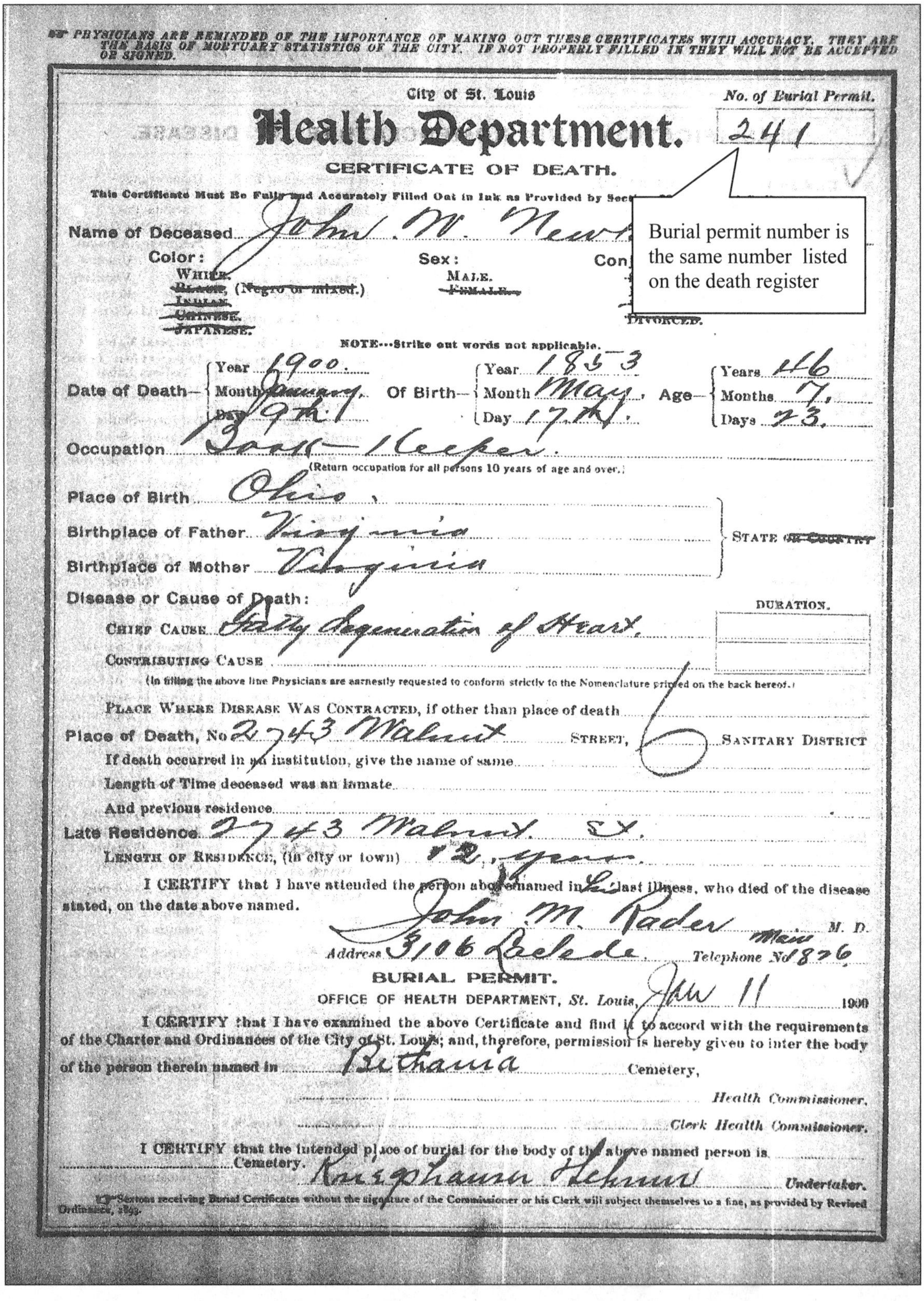

PHYSICIANS ARE REMINDED OF THE IMPORTANCE OF MAKING OUT THESE CERTIFICATES WITH ACCURACY. THEY ARE THE BASIS OF MORTUARY STATISTICS OF THE CITY. IF NOT PROPERLY FILLED IN THEY WILL NOT BE ACCEPTED OR SIGNED.

City of St. Louis

No. of Burial Permit. 241

Health Department.

CERTIFICATE OF DEATH.

This Certificate Must Be Fully and Accurately Filled Out in Ink as Provided by Sect...

Name of Deceased John W. Newl...

Color: White. ~~Black~~, (Negro or mixed.) ~~Indian.~~ ~~Chinese.~~ ~~Japanese.~~

Sex: Male. ~~Female.~~

Con... ~~Divorced.~~

NOTE---Strike out words not applicable.

Date of Death—Year 1900. Month January Day 9th

Of Birth—Year 1853 Month May Day 17th.

Age—Years 46 Months 7. Days 23.

Occupation Book-Keeper.

(Return occupation for all persons 10 years of age and over.)

Place of Birth Ohio.

Birthplace of Father Virginia

Birthplace of Mother Virginia

STATE ~~OR COUNTRY~~

Disease or Cause of Death:

DURATION.

Chief Cause Fatty degeneration of Heart.

Contributing Cause

(In filling the above line Physicians are earnestly requested to conform strictly to the Nomenclature printed on the back hereof.)

Place Where Disease Was Contracted, if other than place of death

Place of Death, No 2743 Walnut Street, 6 Sanitary District

If death occurred in an institution, give the name of same

Length of Time deceased was an inmate

And previous residence

Late Residence 2743 Walnut St.

Length of Residence, (in city or town) 12 years

I CERTIFY that I have attended the person above named in last illness, who died of the disease stated, on the date above named.

John M. Rader M. D.

Address 3106 Laclede Telephone No. Main 826

BURIAL PERMIT.

OFFICE OF HEALTH DEPARTMENT, St. Louis, Jan 11 1900

I CERTIFY that I have examined the above Certificate and find it to accord with the requirements of the Charter and Ordinances of the City of St. Louis; and, therefore, permission is hereby given to inter the body of the person therein named in Bethania Cemetery,

Health Commissioner.

Clerk Health Commissioner.

I CERTIFY that the intended place of burial for the body of the above named person is ... Cemetery.

Kriegshauser Lehmus Undertaker.

Sextons receiving Burial Certificates without the signature of the Commissioner or his Clerk will subject themselves to a fine, as provided by Revised Ordinance, 1893.

Figure 25: Burial Permit, John W. Newland, number 241

BURIAL PERMITS

State law requires burial permits; therefore, funeral directors deliver the permit to the cemetery sexton or director before interment, and within ten days the document is filed with the state registrar. The burial permit provides the name of the deceased, cause of death, date and place of death, place of burial, signature of cemetery official, and place of interment.

Starting in 1882, the death register includes the burial permit number, thus, allowing researchers to cross-reference the two documents. St. Louis City pre-1910 burial permits are available on microfilm at St. Louis County Library, Special Collections and St. Louis Public Library. While some permits are missing, the St. Louis County Library website has an index of the available burial permit dates and numbers.[325] Burial permits continue into the twenty-first century; however, this information is included on the death certificate.

RELIGIOUS RECORDS

Religious records often provide important death-related information. A church or synagogue death register may provide the date of death, place of burial, and the name of the next of kin. Additional information could include date and place of birth. As an example, a death index record, number 2371, from St. Marcus Church in St. Louis provides the following information:[326]

Christian Singer; husband of Christine born Hornung; born 2 April 1864 at Korb, Wuerttemberg; died 26 December 1893; buried 28 December at St. Matthew Cemetery.

Not only does this record provide the date of death and place of burial, it also provides the place of birth and his wife's maiden name. Is this information reliable? The date of death and place of burial should be very reliable. The maiden name of his wife is probably reliable because she was young and still living and most likely the informant. The deceased's place of birth is certainly second-hand information since he did not provide that fact, but it is a good clue and worthy of further research.

SOCIAL SECURITY DEATH INDEX

The Social Security Death Index provides clues for most people who died in the United States since 1962. Exceptions for those not covered under Social Security, such as railroad workers and some teachers. This database provides the date or month of death and the last place of residence for most of the deceased plus the state where the person applied, not the place of birth. The early records have limited information; however, the data improves as time progresses. The database is available on several websites, each offering different search options. One such website that is free to the public is (http://ssdi.rootsweb.com/cgi-bin/ssdi.cgi). The index lists the last place of

---

325. "Burial Permits," Special Collections, St. Louis County Library (http://www.slcl.org).

326. Bob Buecher, transcriber and indexer, *St. Marcus Burial, 1890–1904* (St. Louis: The Author, 2004), 83. This information is also available online at *Genealogy in St. Louis* (http://genealogyinstlouis .accessgenealogy.com/Buecher4.htm).

correspondence, which may or may not be the same place as death. Errors occur in this information just as in any other record source. As an example, the database indicates for one St. Louisan that the last state of residence was Michigan, when actually she and her family lived and she died in St. Louis. Perhaps it was an error reading or entering the zip code state abbreviation.

After reviewing the online information, you may request a copy of the Social Security application as displayed in Figure 26. It provides the name and address of the applicant at that time, the applicant's signature, parents' names, place of birth, and employer at the time. The document may include a woman's maiden name or her name from a previous marriage.

Social Security started in 1935 and Medicare started in July 1966. Some citizens applied immediately for Social Security and later for Medicare, others never applied. As an example, if a woman did not work outside her home and died before 1966, a Social Security number was not important to her, or needed. At that time, people did not apply for a Social Security number until they obtained their first job. Now babies have a Social Security number seemingly before they leave the hospital. Consider these changes when searching for a Social Security number. Since the 1960s, a Social Security number often appears on the death certificate.

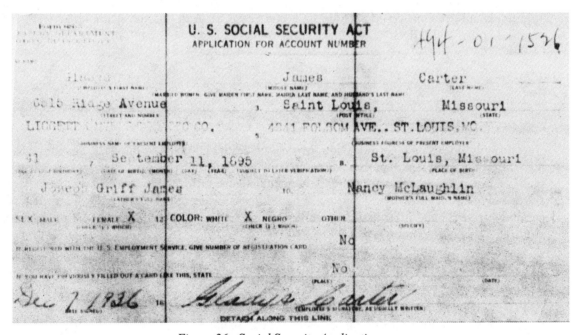

Figure 26: Social Security Application

FUNERAL HOMES

Funeral records often provide unique facts about the service and relatives. Some funeral homes are willing to share their records with family members; others provide limited information at best. Remember, while genealogists think of these as family documents, they are in fact private business records for the funeral home.

The best time to request a funeral home record is while you are visiting one of its current *guests* or better yet, bringing them *new* business. While we do not want to sacrifice a loved one for a few records, be prepared for every opportunity.

Figure 27 is an example of a funeral home record. This document includes the name of the spouse, children, siblings, pall bearers, employment information, music played at the funeral, cemetery layout, and length of time in the city and the United States. This is probably one of the most complete funeral home records that I have seen. Some just tell you the name of the deceased, cemetery, and date of death.

In years past, funeral homes were usually family-operated businesses. If the business closed or merged with another facility, the family may retain the old records. In time, those records may disappear or deteriorate. Other funeral homes in the area may house old records or at least know where the records are located. The business name changed when sons or brothers opened a new facility and moved down the road.

Researchers can trace funeral homes by using a few methods. Many city directories provide a list of undertakers or funeral directors in business during the year of publication. The St. Louis Public Library website has a list of funeral homes compiled from those mentioned in obituaries.[327] To establish a business, corporations file their name with the Secretary of State's office. Those names and records are available online at the Secretary of State's website. The online records date back to 1867.[328]

St. Louis Genealogical Society is attempting to locate and microfilm all available funeral home records. This is not an easy task since there have been more than one thousand funeral homes listed in the city directories since the late 1800s.

Just as their names changed, so did their addresses. The establishments continued to move with the population, their customers. St. Louis Public Library and St. Louis Genealogical Society have a list of St. Louis funeral homes. The microfilmed records listed below are available at the libraries at the time of publication. New records will become available.

St. Louis Genealogical Society published a list of the Local Undertakers Association from 1900–1902. The list provides the name of the facility and their ranking from largest to smallest based on the number of burials. As an example, the 1900 list has 103 funeral homes, which participated in 9,844 burials.[329]

The Funeral Directors' Association Records date from 1881 to1954. Originally named Livery Stable Keepers and Undertakers Association of St. Louis, they changed their name in 1908 to Union Undertakers and Liverymen Association. Then in 1916 the name changed to Mound City Liverymen and Undertakers' Association of St. Louis and the current name St. Louis Funeral Directors' Association was adopted in 1929.[330]

---

327. "Funeral Homes, Parlours, Chapels, Undertakers," *St. Louis Public Library* (http://previous.slpl .org/libsrc/funeral.htm).

328. "Business Services," *Missouri Secretary of State* (http://www.sos.mo.gov/BusinessEntity/ soskb/login.asp).

329. "Local Undertakers' Association," *St. Louis Genealogical Society* (http://www.stlgs.org/ DBlifeBurialsFuneral HomesUndertakers.htm).

330. St. Louis Funeral Directors' Association Records; Missouri Historical Society Research Library.

FUNERAL OF: WOLF, PHILIP J   November 14, 1955   ACCOUNT NO. 55-W-20

IN ACCOUNT WITH: MRS. ANNA M. WOLF, 717 Post, E. St. Louis, Ill

KURRUS UNDERTAKING CO.

NAME	Philip J. Wolf	MILITARY OR NAVAL SERVICE?	
RESIDENCE	717 Post Place	HOW LONG IN U. S.?	Lifetime
Soc. Sec. No.	329-10-7560-mailed PHONE	HOW LONG IN CITY WHERE DEATH OCCURRED?	Lifetime
SINGLE, MARRIED	HUSBAND OF Anna M.	PHYSICIAN (LAST)	Dr. Buser
WIDOWED, DIVORCED Married	(OR) WIFE OF (Baumeister)	CAUSE OF DEATH Arteriosclerotic Heart Disease	
PLACE OF DEATH	717 Post Place		
DATE OF DEATH	November 12, 1955 HOUR 1:20 P M.	CHURCH - MINISTER Rev. Rayburn Dunbar	
DATE OF BIRTH	March 9, 1876	ORGANIZATIONS	
AGE 79 YRS. 8 MOS. 3 DAYS HRS. OR MIN.			
PLACE OF BIRTH E. St. Louis, Ill			
OCCUPATION Grocer - 715 Collinsville - 1914 - 1930			
Water Co., 1935 - 1945			
YRS. ENGAGED DATE LAST WORKED Retired in 1945			

FATHER — NAME Philip Wolf   AGE   / DATE OF FUNERAL Monday, November 14, 1955   2:30 P.M.
FATHER — BIRTHPLACE Germany   / CEMETERY Mt. Hope Cemetery
FATHER — RESIDENCE Deceased / LOT OWNER'S NAME Philip Wolf / LOT NO. #101 - 102 Section "F"

MOTHER — MAIDEN NAME Emma Plappert   AGE / DATE OF SHIPMENT
MOTHER — BIRTHPLACE Unknown / FROM Kurrus Chapel
MOTHER — RESIDENCE Deceased / TO / VIA

CHILDREN	No BROTHERS	SISTERS 11 12 13 14	15 16 17 18 19 20
Philip J. Wolf Jr Greenwich, Conn. (Sales Eng.for Link Belt Co.) Howard M. Wolf 717 Post (Salesman Standard Oil - Serv. Sta.) 2 Grandchildren	Sisters Mrs. D. Glenn (Emma) Rhoades St. Louis, Mo Mrs. Olivette Fox, Cuba, Mo.	Pathway / Rose Reimold (11) / Valentine Plappert (12) / Rose Plappert (13) / Valentine Wolf (14) — John Boyer Lilly #. (1) / Ashes of Alvin Mote (2) / Ashes of Anna Mote (3) / Ashes of Walter Wolf (4)	Emma Wolf (15) / Philip Wolf Sr (16) / Res. for Anna * (17) / Philip J Wolf (18) / 19 / 20 — 5 6 7 8 9 10 Pathway

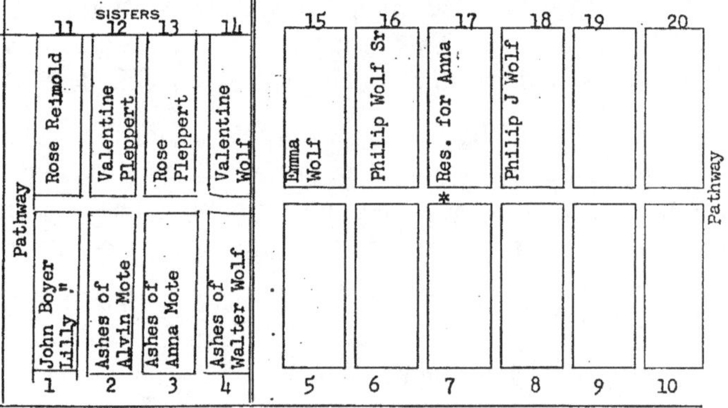

Pallbearers:
Dr. M. W. Dixon, 9432 W. Main St., Belleville, Ill
Ralph W. Hill, 15 Signal Hill
F. H. Lentz, 1312 St. Louis
Herbert Onstott, 525 N. 30th
Jesse H. Fox, 750 Leon St., City
Gene E. James, 112 Julian

"Sweet Peace"
"Come, Ye Disconsolate"
"Softly, Now the Light of Day"

Figure 27: Funeral Home Record

The following funeral home records are available on microfilm in 2008. Abbreviations are used to indicate the current location of the records, SLCL = St. Louis County Library, Special Collection and StLGS = St. Louis Genealogical Society. The library or the Society may acquire additional records at any time.

- Armbruster Funeral Home, 1909 to 1949, SLCL, StLGS
- Armbruster, Edith, Funeral Home, 1927 to 1934, SLCL, StLGS
- Armbruster, Robert, Funeral Home, 1928 to 1950, SLCL, StLGS
- Armbruster, William, Funeral Home, 1909 to 1931, SLCL, StLGS
- Bauman Funeral Home, 1900 to 1934, SLCL, StLGS
- Bopp Funeral Home, 1906 to 1979, SLCL, StLGS
- Buchholz Funeral Home, 1949 to 1999, StLGS
- Crogan Funeral Home, 1922 to 1979, SLCL, StLGS
- Cullen-Kelly Funeral Home, 1879 to 1977, SLCL, StLGS
- Diedrich Funeral Home, 1934 to 1966, StLGS
- Donnelly Funeral Home, 1934 to 1980, SLCL, StLGS
- Fendler Funeral Home, 1914 to 1921, SLCL, StLGS
- Gebken-Benz, 1898 to 1970, SLCL, StLGS
- Hillerman Funeral Home, 1951 to 2001, StLGS
- Hoffmeister Funeral Home, (Broadway facility), 1884 to 1920, SLCL, StLGS
- Howard Funeral Home, 1903 to 1975, SLCL, StLGS
- J. B. Smith Funeral Home, 1932 to 2000, StLGS
- McLaughlin Funeral Home, 1917 to 1981, StLGS
- Mittelberg Funeral Home, 1935 to 1979, StLGS
- Mittelberg Gerber Funeral Home, 1935 to 1980, StLGS
- Parker Funeral Home, 1906 to 1953, StLGS
- Parker Aldrich Funeral Home, 1953 to 1977, StLGS
- Parker Aldrich Funeral Home, 1906 to 1971, SLCL, StLGS
- Peetz Funeral Home, 1905 to 1940, SLCL, StLGS
- Pfitzinger Funeral Home, 1946 to 2002, StLGS
- Roberts Funeral Home (Index only), 1883 to 1952, StLGS
- Schrader Funeral Home, 1898 to 1963, StLGS
- Schumacker Funeral Home, 1905 to 1923, SLCL, StLGS
- Schumacker Funeral Home, 1905 to 1944, StLGS
- Schumacker, Wm., Funeral Home, 1905 to 2000, StLGS
- Schumacker, Wm., Funeral Home, 1944 to 1997, StLGS
- Smith & Crogan Funeral Home, 1916 to 1927, SLCL, StLGS
- Smith & Crogan Funeral Home, 1916 to 1920, StLGS
- Smith, Jay, Funeral Home, 1932 to 1973, StLGS
- Smith, Jay, Funeral Home, 1932 to 2000, StLGS
- Southern Funeral Home, 1908 to 1932, SLCL, StLGS
- Southern Funeral Home, 1962 to 1965, SLCL, StLGS
- Weick Brothers Undertaking, 1911 to 1950, MoHis, SLCL, StLGS
- Witt Funeral Home, 1897 to 1986, StLGS
- Wm. J. Robert Livery & Undertaking, 1893 to 1954, SLCL, StLGS

Monument records are related to both the funeral home records and cemetery records. St. Louis County Library, Special Collections has the Tom Murray Monument Company records available on microfilm dating from 1954 to 1990. St. Louis Genealogical Society has the original ledgers, which consist of newspaper obituaries arranged chronologically. The society is indexing these records.[331]

DEATH NOTICES

The St. Louis Public Library website has the best obituary index in the area. Starting in 1880, the index provides the name and date for the obituary or death notice listed in the *St. Louis Post-Dispatch* and the *St. Louis Argus*. Available online, the index directs you to the correct issue of the newspaper, sometimes even providing a page number. The years completed vary. In addition to the obituaries, the index includes a casualty, missing-in-action, and reburial list for both World War I and World War II.[332]

The Missouri Historical Society Research Library has thirty-two volumes of necrologies dating from 1913 to 1979. Over the years, staff members clipped and photocopied newspaper articles and notices of the deaths of some St. Louisans. Arranged in chronological order and indexed in a card file located in the library, the articles list the name and date of the newspaper where they appeared. When you locate an ancestor, you can note the newspaper name and date, then make a copy directly from the newspaper microfilm onsite or at another facility.[333]

If the obituary is not included in the *St. Louis Post-Dispatch* or the *St. Louis Argus*, other newspapers are available. German ancestors often used the *Westliche-Post*. Residents of St. Louis County may have used the *Watchman-Advocate* or Carondelet residents listed obituaries in the *Carondelet News*. St. Louis County Library is in the process of indexing the obituaries from these publications. Check their website for the most up-to-date information.[334]

Some obituaries appeared in the smaller community publications, perhaps as news articles, not obituaries. This publication provides a list of newspapers and the repositories that hold that microfilm. If the date of death is available, you can request a newspaper search from a local repository. The State Historical Society of Missouri, which has the largest newspaper collection in the state, also provides newspaper research. Their research policy is available online.[335] [See NEWSPAPERS IN ST. LOUIS.]

CORONER RECORDS

Deaths considered an accident, homicide, or suicide are investigated by the coroner and thus a record is produced. Some records are more detailed than others, depending on the circumstances

---

331.   Tom Murray Monument Company records, filmed by St. Louis Genealogical Society, available at the Society office and at St. Louis County Library. The original ledgers are at the Society office.

332.   "St. Louis Obituary Index," *St. Louis Public Library* (http://www.slpl.lib.mo.us/libsrc/obit.htm).

333.   *Necrologies—St. Louis People* (St. Louis: Missouri Historical Society, no date).

334.   "Westliche-Post Obituaries," *St. Louis County Library Special Collections* (http://www.slcl.org/branches/hq/sc/indexes/westliche/westliche-obit-index.htm).

335.   "Research Request Policy," *State Historical Society of Missouri* (http://shs.umsystem.edu/researchrequests.shtm).

and investigation. Newspaper articles often mention the event and provide the name of the victim(s) due to the accident, homicide, or suicide. In some years on 1 January, the newspaper provided a list of those who were temporary guests at the coroner's office.

If the coroner deemed it necessary to investigate a death, he summoned a jury, usually of four to six men who heard the facts about the death at the hearing or inquest. Sometimes the family, police, and witnesses testified about the circumstances surrounding the death. The coroner filed his findings in a report along with the determination of the jury. This information may be on one document or numerous pages. Earlier records tend to be shorter than those in the twentieth century.

In the early years, the sheriff could serve as the coroner. Today, in smaller communities a funeral director may be the coroner. In the 1970s in larger cities, the coroner's office became the medical examiner's office. This includes St. Louis City and County. Medical examiner records are similar to private medical records, which are only available to the next of kin or the estate.

It is important to remember that the records of the coroner's office in any time period are open to the public. Medical examiner records are not.

ST. LOUIS COUNTY — BEFORE 1877

Early coroners' records were handwritten on a plain sheet of paper. In later years, forms helped organize the information. Dennis Northcott's, *St. Louis County Coroner's Records, 1826–1873* provides the names and dates for the records in that time period.[336] Records dating from 1845 to 1876 are available online at the Missouri State Archives website.[337]

ST. LOUIS CITY — AFTER 1876

The St. Louis City Medical Examiner's office (1300 Clark Street, St. Louis 63101; phone 314-622-4971; http://stlouis.missouri.org/government/medex.html) is located downtown across Clark Street from City Hall and next to the Police Headquarters. Submit your request by mail or phone. After the office has time to research your request, they will contact you with the results. If they located a record, they will inform you of the copy fee. You can pick up the documents or pay for postage.

Arranged alphabetically by year, the index cards are accessible only to the staff. If a researcher does not know the exact year, the search is more time consuming. Occasionally, a card may be missing and the staff will search the original records. The journals and other records are stored in chronological order. This card file and the journals are not open to the public. A database for the records produced in the city coroner's office prior to 1900 is available online as mentioned previously.

---

336.   Dennis Northcott, compiler, *St. Louis County Coroner's Records, 1826–1873* (St. Louis: Missouri Historical Society, 1997).

337.   "Coroners' Index," *Missouri State Archives* (http://www.sos.mo.gov/archives/resources/coroners).

ST. LOUIS COUNTY — AFTER 1876

The St. Louis County Medical Examiner's office (6039 Helen Avenue, St. Louis 63134; phone 314-522-3262; http://www.stlouisco.com/doh/medexam/med exam.html) is located near Lambert St. Louis International Airport. County coroners' records started in 1877; however, the records prior to 1944 are missing. Make record request by mail.

You may be hesitant to look at a coroner's record, concerned about the description of the medical findings. Usually that is not a problem. The history and statements included are an asset to any family history as you can see in Figure 28.

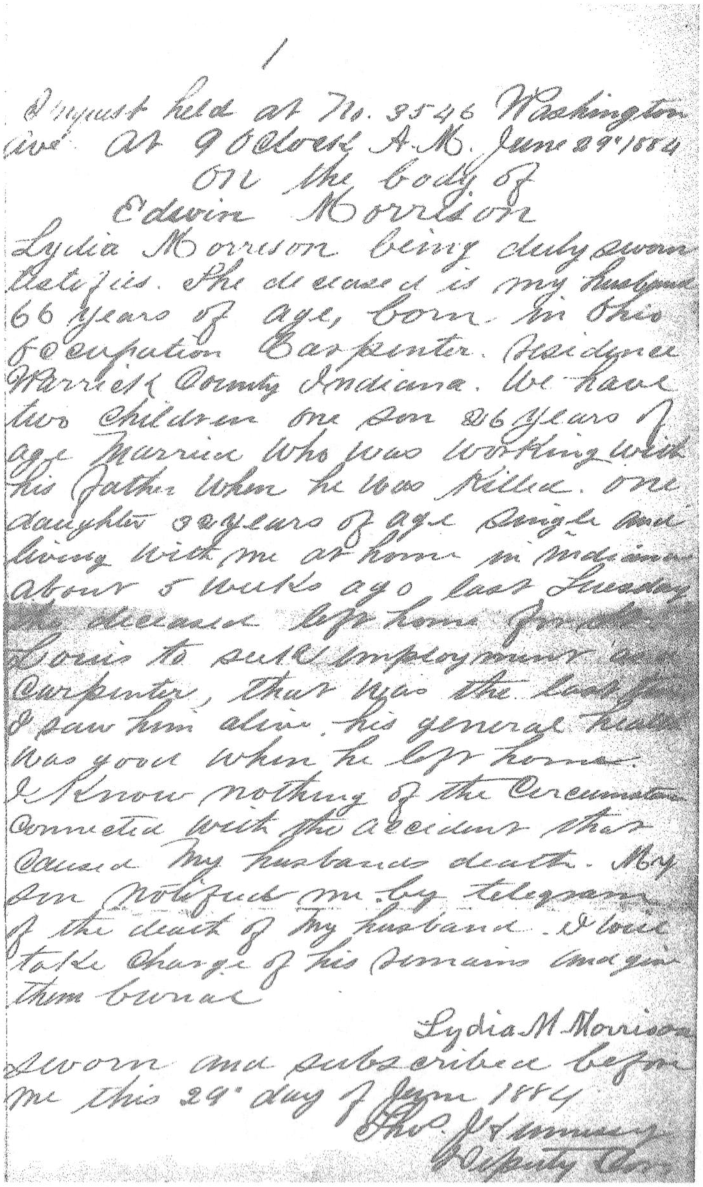

Figure 28: Coroner's record

Directories: City, County, & Social

City or county directories provide a year-by-year address for residents of large metropolitan areas. The directories usually provide the resident's name, address, and occupation and list all residents who worked outside the home. "Widow of ..." identifies the woman of the house starting with the next publication after her husband died. Middle initials are sometimes included, perhaps an initial that does not appear elsewhere.

Carefully review each publication as the information may vary from year to year. A young woman with her first job may appear in the household of her parents before she married. Likewise, young men may first appear at the same address as their parents. While living at the same address does not guarantee or prove the parent-child relationship, it does add weight to your argument.

In most cases, the publishers gathered material for the directories in the year prior to the date of publication. Someone that died in early 1910 may not be in the 1910 census, but may appear in the 1910 city directory. Take all of this into consideration when gathering information on your ancestors. Study the names and addresses in the directories during the lifetime of your ancestors. You may find an example such as this that will help you put together your family groups.

1881 St. Louis City Directory

Hornig, Henry, lab, r 319 S 2d

Hornig, Jacob, porter, r 17 S 2d

Hornig, Philip, porter, r 17 S 2d

Hornig, Valentine, waiter, r 17 S 3d

1884 St. Louis City Directory

Hornig, Catherine, wid. Valentine, r. 21 S 3d

Hornig, Jacob, porter, 417 N. Main

Hornig, Philip, porter, r. 21 S 3d

Hornig, Valentine, porter, r 21 S 3d

Was Valentine, the waiter in 1881, the deceased husband of Catherine in 1884? Did this couple have sons named Jacob, Philip, Valentine, and possibly Henry? The 1884 directory is the only record located that lists the name of Catherine's husband.

City directories are just like any other publication, errors occur. Did the 1881 Valentine really live at 17 S 3d or did he live at 17 S 2d with probable sons Jacob and Philip? Catherine and her two sons lived at 21 S 3d in 1884. By using this information along with other records we could assemble this family group.

St. Louis City directories started in 1821 with sporadic publications until 1865 and usually annual publications thereafter until 1980. St. Louis County directories started publication in 1893 and, with an irregular schedule, concluded in 1979. Additional publications include reverse and business directories. A reverse directory lists the households by address rather than by surname. The Missouri state gazetteers may be helpful for St. Louis research as well. The City directories do not include some citizens who lived in St. Louis County prior to 1893.

A city directory provides many lists. The alphabetical list of residents is the major section. In addition, the publication may identify cemeteries, churches by denomination, hospitals, orphanages, schools, and streets. Business directories group attorneys, carpenters, doctors, funeral homes, schools, and others by business type. At least three St. Louis City directories are available online. Ancestry.com, lists 1889 and 1890, with more to follow.[338] Bob Doerr provides a transcription of the 1860 city directory.[339]

The Gould commercial registers, the Red Books, usually have three sections. The first section is an alphabetical listing of all businesses. The second section is a listing by streets, and the third section is by business type. The St. Louis publications usually covered the entire metropolitan area, including some areas in Illinois. This publication was very common between 1882 and 1908. There are some Red and Blue Books that provide both the commercial and residential information.

The telephone book eventually replaced the St. Louis city directories. The first extant St. Louis white pages are from 1908 and yellow pages from 1956. Starting about 1970, criss-cross directories list the residents by street address rather than alphabetical by surname. This allows researchers to establish the neighborhood. Publication of the early telephone books occurred twice or three times a year. For example, in 1917 the telephone book was printed in the spring, summer, and fall.

St. Louis changed the street numbering system in 1884. Be aware of these changes when using the city directories. Your ancestor may still live in the same house, but the address may be different. A business or a home at 10th and Market before 1884 could be at 1000 or 1050 Market after 1884. The location was the same.

The early settlers provided the names for the streets. Since that time, some street names have changed. Magnan's *Streets of St. Louis* provides a list of the original street names along with the new ones. This publication includes a small amount of biographical information about these early settlers.[340]

Directories are available at Missouri Historical Society Research Library (MoHis), St. Louis County Library, Special Collections (SLCL), St. Louis Public Library (SLPL), and the State Historical Society of Missouri (SHS). The Family History Library has many of the same

---

338.   "1889–1890 St. Louis City Directories," *Ancestry* (http://www.ancestry.com).

339.   "1860 St. Louis City Directory," *Bob Doerr* (http://www.rollanet.org/~bdoerr/1860CyDir/ 1860CD.htm).

340.   William B. Magnan, *Streets of St. Louis* (Groton, Connecticut: Right Press, 1994).

directories on microfilm or microfiche. Some publications are available in their original book form; others are on microfilm and microfiche.

Due to limited space in the chart, the following abbreviations are used: Bk = Book; Fch = Fiche; Flm = Film; and N/A = not applicable.

ST. LOUIS DIRECTORIES

Year	Directory	Publisher	City Before /After 1877	County After 1876	MoHis	SLCL	SLPL	SHS
1821	City Directory	Paxton	Yes	N/A	Fch/Flm	Fch/Bk	Fch	—
1822–1835	No Publications		—	—	—	—	—	—
1836–1837	City Directory	Keemle	Yes	N/A	Fch/Bk	Fch	Fch	Fch
1838–1839	City Directory	Keemle	Yes	N/A	Fch/Bk	Fch	Fch	Fch
1840–1841	City Directory	Keemle	Yes	N/A	Fch/Bk	Fch/Bk	Fch	Fch
1842	City Directory	Chambers &Knapp	Yes	N/A	Fch/Flm	Fch	Fch	Bk/Flm
1843–1844	No Publication	—	—	—	—	—	—	—
1845	City Directory	Green's	Yes	N/A	Fch/Bk/Flm	Fch	Fch	—
1846	No Publication	—	—	—	—	—	—	—
1847	City Directory	Green's	Yes	N/A	Fch/Flm	Fch	Fch	—
	Business Directory	—	—	—	Fch	—	—	—
1848	City Directory	Sloss	Yes	N/A	Fch/Bk	Fch	Fch	Fch
	Business Directory	Taylor	—	—	Bk	—	—	—
1849	No Publication	—	—	—	—	—	—	—
1850	City Directory	Green	Yes	N/A	Fch	Fch	Fch	Fch
	Business Directory	Taylor	—	—	Fch/Bk	—	—	—
1851	City Directory	Green	Yes	N/A	Fch/Flm	Fch	Fch	—
1852	City Directory	Morrison	Yes	N/A	Bk/Fch	Fch	Fch	Bk/Flm
1853	City Directory	—	Yes		Fch/Flm	Fch	Fch	
1853–1854	Business Directory	Montague	Yes	N/A	Bk	—	—	Bk
1854–1855	City Directory	Chambers	Yes	N/A	Bk/Fch	Fch/Bk	Fch	Bk/Flm
1856	No Publication	—	—	—	—	—	—	—
1857	City Directory	Kennedy	Yes	N/A	Fch/Bk	Fch	Fch	Bk
1858	City Directory	—	Yes	N/A	Fch	Fch	Fch	—
1858	Business Directory	StL Pictorial	Yes	N/A	Bk	—	Fch	—
1859	City Directory	Kennedy	Yes	N/A	Fch/Bk	Bk/Fch	Fch	Bk/Flm
	Business Directory	Kennedy	Yes	N/A	Bk	—	—	—
	Business Directory	Heller	Yes	N/A	Bk	—	—	—
1860	City Directory	Edwards	Yes	N/A	Fch	Flm/Fch	Fch	—
(Online)	City Directory	Kennedy	Yes	N/A	Bk	Flm	—	—
	Business Directory	Kennedy	Yes	N/A	Bk	—	Fch	—
1861	City Directory	—	Yes	N/A	—	Flm	Flm	—
1862	No Publication	—	—	—	—	—	—	—
1863	City Directory	Polk	Yes	N/A	Flm	Flm	Flm	—
	Business Directory	Campbell	Yes	N/A	Bk/Flm	—	Flm	Flm
1864	City Directory	Edwards	Yes	N/A	Bk/Flm	Flm	Flm	Bk/Flm
1865	City Directory	Edwards/Polk	Yes	N/A	Bk/Flm	Flm	Flm	—
1866	City Directory	Edwards/Polk	Yes	N/A	Bk/Flm	Bk/Flm	Flm	—
	Business Directory	Holland & Thorp	—	—	—	—	—	Bk
1867	City Directory	Edwards/Polk	Yes	N/A	Bk/Flm	Flm	Flm	—
1868	City Directory	Polk	Yes	N/A	Flm	Flm	Flm	—
	Business Directory	Edwards	Yes	N/A	Bk/Flm	—	—	—

Year	Directory	Publisher	City Before/After 1877	County After 1876	MoHis	SLCL	SLPL	SHS
1868	Business Directory	Tanner & Lee	Yes	N/A	Bk	—	—	—
1869	City Directory	Edwards/Polk	Yes	N/A	Bk/Flm	Flm	Flm	—
	Business Directory	Edward/Polk	Yes	N/A	Bk	—	—	—
1870	City Directory	Edwards/Polk	Yes	N/A	Bk/Flm	Flm	Flm	Bk/Flm
1871	City Directory	Edwards/Polk	Yes	N/A	Bk/Flm	Flm	Flm	Bk/Flm
	Business Directory	DeYongh	Yes	N/A	Bk	—	—	—
1872	City Directory	Gould & Aldrich	Yes	N/A	Bk/Flm	Flm	Flm	Bk/Flm
	Business Directory	Gould	Yes	N/A	Bk	—	—	—
1873	City Directory	Gould	Yes	N/A	Bk/Flm	Flm	Flm	Bk/Flm
	Commercial Dir.	Gould	Yes	N/A	Bk	Flm	—	—
1874	City Directory	Gould	Yes	N/A	Bk/Flm	Flm	Flm	Bk/Flm
	Business Directory	Bakers	Yes	N/A	Bk	—	—	—
1875	City Directory	Gould	Yes	N/A	Bk/Flm	Flm	Flm	Bk/Flm
	Business Directory	Gould	Yes	N/A	Bk	—	—	—
1876	City Directory	Gould	Yes	N/A	Bk/Flm	Flm	Flm	Bk/Flm
1877	City Directory	Gould	Yes	N/A	Bk/Flm	Flm	Flm	—
1878	City Directory	Gould	Yes	N/A	Bk/Flm	Flm	Flm	Bk/Flm
1879	City Directory	Gould	Yes	N/A	Bk/Flm	Flm	Flm	—
1880	City Directory	Gould	Yes	N/A	Bk/Flm	Flm	Flm	Bk/Flm
1881	City Directory	Gould	Yes	N/A	Bk/Flm	Flm	Flm	Bk/Flm
1882	City Directory	Gould	Yes	N/A	Bk/Flm	Flm	Flm	Bk/Flm
1883	City Directory	Gould	Yes	N/A	Bk/Flm	Flm	Flm	Bk/Flm
1884	City Directory	Gould	Yes	N/A	Bk/Flm	Flm	Flm	Bk/Flm
1885	City Directory	Gould	Yes	N/A	Bk/Flm	Flm	Flm	Bk/Flm
1886	City Directory	Gould	Yes	N/A	Bk/Flm	Flm	Flm	—
1887	City Directory	Gould	Yes	N/A	Bk/Flm	Flm	Flm	Bk/Flm
1888	City Directory	Gould	Yes	N/A	Bk/Flm	Flm	Flm	Bk/Flm
1889	City Directory	Gould	Yes	N/A	Bk/Flm	Flm	Flm	Bk/Flm
1890	City Directory	Gould	Yes	N/A	Bk/Flm	Flm	Flm	—
1891	City Directory	Gould	Yes	N/A	Bk/Flm	Flm	Flm	—
1892	City Directory	Gould	Yes	N/A	Bk/Flm	Flm	Flm	Bk/Flm
1893	City Directory	Gould	Yes	N/A	Bk/Flm	Flm	Flm	Bk/Flm
	Business Directory	Edwards	Yes	N/A	Bk	—	—	—
1893	County Directory	Spahn	N/A	Yes	Bk	Flm	Flm	—
	Business Directory	Edwards	—	—	Bk	—	—	—
1894	City Directory	Gould	Yes	N/A	Bk/Flm	Flm	—	Bk/Flm
1895	City Directory	Gould	Yes	N/A	Flm	Flm	Flm	Bk/Flm
	Business Directory	Edwards	Yes	N/A	Bk	—	—	—
1896	City Directory	Gould	Yes	N/A	Bk/Flm	Flm	Flm	Bk/Flm
	County Directory	J.G. Weber Co.	N/A	Yes	Bk	Bk/Flm	—	—
	Business Directory	—	—	—	—	—	—	Bk
1897	City Directory	Gould	Yes	N/A	Bk/Flm	Flm	Flm	Bk/Flm
1898	City Directory	Gould	Yes	N/A	Bk/Flm	Flm	Flm	Bk/Flm
1899	City Directory	Gould	Yes	N/A	Bk/Flm	Flm	—	Bk/Flm
1900	City Directory	Gould	Yes	N/A	Bk/Flm	Flm	Flm	Bk/Flm
	Business Directory	—	—	—	—	—	—	Bk
1901	City Directory	Gould	Yes	N/A	Bk/Flm	Flm	Flm	Bk/Flm
1902	City Directory	Gould	Yes	N/A	Bk/Flm	Flm	Flm	Bk/Flm
	Business Directory	Johnson	Yes	—	—	Bk	—	—
1903	City Directory	Gould	Yes	N/A	Bk/Flm	Flm	Flm	Bk/Flm
	County Directory	Argus	N/A	Yes	—	Bk/Flm	Flm	—
1903–1904	Business Directory	Mercantile	—	—	Bk	Flm	—	—

Year	Directory	Publisher	City Before /After 1877	County After 1876	MoHis	SLCL	SLPL	SHS
1904	City Directory	Gould	Yes	N/A	Bk/Flm	Flm	Flm	—
1905	City Directory	Gould	Yes	N/A	Bk/Flm	Flm	Flm	—
1906	City Directory	Gould	Yes	N/A	Bk/Flm	Flm	Flm	—
1907	City Directory	Gould	Yes	N/A	Bk/Flm	Flm	Flm	Bk/Flm
1908	City Directory	Gould	Yes	N/A	Bk/Flm	Flm	Flm	—
	Phone Book	Bell	—	—	Bk	—	—	—
1909	City Directory	Gould	Yes	N/A	Bk/Flm	Flm	Flm	Bk/Flm
	County Directory	Boo's	N/A	Yes	Bk/Flm	Flm	Online	—
	Red Book	Gould	Yes	—	Bk	—	Bk	Bk
1910	City Directory	Gould	Yes	N/A	Bk/Flm	Flm	Flm	Bk/Flm
	Red Book	Gould	—	—	—	—	Bk	—
1911	City Directory	Gould	Yes	N/A	Bk/Flm	Flm	Flm	Bk/Flm
	Red Book	Gould	—	—	—	—	Bk	Bk
1912	City Directory	Gould	Yes	N/A	Bk/Flm	Flm	Flm	Bk/Flm
	Phone Book	Bell	—	—	Bk	—	Flm	—
1912–1913	Red Book	Gould	—	—	—	Bk/Flm	Bk	Bk
1913	City Directory	Gould	Yes	N/A	Bk/Flm	Flm	Flm	Bk/Flm
	Phone Book	Bell	—	—	Bk	—	Flm	—
1914	City Directory	Gould	Yes	N/A	Bk/Flm	Flm	Flm	Bk/Flm
	Red Book[341]	Gould	—	—	—	Bk/Flm	Bk	—
	Phone Book	Bell	—	—	—	—	Flm	—
1915	City Directory	Gould	Yes	N/A	Flm	Flm	Flm	Bk/Flm
	Phone Book	Bell	—	—	—	—	Flm	—
1916	City Directory	Gould	Yes	N/A	Bk/Flm	Flm	Flm	Bk/Flm
	Red Book	Gould	—	—	—	Flm	Bk	—
1917	City Directory	Gould	Yes	N/A	Flm	Flm	Flm	Bk/Flm
	County Directory	County Dir Co.	N/A	Yes	Bk/Flm	Bk/Flm	Flm	—
	Phone Book	Bell	—	—	Bk	—	—	—
1918	City Directory	Polk/Gould	Yes	N/A	Bk/Flm	Flm	Flm	Bk/Flm
	Red/Blue Bk	Gould	Yes	—	Bk	Flm	—	—
	Phone Book	Bell	—	—	Bk	—	Flm	—
1919	City Directory	Polk/Gould	Yes	N/A	Bk/Flm	Bk/Flm	Flm	Bk/Flm
	Red Book	Gould	—	—	—	Flm	Bk	—
	Phone Book	Bell	—	—	—	—	Flm	—
1920	City Directory	Gould	Yes	N/A	Bk/Flm	Flm	Flm	—
	County Directory	County Dir Co.	N/A	Yes	Bk/Flm	Flm	Flm	—
	Red/Blue Book	Gould	Yes	—	Bk	Flm	Bk	Bk
	Phone Book	Bell	—	—	Bk	—	—	—
1921	City Directory	Gould	Yes	N/A	Bk	Flm	Flm	—
	Red/Blue Book	Gould	Yes	—	Bk	Flm	Bk	—
	Phone Book	Bell	—	—	—	—	Flm	—
1922	City Directory	Polk/Gould	Yes	N/A	Bk/Flm	Flm	Flm	Bk/Flm
	County Directory	Gould	N/A	Yes	Bk/Flm	Flm	Flm	—
	Red/Blue Book	Gould	Yes	—	—	Flm	Bk	Bk
1923	City Directory	Polk/Gould	Yes	N/A	Bk/Flm	Flm	Flm	—
	County Directory	Gould	N/A	Yes	Bk/Flm	Bk/Flm	Flm	—
	Red/Blue Book	Gould	Yes	—	Bk	Bk/ Flm	Bk	Bk
1924	City Directory	Polk/Gould	Yes	N/A	Bk/Flm	Flm	Flm	—
	Red/Blue Book	Gould	Yes	—	Bk	Flm	Bk	Bk/Flm

341. *Gould's St. Louis Red Book* (St. Louis: Gould Directory Company, 1914). [Available online at HeritageQuest.]

Year	Directory	Publisher	City Before /After 1877	County After 1876	MoHis	SLCL	SLPL	SHS
1924	Phone Book	Bell	—	—	—	—	Flm	—
1925	City Directory	Polk/Gould	Yes	N/A	Bk/Flm	Flm	Flm	Bk
	Red/Blue Book	Gould	Yes		Bk	Flm	Bk	Bk/Flm
1926	City Directory	Polk/Gould	Yes	N/A	Bk/Flm	Flm	Flm	Bk
	County Directory	Polk/Gould	N/A	Yes	Bk/Flm	Bk/Flm	Flm	—
	Red/Blue Book	Gould	Yes	—	Bk	Flm	Bk	Bk
	Phone Book	White Pages	—	—	—	—	Flm	—
1927	City Directory	Polk/Gould	Yes	N/A	Bk/Flm	Flm	Flm	Bk/Flm
	Red/Blue Book	Gould	Yes		Bk	Flm	Bk	Bk
	Phone Book	White Pages	—	—	—	—	Flm	—
1928	City Directory	Polk/Gould	Yes	N/A	Bk/Flm	Flm	Flm	Bk/Flm
	County Directory	Polk/Gould	N/A	Yes	Bk/Flm	Flm	Flm	—
	Red/Blue Book	Gould	Yes	—	Bk	Flm	Bk	Bk
	Phone Book	White Pages	—	—	Bk	—	Bk	—
1929	City Directory	Polk/Gould	Yes	N/A	Bk/Flm	Flm	Flm	Bk/Flm
	Red/Blue Book	Gould	—	—	Bk	Flm	Bk	—
1930	City Directory	Polk/Gould	Yes	N/A	Bk/Flm	Flm	Flm	Bk/Flm
	County Directory	Polk	N/A	Yes	Bk/Flm	Bk/Flm	Flm	—
	Phone Book	White Pages	—	—	—	—	Bk	Bk
1931	City Directory	Polk/Gould	Yes	N/A	Bk/Flm	Flm	Flm	Bk/Flm
1932	City Directory	Polk/Gould	Yes	N/A	Bk/Flm	Bk/Flm	Flm	Bk/Flm
	County Directory	Polk	N/A	Yes	Bk/Flm	Bk/Flm	Flm	—
	Phone Book	White Pages	—	—	—	—	Flm	—
1933	City Directory	Gould	Yes	N/A	Flm	Bk/Flm	Flm	Bk/Flm
	Phone Book	White Pages	—	—	—	—	Bk	Bk
1934	City Directory	Polk/Gould	Yes	N/A	Flm	Flm	Flm	—
	County Directory	Polk	N/A	Yes	Bk/Flm	Bk/Flm	Flm	—
	Phone Book	White Pages	—	—	—	—	Flm	Bk
1935	City Directory	Polk/Gould	Yes	N/A	Bk/Flm	Bk/Flm	Flm	Bk
	Phone Book	White Pages	—	—	Bk	—	Bk	Bk
1936	City Directory	Gould	Yes	N/A	Bk/Flm	Bk/Flm	Flm	Bk
	County Directory	Polk	N/A	Yes	Bk	Bk/Flm	Flm	—
	Phone Book	White Pages	—	—	—	Bk	Bk	Bk
1937	City Directory	Gould	Yes	N/A	Bk/Flm	Flm	Flm	Bk
	Phone Book	White Pages	—	—	—	—	Flm	—
1938	City Directory	Gould	Yes	N/A	Bk/Flm	Bk/Flm	Flm	Bk
	County Directory	Polk	N/A	Yes	Bk	Bk/Flm	Flm	—
	Phone Book	White Pages	—	—	Bk	—	Bk	Bk
1939	City Directory	Gould	Yes	N/A	Bk/Flm	Flm	Flm	Bk/Flm
	County Directory	Polk	N/A	Yes	Bk	Bk/Flm	Flm	—
	Phone Book	White Pages	—	—	—	—	Bk	Bk
1940	City Directory	Gould	Yes	N/A	Bk/Flm	Bk/Flm	Flm	Bk/Flm
	Phone Book	White Pages	—	—	—	—	Flm	—
1941	City Directory	Gould	Yes	N/A	Bk/Flm	Bk/Flm	Flm	Bk/Flm
	County Directory	Polk	N/A	Yes	Bk	Bk/Flm	Flm	—
	Phone Book	White Pages	—	—	Bk	—	Bk	—
1942	City Directory	Gould	Yes	N/A	Bk/Flm	Bk/Flm	Flm	Bk
1943	County Directory	Polk	N/A	Yes	Bk	Flm	Flm	Bk
	Phone Book	White Pages	—	—	Bk	—	Flm	—
1944	City Directory	Gould	Yes	N/A	Bk/Flm	Bk/Flm	Flm	—
	Phone Book	White Pages	—	—	—	—	Bk	Bk
1945	Phone Book	White Pages	—	—	Bk	—	Bk	—

Year	Directory	Publisher	City Before /After 1877	County After 1876	MoHis	SLCL	SLPL	SHS
1946	City Directory	Gould	Yes	N/A	Bk/Flm	Bk/Flm	Flm	Bk
	County Directory	Polk	N/A	Yes	Bk	Bk/Flm	Flm	—
	Phone Book	White Pages	—	—	Bk	—	Flm	—
1947–1948	City Directory	PolkGould	Yes	N/A	Bk/Flm	Bk/Flm	Flm	—
	Phone Book	White Pages	—	—	Bk	—	Bk	Bk
1948	Phone Book	White Pages	—	—	Bk	—	Bk	—
1949	County Directory	Polk	N/A	Yes	Bk	Bk/Flm	Flm	—
	Phone Book	White Pages	—	—	Bk	—	Bk	Bk
1950	Phone Book	White Pages	—	—	Bk	—	Bk	—
1951	Phone Book	White Pages	—	—	Bk	—	Bk	—
1952	City Directory	Gould	Yes	N/A	Bk/Flm	Bk/Flm	Flm	Bk
	Phone Book	White Pages	—	—	Bk	—	Bk	—
1953	County Directory	Polk	N/A	Yes	Bk	Bk/Flm	Flm	—
	Phone Book	White Pages	—	—	Bk	—	Bk	—
1954	Phone Book	White Pages	—	—	Bk	—	Bk	Bk
1955	City Directory	Polk	Yes	N/A	Bk/Flm	Bk/Flm	Flm	—
	County Directory	Polk	N/A	Yes	Bk	Bk/Flm	Flm	—
	Phone Book	White Pages	—	—	Bk	—	Bk	
1956	City Directory	Polk	Yes	N/A	Bk/Flm	Flm	Flm	Bk
	Phone Book	White/Yellow	—	—	Bk	—	Bk	Bk
1957	County Directory	Polk	N/A	Yes	Bk	Bk/Flm	Flm	—
1958	City Directory	Polk	Yes	N/A	Bk/Flm	Flm	Flm	Bk
	County Directory	Polk	N/A	Yes	Bk	Bk/Flm	Flm	—
	Phone Bk	White/Yellow	—	—	Bk	—	Bk	—
1959	City Directory	Polk	Yes	N/A	Bk/Flm	Bk/Flm	Flm	Bk
	County Directory	Polk	N/A	Yes	Bk	Bk/Flm	Flm	Bk/Flm
	Phone Book	White/Yellow	—	—	Bk	—	Bk	Bk
1960	City Directory	Polk	Yes	N/A	Bk/Flm	Bk/Flm	Flm	—
1960	Phone Book	White/Yellow	—	—	Bk	—	Bk	—
1961	City Directory	Polk	Yes	N/A	Bk/Flm	Bk/Flm	Flm	—
	County Directory	Polk	N/A	Yes	Bk	Bk/Flm	Flm	—
	Phone Book	White/Yellow	—	—	Bk	—	Bk	Bk
1962	County Directory	Polk	N/A	Yes	Bk	Bk/Flm	Flm	—
	Phone Book	White/Yellow	—	—	Bk	—	Bk	Bk
1963	City Directory	Polk	Yes	N/A	Bk/Flm	Bk/Flm	Flm	—
	County Directory	Polk	N/A	Yes	Bk	Bk/Flm	Flm	—
	Phone Book	White/Yellow	—	—	Bk	—	Bk	Bk
1964	City Directory	Polk	Yes	N/A	Bk/Flm	Bk/Flm	Flm	Bk
	Phone Book	White/Yellow	—	—	Bk	—	Bk	Bk
1965	City Directory	Polk	Yes	N/A	Bk/Flm	Flm	Flm	Bk
	County Directory	Polk	N/A	Yes	Bk	Bk/Flm	Flm	
	Phone Book	White/Yellow	—	—	Bk	—	Bk	Bk
1966	City Directory	Polk	Yes	N/A	Bk/Flm	Bk	Flm	Bk
	County Directory	Polk	N/A	Yes	Bk	Bk/Flm	Flm	—
	Phone Book	White/Yellow	—	—	Bk	—	Bk	Bk
1967–1968	City Directory	Polk	Yes	N/A	Bk/Flm	Bk/Flm	Flm	—
	County Directory	Polk	N/A	Yes	Bk	Bk/Flm	Flm	—
	Phone Book	White/Yellow	—	—	Bk	—	Bk	Bk
1968	County Directory	Polk	N/A	Yes	Bk	Bk/Flm	Flm	—
	Phone Book	White/Yellow	—	—	Bk	—	Bk	Bk
1969	City Directory	Polk	Yes	N/A	Bk/Flm	Bk/Flm	Flm	—
	County Directory	Polk	N/A	Yes	Bk	Bk/Flm	Flm	—

Year	Directory	Publisher	City Before /After 1877	County After 1876	MoHis	SLCL	SLPL	SHS
1969	Phone Book	White/Yellow	—	—	Bk	—	Bk	Bk
1970	City Directory	Polk	Yes	N/A	Bk/Flm	Bk/Flm	Flm	Bk
	County Directory	Polk	N/A	Yes	Bk	Bk/Flm	Flm	—
	Phone Book	White/Yellow	—	—	Bk	—	Bk	Bk
1971	City Directory	Polk	Yes	N/A	Bk/Flm	Bk/Flm	Flm	—
	County Directory	Polk	N/A	Yes	Bk	Bk/Flm	Flm	—
	Phone Book	White/Yellow	—	—	Bk	—	Bk	Bk
1972–1973	City Directory	Polk	Yes	N/A	Bk/Flm	Bk/Flm	Flm	—
1972	County Directory	Polk	N/A	Yes	Bk/Flm	Bk/Flm	Flm	—
	Phone Book	White/Yellow	—	—	Bk	Bk	Bk	Bk
1973	County Directory	Haines	N/A	Yes	Flm	Bk/Flm	Flm	—
	Phone Book	White/Yellow	—	—	Bk	Bk	Bk	—
	Criss-Cross	Haines	—	—	Bk	—	—	—
1974	City Directory	Polk	Yes	N/A	Bk/Flm	Bk/Flm	Flm	—
	County Directory	Polk	N/A	Yes	Bk	Bk/Flm	Flm	—
	Phone Book	White/Yellow	—	—	Bk	Bk	Bk	Bk
1975	City Directory	Polk	Yes	N/A	Bk/Flm	Bk/Flm	Flm	—
	County Directory	Polk	N/A	Yes	Bk	Bk/Flm	Flm	—
	Phone Book	White/Yellow	—	—	Bk	Bk	Bk	Bk
1976–1977	City Directory	Polk	Yes	N/A	Bk/Flm	Bk/Flm	Flm	—
1976	County Directory	Polk	N/A	Yes	Bk	Bk/Flm	Flm	—
	Phone Book	White/Yellow	—	—	Bk	—	Bk	Bk
1977	Phone Book	White/Yellow	—	—	Bk	Bk	Bk	Bk
1978	City Directory	Polk	Yes	N/A	Flm	Bk	—	—
	Phone Book	White/Yellow	—	—	Bk	Bk	Bk	—
1979	City Directory	Polk	Yes	N/A	Flm	—	—	—
	County Directory	Polk	N/A	Yes	Bk	Bk	Flm	—
1979	Street Directory	Phone Co.	Yes	Yes	Bk	Bk	—	—
	Phone Book	White/Yellow	—	—	Bk	Bk	Bk	Bk
1980	City Directory	Polk	Yes	N/A	Bk/Flm	Bk/Flm	Flm	—
	Phone Book	White/Yellow	—	—	Bk	—	Bk	Bk
1981	Phone Book	White/Yellow	—	—	Bk	Bk	Bk	Bk
	Street Directory	Phone Co.	Yes	Yes	Bk	Bk	Bk	—
1982	Phone Book	White/Yellow	—	—	Bk	—	Bk	Bk
1983	Phone Book	White/Yellow	—	—	Bk	—	Bk	Bk
	Street Directory	Phone Co.	Yes	Yes	Bk	Bk	Bk	—
1984	Phone Book	White/Yellow	—	—	Bk	Bk	Bk	Bk
1985	Phone Book	White/Yellow	—	—	Bk	Bk	Bk	Bk
	Street Directory	Phone Co.	Yes	Yes	Bk	Bk	Bk	—
1986	Phone Book	White/Yellow	—	—	Bk	Bk	Bk	Bk
	Criss-Cross	Haines	—	—	Bk	Bk	Bk	—
1987	Phone Book	White/Yellow	—	—	Bk	Bk	Bk	Bk
	Criss-Cross	Haines	—	—	Bk	Bk	Bk	—
1988	Phone Book	White/Yellow	—	—	Bk	Bk	Bk	Bk
	Criss-Cross	Haines	—	—	Bk	Bk	Bk	—
1989	Phone Book	White/Yellow	—	—	Bk	Bk	Bk	Bk
1989	Criss-Cross	Haines	—	—	Bk	Bk	Bk	—
1990	Phone Book	White/Yellow	—	—	Bk	Bk	Bk	Bk
	Criss-Cross	Haines	—	—	Bk	Bk	Bk	—
1991	Phone Book	White/Yellow	—	—	Bk	Bk	Bk	Bk
	Criss-Cross	Haines	—	—	Bk	Bk	Bk	—
1992	Phone Book	White/Yellow	—	—	Bk	Bk	Bk	Bk

Year	Directory	Publisher	City Before /After 1877	County After 1876	MoHis	SLCL	SLPL	SHS
1992	Criss-Cross	Haines	—	—	Bk	Bk	Bk	—
1993	Phone Book	White/Yellow	—	—	Bk	Bk	Bk	Bk
	Criss-Cross	Haines	—	—	—	Bk	Bk	—
1994	Phone Book	White/Yellow	—	—	Bk	Bk	Bk	Bk
	Criss-Cross	Haines	—	—	—	Bk	Bk	—
1995	Phone Book	White/Yellow	—	—	Bk	Bk	Bk	Bk
1996	Phone Book	White/Yellow	—	—	Bk	Bk	Bk	Bk
	Criss-Cross	Haines	—	—	—	Bk	Bk	—
1997	Phone Book	White/Yellow	—	—	Bk	Bk	Bk	Bk
	Criss-Cross	Haines	—	—	—	Bk	Bk	—
1998	Phone Book	White/Yellow	—	—	Bk	Bk	Bk	Bk
	Criss-Cross	Haines	—	—	—	Bk	Bk	—
1999	Phone Book	White/Yellow	—	—	Bk	Bk	Bk	Bk
	Criss-Cross	Haines	—	—	—	Bk	Bk	—
2000	Phone Book	White/Yellow	—	—	Bk	Bk	Bk	Bk
2001	Phone Book	White/Yellow	—	—	Bk	Bk	Bk	—
	Criss-Cross	Haines North	—	—	Bk	Bk	Bk	—
	Criss-Cross	Haines South	—	—	Bk	Bk	Bk	—
2002	Phone Book	White/Yellow	—	—	Bk	Bk	Bk	—
	Criss-Cross	Haines North	—	—	Bk	Bk	Bk	—
	Criss-Cross	Haines South	—	—	Bk	Bk	Bk	—
2003	Phone Book	White/Yellow	—	—	Bk	Bk	Bk	—
2004	Phone Book	White/Yellow	—	—	Bk	Bk	Bk	—
2005	Phone Book	White/Yellow	—	—	Bk	Bk	Bk	—
	Criss-Cross	Haines North	—	—	Bk	Bk	Bk	—
2005	Criss-Cross	Haines South	—	—	Bk	Bk	Bk	—
2006	Phone Book	White/Yellow	—	—	Bk	Bk	Bk	—
	Criss-Cross	Haines North	—	—	Bk	Bk	Bk	—
	Criss-Cross	Haines South	—	—	Bk	Bk	Bk	—
2007	Phone Book	White/Yellow	—	—	Bk	Bk	Bk	—

Other Directories

The *1877 Elite Directory of St. Louis Society* provides a list of the St. Louis movers and shakers in 1877. The *1889 Gilt Edge Citizens' Directory* provides another list.[342] Both publications are available at the Missouri Historical Society Research Library.

Other directories provide additional information. The *Blue Book for the City of St. Louis* [343] provides a list of St. Louis clubs, the membership list, and the business location for each member. This publication provides a list by street name, which shows neighborhoods though every street in the area was not listed in this book. Issued between 1883 and 1916, copies are available at the St. Louis Public Library, the State Historical Society of Missouri, and the Missouri Historical Society Research Library.

---

342. *The 1877 Elite Directory of St. Louis Society* (St. Louis: C.E. Ware, 1877). Also, *1889 Gilt Edge Citizens' Directory* (St. Louis: privately printed, 1889).

343. *Gould's Blue Book for the City of St. Louis* (St. Louis: Gould Directory, 1884–1916). [The 1903, 1907, and 1913 directories are available online at HeritageQuest.]

An 1894 Polk directory, *St. Louis and St. Louis County Directory of Physicians, Druggists, and Dentists,* provides a listing of St. Louis medical personnel, their medical school name, and year of graduation.[344] The St. Louis Public Library website has an index for this publication.

In 1900, the *Official Office Building Directory and Architectural Handbook* presented a view of the downtown business area.[345] The *1914 St. Louis Business Men's League Roster* and the *1917* and *1919 St. Louis Chamber of Commerce* directories provide further details about businessmen of that era.[346]

The 1916 edition provides the following list of St. Louis clubs and the names of their members.

- Automobile Club of St. Louis
- Century Boat Club
- City Club
- Commercial Club
- Elks Club
- Liederkranz Club
- Mercantile Club
- Midland Valley Country Club (Ashby Road at Midland Boulevard)
- Missouri Athletic Association
- Morning Choral
- New England Society
- Noonday Club
- Normandie Golf Club
- Racquet Club
- St. Louis Amateur Athletic Association (Clayton Road in Forest Park)
- St. Louis Club (Lindell Boulevard near Grand Avenue)
- St. Louis Country Club (Price and Ladue Roads)
- St. Louis Symphony Society (Knights of Columbus Building)
- St. Louis Women's Club (4600 Lindell Boulevard)
- Sunset Country Club (Denny and Gravois Roads)
- University Club (607 N. Grand Avenue)
- Wednesday Club (Taylor and Westminster Avenues)
- Westwood Country Club (Glendale)

344. *St. Louis and St. Louis County Directory of Physicians, Druggists, Dentists, etc., Comprising a Complete and Accurate List of All Physicians, Their Correct Office and Residence Addresses, Hours of Consultation at Both Office and Residence, Telephone Number, etc.: Also a Complete and Accurate List of Dentists, Druggists, and Midwives, Arranged Alphabetically and By Streets* (St. Louis: R. L. Polk and Company, 1894).

345. *Official Office Building Directory and Architectural Handbook* (St. Louis: Gould, 1900).

346. *1914 St. Louis Business Men's League Roster* (St. Loius: The League, 1905). Also, *1917* and *1919 St. Louis Chamber of Commerce Directories* (St. Louis: The Chamber, 1917–1919).

The West Directory contains information on eight cities about 1837; St. Louis is one of those cities. The book outlines life on a steamboat traveling to St. Louis and then details the commerce in the city. Just like a city directory, this publication offers advertising for St. Louis merchants in 1837.[347]

Biographical directories were popular in the early twentieth century. Published in 1913 and 1915 by the Press Club of St. Louis, *Men of Affairs in Saint Louis: A Newspaper Reference Book,* provides biographical information on the businessmen of the day.[348]

A national social register association located in New York publishes registers for large cities. *The Social Register, St. Louis, 1914*, provides a list of the St. Louis social elite, their addresses, communities, clubs, and college and graduation dates. An appendix provides a list of women's maiden names.[349] The St. Louis Public Library has a complete set of this publication.

Notable St. Louisans in 1900 by James Cox is a directory of businessmen who contributed to the development of the St. Louis area. The publication provides names, photographs, and occupations. It does not include biographical sketches.[350]

The *Who's Who in St. Louis, 1928–1929* directory provides an independent view of the people of St. Louis. Unlike some other directories, those mentioned in this publication did not pay a fee to influence the author and publisher to include them in the listing.[351] You can also check Who's Who publications for the state and even nationally.

If you are interested in the history of a house, look at the *Gould's Blue Book* directories as they list the property by street and number, then reference the name of the owner. You can see the approximate time the ownership changed. For further details on conducting a real estate search, refer to LAND: DEEDS, GRANTS, & PATENTS.

Printed every two years in the odd-numbered year since 1889, the *State of Missouri Blue Books* provide a comprehensive list of state employees and a biographical description in some cases. If your ancestor was a state employee, his or her name, salary, and department of employment should be available during the years of employment.

If the employee worked less than two years, the book publication date may not coincide with the employment dates. Most St. Louis repositories have a good collection of *Missouri Blue Books.*

---

347.   *The West Directory* (Woodbridge, Connecticut: Research Publications, 1980–1984), FHL fiche 6,044,632.

348.   *St. Louis Press Club, Men of Affairs in Saint Louis: A Newspaper Reference Book* (St. Louis: Press Club of St. Louis, 1913). Also, St. Louis Press Club, *Men of Affairs in Saint Louis: A Newspaper Reference Book* (St. Louis: Press Club of St. Louis, 1915) [Index available at St. Louis Public Library website.]

349.   *Social Register, St. Louis, 1914* volume 28, number 7, 7 November 1913 (New York: Social Register Association, 1913). [Available online at HeritageQuest.]

350.   James Cox, *Notable St. Louisans in 1900: A Portrait Gallery of Men Whose Energy & Ability have Contributed Largely Towards Making St. Louis the Commercial and Financial Metropolis of the West, Southwest, and South* (St. Louis: Benesch Art Publishing, 1900). [Available online at HeritageQuest.]

351.   Samuel T. Larkin, compiler, *Who's Who in St. Louis, 1928–1929* (St. Louis: Civil Union of St. Louis, 1928).

The Blue Books also contain articles on historically significant subjects for Missouri residents. These articles often mention citizens and sometimes contain related photographs. The 2008 edition mentions numerous St. Louis residents.

Some City, County, and State government departments had newsletters. Check catalogs at Missouri Historical Society Research Library, the State Historical Society of Missouri, and the Missouri State Archives for back issues of these newsletters. They offer a wealth of biographical information. For example the highway department had a newsletter which listed anniversaries, births, deaths, and other special events for the employees in each region. This publication is housed at the State Historical Society of Missouri in Columbia.

The librarians at the previously mentioned facilities may have additional directories or publications valuable to your research.

Ethnic Records

During the 1800s, St. Louis became a composite of people from numerous ethnic backgrounds. The earliest citizens were French and Spanish. The population grew with the migration of pioneers from Kentucky, North Carolina, Pennsylvania, Tennessee, Virginia, and other states east of the Mississippi River.

The Germans and Irish soon arrived, followed by immigrants from England, Greece,[352] Italy, Poland, Scotland, and the Scandinavian and Eastern European countries. The immigrants brought with them various religious backgrounds including Catholic, Jewish, and a variety of Protestant denominations.

Each ethnic group has a variety of specialty books to help you. General books on immigration and naturalization provide an overview for all ethnic groups. Some immigrants to the St. Louis area migrated via Castle Garden and then Ellis Island in New York,[353] while others sailed to New Orleans and traveled up the Mississippi River.[354]

Many passenger lists are available online at subscription websites. Most of these websites are available free of charge at local repositories. When using the online databases, use creative ways to spell the given name and the surname of your ancestors. Even if your family *always* spelled the name the same, that does not mean the manifest agreed. The ship's officer recorded the name as he heard it, so consider the pronunciation with the immigrant's heavy accent as well as the nationality of the purser.

The naturalization laws are outlined in John Newman's *American Naturalization Processes and Procedures, 1790–1985.*[355] It is important to determine the laws in effect when your ancestor immigrated and was naturalized. For example, foreign-born women automatically became citizens when they married a U.S. citizen before 1922. These women did not have naturalization forms. After 1922, women had to naturalize on their own. Females also derived citizenship from

---

352. Aphrodite Matsakis Ph.D., *Growing Up Greek* (Chicago: Arcadia Publishing, 2002).

353. "Ellis Island Database." *The Statute of Liberty, Ellis Island Foundation* (http://www .ellisisland.org).

354. Loretto Dennis Szucs, *They Became Americans: Finding Naturalization Records and Ethnic Origins* (Salt Lake City: Ancestry, 1998).

355. John J. Newman, *American Naturalization Processes and Procedures, 1790–1985* (Indianapolis: Indiana Historical Society, 1985).

their fathers. After 1906, the naturalization forms include the name of the spouse and children, often with their birth dates and places.

Because of the variety of ethnic backgrounds, St. Louis has many civil and religious documents in languages other than English. Early land and court records are in Spanish or French. Religious records could be in French, German, Polish, and many other languages. Not only are they in a foreign language, but they also may have colloquialisms developed in this area or from the author's home area. This often causes a problem when you try to read the document. Books such as *A Glossary of Mississippi Valley French, 1673–1850,* provides a list of French words, particularly those brought to this part of the country by those early French settlers.[356] *FamilySearch.org* offers vocabulary lists in many languages, each containing often-used words in genealogical documents.[357]

The Family History Library has a good collection of ethnic finding aids available online at (http://www.familysearch.org) or in booklet format at your local Family History Center. These research outline publications are very inexpensive and provide extensive information.[358]

AFRICAN AMERICAN

Missouri was a border state during the Civil War. Some areas within Missouri had plantations with slaves, others did not. Heard in St. Louis, the Dred Scott case became an important part of the history of the Old Courthouse as well as the nation.

St. Louis City Hall has many unindexed African American records. They include slave marriages starting in 1804 and continuing until the Civil War era. Slave sales and emancipation documents dating from 1784 to 1860 are often found in the deed records, but are usually unindexed. Land records often list the name and birth dates of slaves.[359]

After the Civil War, many African Americans migrated up the Mississippi River from the states of Arkansas, Louisiana, and Mississippi. Some stayed in St. Louis, others moved north to cities like Chicago and Detroit. Many of these same people provided narratives about their lives. Some of this information is included in the *Slave Narratives from the Federal Writers' Project, 1936–1938.*[360] The Missouri Historical Society published a collection of writings by and about African Americans in St. Louis, *Ain't But A Place: An Anthology of African American Writings About St. Louis.*[361]

---

356.   John Francis McDermott, *A Glossary of Mississippi Valley French, 1673–1850* (St. Louis: Washington University, 1941).

357.   "French Vocabulary Guide," *FamilySearch* (http://www.familysearch.org/Eng/Search/RG/frameset_rhelps.asp).

358.   "Research Outline," *Family Search* (http://www.familysearch.org).

359.   *Archives Services: Nearly 250 Years of St. Louis History Thru Public Records* (St. Louis: Recorder of Deeds, no date).

360.   "Slave Narratives from the Federal Writers' Project, 1936–1938," *Library of Congress* (http://memory.loc.gov/ammem/snhtml/snhom.html). George P. Rawick, editor, *The American Slave: A Composite Autobiography, Volume 11, Arkansas Narratives and Missouri Narratives* (1941; reprint, Westport, Connecticut: Greenwood Publishing Company, 1972).

361.   *Ain't But A Place: An Anthology of African American Writings About St. Louis* (St. Louis: Missouri Historical Society Press, 1998).

The Freedman's Savings and Loan records, 1865–1874, list the name of the customer, date of application, where he was born and brought up, place of residence, age, complexion, occupation and who he works for, name of wife, children, father, mother, brothers, and sisters. The record also includes the applicant's signature. Not all fields are complete on all records. Unfortunately, the account numbers that apply to St. Louis only range from 223 to 366; however, if your ancestor is included, the information is very valuable. These microfilmed records are available at local libraries.

John Wright's book, *Discovering African American St. Louis: A Guide to Historic Sites*, provides photographs and history of churches, hospitals, schools, and many other places of interest.[362]

The Colored Aristocracy of St. Louis [363] provides an interesting account of African Americans with a long history in St. Louis. Morgan's *Profiles in Silhouette: The Contributions of Black Women of Missouri,* previously mentioned, chronicles African American women.[364]

The Missouri Historical Society Research Library has a bound volume consisting of newspaper clippings called *Negro Scrapbook,* which starts in 1897 and continues into the 1970s.[365] Another African American resource is a bound volume titled *Free Men and Women of Color in St. Louis, 1821–1860.* Information within this publication came from the city directories and provides the directory year of publication, and the information about citizens: name, occupation, and address.[366] Here are two examples:

> Scott, Dred – whitewasher – alley betw 10th & 11th Sts. [1854–1855]
>
> Scott, Harriet – widow Dred – alley betw Franklin & Wash [1860]

The librarians at St. Louis Public Library authored *African-American Heritage of St. Louis: A Guide,* which is available online.[367] An index for several African American related books is available on the St. Louis Public Library's website.

- Clayton, Sheryl H. *Black Men Role Models of Greater St. Louis.* East St. Louis, Illinois: Essai Seay Publications, 1984.

- *Kinloch: Yesterday, Today, and Tomorrow.* St. Louis: Kinloch History Committee, 1983.

---

362.   John A. Wright, *Discovering African American St. Louis: A Guide to Historic Sites* (St. Louis: Missouri Historical Society, 1994). John A. Wright, *St. Louis: Disappearing Black Communities* (Charleston, South Carolina: Arcadia Publishing, 2004). John A. Wright, *African Americans in Downtown St. Louis* (Chicago: Arcadia Publishing, 2003).

363.   Cyprien Clamorgan, *The Colored Aristocracy of St. Louis* (Columbia: University of Missouri Press, 1999).

364.   Morgan, *Profiles in Silhouette: The Contributions of Black Women of Missouri,* previously cited.

365.   *Negro Scrapbook* (St. Louis: Missouri Historical Society, no date).

366.   *Free Men and Women of Color in St. Louis, 1821–1860* (St. Louis: Missouri Historical Society, no date).

367.   "African-American Heritage of St. Louis: A Guide," *St. Louis Public Library* (http://www .umsl.edu/services/library/blackstudies/slplndx.htm).

- Lipsitz, George. *The Sidewalks of St. Louis: Places, People, and Politics in an American City.* Columbia: University of Missouri Press, 1991.

- Morris, Ann. *North Webster: a Photographic History of a Black Community.* Bloomington, Indiana: Indiana University Press, 1993.

- Pearson, Thomas A., and Anne Watts, compilers, *Biographical Sketches of St. Louisans.* St. Louis: St. Louis Public Library, 1996.

- *Profiles in Silhouette: Contributions of Black Women of Missouri.* St. Louis: Delta Sigma Theta, 1980.

- Smith, JoAnn Adams. *Selected Neighbors and Neighborhoods of North St. Louis and Selected Related Events.* St. Louis: Friends of Vaughn Cultural Center, 1988.

- Wright, John Aaron. *Discovering African-American St. Louis: A Guide to Historic Sites.* St. Louis: Missouri Historical Society Press, 1994.

The index for the employees of the "Black St. Louis Public Schools," *Missouri School Directory,* is available on the St. Louis Public Library website. The volumes extracted were 1925–1926, 1935–1936, 1946–1947, and 1954–1955.[368] The same library has also indexed the freemen of color listed in the 1821 to 1860 city directories.[369]

St. Louis County Library, Special Collections has the Julius K. Hunter and Friends African American Collection. Thanks to sponsor donations, the Library has purchased extensive African American resources. The Library has a free African American guide to assist researchers.[370]

BOHEMIAN–CZECH

About 1848, the Czech immigration to St. Louis began. Most were Catholic, very few Protestant. *The History of the Czechs in Missouri, 1845 to 1904*, by June Sommer, provides details about St. Louis Czechs in the Soulard area and beyond. June also updated this information in a 2006 two-part article, "Bohemian Czechs" published in the *St. Louis Genealogical Society Quarterly*.[371] St. Louis County Library has a *Bohemian, Czech, Moravian and Slovak Genealogy* guide.[372]

---

368. "Missouri School Directory Index," *St. Louis Public Library* (http://www.slpl.lib.mo.us/libsrc/teachers.htm).

369. "Free Men and Women of Color in St. Louis City Directories, 1821–1860 Index," *St. Louis Public Library* (http://www.slpl.lib.mo.us/libsrc/freemen.htm).

370.   St. Louis County Library, *African American Guide* (St. Louis: The Library, 2007).

371.   June Sommer, *The History of the Czechs in Missouri, 1845 to 1904* (St. Louis: St. Louis Genealogical Society, 1988). June Sommer, "Bohemian Czechs," *St. Louis Genealogical Society Quarterly* 39 (Fall 2006): 79–84 and (Winter 2006): 115–120. Eileen NiNi Harris, *Bohemian Hill: An American Story* (St. Louis: St. John Nepomuk Parish, 2004).

372.   St. Louis County Library, *Bohemian, Czech, Moravian and Slovak Genealogy* (St. Louis: The Library, 2007).

CHINESE

The current and previous St. Louis Cardinals' Busch Stadium sits on the former Chinatown of St. Louis. Chinese immigrants came to St. Louis as early as the 1860s.[373] *Chinese St. Louis: From Enclave to Cultural Community* provides background into the Chinese experiences in St. Louis since 1860.[374] Additional information may be available at the Asian Cultural Center, currently housed at St. Louis County Library's Daniel Boone branch.

CREOLE

The early French or Creole citizens helped populate St. Louis. Two publications, *Creoles in St. Louis* and *Glimpses of Creole Life in Old St. Louis,* provide details about the Creoles and their life in early St. Louis.[375]

FRENCH

Founded by the French, St. Louis has a rich French history. French pioneers established St. Louis, Carondelet, and St. Ferdinand. Many were fur traders. After the Louisiana Purchase, many of the street names were changed from their original French names to more American-style names. A book by John Rodabough, *Frenchtown,* provides insight into the life of the French in the area of St. Louis at the time the city was founded and two hundred years beyond.[376] A publication by Rita K. Coulter, *Discover the French Connection Between St. Louis and New Orleans,* describes the French living in New Orleans and various stops along the way to Illinois, Ste. Genevieve, and St. Louis.[377] St. Louis County Library, Special Collections offers helpful research guides, *French, Belgian, and Luxembourger Genealogy* and *French-Canadian Genealogy.*[378]

GERMAN

The St. Louis Public Library has several publications important to German research in St. Louis. On their website, they offer *Lasting Impressions: German-Americans in St. Louis,*

---

373.   Ping Linghu, *Chinese in St. Louis, 1857–2007* (Charleston, South Carolina: Arcadia Publishing, 2007).

374.   Huping Ling, *Chinese St. Louis: From Enclave to Cultural Community* (Philadelphia: Temple University Press, 2004).

375.   Eugenie Berthold, *Glimpses of Creole Life in Old St. Louis* (St. Louis: Missouri Historical Society, 1933). Paul Beckwith, *Creoles in St. Louis* (St. Louis: Nixon-Jones Print Company, 1893). [Digital publication available at HeritageQuest.]

376.   John Rodabough, *Frenchtown* (St. Louis: Sunrise Publishing, 1980).

377.   Rita K. Coulter, *Discover the French Connection Between St. Louis and New Orleans* (Elmhurst, Illinois: Interhouse Publishing, 1977).

378.   St. Louis County Library, *French, Belgian, and Luxembourg Genealogy Including Acadians and Huguenots in France* (St. Louis: The Library, 2007). St. Louis County Library, *Guide to French-Canadian Genealogy* (St. Louis: The Library, 2007).

which gives some suggestions about researching your St. Louis German ancestors.[379] Two other publications, *German-American Heritage of St. Louis: A Guide* and *St. Louis Germans, 1850–1920: The Nature of an Immigrant Community,* provide clues and directions to start this research.[380] If a German ancestor was Catholic, refer to St. Louis German Catholics.[381]

Emigration and Settlement Patterns of German Communities in North America provides some interesting facts and statistics about the German migration. Part of the study and analysis uses St. Louis Germans.[382]

Germans to America may help you locate that immigrant ancestor. Found in this 67-volume publication are immigrants who moved to the United States between 1850 and 1897. Use a variety of spellings when researching this resource. Photocopy ships' lists, as you may find other relatives, family friends, or neighbors who arrived on the same boat.[383]

The German community formed various organizations in St. Louis. The *1937 Directory for St. Louis, St. Louis County, and Vicinity of German-American Societies, Lodges, Unions, Institutions, Churches, Church Societies* provides the name of each organization, contact person, address and phone number. Most of the text is in English, some in German.[384]

St. Louis County Library, Special Collections has information brochures on German research, updated as new information becomes available.[385]

IRISH

St. Louis Irish immigrants were second in population only to the Germans. The Irish established two communities within St. Louis: Dogtown and Kerry Patch.[386] The history of one community is available in Brunsmann's, *Early Irish Settlers in St. Louis, Missouri, and Dogtown*

379. "Lasting Impressions: German-Americans in St. Louis," *St. Louis Public Library* (http://exhibits.slpl.lib.mo.us/germanamerican/index.asp).

380. *German-American Heritage of St. Louis: A Guide* (St. Louis: St. Louis Public Library, 1991). Audrey Olson, *St. Louis Germans, 1850–1920: The Nature of an Immigrant Community* (Ann Arbor, Michigan: UMI, 1978).

381. William B. Faherty, *St. Louis German Catholics* (St. Louis: Reedy Press, 2004).

382. Eberhard Reichman, LaVern J. Rippley, and Jörg Nagler, *Emigration and Settlement Patterns of German Communities in North America* (Indianapolis: Max Kade German-American Center, 1995).

383. Ira A. Glazier and P. William Filby, *Germans to America: Lists of Passengers Arriving at U.S. Ports,* 67 volumes (Wilmington, Delaware: Scholarly Resources, 1988–).

384. Rembert von Muenckhause, *1937 Directory for St. Louis, St. Louis County, and Vicinity of German-American Societies, Lodges, Unions, Institutions, Churches, Church Societies* (St. Louis: The Author,1937).

385. St. Louis County Library, *German Genealogy St. Louis-Area Research* (St. Louis: The Library, 2007). St. Louis County Library, *German Genealogy, German: Regional Resources* (St. Louis: The Library, 2007). St. Louis County Library, *German Genealogy, German Resources* (St. Louis: The Library, 2007).

386. Ellen M. Dolan, *The Saint Louis Irish* (St. Louis: Old St. Patrick's, 1967). [Index available online at St. Louis Public Library's website]. "The Kerry Patch," *St. Louis Irish History* (http://home.earthlink.net/~lilirish/KerryPatch.htm). "Dogtown, St. Louis, Missouri," *Bob Corbett's Dogtown Homepage* (http://www.webster.edu/~corbetre/dogtown/dogtown.html). David Lossos, *Irish St. Louis* (Chicago: Arcadia Publishing, 2004).

Neighborhood.[387] The Catholic Church established several Irish parishes. Father Faherty's *St. Louis Irish: An Unmatched Celtic Community* provides further Irish history.[388] St. Louis County Library, Special Collections has an information brochure for *Irish Genealogy.*[389]

ITALIAN

Most Italians migrated to the United States in the late 1800s and early 1900s and probably came through Ellis Island. Many naturalized after September 1906, thus providing detailed information about the old country and family members. St. Louis County Library, Special Collections has information on naturalizations for that time period. Refer to their finding aid, *Guide to Italian Genealogy.* Publications helpful for Italian research include Colletta's, *Finding Italian Roots: The Complete Guide for Americans.*[390] Gary Mormino's *Immigrants on the Hill* provides great background for Italians in St. Louis.[391] *The Italians in Missouri* starts with a review of the St. Louis Italians. Also, refer to the master's thesis by Walter John Galeis, *The History of the Catholic Italians in St. Louis.*[392]

JEWISH

The St. Louis County Library, Special Collections is the repository for resources for the former Jewish Genealogical Society of St. Louis. Walter Ehrlich wrote two volumes of, *Zion in the Valley: The Jewish Community of St. Louis.* One book covers the 1807–1907 period and the other the twentieth century.[393] The Library has reprinted an old publication, *Jewish Progress in St. Louis: Religious, Charitable, Educational, Social, Mercantile.*[394] The *Guide to Jewish Genealogy* is available at St. Louis County Library.[395]

The same library has a rich collection of Yizkor books, which are memorial books written mostly in the 1950s to document the Jewish communities in Europe that were destroyed by the Nazis during World War II. Very few libraries in the United States have these books.

---

387.   Sandra Brunsmann, *Early Irish Settlers in St. Louis, Missouri and Dogtown Neighborhood* (St. Louis: The Author, 2000).

388.   William B. Faherty, *The St. Louis Irish: An Unmatched Celtic Community* (St. Louis: Missouri Historical Society Press, 2001).

389.   St. Louis County Library, *Irish Genealogy* (St. Louis: The Library, 2007).

390.   John Philip Colletta, *Finding Italian Roots: The Complete Guide for Americans*, 2nd edition (Baltimore: Genealogical Publishing Company, 2003).

391.   Gary Ross Mormino, *Immigrants on the Hill: Italian-Americans in St. Louis, 1881–1982* (Chicago: University of Illinois Press, 1986).

392.   Giovanni Schiavo, *The Italians in Missouri* (New York: Arno Press, 1975). Walter John Galeis, *The History of the Catholic Italians in St. Louis,* master's thesis (St. Louis: privately printed, 1936).

393.   Walter Ehrlich, *Zion in the Valley: The Jewish Community of St. Louis 1807–1907* (Columbia: University of Missouri Press, 1997). Walter Ehrlich, *Zion in the Valley: The Jewish Community of St. Louis, the Twentieth Century* (Columbia: University of Missouri Press, 2002).

394.   Abraham Rosenthal, *Jewish Progress in St. Louis: Religious, Charitable, Educational, Social, Mercantile* (1904; reprint, St. Louis: The Library, 2004).

395.   St. Louis County Library, *Guide to Jewish Genealogy* (St. Louis: The Library, 2007).

Other resources include the St. Louis Genealogical Society website has a timeline of Jewish history in St. Louis and an index to Jewish deaths and burials in St. Louis. It also has *Generations,* the Jewish Genealogical Society publication. The Brodsky Library and the Holocaust Museum may be helpful as well.

POLISH

Polish research may involve Catholics, Jews, and Protestants. Atlases and maps provide a history of the border changes. Dictionaries and guides help with the records and translations. One is available at FamilySearch.org or at a Family History Center. Various guides provide an overview of the records. The Polish Genealogical Society of America (http://www.pgsa.org) provides guidance for research into your Polish roots.

The History of the Catholic Poles of St. Louis offers background information on the citizens, churches, and schools. A more recent title by Eileen NiNi Harris, *Unyielding Spirit: The History of the Polish People of St. Louis,* published by St. Stanislaus Kostka Parish provides may be helpful. Jonathan Shea's book, *Going Home: A Guide to Polish American Family History Research* may be helpful as well.[396] The St. Louis County Library, Special Collections offers the *Guide to Polish Genealogy* to help with your research.[397]

SCANDINAVIAN

Resources for Denmark, Finland, Norway, and Sweden are available at St. Louis County Library, Special Collections. Scandinavian resources such as *Scandinavian-American Genealogical Resources* may be helpful. St. Louis County Library offers an information brochure called *Guide to Scandinavian Genealogy* to help with your research.[398]

SCOTS

If you have Scottish ancestry, St. Louis County Library has just acquired a large collection of Scottish Monumental Records tombstone inscriptions. Divided by counties in Scotland, these books may help you discover a new generation or more in Scotland. To best utilize the books, determine the county of origin and then review the small but powerful books. This collection was a gift to the Library and Scottish researchers, purchased by four donors. This is one of the largest collections of Scottish cemetery books in the country. St. Louis County Library, Special Collections offers the *Guide to Scottish Genealogy* to help with your research.[399]

---

396.   John Stanislaus Mysliwiec, *The History of the Catholic Poles of St. Louis* (St. Louis: St. Louis University, 1936). Eileen NiNi Harris, *Unyielding Spirit: The History of the Polish People of St. Louis* (St. Louis: St. Stanislaus Church, Kostka Parish, 2007). Jonathan Shea, *Going Home: A Guide to Polish American Family History Research* (New Brittan, Connecticut: The Author, 2008).

397.   St. Louis County Library, *Guide to Polish Genealogy* (St. Louis: The Library, 2007).

398.   St. Louis County Library, *Guide to Scandinavian Genealogy* (St. Louis: The Library, 2007).

399.   St. Louis County Library, *Guide to Scottish Genealogy* (St. Louis: The Library, 2007).

Government Records: Courts, Elections, & Taxes

Court records come from different types of courts and different levels of government. They may be federal, state, county, or city records. Different locations house each type of court record. Many federal records are housed at the National Archives. State records for Missouri are often located in Jefferson City and many are available at the Missouri State Archives. Appeals filed in Missouri can go to the Court of Appeals or directly to the Missouri Supreme Court, which is the highest court in the state.

St. Louis City maintains its records in the downtown area. St. Louis County records are at the county seat in Clayton and many of those are available on microfilm at St. Louis County Library, Special Collections.

The court names changed over time; therefore, it is necessary to understand the court system for the time period in which you are interested. To add to the confusion, some records could be filed in various courts. Naturalization records are a good example. The HISTORY chapter provides information about court records during the territorial period. Plus, with the separation of the City and County, any court record at that level after 1876 could be in either of two jurisdictions.

The Recorder of Deeds certainly produces government records. This publication describes some of those records in other chapters.

Birth records	BIRTH chapter
Death records	DEATH chapter
Deed records	LAND chapter
Marriage records	MARRIAGE chapter

The Circuit Court includes the Probate Court office and those records are described in the WILLS AND PROBATE RECORDS chapter.

LEGAL VOCABULARY

Different states use different terms in their court documents. A list of a few general terms may be helpful while conducting research in legal documents.

- DEFENDANT, the person defending the suit filed by the plaintiff.

- DIRECT refers to the plaintiff in a court case and the grantor in land transactions.

- ET AL., means *and others* and is often found in probate cases when there are several heirs. *Et als.* is also used in the court system when there is more than one plaintiff or defendant.

- INDEXES provide a direct and indirect list of participants.

- INDIRECT refers to the defendant in court cases and the grantee in land transactions.

- JUDGMENT DOCKET provides an alphabetical list of judgments and decrees.

- MINUTES are brief entries of the proceedings.

- PLAINTIFF, the person filing the legal action.

- RECORD includes information in the Minutes.

- RELICT means widow or widower.

- RETURN DOCKET has entries for each suit, the order and date of the filing, names of the parties and attorneys.

- TRIAL DOCKET may be called the court docket or the bar docket.

COURTS

Federal Courts

The U.S. District Court in the Missouri Eastern District is located in the Thomas Eagleton Federal Building in downtown St. Louis, currently with seven judges serving the area. The historical records from this court are located at the National Archives Central Region branch in Kansas City, Missouri.

St. Louis is the home of the Eighth Federal Circuit Court of Appeals, which covers the states of Arkansas, Iowa, Minnesota, Missouri, Nebraska, North Dakota, and South Dakota. The Eighth Circuit of Appeals has eleven federal judges located in St. Louis.

Court cases include the federal case filed by Dred and Harriet Scott as well as others seeking their freedom from slavery.

If your ancestor was involved in a federal court case, such as a lawsuit, bankruptcy, a crime against the government, a crime that crossed state lines, or perhaps a witness to a crime, you can locate the records at the National Archives branch in Kansas City. You can contact the Archives by mail or email to determine the status of the records.

State Courts

The Twenty-first Judicial Circuit of the State of Missouri (St. Louis County Circuit Court) handles civil, criminal, family, probate, and traffic court matters. The Twenty-second Judicial Circuit of the State of Missouri (St. Louis City Circuit Court) handles the same matters, but in the City.

The Missouri Court of Appeals, Eastern District hears cases from twenty-five counties and the City of St. Louis. The courtrooms have been in several locations, including the Old Courthouse, Civil Courts Building, and the Old Post Office, all in downtown St. Louis. The Court also has a branch in St. Louis County. Further information about the court system is available online at (http://www.courts.mo.gov).

Early Missouri Supreme Court records are indexed in a database that covers cases during the territorial period, 1804–1820, and after statehood. This ongoing project is currently up to about 1870. [400]

Circuit Court Records

The Circuit Court presides over most civil and criminal cases. Today the Circuit Court has four divisions: Civil, Criminal, Domestic Relations, and Juvenile.

> CIVIL COURT — handles all civil cases between two or more people, including lawsuits, which do not involve a crime. The cases formerly heard by the Chancery and Equity Courts are now heard in the Civil Court.

> CRIMINAL COURT — handles all criminal cases.

> DOMESTIC RELATIONS COURT — handles all matters relating to families and their well being. Sometimes the Department of Welfare becomes involved.

> JUVENILE COURT — handles all matters concerning the welfare of children under the age of seventeen.

St. Louis Circuit Court records are available from the beginning of the court system to the current time. First classified as County records prior to 1877, these records continue as City records. Since 1877, the County government has also had a Circuit Court. [401]

An index to the St. Louis City's Civil Court records is located in the Central File room of the Circuit Clerk's office on the third floor. The records themselves relate to any civil action since 1817, divorce, property dispute, property settlement, name changes, slavery emancipation, liens, and garnishments, or any other type of civil suit.

The alphabetical-by-surname index cards to these records cover the period 1817–1970, using the Soundex coding system. After 1970, these records are filed by case with a plaintiff-defendant cross index using the surnames. Each card has a case number reference to the original document.

The clerk will search the files and complete a File Inspection Request. You can take this slip to the Archives on the second floor where you will view the file. Because some files are located in another building, contact the office prior to your visit to avoid a second trip. Photocopies are available for a fee; take cash, as checks are not accepted.

Some of the St. Louis City Circuit Court Indexes and Case files are on microfilm. The direct index is alphabetical by the first letter of the plaintiff's surname. The ledger gives the plaintiff's name, the defendant's name and the case number, all separated by the Court term. [402] Court was held in February, April, October, and December.

---

400.   "Missouri Supreme Court Database," *Missouri State Archives* (http://www.sos.mo.gov/ archives/judiciary/supremecourt/default.asp).

401.   Joseph Fred Benson, *One Hundred Years of Justice: A History of the Circuit Court of St. Louis County, Missouri, 1877–1978* ([St. Louis]: privately printed, 1978). Family Court of St. Louis County, *Guide to the Family Court* (St. Louis: Community Relations Office of Family Court, 2002).

402.   St. Louis City Case Files; Missouri State Archives film starting C47168.

Researchers may visit the St. Louis City Circuit Clerk (10 North Market, St. Louis 63101; phone 314-614-8309; http://www.stlcitycircuitcourt.com) or contact them by fax. Due to the large number of requests, a response may be slow.

City and County Records

The City maintains a Microfilm Library, established in 1957, and formerly called the Archival Library. This office provides limited public access to the records most for the City, but some for St. Louis County before 1876. However, most records of interest to genealogists are available at the local repositories, Missouri State Archives, and the Family History Library. Check with the City Hall Archivists' research department for further information on these records.

Office of the County Clerk, County Court Minute Books, 1824–1877

There are twenty-three County Clerk Minute Books on six rolls of microfilm. St. Louis County filmed this record, not the City. This film is available at the Missouri State Archives and at St. Louis County Library, Special Collections.

The first roll is an index to the entire set. The index begins with many names indexed by the first letter of the surname. As the index and time progressed, the indexer changed to topics with names included under the topics. The entire set is typed, so this is not the original record; however, the typescript is easy to read.

The records include information on county commissioners, free negro licenses, hospitals, insane, jailors, judges, juries, justices of the peace, parks, poorhouse, railroads, registrations, road overseers, taxes, tobacco inspectors, and more.

St. Louis County Council—County Court Record Books (large books). This record starts in January 1877 and continues until today. The first 100 volumes record the actions from 1877 to the 1950s. St. Louis County Library, Special Collections has the film from 1877 to 1929, the first 34 volumes. You will find an index in the front of some of these books.

Dram shop owners obtained license and paid taxes yearly. The license book is alphabetical. The record includes the owner's name, township, place of business, amount of state and county tax, when due and when paid, and when the license expired.[403]

Other professions used licenses and permits that were recorded in the court record books. The following list is an example of the information available.

Doctors' and Druggists' Permits

Merchants' and Manufacturers' License Statement

Merchants' and Manufacturers' License Tax Books

Merchants' and Manufacturers' Licenses (Meat, Beer, Soda, & Cider Peddlers)

Merchants' Statements

Pauper Ledger

Paupers and Insane

Record of Dental Certificates

---

403.   St. Louis County Clerk, Dram Shop Licenses, 1891–1910; Missouri State Archives film C18161.

Record of Jurors

Record of Pharmacists and Osteopaths

Record of St. Louis County Hospital

Record of State Board Health Certificates

Register of Farm Names

Register of Paupers and Insane, Account Books

Register of School Warrants

Roll of Physicians

School Warrants

Warrant Registers

Recorder of Deeds

Military Discharge Records

When veterans returned home after a war, they often recorded their discharge papers at the courthouse. In Missouri, this filing took place in the Recorder of Deeds' office. These records were filed by the veterans after their discharge. The Recorder of Deeds' office maintains the discharge ledgers; however, at the current time they are not considered public records.

Trademarks

The City Recorder maintains a trademark document file dating from 1865 to 1930. If you feel your ancestor filed a trademark, check this file. Topics include alcohol, dry goods, equipment, foods, medicines, tobacco, and some organizations.

Notarial Records

Some court or governmental types of records need to be signed by a notary public. These records are often called notarial records. Two examples are listed below.

Record of official acts, 1875–1881, St. Louis Notarial records FHL film 981,664, item 6

Commissions to St. Louis County officials, 1875–1877, FHL film 981,664, item 4

Other Records

St. Louis County Library, Special Collections has several indexes that may be helpful in your search.

- St. Louis County Index to Wards (Minors and Incompetent individuals)

- St. Louis County Wards, Books 1–6, 1890–1939 (Dependent on County support)

- St. Louis County Register of Poor Farms

Jurors

Various court actions require jurors. A St. Louis City alphabetical list of jurors from 1860 to 1862 is extant. The original records are available at the Missouri Historical Society Research Library, and the Missouri State Archives has microfilmed these records.[404]

ELECTIONS

Voter registration records provide an assortment of information that is particularly valuable in the time before vital records and as a substitute for the 1890 census. It is important to remember who is eligible to be on the voter lists and those who were ineligible, based on the laws for that time. However, a limited number of voting records exist.

Before 1920, women were not on voter lists in St. Louis or Missouri. Men over the age of twenty-one, either natural-born citizens or immigrants who were naturalized were eligible to vote. When registering, would-be-voters had to provide their birth date and place of birth. Naturalized citizens had to provide their place and date of naturalization. The information often includes the name of the court. All voters had to sign the record.

The City and County are divided into wards and precincts. The political districts changed often with the population growth and migration. The ward and precinct boundaries usually went right down the middle of a street. The people who lived on one side of the street could be in a different ward or precinct than the people across the street.

Locate your ancestor's address for a year when there was a presidential election. More voters registered for the presidential elections than in other years. Then locate that street on the ward maps and identify the correct political division, both ward and precinct. If the area is on the border of two or more wards or precincts, make a note of all possibilities.

St. Louis City — after 1876

Arranged by City ward and precinct, voter registration records between 1896 and 1937 are copies of a journal signed by the voter. An every-name index does not exist.[405]

To utilize the records before 1937 follow these steps:

• Locate your ancestor's address in the city directories if unknown
• Locate the street on the City ward maps, available on CD or in paper format
• Determine the ward and precinct where your ancestor lived
• Check the voter record for that area
• Photocopy the document
• Check other names in the neighborhood for collateral family members

---

404.   St. Louis City Jurors; some originals at Missouri Historical Society; Missouri State Archives film starting with C43724.
405.   St. Louis City voter records; St. Louis County Library microfilm.

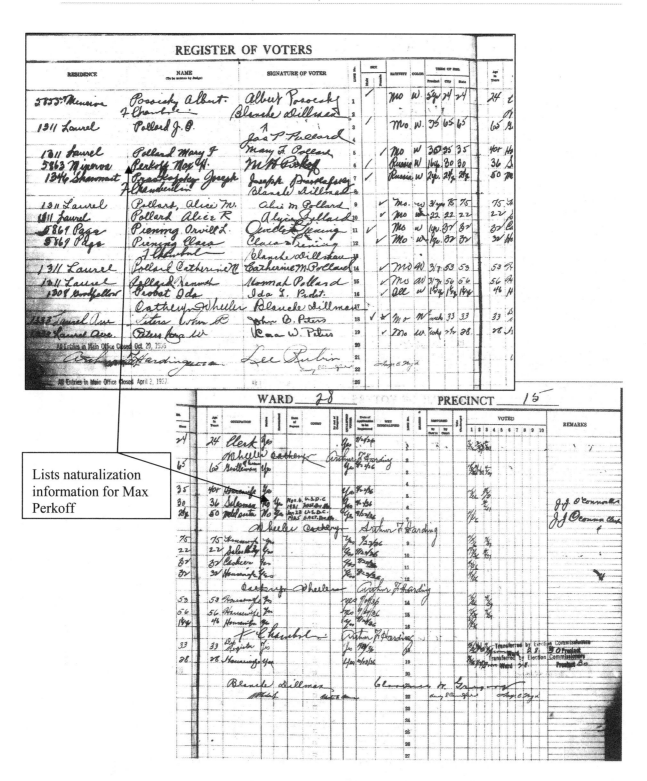

Lists naturalization information for Max Perkoff

Figure 29: Voter Registration Records, pre-1937

Because this is a large set of microfilm, it is often a challenge to use. Some of the pages are easy to read, others are not. Some of the documents were filmed backwards, others go the right direction. However, once you locate your ancestor, his or her information may reveal his or her home town, date of birth, or naturalization information, previously unknown as displayed in Figure 29.

Before 1937, voters had to register every four years. Starting in 1937 voters registered one time and that was valid until they moved to another address or out of town. The post 1937 registration had two original cards: one yellow and one white. When a voter registered, he or she answered questions posed by the registrar who filled out the card. The voter only signed the card. This method leaves room for errors. Figure 30 shows a voter card for Thomas Carter, a painter. This is the right Thomas Carter, but he was never a painter. If others were registering at the same time, it was possible that the registrar recorded the incorrect information and if the voter did not notice and correct the information, it is recorded for history.

The card provides the name, address, ward, precinct, date or registration, date of birth, occupation, naturalization place and date if applicable, and voter's signature. The card was marked each time the person voted.

These yellow cards dating from 1937 to 1971 were placed in alphabetical order and microfilmed. These records are very easy to use. If your ancestor lived after 1937, check this record first. This microfilm is available at the St. Louis County Library, Special Collections.

For voter information after 1971, check with the St. Louis City Board of Election Commissioners (300 North Tucker Boulevard, St. Louis 63101; phone 314-622-4336; http://www.stlelections.com). To help locate recent St. Louis citizens, researchers may check the online inactive voters' list.

Voter registration records for the City of St. Louis are available at St. Louis County Library, Special Collections thanks to a generous donation by Mary F. Berthold.

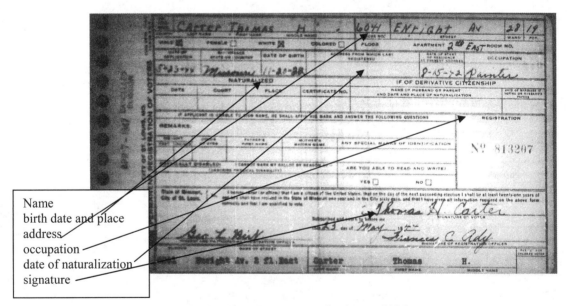

Figure 30: Voter Registration Card, post-1936

ST. LOUIS COUNTY — AFTER 1876

St. Louis County voter registration books, 1924–1936 are located at the Missouri Historical Society Research Library. Each journal represents a precinct within a ward in St. Louis County. The inside front cover of the book has a map and description of the precinct boundaries so that you can easily identify the streets and neighborhood. Women were given the right to vote in 1920; thus the books are full of signatures for new women voters.

Voters registered every four years in a new journal. A check mark on the same page indicates when a person voted within that four-year period. The lack of a check mark may provide a clue as to when someone died or moved. The journal may provide clues as to why that person left the precinct, such as the house burned down or it may list their new address.

St. Louis County Board of Election Commissioners (12 Sunnen Drive, Maplewood 63143; phone 314-615-1800; http://www.co.st-louis.mo.us/elections/FAQ's.html) does not have archival voter records at this time. Records may be located in the future. The County map on this website provides an overview of the County municipalities. Click on the municipality for a more detailed map.

The League of Women Voters published two books pertaining to voting in St. Louis County.[406] Poll books dating from 1838 to 1845 are in the Missouri Historical Society Research Library manuscript collections.

In August 1858, J. Richard Barrett won the election for the seat in the First Congressional district of Missouri for the 36th Congress. However, Frank P. Blair contested the election stating that the election was fraudulent due to the participation of ineligible voters.

The 1,151 page document filed with the court and with the U.S. House of Representatives, provides the names of the voters and often testimony from those men. In most cases, the men provide information about when they came to the United States, how long they had been in St. Louis, and whether they were naturalized citizens. In some cases, men testified for or against other voters. If your ancestors lived in St. Louis in August 1858 they may have participated in this election and be mentioned by name in this document.

This document, which is part of the U.S. Serial Set is available online at HeritageQuest. On the search screen, enter St. Louis as the place and election as the keyword.[407]

TAXES

Early St. Louis citizens paid taxes at the city, county, and state level. Many of the state-level tax records burned in the 1911 Missouri State Capitol fire. Other obstacles include the difficulty in reading the papers or ledgers used by the tax collector.

---

406.   League of Women Voters, *Know Your County, St. Louis County* (St. Louis: League of Women Voters, 1965). Avis D. Carlson, *League of Women Voters in St. Louis: The First Forty Years, 1919–1959* (St. Louis: The League, 1959).

407.   U.S. Congress, *Contesting Seat of J. Richard Barrett, Representative from the First Congressional District of Missouri, Memorial of Frank P. Blair, December 1859*. 36th Congress 1st session, House Miscellaneous Document 8. [Available on HeritageQuest.]

Some tax records date back to 1819 and perhaps even prior to that date. A combined land and property tax list from 1819 for all of St. Louis County and another dated for only the City in 1823 lists the names of early St. Louis-area citizens. Two other lists provide the delinquent St. Louis tax payers for 1822 and 1824.[408] The 1818–1819 delinquent tax lists give us the name of the taxpayer and the dollar amount due. The lists do not mention the taxed property. Remember, this list is of people who did NOT pay their taxes. A few names have PAID written on their lines. The taxpayers were delinquent as of July 1822, the date of the document.

Tax lists dating from 1824 to 1831 are available on microfilm at the Family History Library. The publication, *Ten Thousand Missouri Taxpayers,* includes some St. Louis County residents, dating from 1780 to 1867.[409]

The Assessor's office is the custodian of the tax records in St. Louis. While you can certainly uncover tax records for property owned in St. Louis, you can also follow the history of a house or property.[410] This process is the same used by title companies to provide a clear title during property transactions. [See LAND: DEEDS, GRANTS & PATENTS.]

The first federal income tax system started in 1862.[411] National Archives microfilmed records are available for St. Louis and most of Missouri. Divided into thirteen districts, the first ten are the wards in St. Louis. The eleventh district covers steamboats and corporations. The twelfth district covers South St. Louis County such as Glencoe, Kirkwood, and Mehlville. The thirteenth district covers North County, including Bridgeton, Central, and St. Ferdinand.[412] Surnames and corporate names are listed alphabetically by the first letter only. Review the list carefully to locate your family member.

The National Archives–Central Plains regional facility in Kansas City holds federal tax records for St. Louis dating from 1865 to 1874 and again from 1943–1954. This facility may acquire more information.

The most important aid in your research, other than the address, is the City block number. Block numbers divide the City of St. Louis into manageable parts, outlined on various maps. The St. Louis City ward maps include block numbers.[413] Tax information and deeds list block numbers. The address or street name may have changed over the years, but the block number has remained the same. Figure 7 on page 54 shows the block numbers listed on the City ward maps.

---

408.   Lois Stanley, George F. Wilson, and Maryhelen Wilson, *Missouri Taxpayers, 1819–1826* (Decorah, Iowa: privately printed, 1979), 94–107.

409.   St. Louis Tax books, 1824–1831; FHL film 1,005,418. Sherida K. Eddlemon, *Ten Thousand Missouri Taxpayers* (Bowie, Maryland: Heritage Books, 1996).

410.   James R. Kimmey, *House History in St. Louis: A Guide to Research on Real Estate and Building History* (St. Louis: privately printed, 1991).

411.   "Statutes at Large, 5 August 1861, (12 Stat. 309)," *Library of Congress, Century of Lawmaking* (http:// memory.loc.gov/ammem/amlaw/lwslink.html).

412.   *National Archives, Internal Revenue Assessment Lists for Missouri, 1862–1865*, M776, Record Group 58, 22 rolls (Washington, D.C.: NARA).

413.   St. Louis Genealogical Society, *St. Louis City Ward Maps,* previously cited.

The 1820 assessment book had the following categories followed by the total in whole dollars:[414]

- Vacant lots
- Houses and lots
- Commonfield lots
- Breweries
- Tan-yards
- Slaves
- Horses
- Mules
- Geldings
- Cattle
- Goods and merchandise

The list provides one line for each piece of property. While most taxpayers' names appeared on one or two lines, some prominent, wealthy citizens owned enough property to fill an entire page. John Shackleford, John Mullanphy, William Clark, and Auguste Chouteau are a few examples.

Tax books are available for most years; thus our ancestors had to pay taxes yearly, just like we do. Property owners in the 1800s appealed their taxes. Notations indicate if the Court of Appeals reduced the property valuation for some.

As time progressed, the tax lists name the taxpayer, the street address (as used then) or the name of the village, such as St. Ferdinand. Due to the growth in the area by 1825, the alphabetical tax lists are divided by townships. Tax bills indicate the City block number for the City dwellers. The tax bill may include a wide variety of information including the following:[415]

- City block number
- Book and page number for property transfer
- Number of the bill
- Date of bill
- Name of property owner
- Number of the lot
- Frontage
- Property description (North, East, South, West)
- Character of work
- Name of contractor
- Amount of bill
- Date paid
- Remarks
- Notations

---

414. List of Assessment of the Corporation and Precincts of the Town of St. Louis for the Year 1820; FHL film 980,602.

415. Miscellaneous Records; FHL film 981,653 and City Archives film F538. Likewise the 1844 Real Estate Tax list is on FHL film 980,604 and Missouri State Archives film C2664.

St. Louis City sewer tax records are available for 1853–1855. This difficult-to-read handwritten journal source is divided by sewer districts. It lists the property owners, street name, frontage, depth, and description of the lot. The document lists the value per foot, value of the lot, and value of the improvements, plus the tax assessment. Arranged by city block numbers, the lists provide the property owner's name. It is necessary to know the city block number of the subject property in order to use this record efficiently.[416] This makes it easier for researchers to locate their ancestors. However, some records are easy to read; others are not. These records are available at the Family History Library, some at the City Archives, and some at the Missouri State Archives.

Tax Lists, City of St. Louis:

- 1818–1944 Assessor's Office, Real Estate tax; FHL films starting with 980,602

- 1819–1952 Comptroller's Office, Miscellaneous Real Estate tax; City Archives films starting with C2660

- 1824–1970 Comptroller's Office Personal Property Abstracts of Tax bills; City Archives films starting with A381

- 1824–1970, Comptroller and Assessor's Office, abstracts of tax books and real estate assessments; City Archives films starting with A401

- 1849–1851 Collector's Office, account, real estate assessments and collections 1860–1863, personal property and poll tax, 1862–1866 for Carondelet; FHL films 981,656–981,657

- 1853 Comptroller's Office, account books of collection of taxes, real and personal property, comptroller's office; FHL film 981,642

- 1853–1904 Special Tax, index cards arranged by city block; FHL films 1,001,239–1,001,240

- 1859–1862 Collector's Office, account, city revenue 1851–1870 record of real estate sales, 1859 for Carondelet; FHL film 981,656

- 1861–1922 Special tax bills, FHL 981,653 and City Archives films F535 and F539

- 1863 special tax for improvements of alleys; City Archives film B550

- 1863–1864 Delinquent tax claims for Carondelet; FHL film 981,654, City Archives film F119

- 1864–1865 Assessor's Office, individual tax bills; FHL film 1,005,420

- 1869–1876 Special tax for alleys; City Archives film B557

- 1869–1881 Comptroller's Office, 72 rolls beginning with FHL film 981,637, City Archives films starting with C72.

Court, election, and tax records are not easy to use; however, they may provide information unavailable in other documents. Start with the other records and progress to these.

---

416.   St. Louis City Tax Records for Sewers 1853–1855; Missouri State Archives film C13433, and City Archives film F93.

Historic Homes, Museums, & Parks

S t. Louis has many interesting and noteworthy homes, museums, and parks full of history. Perhaps your ancestor lived in one of these historic homes or visited the museums or parks. Books and articles provide information on many of these places.

Many homes on historic streets provide interesting facts about the families that lived there and about the houses themselves. Books and articles describe many of these homes and some websites offer photos of St. Louis property: the good, bad, and ugly.[417] One website has a map showing the location of each house in the City of St. Louis.[418] Some publications offer historical information about St. Louis structures as well as those in other parts of the metropolitan area.[419]

Julius Hunter authored *Kingsbury Place: The First Two Hundred Years,* sharing the genealogy and details of each house on that street.[420] He then shared the tales about two beautiful streets in the City's Central West End, Westmoreland and Portland Place.[421] St. Louis Landmarks Association focuses on these same streets in some of their publications.[422] *Terrace Tales,* by Jeff Tallent, provides details and photographs of the homes on Washington Terrace.[423] All of these

---

417. Elinor Coyle, *Old St. Louis Homes, 1764–1865: The Stories They Tell* (St. Louis: Folkstone Press, 1964). George Lipsitz, *The Sidewalks of St. Louis: Places, People, and Politics in an American City* (Columbia: University of Missouri Press, 1991).

418. *Built St. Louis* (http://www.builtstlouis.net).

419. St. Louis Regional Commerce and Growth Association, *Mounds to Mansions: Historical Sites of the St. Louis Region* (St. Louis: RCGA, 1976). Timothy J. Fox, editor, *Where We Live: A Guide to St. Louis Communities* (St. Louis: Missouri Historical Society Press, 1995).

420. Julius K. Hunter, *Kingsbury Place: The First Two Hundred Years* (St. Louis: C. W. Mosby Company, 1982).

421. Julius K. Hunter, *Westmoreland and Portland Places; The History and Architecture of America's Premier Private Streets, 1888–1988* (Columbia: University of Missouri Press, 1988).

422. Carolyn Hewes Toft, *St. Louis Landmarks and Historic Districts* (St. Louis: Landmarks Association, 2002).

423. Jeff Tallent, *Terrace Tales: A Contemporary History of Washington Terrace, Street of Mansions* (St. Louis: Finbar Company, 1992).

books list each house and all of its owners. Other books provide information about the architecture of private homes.[424]

Chronicled in *Parkview: A St. Louis Urban Oasis, 1905–2005,* this neighborhood is situated on the City Limits and is part of the City of St. Louis and St. Louis County in the University City municipality. The neighborhood includes the streets of McPherson, Pershing, Washington, Waterman, Westgate, and Westminster. The publication provides photographs and a list of the property owners from 1905 to 2005, the architect, the builder, and date of construction.[425]

Meet Me on Enright consists of two volumes, one describing the homes and the other about the residents of the Enright neighborhood.[426]

Gaslight Square, formerly located in the 4200 block of Olive in the 1960s was a unique dining and nightclub location, is another area that may be mentioned in your more contemporary family history. Many St. Louis residents visited Gaslight Square at least once, if not more often. Thomas Crone, author of *Gaslight Square, an Oral History,* interviewed those who worked and played in this unique area of St. Louis.[427]

Where We Live, published by the Missouri Historical Society provides information on many communities and neighborhoods in St. Louis.[428] This publication started as a series of bi-monthly brochures published from 1992 to 1994, providing information on neighborhoods in the St. Louis area.[429] Available titles are:

- Carondelet
- Central West End/ DeBaliviere Place
- Cherokee/ Lemp
- Fairgrounds & O'Fallon Park
- Ferguson
- Florissant
- Forest Park
- Forest Park Southwest
- Hyde Park
- Kirkwood
- Manchester
- Midtown
- Near South Side
- Penrose
- Shaw
- Skinker/ DeBaliviere
- Soulard
- The Hill
- The Ville
- University City
- Webster Groves

424. Charles Savage, *Architecture of the Private Streets of St. Louis* (Columbia: University of Missouri, 1987). Lawrence Lowic, *The Architectural Heritage of St. Louis, 1803–1891 from the Louisiana Purchase to the Wainwright Building* (St. Louis: Washington University Gallery of Art, 1982).

425. Mary Henderson Gass, Jean Fahey Eberle, and Judith Phelps Little, *Parkview: A St. Louis Urban Oasis, 1905–2005* (St. Louis: Virginia Press, 2005).

426. Enright Neighbors Association, *Meet Me on Enright,* 2 volumes (St. Louis: The Association, no date).

427. Thomas Crone, *Gaslight Square, an Oral History* (St. Louis: William and Joseph Press, 2004).

428 Tim Fox, *Where We Live: A Guide to St. Louis Communities* (St. Louis: Missouri Historical Society Press, 1995).

429. Missouri Historical Society, *Where We Live* (St. Louis: Missouri Historical Society, 1992–1994). The individual publications outline one neighborhood per brochure.

HISTORIC BUILDINGS

Historic Building Survey St. Louis County, Missouri, 1965–1966 catalogs some of the early St. Louis County farms, homes, and churches.[430] The inventory provides the type of construction, location, often with a map, and the name of the original and current (1965) property owners, and property use. In the twenty-first century, private individuals own many of the homes and buildings.[431]

Missouri Historical Society's two-volume publication, *Old Public Buildings,* includes information on St. Louis buildings dating from the 1920s to 1977. The Saint Louis Old Post Office (815 Olive Street) was built in 1884, originally the home of the federal Custom House and Court House. The courtrooms closed in 1935 when the new federal building was available at Twelfth and Market. The Old Post Office is still operational today, but it has a long history ranging from a premier office building to being at risk of the wrecking ball. If your ancestor lived in St. Louis around the turn of the century, he or she probably had reason to visit this building from time to time. In 1968, it was designated a National Historic Landmark. Today the building has a variety of tenants from education, Missouri Court of Appeals, restaurants, and more. Further information on this historic building is available online and in print.[432]

St. Louis had many interesting hotels in the nineteenth and early twentieth centuries, including the Barnum's Hotel, Planter's House, and Southern Hotel.[433] In the era before television, St. Louis residents found entertainment and friends at Casa Loma Ballroom, which is still open today.[434]

Historic Florissant maintains their collection of photographs and documents at the Gittemeier House. This organization specializes in preserving historic homes and other buildings in the Florissant area.

Sports are an important part of the St. Louis community and have been for many years. Baseball came to the area in the nineteenth century and today brings the community together

---

430.   Kenneth E. Coombs, *Historic Building Survey St. Louis County, Missouri, 1965–1966* ([St. Louis]: St. Louis County Commission on Historic Buildings, 1966).

431.   St. Louis County Department of Parks and Recreation, *100 Historical Buildings in St. Louis County* (St. Louis: St. Louis County Parks Department, 1970). St. Louis County Department of Parks and Recreation, *Historic Buildings in St. Louis County* (St. Louis: Parks Department, 1983, 1996). George Lipsitz, *The Sidewalks of St. Louis: Places, People, and Politics in an American City* (Columbia: University of Missouri Press, 1991).

432.   Carolyn Hewes Toft and Osmund Overly, *The Saint Louis Old Post Office: A History and Architectural Guide to the Building and its Neighborhood* (St. Louis: Landmarks of St. Louis, 1979). "The St. Louis Old Post Office and Custom House," *Your Missouri Courts* (http://www.courts.mo.gov/page.asp?id=3502).

433.   Patricia Treacy, *The Grand Hotels of St. Louis* (Charleston, South Carolina: Arcadia Publishing, 2005).

434.   David A. Lossos, *St. Louis Casa Loma Ballroom* (Charleston, South Carolina: Arcadia Publishing, 2005).

more than anything else. Three stadiums: Sportsman's Park, Busch Stadium I, and Busch Stadium II, played an important role in the success of the St. Louis baseball teams.[435]

The 1904 Olympics in conjunction with the World's Fair was another major sporting event in St. Louis history. Many Olympic events took place on the campus of Washington University and on Francis Field, which is a very unassuming structure compared to the massive stadiums of the twenty-first century.[436]

The Old Courthouse (11 North Fourth Street, St. Louis 63102; phone 314-655-1600; http://www.nps.gov/jeff), is part of the Jefferson National Expansion Memorial with a reference library and archival facility. The library is open to the public; however, appointments are preferred. The scope of the library collection includes St. Louis history, westward expansion, Dred Scott and slavery, and the National Park Service. An online catalog is available at the National Park Service website; however, some items, such as the vertical files, are not in the catalog.[437] The bookstores at the Old Courthouse and inside the Arch provide a vast array of publications on St. Louis.[438]

The reference area holds numerous reports about the construction of the Arch including the architectural competition from the 1940s. They have oral interviews from the men who developed the project, politicians who endorsed the plan, engineers, landscapers, park employees, and of course, the construction crew. If your ancestor was involved with the Arch, the interviews may be interesting for family members.[439]

The archival collection includes building histories, some more extensive than others, and photos of exteriors and some interiors of the buildings removed prior to the Arch ground construction, about 1939. In addition to the photos, the collection includes copies of any lawsuits filed regarding this property. If your ancestor lived in one of the buildings destroyed by the park, this collection may provide a glimpse of the structure.

Finding aids provide a list of every name included in the documents in the collection. The finding aids are available online and in book format:

- *Finding Aid to Jefferson National Expansion Monument Research Reports, 1936–1970.* This publication includes reports on the history of the St. Louis area

- *Finding Aid to U. S. Territorial Expansion Memorial Commissions Records, 1933–1973*

- *Finding Aid to Mechanics Institute of St. Louis Records, 1816–1894*

---

435.   Joan M. Thomas, *St. Louis Big League Ballparks* (Charleston, South Carolina: Arcadia Publishing, 2004). Steve Steinberg, *Downtown St. Louis Baseball in: 1900–1925* (Charleston, South Carolina: Arcadia Publishing, 2001).

436.   George Mathews and Sandra Marshall, *St. Louis Olympics, 1904* (Chicago: Arcadia Publishing, 2003). Elana V. Fox, *Inside the World's Fair of 1904: Exploring the Louisiana Purchase Exposition* (St. Louis: The Author, 2003). Bert Minkin, compiler, *Legacies of the World's Fair* (St. Louis: The World's Fair Society, 1998).

437.   *National Park Service* (http://www.mps.gov/Jeff/culture/collections.htm).

438.   Robert J. Moore, *The Old Courthouse Jefferson National Expansion Memorial* (St. Louis: Jefferson National Park Association, 2004). *The Museum of Westward Expansion* (St. Louis: Jefferson National Expansion Historical Association, 1977). Donald F. Dosch, *The Old Courthouse: Americans Build a Forum on the Frontier* (St. Louis: Jefferson National Expansion Historical Association, 1979).

439.   "Oral History Project," *National Park Service* (http://www.nps.gov/jeff/historyculture/oralhistory.htm)

- *Meriwether Lewis Clark Collection*

- *Grace Lewis Miller Papers, 1938–1971*

- *Harold A. Bulger Western Forts Collection*

- *Indian War Widow Project, Records, ca. 1864–1965*

- *Fur Trading Illustration Project, 1845–1948*

The Dred Scott case was by far the event with the greatest impact that took place in the Old Courthouse. Walter Ehrlich wrote an article about the Scott case, "Was the Dred Scott Case Valid?" [440]

HISTORIC HOMES

BISSELL HOUSE (10255 Bellefontaine Road, St. Louis 63137; phone 636-532-7298 [St. Louis County Parks]; http://www.co.st-louis.mo.us/parks/bissell.html) is a historical house built by General Daniel Bissell, a military commander, about 1812 during the territorial era of St. Louis.

CAMPBELL HOUSE (1508 Locust Street, St. Louis 63103; phone 314-421-0325; http://www.campbellhousemuseum.org) provides the history on the Robert Campbell family, about 1850, St. Louis, and lifestyle of the mid-nineteenth century. The Campbell family was involved in fur trading and other businesses. Records are available at the museum.

CHATILLON–DEMENIL MANSION (3352 DeMenil Place, St. Louis 63118; phone 314-771-5828; http://www.demenil.org) houses an extensive collection of 1904 St. Louis World's Fair memorabilia.

EUGENE FIELD HOUSE AND ST. LOUIS TOY MUSEUM (634 South Broadway Street, St. Louis 63102; phone 314-421-4689; http://www.eugenefieldhouse.org/index.html) was the birth place of Eugene Field, the Children's Poet. His father, Roswell Field, was an attorney and instrumental in the Dred and Harriet Scott case. Today the row house is a museum for antique toys and dolls and is designated as a National Historic Landmark.

GITTEMEIER HOUSE (1067 Dunn Road, Florissant 63031; phone 314-921-7055; http://www.historicflorissant.com/about.shtml) provides a museum, resource center, and bookstore operated by Historic Florissant.

MUDD'S GROVE (302 West Argonne Avenue, Kirkwood 63122; phone 314-965-5151; http://www.kirkwoodarea.com/historic/main_frameset.htm) is a Greek Revival home from about 1860 that is on the National Register of Historic Places, operated by the Kirkwood Historical Society.

OAKLAND HOUSE (7801 Genesta Street, Affton 63123; phone 314-352-5654; http://www.afftonoaklandhouse.com), an 1850s vintage home, is owned and restored by the Affton Historical Society.

---

440.   Walter Ehrlich, "Was the Dred Scott Case Valid?" *The Journal of American History* 40 (September 1968).

PAYNE-GENTRY HOUSE (4211 Fee Fee Road, Bridgeton 63044; phone 314-739-5599; http://www.bridgetonmo.com/DesktopDefault.aspx?tabid=60) is located in Bridgeton near Lambert St. Louis International Airport. This restored Victorian house is a good example of a late nineteenth-century structure. The Bridgeton Historical Society maintains its research documents in the house.

SAMUEL CUPPLES HOUSE (3673 West Pine Mall, St. Louis 63103; phone 314-977-3575; http://cupples.slu.edu) is located on the campus of St. Louis University. Records associated with the Cupples house are available through the University.

SAPPINGTON HOUSE (1015 Sappington Road, Crestwood 63126; phone 314-822-8171; http://www.ci.crestwood.mo.us/departments/parks/sapp_house.aspx) originally built by Thomas Sappington about 1808, is one of, if not the, oldest home in St. Louis and today it is a museum, library, and restaurant.

THORNHILL (Faust Park, 15185 Olive Boulevard, Chesterfield 63017; 636-532-7298; http://www.co.st-louis.mo.us/parks/Thornhill.html) is the former home of the second governor of Missouri, Frederick Bates. This residence is the oldest existing home of a Missouri governor. Governor Bates served while St. Charles was the state capital, just down the Missouri River from the governor's home. He reportedly commuted by boat.

WHITE HAVEN (7400 Grant Road, Affton 63123; phone 314-842-3298; http://www .nps.gov/ulsg/index.htm) is a National Historic Site operated by the National Park Service. The library and bookstore contain resources on President U.S. Grant and the Dent Family.

MUSEUMS AND BUILDINGS

CARONDELET HISTORIC CENTER (6303 Michigan Avenue, St. Louis 63111; phone 314-481-6303; http://stlouis.missouri.org/carondelet/history/HisSoc.html) houses a library and museum. This facility also includes the Susan Blow Kindergarten Museum.

CHASE PARK PLAZA HOTEL (212 North Kingshighway Boulevard, St. Louis 63108; phone 314-633-1000; http://www.chaseparkplaza.com) opened in 1922 and operated by the Koplar family with top name entertainment. All U.S. presidents between the 1920s and 1980s stayed at this hotel.[441]

FOX THEATER (527 North Grand Avenue, St. Louis 63103; phone 314-534-1678; http://www.fabulousfox.com/default.aspx) is an icon of St. Louis theaters dating from 1929 to the current day. Ballet, Broadway shows, movies, rock concerts, vaudeville, and special events have graced the stage of the Fox. Family memorabilia may include tickets or playbills for some of these events.[442]

MISSOURI HISTORY MUSEUM (Lindell Boulevard at DeBaliviere Avenue in Forest Park, Post Office Box 11940, St. Louis 63112; phone 314-746-4599; http://www.mohistory .org) displays St. Louis history and artifacts. This museum is part of the Missouri Historical Society.

---

441. Candace O'Conner, *Meet Me in the Lobby: The Story of Harold Koplar and the Chase Park Plaza* (St. Louis: Virginia Publishing Company, 2005).

442. Mary Strauss, *The Fabulous Fox* (St. Louis: The Theater, 1985).

MUSEUM OF WESTWARD EXPANSION (Arch Grounds; http://www.nps.gov/archive/jeff/expansion_museum.html) is a museum inside the Arch. Any associated records are available at the Old Courthouse library.

ST. LOUIS ART MUSEUM (One Fine Arts Drive, St. Louis 63110; phone 314-721-0072; http://www.stlouis.art.museum) is located in Forest Park and was established after the 1904 St. Louis World's Fair.

ST. LOUIS HOLOCAUST MUSEUM AND LEARNING CENTER (12 Millstone Campus Drive, St. Louis 63146; phone 314-442-0020; http://www.hmic.org) includes a chronological list of events between 1933 and 1945 along with a list of refugees.[443]

TRANSPORTATION MUSEUM (3015 Barrett Station Road, Kirkwood 63122; 314-965-7998; http://www.museumoftransport.org) is a museum of transportation vehicles ranging from planes to trains and is owned and operated by St. Louis County Parks Department.[444]

UNION STATION (1820 Market Street, St. Louis 63103; phone 314-421-6655; http://www.stlouisunionstation.com), designated as a National Historic Landmark in 1976, was the largest railroad station in the country in the early to mid-twentieth century. If your ancestors served in World War I or II, or just traveled for pleasure, they probably departed from Union Station. Several publications chronicle the history of this magnificent building.[445]

PARKS

The Forest Park Highlands Amusement Park opened in 1896 and burned down in 1963. The Highlands was an early recreation hub and amusement park in St. Louis, which regularly hosted family outings and school picnics. High school yearbooks mention the Highlands, as do diaries and letters. *Forest Park Highlands* provides photos and narrative about this memorable location in St. Louis.[446]

FOREST PARK (South Kingshighway, St. Louis 63110; phone 314-367-7275; http://stlouis .missouri.org/citygov/parks/forestpark), the premier park in St. Louis, formed in 1876, is larger than Central Park in New York City. Forest Park served as the home of the 1904 World's Fair and Olympics. Many historians theorize that almost all St. Louis citizens in 1904 attended the Fair at least once.[447] Homeowners used lumber from the Fair's

---

443.   Sarah Ogilvie and Scott Miller, *Refuge Denied: St. Louis Passengers and the Holocaust* (Madison, Wisconsin: University of Wisconsin, 2006).

444.   *Collection Highlights of the Transportation Museum* (St. Louis: Transportation Museum Association, 2007).

445.   William F. Handy, *A Historical Guide to Saint Louis Union Station* (St. Louis: Bank Building Corporation, 1975). Norbury Wayman, *St. Louis Union Station and its Railroads* (St. Louis: Evelyn E. Newman Group, 1986). Lesley Barker, *St. Louis Gateway Rail: The 1970s* (Charleston, South Carolina: Arcadia Publishing, 2006). Albert Montesi and Richard Deposki, *St. Louis Union Station* (Chicago: Arcadia Publishing, 2002).

446.   Doug Garner, *Images of America: Forest Park Highlands* (Chicago: Arcadia Publishing, 2007).

447.   Margaret Johanson Witherspoon, *Remembering the St. Louis World's Fair* (St. Louis: Comfort Printing Company, 1973).

demolished structures to build new homes. Fair documentation is available at the Missouri Historical Society and other locations. Today Forest Park includes the Boathouse, Jewel Box, Missouri Historical Society Museum, Municipal Opera (The Muny), St. Louis Art Museum, St. Louis Zoo, and golf courses.[448]

GRANT'S FARM (10501 Gravois Road, Affton 63123; phone 314-843-1700; http://www .grantsfarm.com/GrantsCabin.htm) is the home of Hardscrabble, the historic log cabin home of President U.S. Grant, and across the street from Whitehaven, the Dent and Grant plantation, now operated by the National Park Service.

JEFFERSON BARRACKS HISTORIC PARK (533 Grant Road, St. Louis 63125; phone 314-544-5714; http://www.co.st-louis.mo.us/parks/j-b.html) consists of approximately 450 acres of land that have served as a military outpost and training center. Named in honor of Thomas Jefferson, the Barracks opened in 1826 as the training facility for the Army of the West. Jefferson Barracks played a role during the westward expansion, the Civil War, and on up to World War II. Civil War generals, Robert E. Lee and Ulysses S. Grant, both were stationed at Jefferson Barracks prior to the Civil War. The military abandoned the facility in 1946, calling it surplus. Today the old powder magazine houses the museum. The park rangers and the Friends of Jefferson Barracks Park preserve and interpret the history of the park.

MISSOURI BOTANICAL GARDEN (4344 Shaw Boulevard, St. Louis 63110; phone 314-577-5100; http://www.mobot.org) is a world renowned garden established by Henry Shaw in the 1850s. *The Illustrated History of Missouri Botanical Garden* (http://www .mobot.org/mobot/archives) provides a timeline, history, and important facts about the Garden. The Garden library has the Henry Shaw Collection and the Tower Grove Collection.[449]

ST. LOUIS ZOOLOGICAL PARK (One Government Drive, St. Louis 63110; http://www .stlzoo.org), known as one of the best zoos in the world, it opened before the 1904 World's Fair, and the original bird cage is still in use. Admission is free thanks to the early city fathers and government statutes. Numerous publications describe the Zoo as guests see it.[450] The Zoo has a research facility as well.

TOWER GROVE PARK (4256 Magnolia Avenue, St. Louis 63110; phone 314-771-2679; http://stlouis.missouri.org parks/tower-grove) was a donation to the City by Henry Shaw in 1868.[451]

---

448.   Richard Weiss and Sally J. Altman, *Forest Park: The Jewel of St. Louis* (St. Louis: St. Louis Post-Dispatch, 2007). "Forest Park," *City of St. Louis* (http://stlouis.missouri.org/citygov/parks/forestpark) or (http://www.forestparkforever.org/HTML). Timothy J. Fox, *Where We Live*. Marvin Holdermess, *Curtain Time in Forest Park: A Narrative of the St. Louis Municipal Opera, 1919–1958* (St. Louis: The Muny, 1958). Judith Newmark, *The Muny: Songs of St. Louis* (St. Louis: St. Louis Post-Dispatch, 2007).

449.   William Barnaby Faherty. *A Gift of Glory In The First Hundred Years of the Missouri Botanical Garden, 1859–1959* (Ocean Park, Washington: Harris and Friedrich, 1989).

450.   Zoological Board of Control, *St. Louis Zoological Garden Official Guide Book* (St. Louis: The Zoo Garden, 1939). A map from 1919 shows the Zoo in its early years, "Zoological Park of St. Louis [1919]," *St. Louis Public Library* (http://exhibits.slpl.org/maps/data/dm42512415.asp).

451.   Robert E. Knittel, *Walking in Tower Grove Park: A Victorian Strolling Park* (St. Louis: Grasshopper Press, 1983).

Institutions:
Hospitals, Orphanages, Homes, & Prisons

Various types of institutions produce records on a daily basis. These records are of interest to genealogists and may help determine the lifestyle of one or more of your ancestors. Some of these records are available to the public; however, others are closed. Closed records include mental health facilities, orphanages, and recent records from all institutions.

Prison records are an example of records open to the public. The more than one hundred sixty year old Missouri State Penitentiary opened in 1835 and closed in 2004 leaving records covering more than 160 years to the Missouri State Archives.[452] The records include the register of inmates, 1836–1931, and the penal records index, 1837–1939. Both are currently available in paper format and may be online in the future.[453]

HOSPITALS

The Missouri Historical Society Research Library has a bound volume of newspaper clippings titled, *St. Louis Hospitals,*[454] which includes articles about local hospitals dating from the 1930s to the 1970s.

The 1849 cholera epidemic strained physicians and hospitals. Those that could temporarily moved to areas outside the City limits during that summer. The possibility of contracting cholera while living in the City was much higher compared to those living in the more rural areas.

Listed below are known hospitals and dispensaries. While records may or may not be available for the facility of interest to you, the listed location or affiliation may lead to other records or identifying clues. Death registers and certificates may identify these facilities as a place of death. The hospital location may be a clue to an unknown place of residence.

---

452. "Missouri State Penitentiary," *Welcome to Jefferson City* (http://www.visitjeffersoncity .com/historic_stateprison.html).

453. "Penitentiary Records," *Missouri State Archives* (http://www.sos.mo.gov/archives/resources/ penitentiary.asp).

454. *St. Louis Hospitals* (St. Louis: Missouri Historical Society, no date).

Some St. Louis residents may have been patients at the State Mental Hospital in Fulton, Missouri. The hospital opened in 1849. The Missouri State Archives website offers the history and photographs of the hospital, *Quest for a Cure: Care and Treatment in Missouri's First Mental Hospital* (http://www.sos.missouri.gov/archives/exhibits/quest/intro.asp); however, the patient records are not open to the public.

St. Louis County Hospital, established in 1931, was the first of many to locate in the County. This is just another indicator of the population shift from the City to the County.

The *St. Louis Medical Society*, previously mentioned, also provides a history and summary for the hospitals as of the publication date, 1939.[455] A timeline provides details about numerous hospitals in St. Louis.[456]

Dispensaries

- Children's Free Hospital Dispensary, established in 1885, was located at Jefferson Avenue and Adams Street.
- Good Samaritan Homeopathic Dispensary, established in 1896, was located at Jefferson Avenue and O'Fallon Street.
- Grand Avenue Free Dispensary, established in 1890, was located at Grand Avenue and Caroline Street. It was affiliated with the Marion-Sims Medical College at the same location.
- O'Fallon Dispensary, established in 1882, located at 18th and Locust Streets, was established for free medical assistance.
- St. Louis Dispensary, established in 1877, located on Market Street, near 11th Street in City Hall, provided treatment and medication for the poor. The service was popular with the citizens. An ambulance service started, and by 1896 two branch facilities were in place, one in North City and the other in South City.
- St. Louis Homeopathic Dispensary, established in 1895, located at Jefferson Avenue and Howard Street, was affiliated with the Homeopathic Medical College.
- St. Louis Polyclinic Dispensary, established in 1885, was located at Jefferson and Lucas Avenues.

Hospitals

- Alexian Brothers Hospital, founded in 1870, now located at 2645 Keokuk Street, was formerly located at Broadway Avenue and Osage Street. The hospital is affiliated with St. Louis University and is currently called St. Alexius Hospital.
- Barnes Hospital, founded in 1892, was first located on Garrison Avenue between Glasgow Street and Sheridan Avenue, then moved to its current location on Kingshighway Boulevard in 1912. Since a merger with Jewish Hospital, the facility has been called Barnes-Jewish Hospital.
- Bethesda Hospital, established in 1889, was located at 12th Street and Soulard Street. As Bethesda Maternity, it moved to 3649 Vista Street in 1900.
- Cardinal Glennon Hospital, established in 1956, is located at 1465 South Grand Avenue in St. Louis.[457]
- Christian Hospital, established in 1900 on North Grand Avenue, moved to 4511 North Newstead Avenue in 1924, and eventually to its current location, 11133 Dunn Road in North St. Louis County.

---

455.   *St. Louis Medical Society*, previously cited.

456.   "St. Louis and Washington University 19th Century Timeline," *Bernard Becker Medical Library Digital Collection* (http://beckerexhibits.wustl.edu/mowihsp/stlwu/19thTimeline.htm).

457.   *SSM Cardinal Glennon Children's Hospital* (St. Louis: The Hospital, 2004).

- City Hospital, chartered in 1845 closed in 1980, was formerly located at 14th Street and Lafayette Avenue. The register, starting in 1875, provides an alphabetical list of patients. Some of these records are difficult to read.[458]
- City Infirmary, also called the Poor House and Poor Farm, was formed in 1840. It was eventually located at 5600 Arsenal Avenue along with the City Sanitarium. This facility was called the St. Louis County Insane Asylum before 1876 and St. Louis Insane Asylum after 1876.
- Deaconess Hospital was founded in 1889 by the Evangelical churches in St. Louis. The hospital had several locations 1) 14th and Carr Streets, 2) Sarah Street and West Belle Place, and 3) Oakland and Hampton Avenues, which has been the home of this hospital since 1930, now called Forest Park Hospital.
- DePaul Hospital, established in 1828 is currently located at 12303 DePaul Drive in Bridgeton. It was formerly located at 2415 North Kingshighway Boulevard, and was operated by the St. Vincent de Paul Society until 1977.
- Female Hospital, formerly the House of Industry, opened in 1872 and was razed in 1915.[459]
- Firmin-Desloge Hospital, founded by 1932 on Grand Avenue, is now part of St. Louis University Hospital.
- Frisco Hospital, founded in 1899 at 4960 Laclede Street, cared for railroad employees.
- Good Samaritan Hospital, founded in 1858 by the Evangelical churches, was originally located at 16th and Carr Streets. The hospital expanded and moved to Jefferson Avenue and O'Fallon Street in 1861. The hospital was used by the Union Army during the Civil War and in later years was sometimes called the Good Samaritan Altenheim or "Old People's Home."
- Homer G. Phillips, founded in 1919 as City Hospital 2, moved in 1937 to 2601 Whittier Street and changed its name to Homer G. Phillips Hospital.[460] This facility closed as a hospital in 1979.[461]
- Jewish Hospital, original location was at 5415 Delmar Boulevard, with the move to its current location in 1919. The hospital merged with Barnes forming the Barnes-Jewish Hospital complex.[462]
- Koch Hospital, located about one mile south of Jefferson Barracks, was originally called Quarantine Hospital. It cared for epidemic patients and later patients with tuberculosis.
- Lutheran Hospital, founded in 1858, was originally located at 7th and Sidney Streets, and moved to Potomac and Ohio Streets by 1883.
- McMillan Hospital, founded in 1926, is now part of the Barnes-Jewish complex and Washington University.
- Missouri Baptist Hospital, established in 1890, was located on Taylor Avenue and is currently located on Ballas Road in West County.[463]

---

458. *St. Louis City Hospital Index*; FHL film 980,608. These same records are available at the St. Louis City Archives.

459. Female Hospital registers and discharges, 1876–1905; FHL film 980,264–980,266.

460. *A Jewel in History: The Story of Homer G. Phillips Hospital, St. Louis, Missouri,* Video Cassette (Berkeley, California: University of California Extension Center for Media and Independent Learning, 2000).

461. "Recalled to Life: Homer G. Phillips Hospital," *Built St. Louis* (http://www.builtstlouis .net/homerphillips.html). "A Short History of Homer G. Phillips Hospital," *Ecology of Absence* (http://www.eco-absence.org/stl/hgp/history.htm).

462. David A. Gee, *Working Wonders: A History of the Jewish Hospital of St. Louis, 1891–1992* (St. Louis: The Hospital, 1992). David A. Gee, *A History of the Jewish Hospital of St. Louis* (St. Louis: The Hospital, 1981). Jewish Hospital 1980–1982 journal; State Historical Society of Missouri.

463. Betty Burnett, *One Hundred Years of Caring: Missouri Baptist Hospital* (Gerald: Patrice Press, 1985). *The Second Century: Missouri Baptist Hospital in Transition* (St. Louis: The Hospital, 1984).

- Missouri Pacific Railway Hospital, established in 1876, was at 1600 California Avenue.[464]
- Mount St. Rose Hospital overlooked the Mississippi River in South City at the intersection of Broadway and Hoffmeister Avenues. This facility cared for patients with tuberculosis.
- Polyclinic Hospital, established in 1885, located at Lucas and Jefferson Avenues, was part of the Missouri Medical College.
- Quarantine Hospital was located on Arsenal Island prior to 1854. About 1867, Quarantine Hospital moved to property south of Jefferson Barracks, was later known as Koch Hospital.
- St. Ann's Lying-in Hospital was a maternity facility established in 1853 and was part of the St. Ann's Widows' Home and Foundling Asylum. This facility, run by the Sisters of Charity, was located at 10th and O'Fallon Streets, then was moved to Page Avenue and Union Boulevard.

  The admission journals, starting in 1853, provide a small amount of information about the children. In most cases, they do not provide names of parents. However, in some years they provide the name "by whom placed" and an address, a name that may be one of the parents. In many cases, one of the parents removed the child after a brief stay. In 1885, the ledger indicates where the child was born, usually St. Louis. Occasionally the name of the adoptive parents is given. The admission's questions were date of entry, name of child, age, baptized, died, and left. It also had a column for "Country" which often had a city or county listed, but more often was left blank.[465]
- St. Anthony's Hospital was located at Grand Avenue at Chippewa in 1893 and is currently located on Tesson Ferry Road in South St. Louis County.
- St. John's Hospital was opened in 1856 and is currently located on Ballas Road in Creve Coeur. The hospital has had various locations including 1) 10th and Morgan Streets, 2) 23rd and Locust Streets, and 3) on Euclid Avenue.
- St. Louis Baptist Hospital, founded in 1893, was located at 19th and Carr Streets. The hospital moved to Garrison and Franklin Avenues in 1896.
- St. Louis Children's Hospital, formed in 1879, was located at 2834 Franklin Avenue, then moved to Jefferson Avenue and Adams Streets before moving to its current location on Kingshighway Boulevard in 1914.
- St. Louis Chronic Hospital was also known as the State Mental Hospital.[466]
- St. Louis City Asylum, originally called St. Louis County Insane Asylum, located on Arsenal Street. The name changed to St. Louis City Sanitarium. Patient lists are available from 1869 to 1911. The name changed again to the St. Louis State Hospital and then to St. Louis Psychiatric Rehabilitation Center.[467]
- St. Louis City Hospital, originally located on Soulard Street and St. Ann Avenue, was formerly located on property used by a cemetery.[468]
- St. Louis County Hospital, established in 1931, located on the North-South Road (now Brentwood Boulevard) was the first hospital in St. Louis County. The facility closed in 1986.

---

464.   Hyde and Conard, *Encyclopedia of St. Louis,* 1: 331, 3: 1056.

465.   St. Ann's Hospital and Founding Home; FHL film 1,987,665.

466.   St. Louis Chronic Hospital, 1912–1968 records; Missouri Historical Society, manuscript collection.

467.   St. Louis State Hospital Records; Missouri Division of Mental Health Library (http://www.mimh.edu/library). [Contact this facility for further information.]

468.   St. Louis City Hospital, registers, 1846–1900, 1927 [Index to registers 1866–1876, 1878–1879 1881–1882, 1884–1886, 1893–1894]; FHL film starting with 980,608.

- St. Louis Hospital was founded in 1828 on Spruce Street between 3rd and 4th Streets. It was later called Mullanphy Hospital. The hospital was the first in St. Louis and was run by the Sisters of Charity. In 1872, the hospital relocated to Montgomery Street near Grand Avenue.[469]
- St. Louis Maternity Hospital was formed in 1908 at 4518 Washington Avenue, then moved to what is now the Barnes-Jewish complex in 1924.[470]
- St. Louis Protestant Hospital, formed in 1883, first occupied a building on 11th Street, then moved to 18th Street near Wash Avenue.
- St. Luke's Hospital was founded in 1865 by the Episcopalians. Numerous locations include 1) Ohio Avenue and Sumner Street, 2) 9th and Pine Streets, 3) 19th Street and Washington Avenue about 1881, and 4) Delmar Boulevard at Belt Avenue about 1900. In 1975 it moved to its current location on Woods Mill Road in Chesterfield.
- St. Mary's Hospital was established on Clayton Road in 1924. This institution was previously called St. Mary's Infirmary, located at 3rd and Mulberry Streets, and then 15th Street near Papin Street.[471]
- Shriners' Hospital was founded 1920 as part of Children's Hospital. Today it is located on South Lindbergh Boulevard.
- U.S. Marine Hospital, originally located on Marine and Miami Streets, was founded in 1847 under the supervision of the Secretary of the Treasury. This facility is now called St. Joseph's Hospital, located in Kirkwood. It is moving to Fenton in 2010 and will be named St. Clare.
- Women's Hospital, established in 1894 was located at the corner of 16th and Pine Streets.

ORPHANAGES AND OTHER HOMES

The Catholic Church opened the first orphanage for boys in 1832 on Walnut, near the location of the Old Cathedral. The Sisters of the Sacred Heart opened an orphanage for girls in 1845 with a facility at 15th and Clark Streets.

The records of the St. Louis House of Refuge, 1854–1899, were indexed by Peggy Greenwood and published by St. Louis Genealogical Society. The index from the entry register called the Journal of Commitments is held at the Missouri Historical Society Research Library.[472]

St. Louis Protestant Orphans' Asylum, 1882–1916, a publication of Missouri Historical Society, provides an index of the names listed on the admission and removal pages.[473] The index includes the child's name, age, and year of admission or removal. Missouri Historical Society Research Library owns the original journals.

---

469.   Hyde and Conard, *Encyclopedia of St. Louis,* 1: 331, 3: 1051.

470.   *St. Louis Maternity Hospital: An Account of Three Years' Service in a New Field, May 1908– May 1911* (St. Louis: The Hospital, 1911). St. Louis Maternity Hospital records 1911–1934, manuscript collection.

471.   *A Half Century of Serving, 1924–1974: Saint Mary's Health Center, 6420 Clayton Road, Richmond Heights, Missouri* (Richmond Heights: St. Mary's Hospital, 1974).

472.   "St. Louis House of Refuge, 1854–1899," *St. Louis Genealogical Society Quarterly* 25 (1992) 45–49, 91–94, 121–124; and 26 (1993): 19–22, 45–48, 81–84.

473.   Dennis Northcott, *St. Louis Protestant Orphans' Asylum, 1882–1916* (St. Louis: Missouri Historical Society, 1995).

The book, *German St. Vincent's Orphans' Society of St. Louis, 1850–1925,*[474] provides a history of one of the largest orphanages in St. Louis. This book does not provide a list of the children. It may, however, provide clues for future research.

- Baptist Orphans' Home, established in 1884 and was formerly located on Morgan Street and in 1906 on Lafayette Avenue.[475]
- Bethesda Foundling Home, established in 1889, operated out of several locations including 1) 917 Russell Avenue, 2) Hickory and Gratten Streets, and 3) 3633 Vista Avenue near Grand Avenue.[476]
- Bethesda Home for Old People, was located at 3660 Rutgers Street in 1926.
- Bethesda Maternity Home, established in 1892, was located at 1814 Schild Street and 1210 Gratten Avenue.[477]
- Blind Girls' Home, founded in 1867, was adopted by the St. Louis Women's Christian Association in 1884. The facility, originally located at 5233 Page Boulevard, relocated to Kirkwood on Washington Avenue in 1916.
- Catherine Springer Home was located at 220 North Spring Avenue.
- Christian Orphans' Home, established by the Disciples of Christ Church in 1889, was located first at 2951 North Euclid Avenue, then moved to 915 Aubert Avenue.[478]
- Colored Orphans' Home is now known as the Annie Malone Children's Home, 2612 Annie Malone Drive.
- Convalescent Home, established by the Evangelical Lutheran Missouri Synod, was located at 4359 Taft Avenue.
- Edgewood Children's Home was located at 7th Street near Franklin Avenue.
- Episcopal Orphans' Home, established in 1843, is the oldest Protestant children's home in St. Louis. It was located on Spruce Street and then at 1711 Grand Avenue at Lafayette Avenue.[479]
- Epworth School for Girls, a Methodist facility is located at 25 East Pacific Avenue, Webster Groves.
- Euclid House was located at 1753 Waverly Place.
- Evangelical Lutheran Children's Society was located at 3619 Iowa Avenue.
- German General Protestant Orphans' Home, formerly located at Cass and O'Fallon Streets and then 4447 Natural Bridge Road. Since 1961, it has been located on Olive Boulevard near Mason Road in Creve Coeur.[480]
- German Protestant Evangelical Orphanage is located at 8240 St. Charles Rock Road, near Overland.[481]

474. *German St. Vincent's Orphans' Society of St. Louis, 1850–1925* (St. Louis: privately printed, 1925).
475. Hyde and Conard, *Encyclopedia of St. Louis,* 1: 87–88.
476. Hyde and Conard, *Encyclopedia of St. Louis,* 1: 146.
477. Hyde and Conard, *Encyclopedia of St. Louis,* 1: 146.
478. Hyde and Conard, *Encyclopedia of St. Louis,* 1: 372–373.
479. Hyde and Conard, *Encyclopedia of St. Louis,* 2: 690–691.
480. Glenn J. Sartori, *Still Caring: The Evolution of a St. Louis Orphanage* (St. Louis: G. J. Sartori, 2003).
481. "History," *Evangelical Children's Home* (http://www.evangelicalchildrenshome.org).

- Girls' Industrial Home, established in 1853, merged with Edgewood Children's Home in 1978. This facility was located at 1) 7th Street and Washington Avenue, 2) 718 North 18th Street, and 3) 5501 Von Verson Avenue.[482]

- Good Samaritan Home for Aged was located at 1217 North Jefferson Avenue.

- Hessoum Bohemian Orphans' Home was located in Fenton from 1906 to 1952.[483]

- Home for Aged and Infirm Israelities was located at 3652 S. Jefferson Avenue.

- Home of the Friendless was located at 4431 South Broadway Boulevard.

- House of the Guardian Angel was operated by the Sisters of Charity.[484]

- Jewish Children's Home, established in 1909, was located at 6630 Oakland Avenue.

- Lutheran Orphans' Home, established in 1868 and closed in 1966, was located on Manchester Road at Ballas Road in Des Peres.[485]

- Masonic Home of Missouri, established in 1889, was located at 5351 Delmar Boulevard near Union Boulevard.[486]

- Methodist Orphans' Home, 1895–1992, was located at 3533 Laclede Street, and then at 4385 Maryland Avenue.[487]

- Missouri Baptist Orphans' Home, established in 1882, is located in Bridgeton at 11300 St. Charles Rock Road.[488]

- Mullanphy Home for Emigrants was located at 1609 North 14th Street.

- Old Peoples' Home, located at 1906 Lafayette Avenue, was established by the Evangelical Lutherans.

- Old Soldiers' Orphan Home, 1865–1869, merged with St. Louis Protestant Orphan.[489]

- St. Ann's Hospital and Foundling Home, 1904–1975, was located on Page Avenue west of Union Boulevard.[490]

- St. Elizabeth's Institute, established in 1882 at 3401 Arsenal by the Sisters' of the Precious Blood.

- St. Francis Home for the Girls was established in 1882 and closed in 1965. It was formerly located at 1) 14th and Morgan Streets, 2) 4538 Page Avenue, and 3) in Normandy.[491]

- St. Joseph's Boys' Orphan Asylum, established in 1835 and operated by the Sisters of St. Joseph, was located at 14th and Clark Streets, then 2701 South Grand Avenue at Delor Street.[492]

---

482. Hyde and Conard, *Encyclopedia of St. Louis,* 2: 898–899. Scharf, *History of St. Louis City and County,* 1761. Also, *Western Historical Manuscript Collection* (http://www.umsl.edu/~whc/guides/whm0058.htm).

483. Rowena L. C. Ch'ien, *Backgrounds and Problems of Families Having Children at Hessoum Bohemian Orphanage in Fenton, Fenton, Missouri, July 1949* (St. Louis: St. Louis County Library, Special Collections, 2004).

484. Hyde and Conard, *Encyclopedia of St. Louis,* 1: 331.

485. Hyde and Conard, *Encyclopedia of St. Louis,* 1: 80–88.

486. Hyde and Conard, *Encyclopedia of St. Louis,* 3: 1368–1369

487. Lisa Mecham, *4385 Maryland in the Central West End* (St. Louis: L. Mecham, 1995).

488. Jo Colay Ray, *These Little Ones: The History of Missouri Baptist Children's Home* (St. Louis: The Home, 1986).

489. *Western Historical Manuscript Collection* (http://www.umsl.edu/~whc/guides/whm0058.htm).

490. St. Louis Catholic Services including, St. Ann's Hospital and Foundling Home; FHL film 1,987,665 and at St Louis County Library.

491. Henry A. McGinnis, *History of St. Francis Home for the Girls, Normandy, Missouri, 1887–1950* (St. Louis: St. Louis County Library Special Collections, 2004). [This dissertation does not provide a list of names. It does provide background information on the facility.]

492. Hyde and Conard, *Encyclopedia of St. Louis,* 4: 1950–1951.

- St. Louis City Foundlings operated from 1886 until 1916.[493]
- St. Louis Protestant Orphan Asylum, 1834–1940, has ledger books dating from 1834 to 1916, are at the Missouri Historical Society Research Library. Microfilmed records are available in the Western Historical Manuscript Collection, including annual reports and admissions and departures, 1842–1913.[494]
- St. Louis Russell Home was located at 1214 Garrison Avenue.
- St. Louis Women's Christian Association, established 1868, located at 1814 Washington Avenue.
- St. Mary's Girls Orphans' Asylum, operated from 1843 to 1952 by the Sisters of Charity, was located at 1) 10th and Biddle Streets, 2) 14th and Clark Streets, and 3) Emerson Avenue and Harney Street. The records have been abstracted.[495]
- St. Philomena's Industrial School was operated, 1834–1970, by the Sisters of Charity, located at 1) 3rd and Walnut Streets, 2) 5th and Walnut Streets, and 3) Clark Street and Ewing Avenue.[496]
- St. Vincent's Institution for the Insane, established in 1858 and operated by the Sisters of Charity, was located at 1) 4th and Spruce Streets, 2) 8th and Marion Streets, and 3) St. Charles Rock Road location, about 1895, in St. Louis County.[497]
- St. Vincent's Orphans' Home, established in 1850, was located on Hogan Street between Cass and O'Fallon Streets.

Records for some Catholic homes and orphanages dating from 1853 to 1929 are available on microfilm including St. Ann's Hospital and Foundling Home and for St. Mary's Orphanage.[498]

PRISONS

During the Civil War, St. Louis was home of the Union-controlled Gratiot Street Prison and the Myrtle Street Prison. Some records for these facilities are available on microfilm at the Missouri Historical Society Research Library. These prisons and some of their inmates were mentioned in the Provost Marshal records as well.

The Missouri State Penitentiary opened in 1836 in Jefferson City. The crimes ranged from murders to stealing to making moonshine. In 1836, one man served more than two years in solitary confinement for stealing a $39 watch. The files are arranged alphabetically by the first letter of the inmate's surname. Another set of files is arranged in chronological order of the court orders committing the prisoners. Another set of records consists of a register by county dating from 1880–1967. This register includes the name, color, age, offense, sentence, remarks, and date the sentence began and ended. All these original records are available at the Missouri State Archives.[499]

---

493.   St. Louis City Foundling Home; FHL film 1,987,664, and at St. Louis County Library.

494.   "St. Louis Protestant Orphans' Asylum records, 1834–1940," *Western Historical Manuscript Collection* (http://www.umsl.edu/~whc/guides/whm0058.htm).

495.   Hyde and Conard, *Encyclopedia of St. Louis,* 4: 1975–1976. Emma Theresa Liebig, *The History of St. Mary's Home for Girls in St. Louis, Missouri, 1843–1948,* master's thesis (St. Louis: privately printed, 1948). St. Mary's Orphanages; FHL film 1,987,665.

496.   Hyde and Conard, *Encyclopedia of St. Louis,* 4: 1976–1977.

497.   Hyde and Conard, *Encyclopedia of St. Louis,* 4: 1977.

498.   St. Louis Catholic Services; FHL films 1,987,662–1,987,665.

499.   "Penitentiary Records;" Missouri State Archives manuscript collection.

Land:
Deeds, Grants, & Patents

Land records are a very valuable genealogical source and are often underutilized. Land records may provide the names of various family members and even prove kinship between parents, children, and sometimes grandchildren. Before the every-name census in 1850, land and probate records may be the only records that provide the names of parents and children.

There are numerous ways for property ownership to change from one person to another. Warranty deeds and quit claim deeds may be the most obvious. Conveyance via a will or probate record was also used by many. Deed books record all transactions held by the office of the Recorder of Deeds.

The Land Ordinance of 20 May 1785 established the township and range land survey system.[500] While Missouri is a public land state and uses the township and range land survey system, some early grants used the metes and bounds system. These land parcels, which are askew from the straight lines of the township and range system, are still obvious on maps today.

Many War of 1812 St. Louis veterans, along with veterans from other areas, were eligible for military bounty land warrants in some parts of Missouri.[501] The Missouri property was west of the Mississippi River and north of the Missouri River. Later the Land Acts of 1850 and 1855 allowed veterans to purchase bounty land wherever property was available.

FRENCH AND SPANISH LAND GRANTS

A microfilm set, *Index to the French and Spanish Archives, 1771–1803,* consists of a card file prepared by the WPA. The card labels indicate they are the St. Louis Recorded Archives Index, WPA NPS Transcription Project for JNEM Files. In other words, the Works Progress Administration prepared the cards, in connection with the National Park Service Transcription Project for the Jefferson National Expansion Memorial.

---

500. Continental Congress, Land Ordinance approval, 20 May 1785, 28: 375.
501. Maxine Dunaway, *Missouri Military Land Warrants, War of 1812* (Springfield: M. Dunaway, 1985).

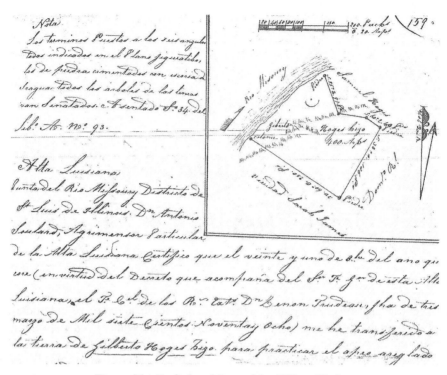

Figure 31: Early Land Record for Gilbert Hodges

Pinpoint the property from land grants and deeds on a map. Figure 31 shows property owned by Gilbert Hodges and Figure 32 shows the same North St. Louis County property outline along the bend in the Missouri River. You can also see several original land grants marked with SUR. [number] on this map.

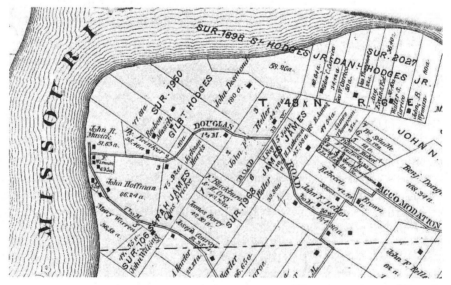

Figure 32: Gilbert Hodges property as shown in 1878 Pitzman's Atlas

The cards provide a variety of information. One lists the name of the person, along with alternative spellings for the surname. Another card lists the same person with the alternative spelling. Each card has columns for the volume, book, page, and instrument numbers, plus an area for remarks. The remark's section indicates the type of record where this person is mentioned, including land transactions, wills, or when listed as a witness. The card may indicate the person's occupation or former place of residence. It also indicates when a person was a grantee or grantor. While the majority of the cards are for men, there are cards for females and free blacks. In this time period, women could own land in their own name.

Example:

Pettier, vol 4, bk 1, pg 186–190, instrument 1402, Dec 20, 1773, buyer of public sale of property to Lammert [—?—] deceased.

There were early French and Spanish land grants with no strings attached. By 1799, immigrants had to agree to support the King of Spain and accept the Catholic Church in order to receive a land grant. (Because of this, you may find a Protestant couple married in the Catholic church.) About this same time, a certificate of survey was required, all of which led to better records for family historians.

The Missouri State Archives microfilm titled "Record of Land Titles or French and Spanish Land Grants" is actually a record of the land claims filed between 1805 and 1829 in volumes A–F, with volume E missing and volume G, dated 1830–1872. The record provides the claim number, the claim statement, and the conclusion along with a survey of the property in question. A printed index provides guidance to this film set.[502]

Example:

James Green, Book A: 256.

Claim 168 – James Green claimed 800 acres

of land in the District of St. Charles

granted by Don Trudeau on 14 January 1799.

LAND MEASUREMENTS

Acre = 43,560 square feet

Arpent = .85 acres

Review the index to see who was buying and selling property at the same time, perhaps with similar names. If you find an entry similar to this, it may be beneficial to print both entries. At the time you review this record, you may not know whether these two men were related, but you will have the documents for a later time. If they have the same name and filed on adjoining pages, it is very likely that they were in the land office at the same time.

James Green, D: 212

John Green, D: 210

Congress decided that fraud was part of the early land claims and appointed a Board of Land Commissioners to review each claim. The owner supplied documents and/or statements regarding his claim. Often witnesses appeared on behalf of the owners. Much of this information is

---

502. Betty Harvey Williams, *Index to French and Spanish Land Grants Recorded in Registers of Land Titles in Missouri* (Warrensburg: B. H. Williams, 1977).

available in the American State Papers.[503] St. Louis Genealogical Society published an index to the minutes of the land commissioners' meetings.[504]

The U.S. Serial Set describes early Missouri land transactions when St. Louis was part of the Louisiana Territory and the Missouri Territory. Two publications to note are the *Land Claims of Missouri, 12th Congress (1812), Document 206*, which describes early land transactions in Missouri and St. Louis,[505] and *Land Claims of Missouri and Arkansas, 19th Congress (1826) House Document 534*, which lists potential land transactions in which the patents were withheld based on the Act of 1815.[506] Both of these books are duplications of the data in the Serial Set, with the addition of an index and some property diagrams.

MISSOURI LAND PATENTS, 1831–1969

The federal government donated millions of acres of land to the state of Missouri. The state in turn sold this land, issuing patents to the new property owner. The Missouri State Archives has an online database listing the name of the grantee, the purchase and patent date, the township and range location, the county, and the number of acres.[507] While property in St. Louis City and County was not included, their citizens purchased property in other parts of Missouri as well. Further information about this process is available in *Missouri Land Claims Proceedings Involving Pioneer Missouri Settlers, 1824–1849.*[508]

ST. LOUIS COUNTY LAND RECORDS, 1804–1876

The Recorder of Deeds office in the St. Louis City Hall has deed records for St. Louis County prior to the City-County separation in 1876. The earliest deed transactions were recorded in French or Spanish. Those transactions were transcribed showing both the English and foreign language versions.

In 1818, surveyors outlined the current St. Louis County boundaries. The surveyors' field notes for each property boundary are available on microfilm. The notes mention claims and land grants.[509]

Oscar W. Collet compiled indexes for early St. Louis deed records. This multi-volume set, divided by the alphabet, has an index for the grantees and another for the grantors. The index provides the grantor's name with his grantees listed below. The list provides the deed book and

503. "American State Papers," *Library of Congress* (http://memory.loc.gov/ammem/amlaw/lwsp.html).

504. St. Louis Genealogical Society, *Index to Minutes of the First and Second Board of Land Commissioners, Missouri 1805–1812, 1832–1835* (St. Louis: The Society, 1981).

505. *Land Claims of Missouri, 12th Congress (1812), House Document 206* (Signal Mountain, Tennessee: Mountain Press, 1999).

506. *Land Claims of Missouri and Arkansas, 19th Congress (1826) House Document 534* (Signal Mountain, Tennessee: Mountain Press, 1999).

507. "Land Patents, 1831–1969," *Missouri State Archives* (http://www.sos.mo.gov/archives/land/#search#search).

508. Charles Butler Barr, *Missouri Land Claims Proceedings Involving Pioneer Missouri Settlers, 1824–1849 in U.S. District Court, Missouri District,* as viewed on FHL film 1,765,087, item 3.

509. Field Notes for St. Louis County; FHL film 981,665 and City Archives film F583.

page number for each transaction, but not the date. All of the land transactions in Collet's index took place before 1876.

The first twenty-six deed book volumes are labeled with letters A to Z. Then the alphabet started over with a superscript number added, for example, A^2, B^2, then on to A^3, B^3. Eventually, the deed books alphabetical indicators and the superscript numbers were replaced by numbers.

JAMES. Samuel

Saml. S. McCullough	C^2 468
Elisha Parke	H^2 528
Mary McCullough.	L^2 92
St. Ferdinand	S^3 125
Same	T^3 366
Barnabas Hanley	U^3 112
Paul Aubuchon	H^4 161
George F. Eichelberger	K^4 136
Eugene Alvarez	N^4 84
Trusten Polk	U^4 257
James Russell	U^4 297
John Cowley	X^4 435
Paul G. Lindsay	Y^4 142
St. Ferdinand	Z^4 199
George F. Eichelberger	A^5 209
Nancy Castello	G^5 189
Michael Castello	B^6 401
John G. James, est.	F^6 351
Edgar B. Forsee*	R...H^6 154

JAMES, Sam'l and wf. Virga. (Robertson)

Jos. Montagne	X^2 273
Pierre Aubuchon, mgee	R..B^3 36
Chas. Kennedy	E^3 33
Andrew Harper	S^3 126
Geo. McCullough	Y^3 594
Presley N. Ross	Z^3 122
Nancy A. James	C^4 539
Bte. Aubuchon	H^4 160
Aberhardt Slarker: Bk. 108 St. Ferd.	P^4 154
Baptiste Hubert, Sur. 125, St. Ferd	Z^4 200
Eugene Alvarez	G^5 189
John F. Baber	R^5 389
Fcis. Mollering	B^6 401
Fcis. Aubuchon	F^6 283
Julia James	N^6 459
James Castello	P^6 219
Geo. Robertson	R^6 478
Edgar B. Forsee	U^6 501

Figure 33: Grantee Index for Samuel James   *Figure 34: Grantor Index for Samuel James*

This example shows that Samuel James had numerous land transactions as the purchaser or grantee shown in Figure 33. You can see the deed book letter and the attached superscript number followed by the page number listed in the Collet's index.

Men could buy land in their name alone, but when they sold land their wife was usually listed. As the grantor, a man needed a dower's release from his wife. Here is a list of land transactions for Samuel James and his wife Virginia (Robertson) James, called Virga in the record, as sellers or grantors in Figure 34. Sometimes the woman's maiden name is included, other times it is not.

Many of these people involved in these transactions are relatives. By reviewing all of the documents you will most likely find new information and prove family relationships. Grantors often named and identified their children in the deeds, sometimes even grandchildren. If you review each land transaction listed for your ancestor, you will be pleasantly surprised.

There were problems with the index. As an example, the name of the wife of the grantor may or may not be listed.[510] The following statement from a brochure distributed by the Recorder of Deeds office in the City of St. Louis, describes the problems with the index. This article was transcribed and used with written permission from the Recorder of Deeds.

INDEX PROBLEMS

In Colonial St. Louis (1764–1803) people lived, worked, played, and worshipped under French and Spanish laws and customs and frontier Catholicism. It was North America without English Common Law and Puritan ways. For forty years, many St. Louisans shared the right to buy or sell, borrow or lend, inherit or bequeath, sue or be sued, regardless of gender, race, age, marital status, parentage. The "Americans" arrived in 1804, after the Louisiana Purchase, and brought cultural and legal changes which removed rights and opportunities afforded to women, children, and people of color under French-Spanish rule.

Researchers will notice the margin note "No Index Card" on many microfilmed pages of early St. Louis records. These records were indexed mid-19th century by Oscar W. Collet. In his day, women, children, and people of color had little legal status. Subsequently and unfortunately, he often dismissed their history by omitting their names from his indexes. Using Collet's indexes alone, St. Louis history becomes the story of primarily only white men. Researchers will also notice the peculiar fifty-year-old indexing of Incorporation Records. Groups may be found under "The," or a company under the first initial of a founder's name.

The Recorder of Deeds conducts research within a limited budget to extract a truer history of St. Louis. Many extraordinary records, otherwise unknown because of the original indexing, are discovered in the course of providing regular customer services. In time, new indexing and computerization will provide greater public access to these historical records.[511]

Microfilms of the deed records prior to 1832 are available at local repositories. Microfilm of the direct deed indexes dating from 1804 to 1895 and the indirect deed indexes from 1804 to 1900 are also available at the repositories. Microfilms of deeds after 1832 are available only at City Hall and at the Family History Library.

ST. LOUIS CITY LAND RECORDS, 1877–PRESENT

The Recorder of Deeds office in the St. Louis City Hall has deed records for the City of St. Louis since 1877. If you have access to the deed indexes and you know the approximate era of the land transactions, you may be able to locate the deed. Deed indexes are available at City Hall and at the Family History Library.

---

510. Oscar W. Collet, compiler, *Collet's General Index to St. Louis County Archives* (St. Louis: Globe-Democrat, 1876). Oscar W. Collet, *Index to Instruments Affecting Real Estate Recorded in the Office of Recorder of Deeds in the County of St. Louis, Missouri: Grantees* (St. Louis: Globe-Democrat Job Printing Company, 1876). Oscar W. Collet, *Index to Instruments Affecting Real Estate Recorded in the Office of Recorder of Deeds in the County of St. Louis, Missouri: Grantors* (St. Louis: Globe-Democrat Job Printing Company, 1876).

511. *Archives Services: Nearly 250 Years of St. Louis History Thru Public Records,* Recorder of Deeds, City of St. Louis. The Recorder of Deeds granted permission to use this quote.

When researching your family history, land records are often an important part of the process. Land records tell us when and where a person owned land and usually where that person lived. Deed records may also indicate the previous county and state where a person resided. Sometimes family historians know when a land transaction took place. Others only know the location of the property.[512] City directories provide St. Louis researchers the opportunity to identify their ancestors' street addresses over a period of several years.

To locate your ancestor's deed or to trace the history of the property located in the City of St. Louis, go to the assessor's office in City Hall, room 114.

Step 1: With a tablet in hand, record the street address in question. Locate the subject address in the *Street Address Directory* located on top of the center island. The directory provides important information; the city block, a nearby cross street, the name of the subdivisions, if any, and possibly some history about the street.

While the street name may change, the city block remains the same. Several research facilities have a St. Louis map showing the city blocks by numbers.

Step 2: After locating and recording the information in the *Street Address Directory*, locate the city block maps on the counter on the east side of the room. Locate the street address on the page with the block number. Record the lot number, dimensions of the lot, and the property description. The description should remain the same on all transactions or explain the difference. For example, one neighbor may purchase part of another neighbor's property, thus changing the dimensions of both properties.

The staff updates the plat map after each sale with the name of the new owner, the date of the sale, and the book and page number of the transaction. Record this information on your tablet.

Step 3: Using the book number for the most recent transaction, locate the book or the microfiche containing that information. The more recent books are located in the center island, older books are available on microfiche. The more recent microfiche is on the south counter and the older books are on the east counter. It is easy to locate the correct microfiche by finding the book number in the fiche header.

Step 4: On your tablet, record the same information again. You need the name of the grantor, and the book and page number. Verify that you are still in the same city block number with the correct address. Record the grantor and grantee.

Repeat this process until you reach your ancestor as the grantor and grantee. Now it is time to move to room 127 which is the office of the Recorder of Deeds. The staff will review your information and help you locate the correct deed.

If your interest is in the house history, not a particular owner, this process provides all of the property owners over the years. The assessor's office lists the grantors and the people that paid the taxes on the property. Renters or others may have lived on the property over the years.

---

512.   James R. Kimmey, *House History in St. Louis: A Guide to Research on Real Estate and Building History* (St. Louis: privately printed, 1991). Edna Campos Gravenhorst, *Historical Home Research in the City of St. Louis* (St. Louis: E. C. Gravenhorst, 2003).

ST. LOUIS COUNTY LAND RECORDS 1877–PRESENT

St. Louis County Library, Special Collections has St. Louis County deeds on microfilm starting in 1877, continuing to 1931. Each of the more than 1,100 volumes has an index; however, no name index for the entire period exists. The deed indexes are available on CD-ROMs.

For further information on land records, read Hatcher's, *Locating Your Roots: Discover Your Roots Using Land Records*.[513] Other information is available at the Bureau of Land Management (http://www.glorecords.blm.gov).

TERMS FOR LAND RECORDS

Direct = seller or grantor

Grantee = buyer

Grantor = seller

Indirect index = buyer or grantee index

Inverted index = buyer or grantee index

---

513.   Patricia Law Hatcher, *Locating Your Roots: Discover Your Roots Using Land Records* (Cincinnati: Betterway Books, 2003).

Marriage & Divorce Records

While marriage and divorce records go hand in hand, they are the responsibility of different record keepers in Missouri. The Recorder of Deeds maintains the marriage documents and the Circuit Court is responsible for divorce records.

ST. LOUIS CITY HALL

RECORDER OF DEEDS OFFICE (City Hall, Archives Department, Room 127; phone 314-622-4610; http://stlouis.missouri.org/citygov/recorder) maintains and houses the marriage records. Researchers may visit City Hall or send requests by mail.

CIRCUIT COURT OFFICE (Civil Courts Building, 1st floor; phone 314-622-4405) stores some records offsite. Contact the clerk to order records prior to your visit for the most efficient use of your time.

ST. LOUIS COUNTY GOVERNMENT CENTER

RECORDER OF DEEDS OFFICE (Administration Building; phone 314-615-3747; http://revenue.stlouisco.com/RecorderOfDeeds) houses marriage records. They will search for and mail most copies, eliminating the need for an onsite visit.

CIRCUIT COURT RECORDS (Courts Building; phone 314-615-8015; http://stlouisco.com/circuitcourt/circlerk.html) includes an online searchable database that has some, but not all divorces.

MARRIAGE

Marriage laws have been in effect since the Louisiana Purchase and the territorial days. Louisiana District marriage laws required males to be 17 years old and females 14, "unless prohibited by the laws of God." Males under 21 and females under 18 were required to obtain the consent of their fathers if living, or mothers if living in the Louisiana District.[514]

Starting in 1865, the Missouri legislature enacted private laws legalizing certain marriages. This included divorced individuals and those not fully complying with the state law.

The state of Missouri adopted new marriage laws in 1881. A marriage license was not required in Missouri prior to 1881. Marriage registers consisted of a two or three line statement

---

514. *Louisiana District Law, 1805,* 65–67.

listing the date, name of the bride, groom, and official. On 26 March 1881, the state legislature passed an act requiring a license.[515] The marriage application began at the same time. After 1881, verbal or written parental consent was legal. After 1919, the state required a written statement. The written consent included the signature and place of residence of the parent or guardian.[516] Common-law marriage was still valid until 1921.[517] When researching an ancestor's marriage, request all related documents including: license, application, and parental consent.

Bridal couples may use their marriage license in any county in Missouri. Therefore, a person could apply for a marriage license in one county and marry in another. After the marriage ceremony, the clergy returned the license to the original county for filing. For many years, the couple filed their application and then had to wait three days before they could pick up the license. This was often an inconvenience for the bridal couple.

The law indicated the wording on the license:

> *This license authorizes any judge, justice of the peace, licensed or ordained preacher of the gospel, or other person authorized under the laws of the State, to solemnize marriage between A. B. of _____ county of _____ and State of _____ who is_ [groom]_the age of 21 years, and C. D., of _____ in the county _____, State of Missouri, who is _[bride]_ the age of eighteen years.*

One St. Louis couple who were completing their college education in the state of Kansas with a wedding date just days away in St. Louis, decided to apply for their Missouri marriage license in Kansas City the week before the wedding so that they could comply with the three-day waiting requirement. While they were moving back to St. Louis just two days before the wedding, they stopped in Kansas City, picked up their marriage license, and proceeded home. On one Saturday in May, the marriage took place in St. Louis County and the clergy and witnesses signed the license. The clergy mailed the license to Kansas City. Future genealogists may not understand why this native-born St. Louis couple filed their marriage license in Kansas City, even though they married in St. Louis.

In 1943, the law required a blood test prior to marriage. The couple had to make application and submit to the blood test, then wait three days before they could marry. Missouri eliminated the blood test and in August 2007 eliminated the three-day waiting period.

Marriage records vary over time, but some are available as early as the late 1700s up to the time of the Louisiana Purchase in 1803. Marriage registers started in 1804 and continued to 1881. The information in those records is limited, usually just a two-line handwritten statement naming the bride and groom, the date, and name of the clergy or justice of the peace. If needed, the license lists the name of the parent providing consent.

---

515. *Laws of Missouri, Thirty-First General Assembly,* 1881, 161, section 1.

516. *Laws of Missouri, Fiftieth General Assembly* (Jefferson City: Secretary of State, 1919), 494, section 1.

517. *Laws of Missouri, Fifty-First General Assembly* (Jefferson City: Secretary of State, 1921), 468, section 1, (7302).

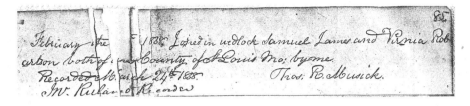

Figure 35: Samuel James & Virginia Robertson, 1838 marriage record

If you can not locate a post-1948 marriage or divorce record in St. Louis, contact the Missouri Vital Records' Office (Vital Records, Post Office Box 570, Jefferson City 65102; phone 573-751-6387;   http://www.dhss.mo.gov/BirthAndDeathRecords/applications.html#MD).   This office maintains a state-wide index for marriage and divorce records starting on 1 July 1948. To utilize this index, submit the online application form available on their website.

The Missouri legislature passed a law in 1865 allowing former slaves to marry and to provide a means for the legitimizing of all children born before the marriage. The officials who performed the ceremonies between 1865 and 1879, recorded the marriages with the Recorder of Deeds. The document usually recorded the name and age of the couple and each of their children.[518]

ST. LOUIS COUNTY — BEFORE 1877

Marriage contracts were popular among the French inhabitants in the late 1700s and early 1800s. They are available on microfilm and included in Collet's index. If the husband or wife died, the marriage contract may be included in the probate packet.

St. Louis used the marriage register, previously mentioned, in the mid-1800s. Listed alphabetically by male or female, the pre-1883 indexes are available on microfilm. The St. Louis Genealogical Society has a printed index dating from 1804 to 1876, covering the time when the City and County split.[519] An additional printed index is available from 1877 to 1881 for City records.[520] St. Louis marriages are available on microfilm via the Family History Library. Records dated 1883 or before are available at local libraries.

A printed index for early Catholic marriages dating from 1774 to 1840 provides the name of the bride and groom and often the name of their parents.[521] This index includes many of the early French settlers and other early residents.

---

518. *Laws of the State of Missouri, Twenty-Third General Assembly* (Jefferson City: W. A. Curry, 1865), 68, sections 1–4.

519. St. Louis Genealogical Society, *Index to St. Louis, Missouri, Marriages: Volume I, 1804–1859, Volume II, 1860–1876* (St. Louis: The Society, 1999).

520. Edward Mochel, *Index to Marriages Recorded in the City of St. Louis, Marriages 1 January 1877–31 December 1880* (O'Fallon: E. F. Mochel, 2001).

521. St. Louis Genealogical Society, *Catholic Marriage Saint Louis, Missouri, 1774–1840* (St. Louis: The Society, 1982).

ST. LOUIS CITY — AFTER 1876

In 1881, the state marriage law changed, as did the marriage documents. At that time the new law required a marriage application and license. The marriage applications provide the signature of the bride and groom and usually their street addresses. When requesting a post-1881 marriage license, also request a copy of the marriage application. Some parental consent affidavits, 1881–1920, are available at St. Louis City Hall.

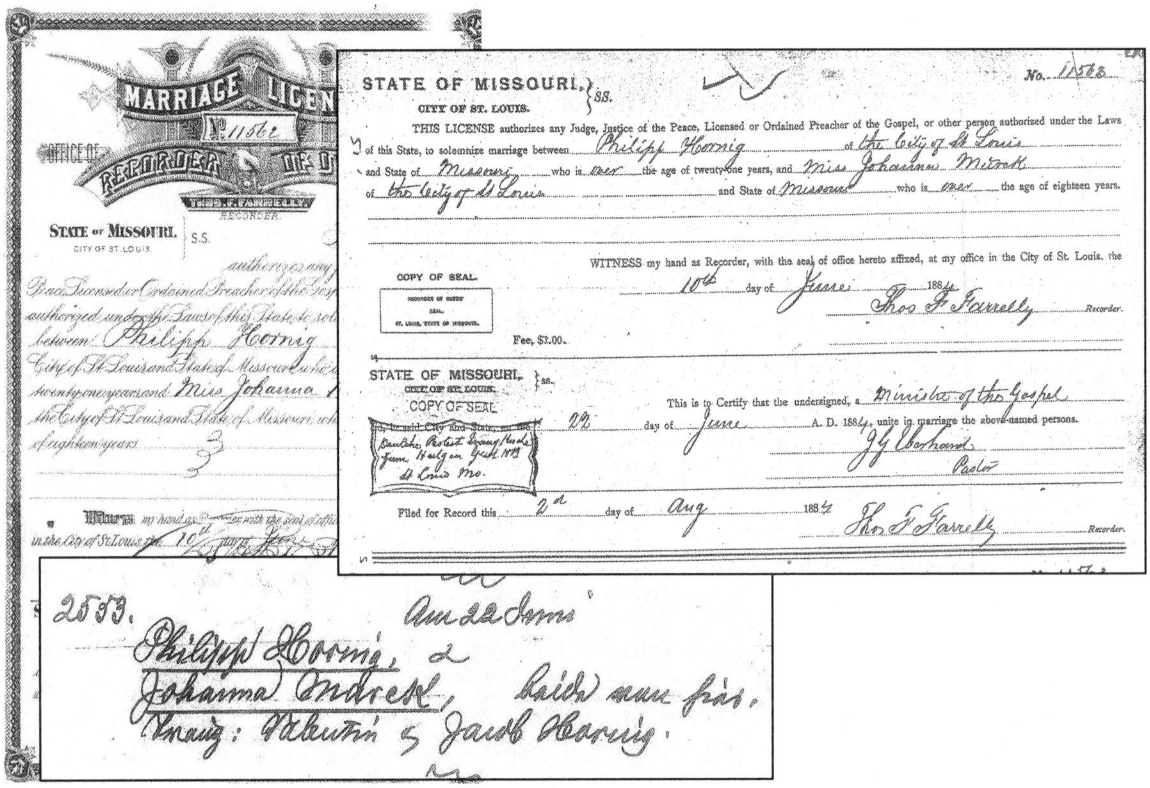
STATE OF MISSOURI, } SS.
CITY OF ST. LOUIS.
No. 11568
THIS LICENSE authorizes any Judge, Justice of the Peace, Licensed or Ordained Preacher of the Gospel, or other person authorized under the Laws of this State, to solemnize marriage between Philipp Hornig of the City of St Louis and State of Missouri who is over the age of twenty-one years, and Miss Johanna Mitrek of the City of St Louis and State of Missouri who is over the age of eighteen years.

WITNESS my hand as Recorder, with the seal of office hereto affixed, at my office in the City of St. Louis, the 10th day of June 1884. Thos F. Farrelly Recorder.

COPY OF SEAL.

Fee, $1.00.

STATE OF MISSOURI, } SS.
CITY OF ST. LOUIS.
COPY OF SEAL

This is to Certify that the undersigned, a Minister of the Gospel, ... 22 day of June A. D. 1884, unite in marriage the above-named persons.
J. G. Eberhardt
Pastor

Filed for Record this 2d day of Aug 1884 Thos F. Farrelly Recorder.

Figure 36: Civil Marriage License, Civil Register, amd Religious Record

Figure 36 shows three documents for the same marriage. Two civil documents, the marriage license, and marriage register, plus the religious record from the Evangelical church book. The minister signed the license and by locating his name on the clergy list, we determined the church where this marriage took place. The register contains the marriage application information and it shows the marriage return. Note that the register has three dates: the application date, the marriage date, and the date the clergy returned the license to the Recorder of Deeds.

Post-1883 St. Louis City marriage records are only available at City Hall and on film at the Family History Library. You can rent the microfilm from the Family History Library and make copies of the needed documents or contact the Archivist at City Hall for assistance with the marriage record search. If you visit City Hall, you can make a photocopy of the marriage register for one dollar. The information on the register is the same as appears on the application and license. This is a good way to obtain a photocopy of collateral marriages without spending a lot of money. You can obtain the original license and application for your direct lines.

ST. LOUIS COUNTY — AFTER 1876

St. Louis County marriage records are available at the St. Louis County Government Center (Recorder of Deeds Office, 41 South Central Avenue, Clayton 63105; phone 314-615-7181; http://revenue.stlouisco.com/RecorderOfDeeds). The records are computerized; to date they are not available online and a printed index does not exist. However, researchers can contact the office by phone and the staff will search the records. If a record is located, they will notify you and send the document with an invoice.

St. Louis County Library and St. Louis Public Library have microfilm for St. Louis County marriages dating from 1877 to 1980. The microfilm set includes the alphabetical card file as shown in Figure 37, copies of the marriage license, and the marriage application. Some of the older documents are dark and hard to read. Figure 37 shows a sample of the marriage card index.

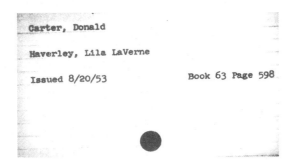

Figure 37: St. Louis County Marriage Card Index

DIVORCE

Prior to 1825 the Superior Court of Missouri granted divorces. Since 1825, Missouri law authorizes the Circuit Clerk's office to process divorce cases for residents of a given county. Prior to 1853, the General Assembly could grant a divorce via a private act. The parties were required to give written notice to the legislature. Ruled invalid, legislative divorces stopped in 1853.[522]

Late eighteenth- and early nineteenth-century documents for early St. Louis divorces or separations, called Separation of Property Agreements, may be viewed onsite at St. Louis City Hall.[523] Before 1876, the Missouri Supreme Court heard more than 100 divorces, some from St. Louis. These records are available online.[524]

City of St. Louis and St. Louis County divorce records are not available via an index. It is necessary to contact the Circuit Clerk's office. Provide the name and a time frame for the event as an overall index does not exist.

---

522. *Missouri Legislature 1852–1853* (2nd session), pages 3–4; revised statutes 1855, page 96 article 9.

523. *Archives Services: Nearly 250 Years of St. Louis History Thru Public Records* (St. Louis: Recorder of Deeds, no date).

524. "Supreme Court Records," *Missouri State Archives* (http://www.sos.mo.gov/archives/judiciary/supremecourt).

The following chart provides guidelines for a marriage record search in St. Louis.

If the marriage occurred before 1877: ⟶ | • Marriage records are available at City Hall with microfilm copies available at St. Louis County Library and St. Louis Public Library. The marriage record is a two- or three-line written statement.

After 1876:

If the marriage occurred after 1876: ⟶ | • After the separation of the City and County marriage records were retained by the Recorder of Deeds at City Hall and the County Government Center.
• Contact either by mail or email. Send a money order to the City before the document is mailed.
• The County will search for the record, mail the document, and include the invoice in the envelope.

Also, after 1876:

If the marriage occurred after 1881: ⟶ | • State laws changed in 1881. Several documents including the application, license, parental consent, and register are available.

Also, after 1881:

If the marriage occurred in the County between 1881 to 1980: ⟶ | • The County marriage index cards and a poor copy of the licenses on microfilm are available at St. Louis County Library. Search for direct and collateral family members. Contact the County Recorder of Deeds office directly for known records and those after 1980. They will conduct a search based on an email request.

City Records:

If the marriage occurred after 1883 in the City: ⟶ | • Visit City Hall for marriage records after 1883. Only the indexes are available at local libraries. The Family History Library in Salt Lake City is the only facility other than City Hall that has microfilm of the marriage records. You can order the film from the Family History Library.

Migration, Immigration, & Naturalization

S t. Louis is and was the home of many families from foreign lands. Some of those pioneers sailed to this country and moved directly to St. Louis. Many German families arrived at the port of New Orleans and then took a steamboat up the Mississippi River to St. Louis. Other St. Louis citizens migrated from other states, perhaps with earlier generations living in the United States.

MIGRATION

Knowledge about the migration paths in and out of St. Louis is important to family historians. Why did your ancestors move to St. Louis and why did they depart? Freedom, employment, the Gold Rush, and free or inexpensive land played important roles in the development of this country and St. Louis in particular.

Some early St. Louis residents moved west for inexpensive or free land. The Springfield, Missouri, federal land office opened in 1835 drawing many pioneers, including some St. Louis residents. Marsha Rising compiled *Opening the Ozarks 1835–1839,* about the first 1,000 people who purchased federal land from the Springfield office. The genealogies of these land owners reveal numerous connections to St. Louis. If your ancestor or his children disappeared in that era, this compilation may be helpful.[525]

While researching those St. Louis ancestors, family historians can expand their search to other states. The Missouri Historical Society Research Library, St. Louis County Library, St. Louis Public Library, and Washington University West Campus have outstanding collections of resources from other states. Many of these resources are old publications, and complete sets may not be available in newer libraries. Because these unique resources are often housed in closed shelves, it is necessary to check the catalog and talk to a librarian or archivist to use these publications.

---

525.   Marsha Hoffman Rising, *Opening the Ozarks: First Families in Southwest Missouri 1835–1839,* 4 volumes (Derry, New Hampshire: American Society of Genealogists, 2005).

State publications include:

Arkansas	*Arkansas Historical Quarterly*
Georgia	*Colonial Records of Georgia*
Illinois	*Journal of the Illinois State Historical Society*
Maryland	*Archives of Maryland*
Massachusetts	*Colonial Society of Massachusetts*
New Hampshire	*State Papers of New Hampshire*
New Jersey	*New Jersey Archives*
New York	*New York Genealogical and Biographical Register*
North Carolina	*State Records of North Carolina*
Pennsylvania	*Pennsylvania Archives*
South Carolina	*South Carolina Historical Magazine*
Virginia	*Virginia Magazine of History and Biography*

Similar collections are available for California, Colorado, Connecticut, Indiana, Iowa, Louisiana, Maine, Michigan, Minnesota, Montana, Nebraska, Oklahoma, Oregon, Utah, Washington, and Wisconsin.

Many journals and articles outline the reasons why people left one area and moved to another. While your ancestor's names may not be listed specifically, they may have been part of a large migration group.

The Periodical Source Index (PERSI) indexes most of these publications. PERSI is available online at HeritageQuest and Ancestry. These databases are probably available at your local library.

IMMIGRATION

Whether your ancestors were immigrants in the 1700s or the 1900s, some arrival locations and dates are elusive. Many passenger lists are available online, but the search is only as good as the person preparing the index. Did the immigrants spell their name the same then as today? Be very flexible and creative with the spelling when searching passenger lists. Immigrants had accents that may have influenced the spelling of their names.

Germans to America and the *Wuerttemberg Emigration Index* are just two examples of indexes that provide immigration clues.[526] The Filby *Passenger and Immigration Lists Index*,[527] in multi-volumes, provides lists of previously-published passenger lists. The material is not in chronological order, just published in any order, as material becomes available. Some libraries offer CD versions of these lists.

526.　Ira Glazier and P. William Filby, *Germans to America* (Wilmington, Delaware: Scholarly Resources, 1988–2002). Trudy Schenk, *Wuerttemberg Emigration Index* (Salt Lake City: Ancestry, 1986–).

527.　P. William Filby, *Passenger and Immigration Lists Index,* 67 volumes (Detroit: Gale Research Company, 1982–).

PASSENGER LISTS

Passenger lists are available on microfilm and online at subscription databases; however, the Ellis Island and Castle Garden websites are free. There were numerous ports of entry along the east coast and the Gulf Coast, including New Orleans. Most libraries have indexes to these passenger lists and some have the microfilm of the actual passenger lists. You can preview the entire passenger list online while looking for other relatives. Some people find it easier to review the list on microfilm. You can also print from the scanned images and from the microfilm.

The early lists only provide the name, age, and country of birth. The twentieth-century passenger lists provide more details including the place of last residence and a relative still living there. They also give the passenger's destination, with a specific city often listed.

If you cannot uncover your ancestor in the computer indexes, refer back to the microfilm. St. Louis libraries have passenger lists and the following indexes:

Atlantic and Gulf Coast Index, 1820–1873, SLPL and SLCL

Baltimore Index, 1820–1891, SLPL; 1897–1952, SLCL

Boston Index, 1820–1891, SLPL; 1902–1920, SLCL

New Orleans Index, 1820–1875, SLPL; 1853–1899, SLCL

New York Index, 1820–1904, SLPL

Philadelphia Index, 1800–1882, SLPL

NATURALIZATION

Naturalization occurred in many ways. In 1803, the United States granted citizenship automatically to those living in the Louisiana Purchase area, which included all St. Louis citizens. A naturalization document is not available in this case. Many citizens in other parts of the country took an oath of loyalty to the United States at the time of the American Revolution. Some of these oaths are extant, others are not. Special naturalization rules applied to men who served in the military.

When the male head-of-household took the naturalization oath, the process included his wife and children, even though their names did not appear on the document. An immigrant often filed his original documents, called first papers, in one location and the next set of papers, called second papers, in another location, thus making it difficult to locate all of the documents. When searching for naturalization documents, it is necessary to look at the circumstances and the laws for that era.

Loretto Dennis Szucs' *They Became Americans: Finding Naturalization Records and Ethnic Origins,* provides an overview of the immigration and naturalization process.[528] John Newman's *American Naturalization Processes and Procedures, 1790–1985,* chronicles the ever-changing

---

528. Loretto Dennis Szucs, *They Became Americans: Finding Naturalization Records and Ethnic Origins* (Salt Lake City, Utah: Ancestry, 1998).

naturalization laws. Researchers can use this book to determine the laws that applied when their ancestors started the naturalization process.[529]

Naturalizations could and did occur in any court, in both federal and many St. Louis courts, including, but not limited to, the Circuit Court, Court of Appeals, Court of Common Pleas, Court of Criminal Correction, Land Court, and Law Commissioner's Court. Do not become concerned if your ancestor's papers were filed in the Court of Criminal Correction. It was just another court and no reflection on the people that used it.

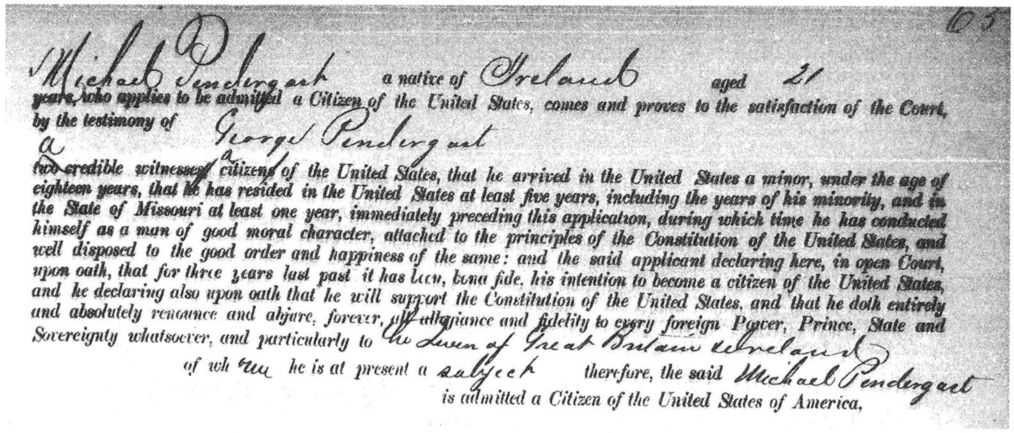

65

Michael Pendergast a native of Ireland aged 21 years, who applies to be admitted a Citizen of the United States, comes and proves to the satisfaction of the Court, by the testimony of George Pendergast a ~~two~~ credible witness~~es~~ a citizen~~s~~ of the United States, that he arrived in the United States a minor, under the age of eighteen years, that he has resided in the United States at least five years, including the years of his minority, and in the State of Missouri at least one year, immediately preceding this application, during which time he has conducted himself as a man of good moral character, attached to the principles of the Constitution of the United States, and well disposed to the good order and happiness of the same: and the said applicant declaring here, in open Court, upon oath, that for three years last past it has been, bona fide, his intention to become a citizen of the United States, and he declaring also upon oath that he will support the Constitution of the United States, and that he doth entirely and absolutely renounce and abjure, forever, all allegiance and fidelity to every foreign Power, Prince, State and Sovereignty whatsoever, and particularly to the Queen of Great Britain & Ireland of whom he is at present a subject therefore, the said Michael Pendergast is admitted a Citizen of the United States of America,

Figure 38: Naturalization Document

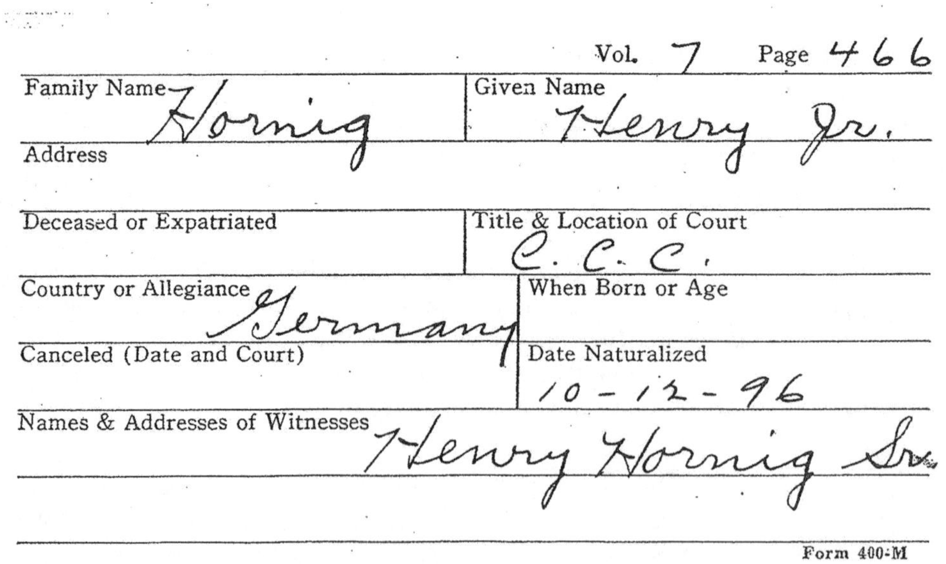

Vol. 7 Page 466

Family Name Hornig

Given Name Henry Jr.

Address

Deceased or Expatriated

Title & Location of Court C. C. C.

Country or Allegiance Germany

When Born or Age

Canceled (Date and Court)

Date Naturalized 10-12-96

Names & Addresses of Witnesses Henry Hornig Sr.

Form 400-M

Figure 39: WPA Naturalization Index Card

529. Newman, *American Naturalization Processes and Procedures, 1790–1985.*

Figure 38 is an example of the surviving naturalization documents for most of the pre-September 1906 naturalization records. Figure 39 is an example of the WPA index cards that show the abbreviation for the local courts used in this process. Usually the information on the card is a duplication of what is on the actual record.

Pre-September 1906 Records

In the pre-1900 era, St. Louis was the home of many immigrants from various ethnic backgrounds. Many became U.S. citizens while living in St. Louis. The Missouri State Archives microfilmed naturalization records housed at the Circuit Court's office and this microfilm is available at local libraries. Library finding aids will help locate the naturalization record for your ancestor. Be aware that most of these documents only contain the name of the new citizen, his country of origin, the date, and possibly some witnesses. It does not include his place of birth or list other family members.

In the 1930s, the WPA prepared index cards for each naturalization record, as shown in Figure 39. Over time some index cards were lost, destroyed, and misfiled; however, an index of the remaining cards is available. The local repositories have the microfilm for the surviving WPA index cards. An electronic database, prepared by St. Louis Genealogical Society, is available online.[530] Another printed index provides information on St. Louis naturalizations dating from 1860 to 1876, which were filed with the Missouri Supreme Court.[531]

The National Archives in Kansas City has two indexes dating from 1846 to 1930. One index includes the declarations of intent and the other the petitions for naturalizations. Arranged by court, year, and first letter of the surname; researchers should allow ample time in Kansas City to look at this textual record. It is not available on microfilm. There is an online database, 1846–1890, from the naturalization book.[532]

The naturalization card file, 1890–1991, previously housed in St. Louis, is located at the National Archives in Kansas City. This resource is not available on microfilm; however, researchers may make a request online.

Post-September 1906 Federal Records

The federal courts house most naturalization records since 27 September 1906. The original journals and the card index, 1890–1991, for naturalizations filed in St. Louis, previously located at the St. Louis federal courthouse, are currently housed at the National Archives Regional Office in Kansas City. Figure 40 is an example of the first papers or declaration of intent as filed in 1923. Microfilm is available for some of these records.[533]

---

530.   "St. Louis Naturalization Index," *St. Louis Genealogical Society* (http://www.stlgs.org/natSearch.aspx).

531.   Alice Henson, *Naturalization Dockets, St. Louis, Missouri, Supreme Court* (Jefferson City: Mid-Missouri Genealogical Society, 1991).

532.   "Name Index to Naturalizations for St. Louis, 1846–1890," *National Archives–Central Plains Region* (http://www.archives.gov/central-plains/kansas-city/finding-aids/naturalization-st-louis.html).

533.   "Online Finding Aids for Archival Holdings at Central Plains Region (Kansas City),"*National Archives–Central Plains Region* (http://www.archives.gov/central-plains/kansas-city/finding-aids/index.html#naturalization).

Microfilm of federal naturalization records have a stub that provides the naturalization number, name of the new citizen, age, declaration of intent, petition volume and page number, and the date the order was signed. It also provides the name, age of the wife and minor children, plus the signature of the new citizen. St. Louis County Library, Special Collections has these records on microfilm with an online index for the post–27 September 1906 records.[534]

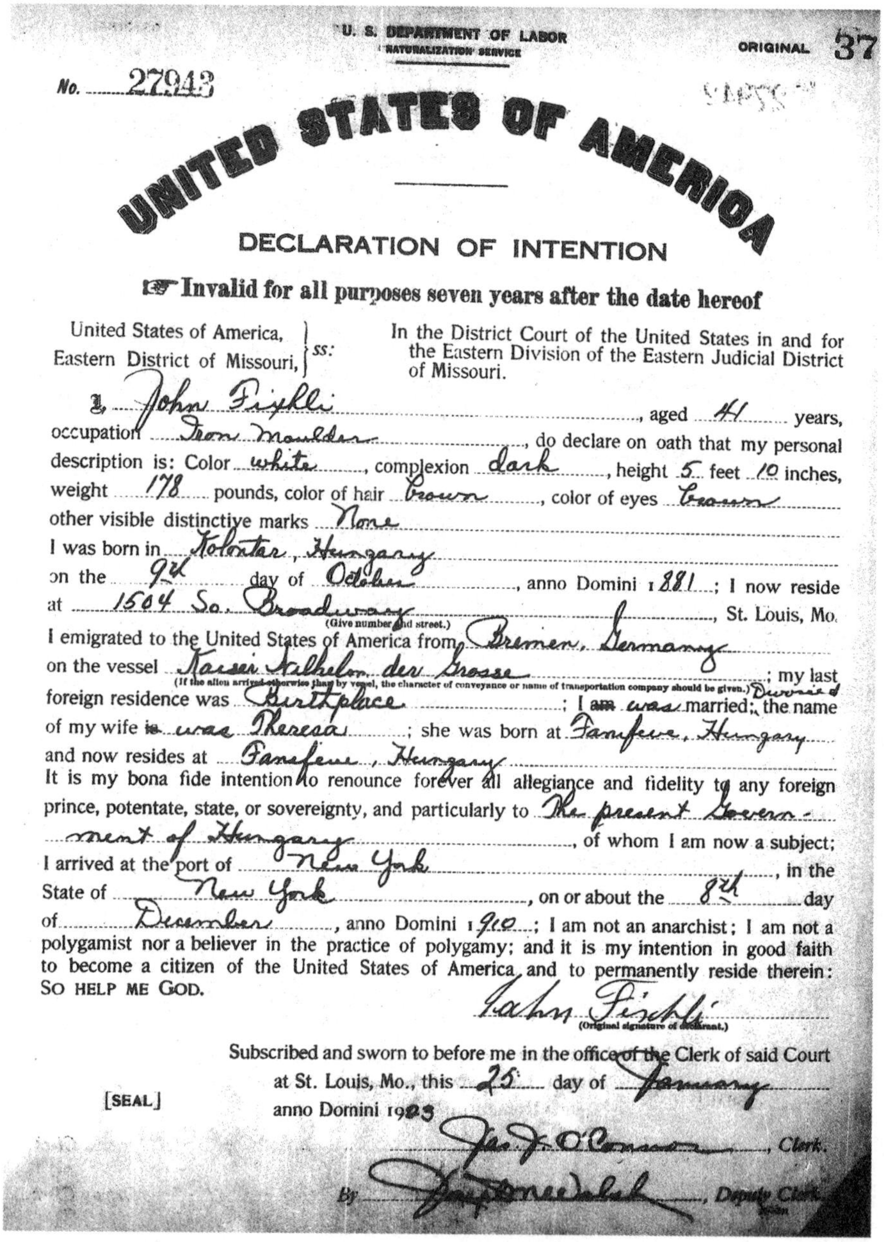
U. S. DEPARTMENT OF LABOR
NATURALIZATION SERVICE
ORIGINAL 37

No. 27943

UNITED STATES OF AMERICA

DECLARATION OF INTENTION

Invalid for all purposes seven years after the date hereof

United States of America, Eastern District of Missouri, } ss: In the District Court of the United States in and for the Eastern Division of the Eastern Judicial District of Missouri.

I, John Fischli, aged 41 years, occupation Iron moulder, do declare on oath that my personal description is: Color white, complexion dark, height 5 feet 10 inches, weight 178 pounds, color of hair brown, color of eyes brown other visible distinctive marks None

I was born in Kolontar, Hungary on the 9th day of October, anno Domini 1881; I now reside at 1504 So. Broadway (Give number and street.), St. Louis, Mo.

I emigrated to the United States of America from Bremen, Germany on the vessel Kaiser Wilhelm der Grosse (If the alien arrived otherwise than by vessel, the character of conveyance or name of transportation company should be given.); my last foreign residence was Birthplace; I am was married; divorced the name of my wife is was Theresa; she was born at Fanefene, Hungary and now resides at Fanefene, Hungary

It is my bona fide intention to renounce forever all allegiance and fidelity to any foreign prince, potentate, state, or sovereignty, and particularly to The present Government of Hungary, of whom I am now a subject; I arrived at the port of New York, in the State of New York, on or about the 8th day of December, anno Domini 1910; I am not an anarchist; I am not a polygamist nor a believer in the practice of polygamy; and it is my intention in good faith to become a citizen of the United States of America and to permanently reside therein: SO HELP ME GOD.

John Fischli
(Original signature of declarant.)

Subscribed and sworn to before me in the office of the Clerk of said Court at St. Louis, Mo., this 25 day of January anno Domini 1923

[SEAL]

Jas. J. O'Connor, Clerk.

By [illegible], Deputy Clerk.

Figure 40: Federal Declaration of Intent, post-1906

534. "St. Louis Naturalization Index," *St. Louis County Library* (http://www.slcl.org).

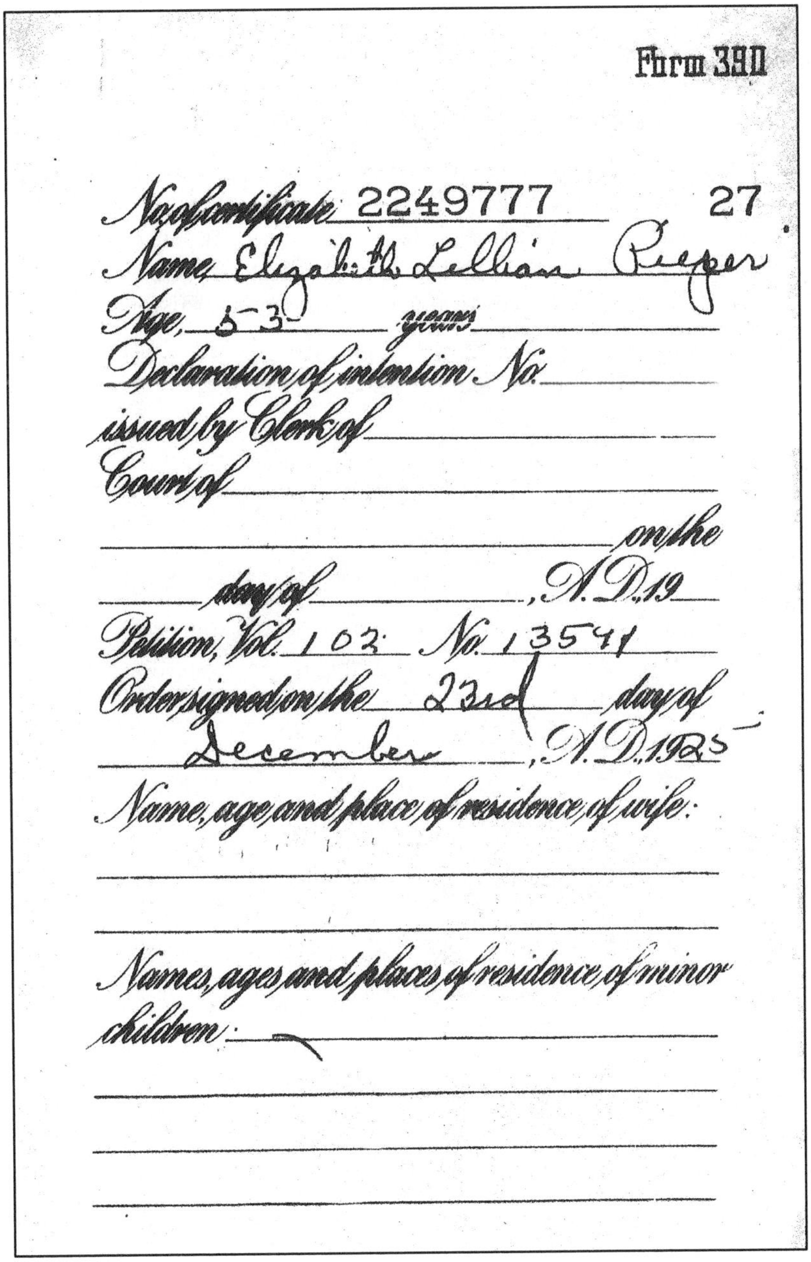

Form 390

No. of Certificate 2249777   27.

Name Elizabeth Lillian Rieger

Age, 5-3   years

Declaration of intention No.

issued by Clerk of

Court of

                                        on the

        day of   , A.D. 19

Petition, Vol. 102 No. 13541

Order signed on the   23rd   day of

    December   , A.D. 1925

Name, age, and place of residence, of wife:

Names, ages, and places of residence, of minor

children:

Figure 41: Federal Naturalization Stub Record, post-1906

Passports

The U.S. government did not require passports until 1941; however, many immigrants applied for a passport long before that. While visiting the *old country*, the immigrant wanted assurance he or she could return to the United States.

Passport applications dating from 1810 to 1906 are available at St. Louis County Library, Special Collections on thirteen rolls of film.[535] Passport applications, 1906–1925, are available at the National Archives, at the Family History Library, and online at Ancestry.com.[536] If you locate a passport application, you may want to obtain a copy of the certificate or passport. These too are available on microfilm from the National Archives and the Family History Library.

Images of some passports dating from 1795 to 1925 are available at Ancestry.com. This database is available at most libraries.

---

535.   *Registers and Indexes for Passport Applications, 1810–1906*, NARA, M1371, Record Group 59, 13 rolls (Washington, D.C.: NARA, No date), available at St. Louis County Library.
536.   *Passport Applications 1906–1925*; FHL beginning film 1,521,724.

Military Events & Records

Most of us have a family member who served in the military, perhaps as far back as the American Revolution, others in far more recent military action. Sometimes the experience of the family veteran(s) is common family knowledge, and other times it is a surprise. Military records are full of genealogical facts and clues on direct-line ancestors, as well as collateral lines. Do not overlook this valuable resource.

A list of the males, and more recently females, along with their birth year, may help determine who served in a particular war. For example, if one of your male ancestors was born between 1810 and 1850, he could have served in the Civil War, which occurred from 1861 to 1865. And, all males born between 1871 and 1899 and still living in 1916 and 1917 were required to register for the World War I draft, unless already in the military service. Those registering for the draft may or may not have actually entered the military.

In addition to the military service records, there are bounty land records, pension records, and lineage society information. These records vary from one war to another. However, numerous publications and websites offer details about each war.

The National Archives maintains most federal military records at one of several locations. *Guide to Genealogical Research in the National Archives of the United States* provides an overview of military records, listing what is available and how to access it. In addition, the National Archives website has a wealth of information to assist family historians.[537]

The Department of Veterans' Affairs turns over military records sixty-two years to the day after the discharge date. Therefore, records for World War II veterans are moving into the custody of the National Archives Military Personnel Records Center in St. Louis and then opened to the public. The 1973 fire destroyed some records, but it is always worthwhile to check for your ancestor's record.[538]

There were several St. Louis military facilities important to the area and the U.S. military overall. Jefferson Barracks was by far the largest, and nationally known, from this area. Benton

---

537. Anne B. Eales and Robert M. Kvasnicka, editors, *Guide to Federal Research in the National Archives of the United States,* 3rd edition (Washington, D.C.: NARA, 2000).

538. "National Military Record Center," *National Archives* (http://www.archives.gov/press/press-releases/2008/nr08-14.html).

Barracks was important during the Civil War, today it is Fairgrounds Park in North St. Louis. The United States established an armory or arsenal by the Mississippi River in South St. Louis.[539]

The Old Courthouse has *Finding Aid to the Indian Wars Widows' Project Records, Circa 1864–1965* compiled by Harry G. Heiss. The records held at the Jefferson National Expansion Memorial Archives are based on a 1962 questionnaire sent to surviving widows of veterans from the Indian Wars that took place between 1865 and 1898. The widows are listed by name along with that of their spouse and his unit information.[540]

The Missouri State Archives has an online military database for Missouri veterans dating from the War of 1812 to World War I.[541] However, many veterans and their families that served from other locations migrated west to the St. Louis area. Some veterans received pensions or bounty land, others did not.[542]

About 1832, the St. Louis Grays formed to fight in the Black Hawk War and then moved on to the Mexican War. By the time of the Civil War, many had joined the Confederate Army. The Missouri Historical Society Research Library has a manuscript collection on the St. Louis Grays.[543]

Lineage societies were formed after most military events. If your ancestor was in the American Revolution, check the National Society, Daughters of the American Revolution (DAR) or Sons of the American Revolution (SAR) records. Another organization, Sons of the Revolution, follows the male direct line from American Revolution soldiers. The Society of the Cincinnati is open to descendents of officers from the American Revolution and only follows the line of the eldest son. Descendents of the Civil War participants had an opportunity to join several organizations, including the Daughters of Union Veterans of the Civil War or the Daughters of the Confederacy.

COLONIAL WARS (PRE–1776)

While St. Louis area was not involved in the Colonial Wars, some of its future residents or their descendents were. The Missouri Historical Society Research Library houses the completed membership applications for the Society of Colonial Wars in Missouri. Other lineage societies, such as the Society of Colonial Dames document these patriots.

---

539.   Randy McGuire, *St. Louis Arsenal: Armory of the West* (Chicago: Arcadia Publishing, 2001).

540.   Harry G. Heiss, *Finding Aid to the Indian Wars Widows' Project Records, Circa 1864–1965,* Record Unit 101, Museum Catalog no. 9015 (St. Louis: National Park Service, 1989).

541.   "Soldier Database: War of 1812–World War I," *Missouri State Archives* (http://www .sos.mo.gov/archives/soldiers).

542.   Lucy Kate McGhee, *Missouri Revolutionary War Soldiers, War of 1812, and Indian Wars Pension List* (Washington, D.C.: n.p., 1957). Also, *The Pension Roll of 1835,* 4 volumes (Baltimore: Genealogical Publishing Company, 1992). Also, U.S. Census Office, *A Census of Pensioners for Revolutionary or Military Services; with Their Names, Ages, and Place of Residence, as Returned by the Marshals of the Several Judicial Districts in 1840* (Baltimore: Genealogical Publishing Company, 1967).

543.   St. Louis Grays manuscript collection; Missouri Historical Society.

AMERICAN REVOLUTION (1776–1783)

St. Louis was the site of one battle during the American Revolution, Fort San Carlos.[544] Also some of the residents of Kaskaskia that served with George Rogers Clark were patriots. Those men were listed as Virginia patriots in that era. Service records and pension records provide clues for these patriots.[545] After the war, many veterans from other states migrated to the St. Louis area, some staying, others moving on.

Daughters of the American Revolution applications and publications often outline the burial site for American Revolution veterans.[546] DAR Lineage Books and the DAR magazine provide further clues for your patriot.[547] The Sons of the American Revolution also provide a patriot index.[548]

An index of the American Revolution pension files and a partial set of documents is available on the HeritageQuest website via St. Louis County Library, St. Louis Public Library, or many other libraries across the country. Footnote.com provides scanned images of the complete federal pension file.[549]

The *Centennial History and Registry of Missouri Society Sons of the American Revolution, 1889–1989,* has a list of members with each patriot named. The appendix provides a cross reference from the patriot to the member.[550]

WAR OF 1812 (1812–1815)

Many St. Louis residents participated in the War of 1812. Betty Harvey Williams's publication, *Soldiers of the War of 1812,*[551] provides the names of St. Louis soldiers and often includes the names of their spouses and children. The Missouri State Archives soldiers' website lists War of 1812 veterans.

---

544.   "Attack on St. Louis," *Scott K. Williams* (http://www.usgennet.org/usa/mo/county/stlouis/attack.htm).

545.   Virgil D. White, *Genealogical Abstracts of Revolutionary War Pension Files,* 4 volumes (Waynesboro, Tennessee: National Historical Publishing Company, 1990–1992). Virgil D. White, *Index to Revolutionary War Service Records,* 4 volumes (Waynesboro, Tennessee: National Historical Publishing Company, 1995).

546.   Daughters of the American Revolution, *Revolutionary Soldiers Buried in Missouri* (Kansas City: DAR, 1966).

547.   Daughters of the American Revolution *DAR Patriot Index,* 3 volumes (Washington, D.C.: The Society, 2003). *Lineage Books, National Society of the DAR, 1890–1921* (Harrisburg, Pennsylvania: Harrisburg Publishing, 1890–1921). *Daughters of the American Revolution Magazine,* 1896–2001 (Washington, D.C.: The Society, 1896–2001).

548.   *National Society of the Sons of the American Revolution* (White Plains, New York: Harris Publishing Company, 1993).

549.   "Revolutionary War Pensions," *Footnote.com* (http://www.footnote.com).

550.   James Shelby and Richard Yohe, *Centennial History and Registry Missouri Society Sons of the American Revolution, 1889–1989* (Shawnee Mission, Kansas: The Society, 1989).

551.   Betty Harvey Williams, *Soldiers of the War of 1812 with Missouri Connections,* 2 volumes (Independence: Trails Publishing, 2002).

Figure 42 shows an example of the compiled service records for the War of 1812. The *Index to Compiled Service Records of Volunteer Soldiers Who Served During the War of 1812* is available at St. Louis Public Library on microfilm.[552]

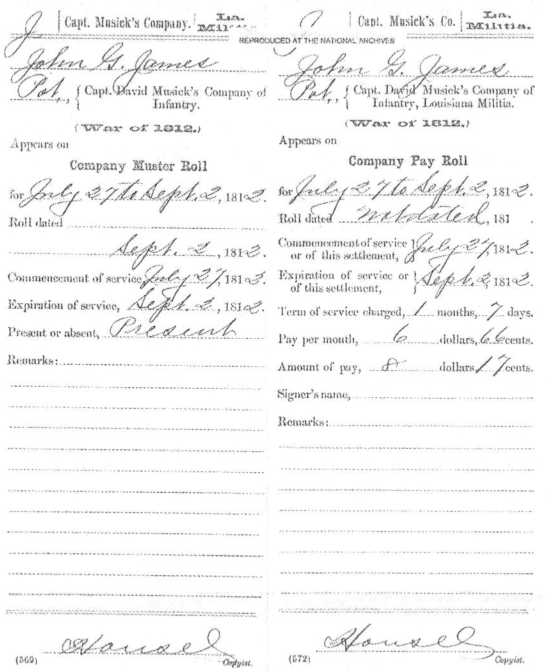

J | Capt. Musick's Company. | La. Mil.

John G. James

Pvt., Capt. David Musick's Company of Infantry.

(War of 1812.)

Appears on Company Muster Roll for July 27 to Sept. 2, 1812.

Roll dated Sept. 2, 1812.

Commencement of service July 27, 1812.

Expiration of service, Sept. 2, 1812.

Present or absent, Present

Remarks:

(569) Housel Copyist.

J | Capt. Musick's Co. | La. Militia.

John G. James

Pvt., Capt. David Musick's Company of Infantry, Louisiana Militia.

(War of 1812.)

Appears on Company Pay Roll for July 27 to Sept. 2, 1812.

Roll dated not dated, 181

Commencement of service or of this settlement, July 27, 1812.

Expiration of service or of this settlement, Sept. 2, 1812.

Term of service charged, 1 months, 7 days.

Pay per month, 6 dollars, 66 cents.

Amount of pay, 8 dollars, 17 cents.

Signer's name,

Remarks:

(572) Housel Copyist.

Figure 42: War of 1812 records

Many War of 1812 veterans, perhaps one of your ancestors, migrated to Missouri for bounty land. The Descriptive Pamphlet for the *War of 1812 Military Bounty Land Warrants, 1815–1858,* M848, is available online at St. Louis County Library's website. This finding aid may help in your search.[553] Bounty land records are important because the War of 1812 pensions became available after 1878; however, many veterans died before that date.[554]

Bounty land in Michigan, Illinois, and Arkansas was available for War of 1812 veterans. The Michigan property was not suitable, so the federal government selected property in Missouri instead of Michigan.

The Missouri property was west of the Mississippi River and north of the Missouri River. Later the Land Acts of 1850 and 1855 allowed veterans to purchase bounty land wherever it was available. Bounty land records provide genealogical information. See LAND RECORDS for information on bounty land in Missouri.

Parkin's, *Missouri Rangers in the Indian War, War of 1812,* provides a list of soldiers.[555] Because Missouri was new and unsettled in many areas, a large number of veterans listed in this publication had a St. Louis connection.

St. Louis County Library, Special Collections has a three-roll microfilm set titled *War of 1812—Missouri Soldiers*. This set is a compilation of three types of records the muster rolls of men who served from Missouri, bounty land forms, and War of 1812 veterans buried in Missouri. Men who served from any state are included in the last two record types.[556]

---

552. *Index to Compiled Service Records of Volunteer Soldiers Who Served During the War of 1812,* M602, Record Group 94, 234 rolls.

553. *War of 1812 Military Bounty Land Warrants, 1815–1858,* M848, Record Group 49, 14 rolls (Washington, D.C.: NARA).

554. Virgil D. White, *Index to War of 1812 Pension Files,* 2 volumes (Waynesboro, Tennessee: National Historical Publishing, 1992). *Index to War of 1812 Pension Applications Files*, M313, Record Group 15, 102 rolls (Washington, D.C.: NARA).

555. Robert Parkin, *Missouri Rangers in the Indian Wars, War of 1812* (St. Louis: The Author, 1961).

556. War of 1812—Missouri Soldiers; St. Louis County Library microfilm.

INDIAN WARS (1832–1837)

Missouri citizens fought in several Indian Wars including the Black Hawk War, Heatherly War, Second Seminole War, and the Osage War. St. Louis citizens may have volunteered for any of these encounters. The Missouri State Archives military database includes these veterans.[557]

MEXICAN WAR (1847–1849)

The *Republican* newspaper, dated 15 August 1880, printed a complete list of St. Louis troops that mustered in on 18 May 1846 departing for the Mexican War.

St. Louis County Library, Special Collections has the National Archives microfilm and printed index, *Index to Mexican War Pension File, 1887–1926* [558] listing veterans who received pensions and bounty land.[559] The *Index to Compiled Service Records of Volunteer Soldiers Who Served During the Mexican-American War* is available at some local repositories on microfilm.[560] The *Mexican War Index for Missouri Militia Muster Records* provides a list of the Missouri men that served in this conflict. It is easy to identify the St. Louis men. For example, the men in the St. Louis Legion served under Alton Easton and others from St. Louis. Most units had men from St. Louis.[561]

Many of the Mexican War veterans also served in the Civil War. For those veterans, the National Archives combined their Mexican War and Civil War pension files. The Mexican War pension files contain a family questionnaire. Barbara Schull Wolfe transcribed the Mexican War Pension Applications and they are available in book format. Entries include the name, state where the veteran was living at the time of application, date of application, and application or certificate number.[562] You can also check Virgil White's *Index to Mexican War Pension Files*. Entries include the name of the veteran and widow, certificate number, date of application, and unit served.[563]

CIVIL WAR (1861–1865)

St. Louis was in a unique position during the Civil War. The governor and others wanted Missouri to secede from the Union. The governor eventually left the state. Missouri did not

---

557. "Soldiers Database: War of 1812–World War 1," *Missouri State Archives* (http://www.sos.mo.gov/archives/soldiers).

558. *Index to Mexican War Pension File, 1887–1926,* T317, Record Group 15, 14 rolls (Washington, D.C.: NARA).

559. Virgil D. White, *Index to Mexican War Pension Files* (Waynesboro, Tennessee: National Historical Publishing Company, 1989).

560. *Index to Compiled Service Records of Volunteer Soldiers Who Served During the Mexican-American War,* M616, Record Group 94, 41 rolls (Washington, D.C.: NARA).

561. Kenneth Weant, *Mexican War Index for Missouri Militia Muster Records* (Arlington, Texas: The Author, 2005).

562. Barbara Schull Wolfe, transcriber, *An Index to Mexican War Pension Applications* (Indianapolis: Heritage House, 1985).

563. Virgil D. White, *Index to Mexican War Pension Files* (Waynesboro, Tennessee: National Historical Publishing, 1989).

secede from the Union, but it did become a border state. Some men joined the Union Army; others joined the Confederates. A useful tool to sort out a soldier's service is the Civil War Soldiers and Sailors System hosted by the National Park Service (http://www.itd.nps.gov/cwss). The database provides very basic facts on the service of 6.3 million soldiers including men that served on both sides.

War Papers and Personal Reminiscences, 1861–1865 provides narrative about the life and times of Missouri soldiers involved in Civil War battles.[564] Some St. Louis men and others from across the state joined the Missouri State Guard fighting for their cause. *The Forgotten Men, Missouri State Guard* provides a list of men that served in the Guard. It lists, in alphabetical order, the name of the veteran and any other information available from National Archives records used in the compilation of the book.[565]

St. Louis and the entire state of Missouri were under Provost Marshal control during the Civil War due to the internal strife. Many documents from that era are available in two NARA microfilmed series: *Union Provost Marshal's File of Papers Relating to Individual Civilians* [566] and *Union Provost Marshal's File of Papers Relating to Two or More Civilians.*[567] Missouri citizens included in the *Individual Civilian* record set are indexed and available online at the Missouri State Archives website.[568]

While only a limited number of battles took place in St. Louis, the city was part of the overall conflict. *Civil War St. Louis* and *The Civil War in St. Louis* provide details of the city, the soldiers, and the tension in this area.[569] *The Roster of Union Soldiers* is available, divided by state, with Missouri soldiers in volumes 21 and 22. This roster provides the soldier's name, unit, and company. There may be more than one person with the same name, thus requiring a record search for each to determine the correct veteran.[570] The *Register of Enlistments in the U.S. Army, 1798–1897* for the entire army shows those from Missouri.[571]

The Union Cause in St. Louis in 1861: A Historical Sketch provides an analysis of the St. Louis area in 1861. It gives background information on the immigrants and other citizens

---

564.   *War Papers & Personal Reminiscences, 1861–65* (1892; reprint, Wilmington, North Carolina: Broadfoot Publishing Company, 1992).

565.   Carolyn M. Bartels, *The Forgotten Men, Missouri State Guard* (Shawnee Mission, Kansas: Two Trails Publishing, 1995).

566.   *Union Provost Marshals' File of Papers Relating to Individual Civilians*, M345, Record Group 109, 300 rolls (Washington, D.C.: NARA, No date).

567.   *Union Provost Marshal's File of Papers Relating to Two or More Civilians*, M416, Record Group 109, 94 rolls (Washington, D.C.: NARA, No date).

568.   "Missouri's Union Provost Marshal Papers: 1861–1866," *Missouri State Archives* (http://www.sos.mo.gov/archives/provost).

569.   Louis S. Gerteis, *Civil War St. Louis* (Lawrence: University Press of Kansas, 2001). William C. Winter, *The Civil War in St. Louis* (St. Louis: Missouri Historical Society Press, 1994).

570.   Janet B. Hewett, *The Roster of Union Soldiers* (Wilmington, North Carolina: Broadfoot Publishing Company, 1997).

571.   *Register of Enlistments in the U.S. Army, 1798–1897*, M233, 81 rolls (Washington, D.C.: NARA, 1956). St. Louis County Library has rolls 25–81. The St. Louis enlistees from 1855 are available in an index on the Special Collection's website.

regarding their position on slavery. The book lists all of the Union units from St. Louis and each soldier in the units.[572]

A list of Missouri Confederate soldiers is available in *The Roster of Confederate Soldiers*.[573] The state required professional men to sign a loyalty oath before they could interact with the public as attorneys, clergy, physicians, and politicians, to name a few examples. While the documents are held at various locations in the state, the original oaths pertaining to St. Louis citizens are available at the Missouri Historical Society Research Library.[574] "Disenfranchised" is a publication available at the same Library and lists St. Louis citizens who would not sign the loyalty oath.[575]

Trans-Mississippi Men at War is a publication compiled from an assortment of sources, including payroll and discharge records, Confederate States of America pensions, biographical sources, and burial and casualty lists.[576]

Many soldiers served in more than one unit during the Civil War; some even served on both sides. It is necessary to review all sources carefully. The *Compiled Service Records of Confederate Soldiers Who Served in Organizations from the State of Missouri* is available at St. Louis Public Library.[577] Volume twelve of the *Confederate Military History, Extended Edition* provides information about the battles in which Missouri soldiers participated.[578]

POST-CIVIL WAR RECORDS

Service records, pension files, census documents, military organizations' records, and soldiers' home records provide possible sources for veterans. By using a combination of these records, researchers should be able to locate their Civil War ancestors.

The National Archives microfilmed the compiled service records for all Union soldiers. *Compiled Service Records of Volunteer Union Soldiers Who Served in Organizations from the State of Missouri* and the index[579] are available at St. Louis Public Library and at the National Archives in Washington, D.C. and Kansas City.

---

572.   Robert J. Rombauer, *The Union Cause in St. Louis in 1861 an Historical Sketch* (St. Louis: St. Louis Municipal Centennial Year, 1909).

573.   Janet B. Hewett, *The Roster of Confederate Soldiers* (Wilmington, North Carolina: Broadfoot Publishing Company, 1995).

574.   Oaths of Loyalty; Dexter Tiffany Collection, Missouri Historical Society, St. Louis.

575.   *A List of Disloyal and Disenfranchised Persons, St. Louis County: 1866* (St. Louis: Missouri Democrat Print, 1866).

576.   Carolyn M. Bartels, *Trans-Mississippi Men at War,* volume 1, Missouri CSA (Independence: Blue and Grey Book Shoppe, 1998).

577.   *Compiled Service Records of Confederate Soldiers Who Served in Organizations from the State of Missouri*, M322, Record Group 109, 193 rolls (Washington, D.C.: NARA, No date).

578.   *Confederate Military History Extended Edition, Volume 12, Missouri* (1899; reprint, Wilmington, North Carolina: Broadfoot Publishing Company, 1988).

579.   *Index to Compiled Service Records of Volunteer Union Soldiers Who Served in Organizations from the State of Missouri, M390, Record Group 94, 54 rolls (Washington, D.C.: NARA). Compiled Service Records of Volunteer Union Soldiers Who Served in Organizations from the State of Missouri*, M405, Record Group 94, 854 rolls (Washington, D.C.: NARA, No date).

Many St. Louis Union veterans were eligible for pensions. Marie Concannon compiled *Index to Missouri Pensioners, 1883.* This publication names all Union veterans living in Missouri in 1883, even those who previously lived in and served from other states during the War.[580] A subscription database provides access to the index to pensions for the Civil War. If you locate your ancestor on this list, you will probably want to order his pension record from the National Archives in Washington, D.C.[581] You can also check the subscription service, Footnote.com, for a scanned image of the Civil War Pension Index card as shown in Figure 43. This card provides the pension application and certificate numbers for the veteran, his widow, and any minors, if applicable. The card provides the pension file numbers. [582]

The Daughters of Union Veterans of the Civil War, 1861–1865 published *St. Louis: Our Civil War Heritage,* which provides biographical data and some tombstone photographs for many St. Louis Union soldiers. This publication also provides an overview of the community during the Civil War period.[583]

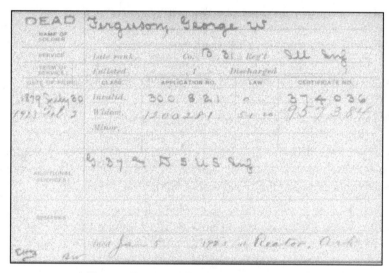

Figure 43: Union Civil War Pension Card

In 1906, the Department of the Interior, Bureau of Pensions, instructed surgeons to examine some of the pensioners. The surgeons provided a certificate and a detailed report of each examination. These documents provide the name of the pensioner, pension number, date, 1906 address, birthplace, age, height, weight, complexion, eyes, permanent marks and scars, and occupation. St. Louis County Clerk's office filed this information.[584]

---

580.   Marie Concannon, *Index to Missouri Military Pensioners, 1883* (Columbia: State Historical Society of Missouri, 1997). Web version, *Virtually Missouri* (http://www.virtuallymissouri.org).

581.   National Archives Pension order form, NATF 85. National Archives Service Record order form, NATF 86; "Obtaining Copies of Records," *National Archives* (http://www.archives.gov/researcher/order).

582.   "Civil War Pensions Index," *Footnote.com* (http://www.footnote.com).

583.   Daughters of Union Veterans of the Civil War, 1861–1865, Julia Dent Grant, Tent 16, *St. Louis: Our Civil War Heritage,* 2 volumes (St. Louis: The Society, 1992).

584.   "Examining Surgeons," St. Louis County Clerk, 1906–1907; Missouri State Archives film, C18169.

The *1890 Special Census of Civil War Veterans and Their Widows* is available for Missouri. The records for some other states were lost in a fire in Washington, D.C. While designated to count Union veterans and their widows, researchers will find some former Confederate soldiers on the census list as well.

Many Union soldiers joined the Grand Army of the Republic (GAR) after the war. The GAR had several lodges in the St. Louis area.[585] The GAR ledgers not only indicated the veteran's membership, but it also listed his death date, which may or may not be available in other records. An 1895 roster of GAR members provides important clues and serves as a census alternative or replacement record.[586]

In 1861, the state of Missouri required an oath of loyalty, as shown in Figure 44, from professional men, such as attorneys, the clergy, government employees, physicians, and others. This oath was signed at the beginning of the war to ensure those men were loyal to the Union. Another oath was signed in 1867 for the same reason. The original documents for St. Louis residents are housed at the Missouri Historical Society Research Library.

Other Union veterans joined the Military Order of the Loyal Legion of the United States, an organization for officers only.[587] When a member moved to another area, he used a transfer card for identification in the new area. The Missouri Historical Society Research Library and Mercantile Library each have a collection of memorial sketches for Loyal Legion members.

Published monthly from 1893 to 1932, the *Confederate Veteran Magazine* provided articles about and of interest to Confederate veterans. This magazine was reprinted in the 1980s. If you have a Confederate veteran, you may find some biographical information including obituaries, history, and unique records. The index provides guidance for articles pertaining to St. Louis and Missouri.[588] This publication is available at local repositories.

In 1913, the Missouri Legislature passed an act granting pensions to Confederate veterans living in Missouri. The original pension files are at the Missouri State Archives. *Missouri Confederate Pensions and Confederate Home Applications' Index* provides a listing of those soldiers.[589] There is a listing of the Confederate Roll of Honor in Missouri, including some St. Louis names.[590]

---

585.   Marie Concannon, compiler, *Grand Army of the Republic, Missouri Division: Index to Death Rolls, 1882–1940* (Columbia: State Historical Society of Missouri, 1995). Web version, *Virtually Missouri* (http://www.virtuallymissouri.org). "Grand Army of the Republic (GAR) Posts in Missouri by Town (1893)," *Mollus* (http://home.usmo.com/~momollus/GARtown.htm).

586.   Grand Army of the Republic, Department of Missouri, *Roster of the Department of Missouri, Grand Army of the Republic and Its Auxiliaries, 1895* (Kansas City: Western Veteran, 1895). [The Phelps Camp #66, Sons of Union Veterans of the Civil War indexed this publication in Springfield, Missouri, in 1999].

587.   *Military Order of the Loyal Legion of the United States* (Wilmington, North Carolina: Broadfoot Publishing Company, 1997).

588.   *Confederate Veteran* (1893; reprint, Wilmington, North Carolina: Broadfoot Publishing Company, 1986–1988).

589.   Peggy Barnes Fox, *Missouri Confederate Pensions and Confederate Home Applications' Index* (Hillsboro, Texas: Hill College Press, 1990).

590.   Peggy Barnes Fox, *Confederate Pensions and Confederate Home Applications Index* (Hillsboro, Texas: Hill College Press, 1996). Leslie Anders, editor, *Confederate Roll of Honor: Missouri* (Warrensburg: West Central Missouri Genealogical Society and Library, 1989).

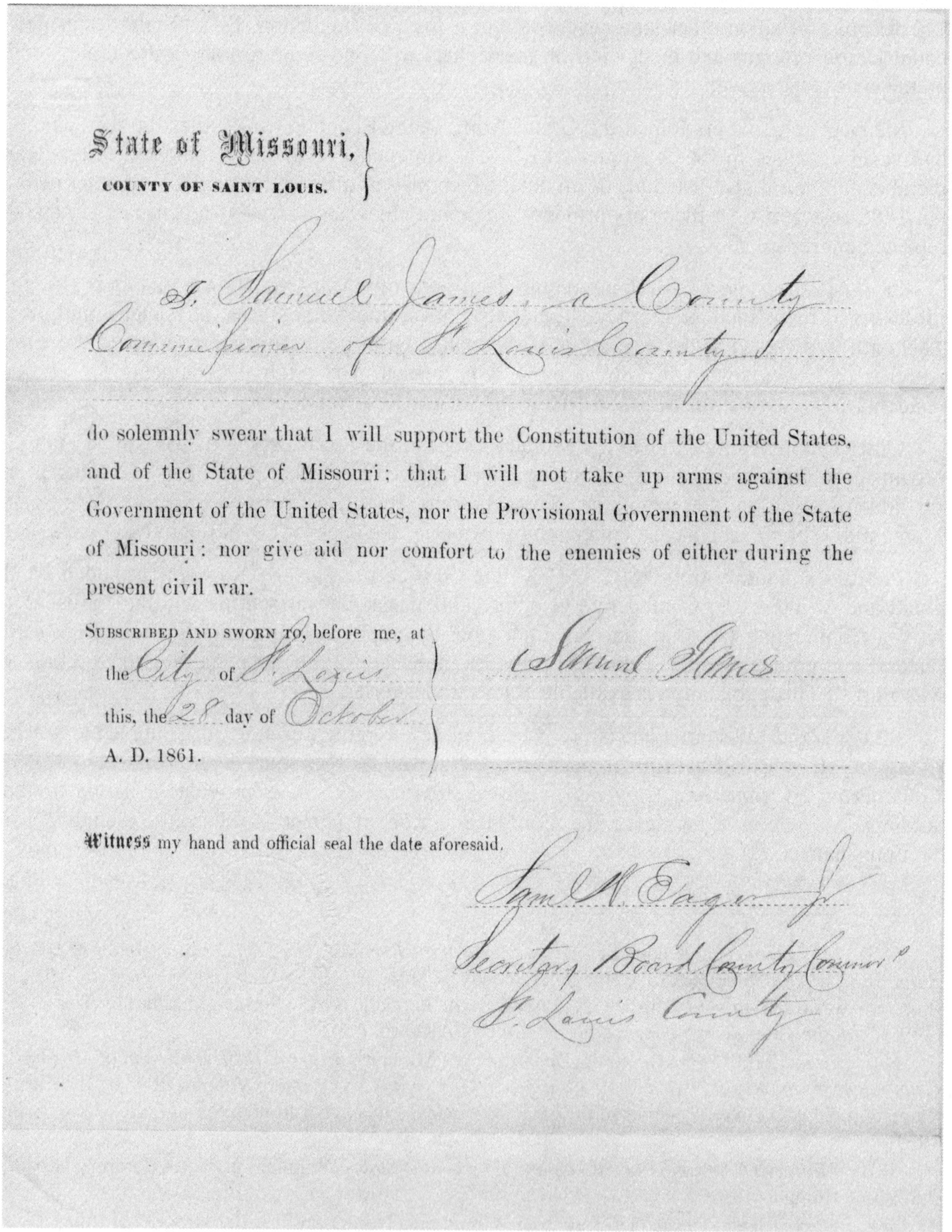

State of Missouri,
COUNTY OF SAINT LOUIS.

I, Samuel James, a County Commissioner of St. Louis County

do solemnly swear that I will support the Constitution of the United States,
and of the State of Missouri: that I will not take up arms against the
Government of the United States, nor the Provisional Government of the State
of Missouri: nor give aid nor comfort to the enemies of either during the
present civil war.

SUBSCRIBED AND SWORN TO, before me, at
the *City of St. Louis*   *Samuel James*
this, the *28* day of *October*
A. D. 1861.

Witness my hand and official seal the date aforesaid.

Saml N Eager Jr
Secretary Board County Commr
St. Louis County

Figure 44: Oath of Loyalty, 1861

The closest branches to St. Louis of the National Home for Disabled Volunteer Soldiers were the Western Branch located in Leavenworth, Kansas, and the Danville Branch in Danville, Illinois. The admission records are available from the National Archives in film series M1749.[591]

The State Federal Soldiers' Home of Missouri was established in St. James, Missouri. Also the State of Illinois operated a soldiers' home in Quincy. Some St. Louis veterans lived in these facilities in their waning years. Even today, some St. Louis veterans retire to the facility in St. James.[592] In 1891, the Confederate Soldiers Home in Higginsville was established, and Missouri took over the facility in 1897.

In 1922–1923, the United Daughters of the Confederacy distributed a four-page questionnaire to veterans and their families. The Western Historical Manuscript Collection–Columbia holds the collection and the findings were published.[593] St. Louis Public Library holds lineage publications for the United Daughters of the Confederacy.

Upon request, the federal government provided tombstones for Union veterans. The first act provided tombstones for requests made between 1879 and 1903. Later acts broadened this time frame.[594] The associated microfilm provides a copy of each index card and is available at St. Louis County Library, Special Collections.

SPANISH–AMERICAN WAR (1898–1902)

In 1898, tension arose between Spain and the United States over the Spanish colony of Cuba, which was trying to gain its independence from Spain. The USS *Maine* sank while in Havana's harbor, after which the U.S. declared war. Jefferson Barracks served as a rendezvous point during the Spanish-American War. Missouri rosters are available and they include the names of St. Louis soldiers.[595]

Information about St. Louis Spanish-American War veterans is available in the Soldiers Database on the Missouri State Archives website.[596] The Archives used the original service cards to compile the database. If the veteran was eligible for a pension, it is available at the National Archives in Washington, D.C.

---

591.   Department of Veterans' Affairs, M1749, Record Group 15.

592.   *Biennial Reports, 1901–1946* (Jefferson City: Mid-State Publishing Company, 1902–1947). [Missouri Government Documents provide details about the Federal Soldiers' Home of St. James, Missouri.] Also, Missouri Confederate Home Applications, available at Missouri State Archives. Marie Concannon, compiler, *Index of Residents, State Federal Soldiers' Home of Missouri, St. James, Missouri, 1899–1946* (Columbia: State Historical Society of Missouri, 1998).

593.   Joanne Webb Chiles Eakin, *Confederate Records from the United Daughters of the Confederacy Files*, volumes 1–8 (Independence: J. C. Eakin, 1995–2001).

594.   *Card Records of Headstones Provided for Deceased Union Civil War Veterans, 1879–1903* M1845, Record Group 92, 22 rolls (Washington, D.C.: NARA, No date).

595.   Missouri, Adjutant General's Office, *Military Records, Spanish-American War, 1897–1898* (Jefferson City: Adjutant General's Office, 1898).

596.   "Soldiers Database: War of 1812–World War I," *Missouri State Archives* (http://www.sos .mo.gov/archives/soldiers).

PHILIPPINE INSURRECTION (1899–1902)

Many of the same soldiers participated in both the Spanish-American War in Cuba and the Philippine Insurrection in the Philippine Islands. St. Louis Public Library has the service cards for this encounter.[597]

WORLD WAR I (1916–1918)

The United States government rules and regulations required all men between the ages of 18 and 45 to register for the draft for World War I. Some of those men later served in the military, most did not. If your male ancestor was born between 1872 and 1899, you want to check this record. There were three drafts and the age limit for each draft varied. Some subscription databases offer an online index. Scanned images of the original records are available online, but are often hard to read.

The original draft cards are available at the National Archives in Atlanta, but the microfilmed records are usually in good condition and very readable. The NARA microfilmed draft board cards, usually arranged alphabetically. They are available at St. Louis County Library, Special Collections and St. Louis Public Library. Rural counties usually only have one draft board, but large cities have numerous draft boards, which makes the search more difficult on microfilm.[598]

When searching for the draft cards, first check the index at Ancestry.com. While their images are difficult to read, if you find your ancestor, you can then go to the microfilm and make a much better photocopy. Remember the card has a front and back, both with valuable information.

Local newspapers published lists of those drafted with each soldier's draft lottery number. They also published a list of those that did not register.[599]

World War I Draft Boards

City Draft Boards

Board	Address
1	4551 North Broadway
2	Blair Avenue and Salisbury
3	1909 St. Louis Avenue
4	14th and Cass Avenue
5	Care of Jefferson Hotel
6	125 South Fourth Street
7	1328 South Broadway
8	714 Soulard Street
9	18th and Shenandoah Avenue
10	3373 South 7th Street
11	3548 South Grand Avenue
12	6818 Michigan Avenue
13	3155 South Grand Avenue
14	Grand and Magnolia
15	Northwest corner Lafayette & Mississippi
16	3132 Park Avenue
17	3688 Olive Street
18	1800 North 23rd Street
19	Jefferson Avenue and Dayton
20	Grand and Franklin
21	3126 North Grand Avenue
22	4103 Easton Avenue
23	14 North Newstead Avenue
24	Magnolia and Clifton Avenue
25	Washington Hotel
26	4503 Page Avenue
27	1902 North Union Boulevard
28	218 Delmar Building

County Draft Boards

Board	Address
1	Clayton
2	Ferguson
3	Kirkwood

597. *Index to Compiled Service Records of Volunteer Soldiers Who Served during the Philippine Insurrection*, M872, Record Group 94, 24 rolls microfilm (Washington, D.C.: NARA, No date)..

598. *World War I Draft Registration Cards Microfilm Numbers for Missouri Films*, M1509, Record Group 163, rolls 1769–1805 apply to St. Louis (Washington, D.C.: NARA, No date).

599. *Complete List of* the *St. Louisans in First Draft for National Army: Names in Alphabetical Order—St. Louis County Included: City's Quota of 4696 and County's 509 will be Taken From This List* (St. Louis: St. Louis Post-Dispatch, 1917).

Newspaper accounts give the reader a flavor of the time and the importance of the registration. Men who were out-of-town were required to register on the designated date in whatever city they were that day. The out-of-town draft board was supposed to return the card to the hometown draft board. The draft law even required men in hospitals and prisons to register.

The City of St. Louis had twenty-eight draft boards that match the boundaries of the same number of political wards. Maps are available to show the boundaries. St. Louis County consisted of three draft boards, in the North, Ferguson; in the middle of the County, Clayton, and to the South, Kirkwood.

The St. Louis Public Library offers an online database for St. Louis area soldiers killed during World War I. This database, compiled by Tom Pearson, is on the same website as the *St. Louis Post-Dispatch* obituary index.[600]

Missouri World War I Army discharge cards, as seen in Figure 45, are available,[601] as are the discharge cards for those who served in the Navy.[602] A copy of the veteran's service card is

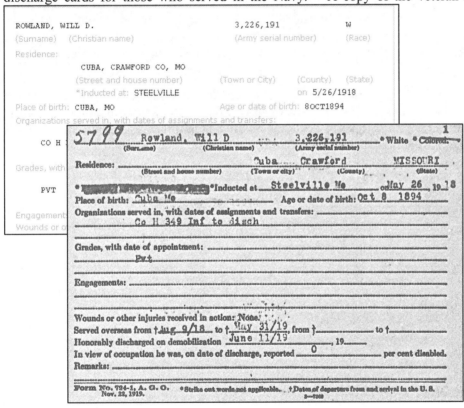

Figure 45: World War I Discharge Record

---

600. "St. Louis City and County Men Killed in World War I," *St. Louis Public Library* (http://www.slpl.lib.mo.us/libsrc/obit.htm).

601. Missouri World War I Army Discharge Cards; Missouri State Archives microfilm, 96 rolls.

602. Missouri World War I Navy Discharge Cards; Missouri State Archives microfilm, 7 rolls.

available for those who served in the Missouri National Guard.[603] All of these records are available on microfilm at local libraries. These records, maintained by the Missouri Adjutant General's office and the Missouri State Archives, still exist and were not destroyed by the 1973 fire at the National Military Personnel Records Center. The Missouri military database includes their names and basic information about the soldiers.[604] Here is an example of the information from the database and the actual card for the same Army veteran.

The Adjutant General's office of Missouri distributed a form statewide for discharged World War I soldiers. The St. Louis City and County forms are available at the Missouri Historical Society Research Library. They provide the name of the veteran, the name of his parents, date and place of birth, military information and history, and his current (1919) occupation and employer. Families participated in this survey voluntarily; therefore, information is not available on all veterans from St. Louis City and County. Any photos submitted with the survey are available at the Missouri Historical Society Research Library.[605]

In addition to the previously mentioned World War I soldiers form, the Women's Committee Council of National Defense, Missouri Division, distributed forms statewide. About 3,000 of the forms are available at the Missouri Historical Society Research Library. This form contains the soldier's name, rank, county of residence, place of birth and enlistment or draft, present address, branch of service, and commanding officer.[606]

Missouri's World War I veterans, or their heirs, received a "bonus pay" from the state in 1922. They received ten dollars for every month of service during the war, with a limit of twenty-five months. The original cards, housed at the Missouri State Archives, provide the veteran's address in 1922 and indicate that he received the payment. If the veteran was deceased, his heirs were eligible and received the payment.[607]

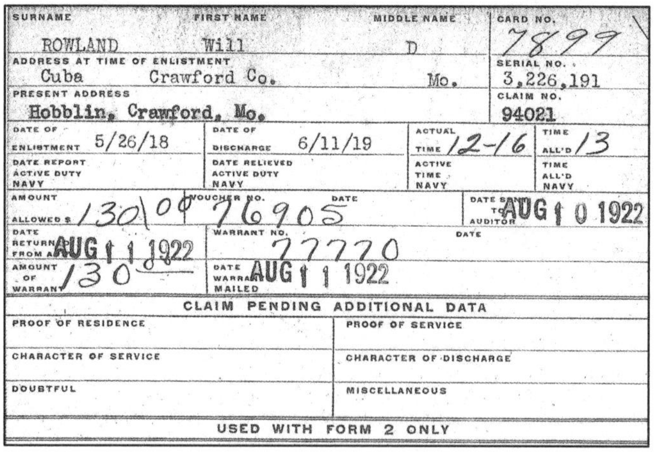
SURNAME ROWLAND FIRST NAME Will MIDDLE NAME D CARD NO. 7899
ADDRESS AT TIME OF ENLISTMENT Cuba Crawford Co. Mo. SERIAL NO. 3,226,191
PRESENT ADDRESS Hobblin, Crawford, Mo. CLAIM NO. 94021
DATE OF ENLISTMENT 5/26/18 DATE OF DISCHARGE 6/11/19 ACTUAL TIME 12-16 TIME ALL'D 13
DATE REPORT ACTIVE DUTY NAVY DATE RELIEVED ACTIVE DUTY NAVY ACTIVE TIME NAVY TIME ALL'D NAVY
AMOUNT ALLOWED $ 130\00 VOUCHER NO. 76905 DATE DATE SENT TO AUDITOR AUG 10 1922
DATE RETURNED FROM AUDITOR AUG 11 1922 WARRANT NO. 77770 DATE
AMOUNT OF WARRANT 130— DATE WARRANT MAILED AUG 11 1922
CLAIM PENDING ADDITIONAL DATA
PROOF OF RESIDENCE PROOF OF SERVICE
CHARACTER OF SERVICE CHARACTER OF DISCHARGE
DOUBTFUL MISCELLANEOUS
USED WITH FORM 2 ONLY

Figure 46: World War I Bonus Pay Record

603. Missouri World War I National Guard Service Cards; Missouri State Archives, microfilm, 7 rolls.

604. "Soldiers Database: War of 1812–World War I," *Missouri State Archives* (http://www.sos.mo.gov/archives/soldiers).

605. World War I State of Missouri Adjutant General Forms (St. Louis: Missouri Historical Society, 1919).

606. World War I soldiers form, the Women's Committee Council of National Defense, Missouri Division, 1917–1919; Missouri Historical Society, manuscript collection.

607. "World War I Bonus Pay cards;" Missouri State Archives, manuscript collection.

St. Louis established a memorial for the local soldiers who sacrificed their lives during World War I. The city placed a plaque and a tree along Kingshighway Boulevard for each man that died in service. Over the years, construction destroyed or removed several of the plaques and some of the trees. Some surviving plaques are on display at Jefferson Barracks.[608]

In addition to the soldiers' records, there are military histories for various units that served in World War I. The *History of the Twelfth Engineers U.S. Army: Mobilized at St. Louis, Missouri, June 1917...* is one example. A military history tells the reader about the unit and its activities. It may or may not mention the veterans by name.[609]

St. Louis is the home of the National Personnel Records Center Military Personnel Records mentioned in the REPOSITORIES chapter. This facility houses records for soldiers that were in World War I and World War II. A devastating fire in 1973 destroyed approximately eighty-five percent of the Army and Air Force records. However, the staff has replaced basic information for some lost records. The fire did not affect the records for the Navy, Marines, and Coast Guard personnel.

Even if your ancestor was in the Army or Air Force, submit a request for the records. You may be pleasantly surprised with the answer. If you know the soldier's service number, it will greatly expedite the search. Make the request online (http://vetrecs.archives.gov). Or, by mail submit form 180, which is available online (http://archives.gov/veterans/military-service-records/get-service-records.html). A book by Christina Schaefer, *The Great War: A Guide to the Service Records of All the World's Fighting Men and Volunteers,* provides an overview of the available information.[610]

WORLD WAR II (1941–1945)

Many World War II soldiers from around the country passed through Jefferson Barracks for training on their way to the War. Records and memorabilia are on display at the museum in Jefferson Barracks. Betty Burnett's publication, *St. Louis at War: The Story of A City, 1941–1945* provides photographs and describes the city during World War II.

The National Archives has the Army Enlistment Records database online (http://www.archives.gov/add) listed under the *World War II* link. The National Archives–Central Plains Region and Ancestry.com has the Selective Service card file for the "Old Man's draft" which took place in April 1942 for men ages 45 to 64. Registration cards for younger men will be open to the public in the future. The U.S. government published the war casualties for Missouri in

---

608. "WWI article," *St. Louis Post-Dispatch*, November 23, 2007.

609. John A. Laird, *History of the Twelfth Engineers U.S. Army: Mobilized at St. Louis, Missouri, June 1917, Returned to the U.S. for Demobilization April 27, 1919, Mustered Out at Camp Funston, May 16, 1919* (St. Louis: privately printed, 1919).

610. Christina Schaefer, *The Great War: A Guide to the Service Records of All the World's Fighting Men and Volunteers* (Baltimore: Genealogical Publishing Company, 1998).

1946.[611] The online obituary index at St. Louis Public Library provides a list of deceased St. Louis veterans.[612]

As part of their World War II collection, the Western Historical Manuscript Collection and the *St. Louis Post-Dispatch* distributed a survey to some WWII St. Louis veterans. The list of the participating veterans is online. This collection includes books, correspondence, and family memorabilia. *Finding Your Father's War* also provides data about military memorabilia and medals.[613]

SUBSEQUENT WARS

St. Louisans participated in military conflicts, such as those in Korea and Vietnam. Some records are available online, but most remain closed due to privacy issues. The veteran or his heirs may request a copy of the associated records. The Virtual St. Louis Korean War Memorial website provides the names of local men who died during combat.[614] Thomas Pearson from St. Louis Public Library compiled a list of *St. Louis City Men Killed in the Vietnam War,* which is available on the library's website.[615] Another website, St. Louisans Killed in Vietnam, provides the names of St. Louis-area residents killed in combat.[616]

The City of St. Louis maintains the Soldier's Memorial (1315 Chestnut Street, St. Louis; phone 314-622-4550; http://stlouis.missouri.org/government/solmem.html). This facility offers memorabilia and history about various wars.

---

611.   *Navy Department of Information, State Summary of War Casualties, Missouri* (Washington, D.C.: U.S. Government Printing Office, 1946).

612.   "St. Louis Post-Dispatch Newspaper Obituaries," *St. Louis Public Library* (http://www.slpl .lib.mo.us).

613.   "World War II Veteran Survey, 1939–1945," *Western Historical Manuscript Collection* (http://www.umsl.edu/~whc/guides/whm0647.htm). Jonathan Gawne, *Finding Your Father's War: A Practical Guide to Researching and Understanding Service in the World War II, U.S. Army* (Philadelphia: Casemate Publishing, 2006).

614.   *The Virtual St. Louis Korean War Memorial* (http://www.usgennet.org/usa/mo/county/ stlouis/korea).

615.   "St. Louis City Men Killed in the Vietnam War," *St. Louis Public Library* (http://www .slpl.lib.mo.us).

616.   "St. Louisans Killed in Vietnam," *History Time Portal to Old St. Louis* (http://www .usgennet.org/usa/mo/county/stlouistribute/vietnam.htm).

Newspapers in St. Louis

Newspaper research can be very rewarding as articles throughout a newspaper can provide clues and helpful information to genealogists. While not every fact may be accurate, it is information contemporary to the event. Review your ancestor's hometown newspapers as well as papers of the out-of-town extended family. Obituaries and vital event notices provide clues to family information. Legal notices such as probate notices, divorce cases, and delinquent tax lists, may provide further clues for your family history. News articles and social event notices remind us of the daily activities of our ancestors. Many St. Louis newspapers had social columns specific to local communities.

Newspaper advertisements provide a glimpse into the past including clothes, furniture, automobiles, weather, and travel. Perhaps your ancestor owned a business that advertised in the newspaper. The classified ads offer information about real estate and businesses. The business section also provides information on stocks and farm products. Many St. Louis families had small farms, on maybe forty acres or less locally known as truck farms; therefore, the market price for their crops provides some history of their farm.

There were three important newspapers in St. Louis in the nineteenth and twentieth centuries: the *Globe*, the *Post*, and the *Star-Times*. The History of the St. Louis Globe-Democrat, 1896, and another, *A History of the St. Louis Globe-Democrat,* published in 1961, provide interesting information about that newspaper.[617] *The Story of the St. Louis Post-Dispatch,* outlines the history of the only surviving newspaper in St. Louis.[618] A master's thesis, *A History of the St. Louis Star-Times* provides information about the third local newspaper.[619] Review all three newspapers for information on family events that took place during their time of publication.

Before starting your newspaper research, make a list of your ancestors, their residential areas, and time periods. Then compare the list to the available newspapers to identify which papers to review. Include the community, county seat, ethnic, and religious newspapers as well as the daily

---

617. *History of the St. Louis Globe-Democrat* (St. Louis: Woodward and Tiernan Printing Company, 1896). Jim Allee Hart, *A History of the St. Louis Globe-Democrat* (Columbia: University of Missouri Press, 1961).

618. *The Story of the St. Louis Post-Dispatch*, 8th edition (St. Louis: St. Louis Post-Dispatch, 1965).

619. Charles Robert Suits, *A History of the St. Louis Star-Times*, master's thesis (Columbia: University of Missouri, 1970).

papers. St. Louis Mercantile Library offers an online *Research Guide to St. Louis Newspapers* and a link to the *St. Louis Reference Record* by W. A. Kelsoe.[620]

NEWSPAPER INDEXES

There have been numerous St. Louis newspapers. Researchers should start with indexes from the *St. Louis Post-Dispatch, St. Louis Globe-Democrat*, and *St. Louis Star-Times*. Other important newspapers are the *St. Louis Argus, Watchman-Advocate,* and *Westliche-Post*. The *Missouri Gazette* and *Missouri Republican* were the earliest St. Louis newspapers starting in 1808.

The *Westliche-Post* was probably the most well read German newspaper in the area and was published from 1857 to 1938. Their obituaries usually have a black bar at the top and bottom, making the obituary easy to locate, even if you do not read German. The name of the deceased is easy to read. Harvey Sealberg's 1967 dissertation on this newspaper, *Westliche-Post of St. Louis: A Daily Newspaper for German-Americans 1857–1938* includes social information on Germans in St. Louis during that era.[621] The Missouri Historical Society Research Library has the *Abend Schule* German newspaper in bound volumes dating from 1854 to 1940.

The *St. Louis Argus* is the premier African-American newspaper. An index to the obituaries is available on the St. Louis Public Library website.[622] The *St. Louis American* started publishing in 1936 and continues today.

The *St. Louis Post-Dispatch* started publication in 1878 and continues today, providing the liberal viewpoint on most issues. An obituary index is available at the St. Louis Public Library website.[623] The *St. Louis Globe-Democrat,* published from 1875 to 1986, provided the conservative viewpoint. Mercantile Library houses the *Globe's* newspaper morgue, which includes photographs and clippings. A topic and surname index dating from 1920s to 1986 is available online at the Mercantile Library website.[624] If you know the political views of your ancestors, it may help determine which newspaper holds their obituaries. Given the choice, the family probably selected the newspaper they read every day, which was the one with similar political viewpoints.

The *St. Louis Star-Times,* published from 1885 to 1951, is often the forgotten newspaper. Among other things, this newspaper published articles about cemeteries, churches, and other local facilities and events of interest to family historians.

---

620. "Research Guide to St. Louis Newspapers," *St. Louis Mercantile Library* (http://www.umsl.edu/ mercantile/mguides/newspaper_guide.rtf).

621. Harvey Sealberg, *Westliche-Post of St. Louis: A Daily Newspaper for German Americans, 1857– 1938* (St. Louis: St. Louis County Library, 2006). [This publication is an authorized facsimile from UMI.]

622. "*St. Louis Argus* Obituaries," *St. Louis Public Library* (http://previous.slpl.org.libsrc/ argusobit.htm).

623. "*St. Louis Post-Dispatch* Obituaries," *St. Louis Public Library* (http://www.slpl.lib.mo.us/ libsrc/obit.htm).

624. "St. Louis Globe-Democrat," *Mercantile Library* (http://www.umsl.edu/mercantile/special_ collections/directory/slma-112_Images.html).

The *St. Louis Christian Advocate* was a weekly publication of the Methodist Episcopal Church South. One publication compiles an index of 6,500 names from Methodist-related obituaries statewide and provides abstracts of the obituaries dating from 1851 to 1882.[625]

The Missouri Historical Society Research Library has a thirty-two volume publication, *Necrologies,*[626] dating from 1913 to 1979. Each article contains the name of the newspaper and the publication date. Researchers can easily locate and print the article from newspaper microfilm. The articles are arranged chronologically and indexed in the information card file.

Many of the following newspapers are available on microfilm, a few are in bound volumes, at various research facilities; however, the available dates vary by facility. The following chart uses these abbreviations: Mercantile Library = Merc; Missouri Historical Society = MoHis; State Historical Society of Missouri = SHS; St. Louis County Library = SLCL; St. Louis Public Library = SLPL

ST. LOUIS NEWSPAPERS

NEWSPAPER	DESCRIPTION	SCHEDULE	YEARS	ARCHIVED
Abend-Anzeiger	German	Daily	1901–1909	MoHis; SHS
Abend Schule	German	Weekly	1854–1940	MoHis
Altruist		Monthly	1885–1917	SHS
American	African American	Weekly	1944–present	SHS
American Tribune			1883–1887	SHS
Amerika	German Catholic	Daily	1872–1924	MoHis; SHS; SLCL; SLPL
Anzeiger des Westens	German	Weekly	1835–1912	MoHis; SHS; SLCL; SLPL
Arbeiter Zeitung	German		1898–1912	MoHis
Baden News Press	Baden	Weekly	1948–1964	SHS; SLCL
Brentwood Scope	Brentwood	Bi-monthly	1963–1974	SHS
Carondelet New Era	Carondelet	Weekly	1859–1860	MoHis
Carondelet News	Carondelet	Weekly	1900–1935	MoHis; SHS; SLCL (index); SLPL; Carondelet
Carondelet Progress	Carondelet	Weekly	1898–1899	SHS; SLCL
Catholic News Letter	Catholic	Weekly	1845–1846	MoHis; SHS
Central Baptist	Baptist	Weekly	1876–1912	MoHis; SHS
Central Christian Advocate	Methodist	Weekly	1853–1910	MoHis; SHS
Central West End Journal	Central West End	Weekly	1984–1987	SLPL

---

625. Mrs. Howard W. Woodruff, compiler, *State-Wide Missouri Obituaries, From "The St. Louis Christian Advocate" Methodist, 1851–1882* (Independence: The Author, 1986).

626. *Necrologies* (St. Louis: Missouri Historical Society, [1979]).

NEWSPAPER	DESCRIPTION	SCHEDULE	YEARS	ARCHIVED
Church Progress	Catholic	Weekly	1903–1929	SHS
Clayton Argus	Clayton	Weekly	1891–1920	MoHis; SHS
Clayton Citizen	Clayton	Weekly	1979–1987	SLPL
Coleman's Rural World	St. Louis	Weekly	1865–1912	SHS
Community Courier		Weekly	1922–1935	SLPL
Community Press	Ellisville	Weekly	1962–1974	SHS
County Star Journal	St. Louis	Weekly	1884–1990	SHS
Courier	United Church of Christ	Monthly	1987–present	SHS
Daily Commercial Bulletin		Daily	1838–1841	MoHis
Daily Globe	St. Louis	Daily	1872–1875	SHS
Daily Missouri Democrat	St. Louis	Daily	1853–1872	Merc; SHS; SLCL
Daily Missouri Republican	St. Louis	Daily	1848	SLPL
Daily Morning Herald	St. Louis	Daily	1841–1860	SHS
Der Lutheraner	German Lutheran	Various	1844–1911	SHS
Der Vorsteher	German		1907–1908	MoHis
Deutsche WochenSchrift	German	Weekly	1969–1982	SHS
Die Deutsche Tribune	German	Daily	1844–1852	MoHis; SHS
Die Neue Zeit	German	Weekly	1863–1864	MoHis
Dispatch	St. Louis	Daily	1864–1877	SHS
Es Videke	Hungarian	Weekly	1958–1969	SHS
Evening News	St. Louis	Daily	1852–1867	SHS
Ferguson Blade	Ferguson	Weekly	1916	MoHis
Florissant News	Florissant	Weekly	1913	MoHis
Florissant Valley Journal	Florissant	Weekly	1990–1991	SHS
Florissant Valley Reporter	Florissant	Weekly	1951–1998	SHS
Flying Dutchman			1976–1980	SLPL
Free Press	Jewish	Weekly	1885–1887	SHS; SLCL
Grand-Arsenal News	Grand/Arsenal	Weekly	1922–1933	SHS
Grand-Gravois Booster	Grand/Gravois	Weekly	1928–1933	SHS
Grocer & General Merchant		Weekly	1881–1900	SHS
Herald	Ferguson	Weekly	1956–1964	SHS
Herold des Glaubens	German Catholic	Weekly	1850–1920	SHS; SLCL; SLPL
Hlas	Bohemian-Czech Catholic	Weekly	1901–1945	MoHis; SHS
Il Pensiero	Italian	Semi-monthly	1969–present	SHS; SLPL
Jefferson–Gravois	Jefferson/Gravois	Weekly	1925–1935	SHS
Jewish Light	Jewish	Weekly	1947–present	MoHis; SHS; SLCL; Brodsky
Jewish Tribune	Jewish	Weekly	1879–1881	SHS; SLCL
Jewish Voice	Jewish	Weekly	1888–1922	MoHis; SLCL
Kirkwood Advertiser	Kirkwood	Weekly	1951–1971	SHS
Kirkwood Leader	Kirkwood	Weekly	1917	MoHis

NEWSPAPER	DESCRIPTION	SCHEDULE	YEARS	ARCHIVED
Kirkwood Monitor	Kirkwood	Weekly	1915–1944	SHS
Labor	Labor	Weekly	1894–1896	SHS
Lafayette Square Marquis			1978–2000	SLPL
La Lega Italiana	Italian	Weekly	1914–1920	SHS; SLCL
La Revue de l'Ouest	French	Weekly	1854–1865	SHS; SLCL (Index)
Le Patriote	French	Weekly	1878, 1884, 1886–1887	Merc; SLCL (Index); SLPL
Lutheran Witness Reporter	Lutheran	Bi-monthly	1965–1975	SHS
Manchester–Chouteau Neighborhood News	Manchester Chouteau	Weekly	1934–1946	SHS
Maplewood Champion	Maplewood	Weekly	1912–1935	SLCL
Maplewood Journal	Maplewood	Weekly	1911–1913	MoHis; SHS
Market Reporter	St. Louis	Daily/Weekly	1875–1931	SHS
Messenger	Kirkwood	Weekly	1928–1959	SHS
Mid-Continent	Presbyterian	Weekly	1888–1896	SHS
Midwest Labor World	Labor	Bi-monthly	1943–1963	SHS
Mill Creek Valley Intelligencer	St. Louis	Weekly	1968–1971	SLPL
Missouri American	St. Louis	Weekly	1916–1971	SHS
Missouri Argus	St. Louis	Weekly	1835–1840	MoHis; SHS; SLPL
Missouri Democrat	St. Louis	Daily	1852–1875	SHS; SLCL; SLPL
Missouri Free Press	St. Louis	Weekly	1833	MoHis
Missouri Gazette	St. Louis	Weekly	1808–1822	Merc; MoHis; SHS; SLPL
Missouri Presbyterian	Presbyterian	Weekly	1866–1870	SHS
Missouri Republican News	St. Louis	Daily/Weekly	1822–1885	MoHis; SHS; SLCL; SLPL
Missourian	St. Louis	Weekly	1843–1845	SHS
Modern View	Jewish	Weekly	1902–1943	SHS; SLPL
Monitor	Kirkwood	Weekly	1915–1944	SHS
Naborhood Link News	Lemay	Weekly	1930–1998	SHS; SLCL; Carondelet
Neighborhood Journal		Weekly	1986–1988	SLPL
Network News	Fenton	Weekly	1992–1995	SHS
News	Baden	Monthly/Wkly	1931–1941	SHS
News Champion	Maplewood	Weekly	1914–1935	SHS
News of St. Louis Hills	St. Louis Hills	Weekly	1951–1952	SLPL
News Press	Baden	Weekly	1948–1980	SHS
News Times	Webster Groves	Weekly	1951–1961	SHS
Normandy Area Advocate	Normandy	Weekly	1990–1997	SHS
North County Journal	North County	Weekly	1957–1995	SHS; SLPL
North St. Louis Community News	Hodiamont–Bartmer	Weekly	1931–1968	SHS; SLCL; SLPL
North Side Journal	North St. Louis	Weekly	1984–1988	SLPL
Northwest County Journal	North County	Weekly	1982–1983	SLPL
Northwest Journal	North County	Weekly	1984–1990	SLPL

NEWSPAPER	DESCRIPTION	SCHEDULE	YEARS	ARCHIVED
Observer	Presbyterian	Weekly	1934–1971	SHS; SLPL
Old School Presbyterian	Presbyterian	Weekly	1870–1874	SHS
Przewodnik Polski	Polish	Weekly	1899–1945	MoHis; SHS
Register	Catholic	Weekly	1941–1957	SHS
Republic	St. Louis	Weekly	1890–1895	SHS
Riverfront Times	St. Louis	Weekly	1987–present	SHS; SLPL
Shepherd of the Valley	Catholic	Weekly	1832–1854	SHS
Spirit of Ferguson	Ferguson	Weekly	1962–1964	SHS
St. Louis American	African-American	Daily	1936–present	MoHis; SHS; SLPL
St. Louis Argus	African-American	Weekly	1912–present	Merc; MoHis; SHS; SLCL; SLPL
St. Louis Beacon	St. Louis	Weekly	1829–1832	SHS; SLPL
St. Louis Bugle	Lemay/Carondelet	Weekly	1945–1996	SHS; SLCL; Carondelet
St. Louis Business Journal	Business	Weekly	1980–present	Merc; MoHis; SHS; SLPL
St. Louis Christian Advocate	Methodist	Weekly	1852–1931	SHS; SLCL; SLPL
St. Louis Chronicle	St. Louis	Daily	1880–1900	SHS; SLPL
St. Louis Commercial Gazette	St. Louis	Weekly	1873–1883	MoHis; SHS
St. Louis Community News	Overland	Weekly	1963–1981	SHS
St. Louis Countian	Clayton/Kirkwood	Daily/Weekly	1919–present	SHS; SLCL; SLPL
St. Louis County Herald	Wellston	Monthly	1903–1924	SHS
St. Louis County Leader	Clayton		1923–1954	SHS
St. Louis County Legal Record	Legal		1861–1866	MoHis
St. Louis County Observer	Maplewood	Weekly	1934–1971	SHS
St. Louis County Sentinel	Clayton		1921–1924	SHS
St. Louis County Star	St. Louis County	Weekly	1984–1988	SLPL
St. Louis County Watchman	Clayton	Weekly	1881–1903	SHS
St. Louis Daily Dispatch	St. Louis	Daily	1864–1877	MoHis; SHS
St. Louis Daily Evening News	St. Louis	Daily	1852–1867	MoHis; SHS
St. Louis Daily Globe	St. Louis	Daily	1872–1875	Merc; SHS
St. Louis Daily Market Reporter	St. Louis	Daily	1902–1931	MoHis; SHS; SLPL
St. Louis Daily Morning Herald	St. Louis	Daily	1852–1858 1906–1907	MoHis; SHS
St. Louis Daily News	St. Louis	Daily	1978–1979	SLPL
St. Louis Daily Press	St. Louis	Daily	1978–1979	SLPL
St. Louis Daily Record	St. Louis	Daily	1890–present	SHS; SLCL; SLPL
St. Louis Daily Reveille		Daily/Weekly	1844–1850	Merc: MoHis; SHS
St. Louis Daily Times	St. Louis	Daily	1850–1879	Merc; MoHis; SHS; SLPL
St. Louis Daily Union	St. Louis	Daily	1846–1849	MoHis; SHS; SLPL
St. Louis Democrat	St. Louis	Daily	1842–1875	Merc; MoHis; SHS
St. Louis Dispatch	St. Louis	Daily	1864–1878	Merc; SHS; SLPL
St. Louis Enquirer	St. Louis	Weekly	1815–1829	MoHis; SHS; SLPL

NEWSPAPER	DESCRIPTION	SCHEDULE	YEARS	ARCHIVED
St. Louis Evangelist	Presbyterian	Weekly	1875–1887	MoHis; SHS
St. Louis Evening Chronicle	St. Louis	Daily	1891–1900	SLPL
St. Louis Evening News	St. Louis	Daily	1852–1867	SHS
St. Louis Evening Post	St. Louis	Daily	1878	Merc; SHS
St. Louis Globe-Democrat	General News	Daily	1853–1986	Merc; MoHis; SHS; SLCL; SLPL
St. Louis Home Journal	St. Louis	Weekly	1868–1871	MoHis; SHS
St. Louis Intelligencer	St. Louis	Daily/Weekly	1850–1857	MoHis; SHS; SLPL
St. Louis & Jefferson County News	Jefferson County	Weekly	1960–1978	SHS
St. Louis Jewish Record	Jewish	Weekly	1916–1951	MoHis
St. Louis Labor	Labor	Weekly	1893–1912	SLPL
St. Louis Labor Tribune	Labor	Weekly	1937–1985	MoHis; SHS; SLPL
St. Louis Labor Union	Labor	Daily	1846–1867	MoHis; SHS
St. Louis Legals	Legal	Daily/Weekly	1995–1998	SHS
St. Louis Lutheran	Lutheran	Weekly	1948–1960	MoHis; SHS; SLCL
St. Louis Missouri Reporter	St. Louis	Daily	1842–1845	MoHis; SHS
St. Louis Morning Herald	St. Louis	Daily	1858–1860	MoHis; SHS
St. Louis Neighborhood News	St. Louis	Weekly	1927–1963	SHS
St. Louis News	St. Louis	Weekly	1901–1945	SHS
St. Louis News	St. Louis	Daily	1978–1979	SHS; SLPL
St. Louis Palladium	African-American	Weekly	1903–1907	MoHis; SHS; SLCL; SLPL
St. Louis Pilot		Weekly	1855–1856	MoHis; SHS
St. Louis Post-Dispatch	General News	Daily	1878–present	Merc; MoHis; SHS, SLCL; SLPL
St. Louis Presbyterian	Presbyterian	Weekly	1853–1894	MoHis; SHS
St. Louis Register	Catholic	Register	1941–1957	SHS; SLPL
St. Louis Republican	St. Louis		1850–1851, 1854	MoHis; SLCL
St. Louis Republic	St. Louis	Daily	1888–1919	SHS; SLPL
St. Louis Review	Catholic	Weekly	1957–present	SHS; SLPL
St. Louis Sentinel	African American	Weekly	1968–present	MoHis; SHS; SLPL
St. Louis Small Business	Business		1989–2000	SLPL
St. Louis Sporting News	Sports	Weekly	1886–present	SHS
St. Louis Star-Times	General News	Daily	1885–1951	MoHis; SHS; SLCL; SLPL
St. Louis Sun	General News	Daily	1989–1990	Merc; SHS; SLPL
St. Louis Times	St. Louis	Daily	1866–1932	SHS; SLPL
St. Louis Tribune	German	Daily	1880–1897	SHS; SLPL
St. Louis Weekly Market Reporter	Business	Weekly	1877–1880, 1883–1889, 1895	SLPL
St. Louis Weekly Reveille		Daily/Weekly	1844–1850	Merc; MoHis; SHS
St. Louis World	St. Louis	Daily	1903–1906	SHS; SLPL
St. Louiske' Listy	Czech	Weekly	1901–1923	SHS
South County Journal	South County	Weekly	1986–1988	SLPL

NEWSPAPER	DESCRIPTION	SCHEDULE	YEARS	ARCHIVED
South County News	South County	Weekly	1989–2000	SHS; SLPL
South County Times	South County	Weekly	1992–present	SHS
South Side Journal	Affton	Weekly	1935–1988	MoHis; SHS; SLPL
South St. Louis County News	Affton	Weekly	1855–1873	SHS
South St. Louis Neighborhood News	South St. Louis	Weekly	1937–1969	SHS
Spectator	St. Louis	Weekly	1880–1893	Merc; MoHis; SHS; SLPL
Spirit of Ferguson	Ferguson	Weekly	1960–1964	SHS; SLPL
Sunday Watchman	Catholic	Weekly	1888–1904	SHS
Times	Webster Groves	Weekly	1909–1914	MoHis; SHS
Town Talk	Ferguson	Weekly	1928–1960	SHS
Tri County Journal	Eureka–Pacific	Weekly	1969–1984	SHS
Tri-Weekly Missouri Republican	Pacific/Eureka	Weekly	1835–1868	SHS
Union Labor Advocate	Labor	Weekly	1934–1958	MoHis; SHS
Valley Reporter	Florissant	Weekly	1951–1998	SHS
Volkstimme des Westens	German	Weekly	1877–1880	SHS; SLPL
Watchman Advocate	County/Republican	Daily/Weekly	1881–1985	Merc; SHS; SLCL (Index)
Webster Advertiser	Webster Groves	Weekly	1963–1971	SHS
Webster Groves News	Webster Groves	Weekly	1916–1960	SHS; SLCL
Webster-Kirkwood Times	Webster Kirkwood	Weekly	1979–present	SHS
Webster News-Times	Webster	Weekly	1914–1951	SHS
Webster Times	Webster	Weekly	1896–1898	MoHis; SHS
Wellston Journal	Wellston	Weekly	1950–1959	SHS; SLPL
West Citizen Journal	West County	Weekly	1986–1987	SLPL
West Countian	West County	Bi-weekly	1994–1996	SHS
West County Citizen	West County	Weekly	1982	SLPL
West End Word	Central West End	Weekly	1972–1988	MoHis; SHS; SLPL
Western Watchman	Baptist	Weekly	1849–1859	SHS
Western Watchman	Catholic	Weekly	1869–1933	SHS
Westliche-Post	German	Daily/Weekly	1857–1938	MoHis; SHS; SLCL (Index); SLPL
Wochenblatt der Amerika	German Catholic	Weekly	1878–1886	SHS
Women's National Daily	University City	Daily	1906–1911	SHS
Women's National Weekly	University City	Weekly	1911–1916	SHS

Religions in St. Louis

Religious records can provide family information about baptisms, confirmations, marriages, and deaths. Membership lists, minute books, and other organizational records can also provide additional family clues.

You can often document a baptismal date, parents' names, and names of the witnesses. The document often provides the actual birth date as well. Marriage records provide the name of the bride and groom, the marriage date, and the names of the witnesses. The names of the bride's and groom's parents are often included. The document may include the date and place of baptism if it occurred outside that parish. Other records may indicate a date of death and the cemetery.

St. Louis is a multi-denominational city. The French and Spanish opened the doors for the Catholic Church; Germans brought Catholics, Lutherans, and Protestant denominations now included in the United Church of Christ; Kentucky and Tennessee immigrants introduced the Baptist and Methodist faiths. Judaism came to St. Louis before 1850. In the 1800s, other religious denominations arrived and flourished in St. Louis.

Many denominations split forming various groups based on political or regional beliefs. The *Handbook of Denominations in the United States* outlines denominational development.[627] Another publication, A *Yearbook of American and Canadian Churches* provides a concise denominational history outline. *Yearbook of American Churches* was published from 1915–1972.[628]

Religious Sources

Numerous publications provide the history and sometimes photographs about religious denominations and their facilities in St. Louis. Mary Stiritz and the Landmarks Association published *St. Louis: Historic Churches and Synagogues*. This publication provides photos of many places of worship used by various congregations.[629] With the Soulard area dating back to

---

627. Frank S. Mead, *Handbook of Denominations in the United States* (Nashville: Abingdon Press, 1985).

628. National Council of Churches of Christ, *Yearbook of American and Canadian Churches* (Nashville: Abingdon Press, 1973–). National Council of Churches of Christ, *Yearbook of American Churches* (New York: The National Council, 1915–1972).

629. Mary M. Stiritz, *St. Louis: Historic Churches & Synagogues* (St. Louis: St. Louis Public Library and Landmarks Association of St. Louis, 1995).

1779, *The Churches of Soulard* provides information about fourteen early south side churches.[630]James Schild's, *House of God*,[631] is another publication that provides an overview and photographs of religious facilities in St. Louis.

St. Louis history books and many printed histories for various local communities offer background information on churches and synagogues in the area.

The *Blue Book: A Manual and Directory of the Protestant Evangelical Churches and Related Organizations of the Metropolitan Area of St. Louis, Missouri, Including the City and County of St. Louis, Missouri, Madison and St. Clair Counties, Illinois* published for the first time in 1926, provides the name and usually the address of many St. Louis churches.[632] Other publications also provide an overview of various religious denominations in the St. Louis area.[633] Listed later in this chapter, are denomination specific publications.

Newspapers provide timely articles about churches and synagogues. St. Louis County Library, Special Collections and St. Louis Public Library have local newspaper clipping files, which contain articles about the establishment, celebrations, special events, and closing for some of these churches. Most of the church clippings come from the *St. Louis Star-Times*, the *St. Louis Post-Dispatch*, and the *St. Louis Globe-Democrat* dating from the 1930s through the 1960s. The Missouri Historical Society Research Library has photocopied their church clippings file and placed the clippings chronologically in ten bound volumes. Within these volumes, the first articles are dated 1901 and continue to the 1970s.

The *St. Louis Star-Times* ran a series of articles about churches of various denominations that were open in the 1930s. The articles provide background information and a photo or drawing for each facility.

Many churches and synagogues have their own website offering the history of the facility. The St. Louis Genealogical Society website provides a list of local clergy and the name of their congregation. This list is in progress; therefore, check back for new updates periodically.[634] Some of the denominational publications, church histories, and websites offer lists of clergy as well.

The following information comes from a collection of sources including city and county directories, church histories, church publications, newspaper articles, and St. Louis history books. The church organizational dates sometimes vary slightly from record to record. In addition to the selected resources listed in this chapter, there are other publications on St. Louis churches.

---

630. *The Churches of Soulard: Celebrating 14 Churches In and Around the Historic Soulard District of St. Louis* (St. Louis: The Churches of Soulard Foundation, 1998).

631. James J. Schild, *House of God: Historic Churches and Places of Worship of the St. Louis Area* (Florissant: Auto Review, 1995).

632. *Blue Book: A Manual and Directory of the Protestant Evangelical Churches and Related Organizations of the Metropolitan Area of St. Louis, Missouri, including the City and County of St. Louis, Missouri, Madison and St. Clair Counties, Illinois* (St. Louis: Metropolitan Church Federation of St. Louis, 1926).

633. David A. Lossos, *Early St. Louis Area Places of Worship: Chapels, Churches, Missions, and Synagogues: Genealogy in St. Louis* (St. Louis: D. Lossos, 2001).

634. "Clergy," *St. Louis Genealogical Society* (http://www.stlgs.org/religionsClergy.htm).

Selected List of St. Louis Congregations

Grouped by denomination are religious congregations in the St. Louis area. This selected list includes only congregations described in a book, pamphlet, or article that could be helpful to researchers. There are many other churches in each denomination. The St. Louis Public Library has a list of area churches available on their website, as does the St. Louis Genealogical Society.

BAPTIST

The Baptist church was the earliest Protestant denomination established in St. Louis. Formed about 1807, Fee Fee Baptist Church was the first Baptist church in the St. Louis area. *The Central Baptist* periodical, 1895–1912 is available at the Missouri Historical Society Research Library. This periodical covers Missouri, Kansas, and Illinois and includes obituaries and marriage notices for the clergy and members of the congregation.

ANTIOCH BAPTIST, established in 1879, located at 18319 Wild Horse Creek, Chesterfield.[635]

CALVARY BAPTIST, established in 1916, located at Lillian Street and Emerson Avenue.[636]

CARONDELET BAPTIST, established in 1867, located at 2nd Street and Taylor Avenue, now called Pennsylvania Avenue and Robert Avenue in Carondelet.[637]

CENTRAL BAPTIST, established in 1941, located at 2842 Washington Avenue, formerly named Eighth Street Baptist and located at 8th Street and Lucas Avenue. This is the second oldest African American Baptist church in St. Louis.[638]

DELMAR BAPTIST, established in 1877, currently located at 1001 Municipal Drive, Town and County, formerly located at 6195 Washington Avenue at Skinker Boulevard in St. Louis.[639]

FEE FEE BAPTIST, established 1807, located at 11330 St. Charles Rock Road.[640]

FOURTH BAPTIST, established in 1851, formerly located at 13th and Sullivan Streets.[641]

---

635. *100th Anniversary Celebration of Antioch Baptist Church: St. Louis, Missouri, March 22–23–24–25, 1979* (St. Louis: The Church, 1979).

636. Calvary Baptist Church: *Lillian and Emerson Avenues, St. Louis, Missouri: Where Everybody is Somebody and the Gospel is Preached to All* (St. Louis: The Church, 1960).

637. "Carondelet's Oldest Baptist Church," *St. Louis Star-Times*, November 19, 1934, page 7.

638. Elizabeth Maddox Huntley, *A History of Central Baptist Church, 1941–1982: Revealing the Local, National, and International Impact of Her Ministries* (St. Louis: E. M. Huntley, 1988). George E. Stevens, *History of the Central Baptist Church, Showing Her Influence Upon Her Times* (St. Louis: King Publishing, 1927).

639. Elva Kuykendall Norman, *Biography of a Church: A History of the Early St. Louis Baptist Community, 1817–1877 and Delmar Church Which Emerged From It, 1877–1977* (St. Louis: Delmar Baptist Church, 1978). "A Center of Baptist Faith in West End," *St. Louis Star-Times*, May 8, 1933, page 4.

640. "Centennial Celebration of Old Fee Fee Baptist Church," *St. Louis Genealogical Society Quarterly* 39 (Spring 2006): 25–26. [This is reprint of an article dated 11 October 1907 from the newspaper, *St. Louis County Watchman*.]

641. *Fourth Baptist Church Centennial, 1851, September 15, 1951, St. Louis, Missouri: 100 Years of Trials and Triumphs* (St. Louis: The Church, 1951). "Fourth Baptist Thrived on Hardships," *St. Louis Star-Times*, February 6, 1933, page 11.

HANLEY HILLS BAPTIST, established in 1952, formerly located in Hanley Hills.[642]

IMMANUEL BAPTIST, established in 1891, formerly located at 5850 Cates Avenue.[643]

KINGSHIGHWAY BAPTIST, established in 1907, located at 5401 Kingshighway Boulevard.[644]

LAFAYETTE PARK BAPTIST, established in 1889, located at 1710 Mississippi Avenue.[645]

MAPLEWOOD BAPTIST, established in 1892, formerly located at 7241 Maple Avenue.[646]

PLEASANT GREEN BAPTIST, established in 1866, located at 2411 Belle Glade Street.[647]

SECOND BAPTIST, established in 1833, located at 9030 Clayton Road in Ladue, formerly located at Washington Avenue and Kingshighway Boulevard, and at 5th and Walnut Streets.[648]

THIRD BAPTIST, established in 1850, located at 620 North Grand Avenue, originally located 6th and Locust Streets.[649]

TOWER GROVE BAPTIST, established in 1890, located at 4257 Magnolia Avenue.[650]

WATER TOWER BAPTIST, established in 1886, formerly located at 2115 East Grand Avenue.[651]

WEBSTER GROVES BAPTIST, established in 1913, located at 308 Summit Street in Webster Groves.[652]

---

642. Littleton P. Bradley, *Hanley Hills Baptist Church, St. Louis, Missouri, 1952–1985* (Ferguson: L. P. Bradley, 1986).

643. "Immanuel Baptist Church Growing West End Center," *St. Louis Star-Times,* July 15, 1935, page 13.

644. "A Church Founded by German Baptists," *St. Louis Star-Times,* January 7, 1935, page 15.

645. "South Side Stronghold of Baptist Faith," *St. Louis Star-Times,* September 4, 1933, page 11.

646. *Maplewood Baptist Church: Celebrating One Hundred Years, 1892–1992* (St. Louis: The Church, 1992).

647. *Pleasant Green Baptist Church in Seventy-nine Years: A Story of Progress Presented in Picture and Written Materials Depicting the History of Our Church from its Very Beginning Down Through the Ages* (St. Louis: The Church, 1945).

648. Neola McCorkle Koechig, *The Story of the Second Baptist Church of Greater St. Louis* (St. Louis: N. M. Koechig, 1982). *Second Baptist Church, St. Louis, Missouri: Souvenir Volume* (St. Louis: The Church, 1908). "100-Year-Old Church," *St. Louis Star-Times,* December 22, 1932, page 15. Second Baptist Church records; St. Louis County Library, microfilm.

649. *1850–1900 Souvenir Program of Fiftieth Anniversary of Third Baptist Church, St. Louis, Missouri: With Historical Sketch of the Church* (St. Louis: The Church, 1900). Dorothy Ferguson Wofford, *Thou Hast Given a Banner: A History of the People and Times of the Third Baptist Church* (St. Louis: The Church, 1985). Norman Eugene Nygaard, *Where Cross the Crowded Ways: The Story of the Third Baptist Church of St. Louis, Missouri, and its Minister, Dr. C. Oscar Johnson* (New York: Greenberg, 1950). Alexander W. Payne, *Third Baptist Church, Saint Louis, 1850–1920: A Condensed History of Seventy Years* (St. Louis: Buschart Brothers, 1921). "A Church on a Million-Dollar Site," *St. Louis Star-Times,* October 24, 1932, page 2.

650. *Tower Grove Baptist Church, 4257 Magnolia Avenue, St. Louis, Missouri: Yearbook 1962* (St. Louis: The Church, 1962). "Tower Grove Baptist a Thriving Church," *St. Louis Star-Times,* February 12, 1934, page 6.

651. "A North Side Center of Baptist Faith," *St. Louis Star-Times,* March 26, 1934, page 5.

652. "A Church That Grew Under One Pastor," *St. Louis Star-Times,* January 8, 1934, page 5.

WEST PARK BAPTIST, established in 1893, formerly located at Hodiamont and Wells Avenues in Wellston.[653]

CATHOLIC

The Archives of the Archdiocese of St. Louis (20 Archbishop May Drive, St. Louis 63119; phone 314-792-7021) governs Catholic parishes and most Catholic cemeteries in St. Louis. Several years ago, the Archdiocese allowed the Family History Library to microfilm the original parish records and granted permission for St. Louis County Library to purchase the film. This microfilmed set is only available at the Family History Library and St. Louis County Library. The original records are housed at the parish or at the Archives of the Archdiocese.

To utilize these records successfully, it is necessary to know the name of the parish. An overall name index does not exist. Some parish records provide an index for a particular record type.

If you do not know the parish, determine where your ancestor lived by using a city directory. Then locate some parishes within that area of town and particularly those with the same ethnic background as your ancestor. Christine Hughes' *Guide to St. Louis Catholic Archdiocesan Parish Records*[654] tells you the original ethnic background of each parish, which records are available for each parish, and the dates that apply. The publication provides the Family History Library film number and the same for St. Louis County Library.

St. Louis Genealogical Society published early Catholic baptisms, 1765–1840 and early Catholic marriages.[655] The *Index to the St. Louis Cathedral and Carondelet Church Marriages*, by Oscar Collet provides early marriage data.[656] Figure 47 the first church in St. Louis, the Old Cathedral or officially the Basilica of St. Louis, King of France.

There is an online index to *The History of the Archdiocese of St. Louis: A Condensed History of the Catholic Church in Missouri and Saint Louis*. This index provides the names of the individuals and families mentioned in this history and may include a family portrait.[657]

Review several publications for the history of Catholics in St. Louis including, *Dream by the River: Two Centuries of Saint Louis Catholicism, 1766–1980,* and *The Notable Catholic Institutions of Saint Louis and Vicinity.*[658] An index, consisting of more than 10,000 names, is

---

653. *Fiftieth Anniversary of the West Park Baptist Church, Hodiamont and Wells Avenues, Saint Louis, Missouri, 1893–1943* (St. Louis: The Church, 1943).

654. Christine Human Hughes, compiler, *Guide to St. Louis Catholic Archdiocesan Parish Records* (St. Louis: Friends of St. Louis County Library, 2001).

655. St. Louis Genealogical Society. *Catholic Baptisms Saint Louis, Missouri, 1765–1840* (St. Louis: The Society, 1982). St. Louis Genealogical Society. *Catholic Marriages Saint Louis, Missouri, 1774–1840* (St. Louis: The Society, 1982).

656. Oscar W. Collet, *Index to the St. Louis Cathedral and Carondelet Church Marriages: And Index to the Marriage Contracts from the Records in the Recorder's Office of St. Louis County*; volume 1, miscellaneous A to Z (St. Louis: St. Louis County Library, Special Collections, 2004).

657. "Index to the History of the Archdiocese," *St. Louis County Library* (http://www.slcl.org/branches/hq/sc/archdio-hist/archdio-index-main.htm).

658. William Barnaby Faherty, *Dream by the River: Two Centuries of Saint Louis Catholicism, 1766–1980* (St. Louis: River City Publishers, 1981). Francis A. Thornton, *The Notable Catholic Institutions of Saint Louis and Vicinity* (St. Louis: St. Louis County Library Special Collections, 2004).

available on the St. Louis County Library website for *The History of the Archdiocese of St. Louis: A Condensed History of the Catholic Church of Missouri and St. Louis.*[659] Douglas Antoinette, *Index to St. Louis Register, 1766–1781: Baptisms, Marriages, and Burials,* provides data about early St. Louis citizens. Parishes represented in this index are not apparent by the records.[660]

Microfilm, including the *Catholic Parish Jubilee Histories*, is available at St. Louis County Library. An index listing the parishes and microfilm roll numbers is available on the library's website.[661]

ASSUMPTION CATHOLIC, established in 1843, located at 4725 Mattis Road in the Mattese area in South St. Louis County.[662]

BASILICA OF ST. LOUIS, KING OF FRANCE "Old Cathedral," established in 1770, located at 209 Walnut Street adjacent to the Arch grounds.[663]

CATHEDRAL BASILICA OF ST. LOUIS "New Cathedral," established in 1908, located at 4431 Lindell Boulevard. This magnificent structure has the largest mosaic collection in the world.[664]

CHURCH OF THE ANNUNCIATION, established in 1861, closed in 1951, formerly located at 6th and LaSalle Streets.[665]

HOLY CROSS CATHOLIC, established in 1863, closed in 1993, formerly located on 8115 Church Road.[666]

HOLY FAMILY CATHOLIC, established in 1898, closed in 2005, formerly located on 4125 Humphrey Street.[667]

HOLY GUARDIAN ANGELS CATHOLIC, established in 1866, closed in 1992, formerly located at 1000 South 14th Street.[668]

HOLY INFANT CATHOLIC, established in 1954, located at 627 Dennison Drive in Ballwin.[669]

---

659   *The History of the Archdiocese of St. Louis: A Condensed History of the Catholic Church of Missouri and St Louis* (St. Louis: Western Watchman Publishing Company, 1924). The index is online, St. Louis County Library (http://www.slcl.org/branches/hq/sc/archdio-hist/archdio-index-main.htm).

660.   Douglass Antoinette, *Index to St. Louis Register, 1766–1781; Baptisms, Marriages, and Burials* ([St. Louis]: privately printed, no date).

661.   "Catholic Parish Jubilee Histories," *St. Louis County Library* (http://www.slcl.org/branches/hq/sc/sc-j-par.htm).

662.   "Old Assumption Church a County Landmark," *St. Louis Star-Times*, August 19, 1935, page 20.

663.   Paul C. Schulte, *The Catholic Heritage of St. Louis: A History of the Old Cathedral Parish, St. Louis, Missouri* (St. Louis: Catholic Herald, 1974). Gregory Franzwa, *The Old Cathedral*, 2nd edition (Gerald, Missouri: Patrice Press, 1980). Elmer H. Behrmann, *The Story of the Old Cathedral Parish of St. Louis IX, King of France, St. Louis, Missouri* (St. Louis: The Church, 1949).

664.   William Barnaby Faherty, *The Great Saint Louis Cathedral* (St. Louis: Archdiocese of St. Louis, 1988).

665.   "Old Annunciation Church Nears Its 75th Year," *St. Louis Star-Times*, May 5, 1934, page 8.

666.   *A Souvenir of the Diamond Jubilee of Holy Cross Parish, 1864–1939, St. Louis, Missouri* (St. Louis, The Church, 1939). *The Centennial of Holy Cross Parish, 1864–1964* (St. Louis: The Church, 1964).

667.   "Holy Family Church Now in Third Home," *St. Louis Star-Times,* October 14, 1935, page 9.

668.   "Holy Angels Parish 69 Years Old," *St. Louis Star-Times,* September 9, 1935, page 13.

669.   *Holy Infant Church, Ballwin, Missouri: Welcome to Our Parish Family* (Galion, Ohio: United Church Directories, 1992).

HOLY ROSARY CATHOLIC, established in 1891, closed in 1994, formerly located at 3905 Clarence Street.[670]

MOST HOLY NAME OF JESUS CHRIST CATHOLIC, "Holy Name," established in 1865, closed in 1992, formerly located at 2047 East Grand Avenue.[671]

OUR LADY OF MOUNT CARMEL CATHOLIC, established in 1871, closed in 1993, formerly located at 8747 Annetta Street.[672]

OUR LADY OF SORROWS CATHOLIC, established in 1907, located at 5020 Rhodes Avenue.[673]

SACRED HEART CATHOLIC, established in 1866, located at 751 North Jefferson Avenue, Florissant.[674]

ST. AGATHA CATHOLIC, established in 1879, located at 3239 South 9th at Utah Street.[675]

ST. AGNES CATHOLIC, established in 1891, closed in 1993, formerly located at Sidney and Salena Streets.[676]

ST. ALPHONSUS LIGUORI CATHOLIC "The Rock Church," established in 1867, located at 1118 North Grand and Finney Avenues.[677]

ST. AMBROSE CATHOLIC, established in 1903 with an Italian congregation, located 5130 Wilson Avenue, on "The Hill."[678]

ST. ANTHONY OF PADUA CATHOLIC, established in 1863, located at 3140 Meramec Street.[679]

ST. BARBARA CATHOLIC, established in 1893 with a German congregation, closed in 1992; formerly located at 1371 Hamilton Avenue at Minerva Street.[680]

---

670. E. Louise King, *The Parish Family of Holy Rosary: October 6, 1991* (St. Louis: The Church, 1991).

671. *Most Holy Name of Jesus Christ, 1875–1975* (Hackensack, New Jersey: Custombook, 1975).

672. *Seventy-fifth Anniversary Year Diamond Jubilee, 1872–1947, Our Lady of Mt. Carmel Church* (St. Louis: The Church, 1947). R. K. Barry, *The History of Our Lady of Mount Carmel Parish, Baden, Missouri* (St. Louis: privately published, 1972).

673. *Our Lady of Sorrows Parish Silver Jubilee 1907–1932* (St. Louis: The Church, 1932). *Our Lady of Sorrows Parish, 1907–1957* (St. Louis: The Church, 1957).

674. *Sacred Heart Parish, Florissant, Missouri, 1866–1966: A Century of God and Country* (St. Louis: The Church, 1966).

675. *Diamond Jubilee of St. Agatha Church, 1946* (St. Louis: The Church, 1946). *In Commemoration of the Golden Jubilee St. Agatha Parish, 1871–1921* (St. Louis: privately printed, 1921). "St. Agatha's—A Church Built by Thrifty Germans," *St. Louis Star-Times,* September 23, 1935, page 18.

676. "Church Owes Birth to Misunderstanding," *St. Louis Star-Times,* May 20, 1935, page 20.

677. *St. Alphonsus Church. Leaves From the History of St. Alphonsus Church, St. Louis, Missouri, 1875: Compiled in Commemoration of the Completion of the Church* (St. Louis: The Church, 1895). "Years of Heart-Breaking Efforts Marked Building of Rock Church, Famous for Its Marble Shrine," *St. Louis Star-Times,* December 15, 1932, page 13.

678. *St. Ambrose Church, Fortieth Anniversary: Historical Review, Brief Historical Sketches and Data of Saint Ambrose Parish, Marconi and Wilson Avenues, St. Louis, Missouri, U.S.A.: Past and Present Achievements by Italians in America, 1903–1943* (St. Louis: Boggiano Brothers Printing, 1943). *St. Ambrose Church In Memory of Our Boys Who Died in Service* (St. Louis: The Church, 1946).

679. *St. Anthony of Padua Church, Souvenir of the Diamond Jubilee of St. Anthony Parish, 1863–1938, Saint Louis, Missouri* (St. Louis: The Church, 1938).

680. *St. Barbara's Parish, 1893–1943* (St. Louis: The Church, 1943).

ST. BERNARD CATHOLIC, established in 1874 with primarily a German congregation, closed 1973, formerly located on Gratiot Street.[681]

ST. BONIFACE CATHOLIC, established in 1859, closed in 2005, formerly located at 7622 Michigan Avenue and Schirmer Street.[682]

ST. BRIDGET OF ERIN CATHOLIC, established in 1853 in an Irish area known as "Kerry Patch," closed in 2003, formerly located on 2401 Carr Street at Jefferson Avenue.[683]

ST. CASIMIR CATHOLIC, established in 1889 with a Polish congregation, closed in 1955, formerly located at 8th and Mullanphy Streets.[684]

ST. CECILIA CATHOLIC, established in 1908, located at 5418 Louisiana Avenue.[685]

ST. CHARLES BORROMEO CATHOLIC, established in 1899 with an Italian congregation, closed in 1982, formerly located at 29th and Locust Streets.[686]

ST. ELIZABETH CATHOLIC, established in 1873, with an African American congregation, closed in 1951, formerly located at 14th and Gay Streets.[687]

ST. FERDINAND OF FLORISSANT CATHOLIC, established in 1789, located at 1765 Charbonier Road in Florissant.[688]

ST. FRANCIS DE SALES CATHOLIC, established in 1867 to serve Germans, closed as a parish in 2005, open as an oratory at 2653 Ohio Avenue.[689]

ST. FRANCIS XAVIER CATHOLIC "The College Church," established in 1837, located at Grand Avenue and Lindell Boulevard on the campus of St. Louis University, originally at 9th Street and Christy Avenue.[690]

ST. HENRY CATHOLIC, established in 1885, closed in 1977, located at California Avenue and Rutger Street. This church merged with Immaculate Conception Parish located on Lafayette Avenue.[691]

---

681. "St. Bernard's Church Near 60th Milestone," *St. Louis Star-Times,* September 3, 1934, page 5.

682. *St. Boniface Parish: The Record of the Growth of a Mustard Seed* (St. Louis: The Church, 1935). "Church to Celebrate 75th Birthday," *St. Louis Star-Times,* May 6, 1935, page 24.

683. Helen Smith and Gerald J. Kleba, *Saint Bridget of Erin 140th Anniversary, 1853–1993* (St. Louis: The Church, 1994). "St. Bridget's—A Church the Irish Built," *St. Louis Star-Times,* June 5, 1933, page 4.

684. "St. Casimir's Church a Polish Center," *St. Louis Star-Times,* March 25, 1935, page 15.

685. *Souvenir of Silver Jubilee, 1908–1933, St. Cecilia's Parish* (St. Louis: The Church, 1933). *St. Cecilia's Parish Golden Jubilee* (St. Louis: The Church, 1960).

686. "A Catholic Church That One May Built," *St. Louis Star-Times,* November 20, 1933, page 15.

687. *Diamond Jubilee: The Priests and People of St. Elizabeth's Mark the Seventy-fifth Anniversary of the Founding of their Parish* (St. Louis: The Church, 1949).

688. *Saint Ferdinand of Florissant, 1789–1961: The Story of an Historic Parish* (Florissant: St. Ferdinand of Florissant, 1961).

689. *St. Francis de Sales Parish 125th Anniversary, 1867–1992* (St. Louis: The Church, 1992). Also, *Diamond Jubilee, St. Francis de Sales Parish, 1867–1942* (St. Louis: Roling Printing Company, 1942).

690. Urban James Kramer, *History of St. Francis Xavier (College) Church St. Louis, 1837–1943* (St. Louis: St. Louis County Library Special Collections, 2004). "The College Church Rich in Tradition," *St. Louis Star-Times,* February 9, 1933, page 20.

691. "St. Henry's Church to Observe Golden Jubilee," *St. Louis Star-Times,* July 22, 1935, page 20.

ST. JAMES THE GREATER CATHOLIC, established in 1861, located at 6401 Wade Avenue.[692]

ST. JOHN NEPOMUK CATHOLIC, established in 1854, closed as a parish in 2005, located at 1625 South 11th Street, was primarily a Bohemian congregation. Today this facility is open as a chapel.[693]

ST. JOHN THE APOSTLE AND EVANGELIST CATHOLIC, established in 1847, located at 16th and Chestnut Streets.[694]

ST. JOSEPH CATHOLIC "The Shrine of St. Joseph," established in 1844 with a German congregation, closed as a parish in 1979, located at 1220 11th at Biddle Streets. This facility is open as a Shrine.[695]

ST. JOSEPH CATHOLIC, established in 1842, located at 106 North Meramec Street in Clayton.[696]

ST. JUDE CATHOLIC, established in 1953, located at 2218 North Warson Road in Overland.[697]

ST. LAWRENCE O'TOOLE CATHOLIC, established in 1855 with an Irish congregation, closed in 1948, formerly located at 14th and O'Fallon Streets.[698]

ST. LEO CATHOLIC, established in 1888 with an Irish congregation, closed in 1978, formerly located at 23rd and Mullanphy Streets.[699]

ST. LIBORIUS CATHOLIC, established in 1856 with a German congregation, closed in 1991, formerly located at 18th and Hogan Streets.[700]

ST. MALACHY CATHOLIC, established in 1858, with an Irish congregation, closed in 1959, formerly located at 2904 Clark Street at Ewing Avenue.[701]

ST. MARY OF VICTORIES CATHOLIC, established in 1843, with a German and later Hungarian congregation, closed in 2005, located at 744 South 3rd Street as a chapel.[702]

---

692. *St. James the Greater Church, 1861–1986* (St. Louis: The Church, 1986). P. J. O'Connor, *History of Cheltenham and St. James Parish: Commemorating the Diamond Jubilee of St. James Parish and the Twenty-fifth Anniversary of the Coming to the Parish of Rev. P. J. O'Connor, Pastor* (St. Louis: P. J. O'Connor, 1937).

693. *Centennial of St. John Nepomuk Church, St. Louis, Missouri: History of First Czech Catholic Church in the United States and the Priests who Served This Congregation, Together with Congratulatory Messages, Program of Celebration, and Other Items* (St. Louis: The Church, 1954). *St. John Nepomuk Church, Souvenir of the Diamond Jubilee of St. John Nepomuk Parish, Sunday November 24 to Thursday November 28, 1929* (St. Louis: The Church, 1938). "Fountainhead of Bohemian Catholic Faith in U.S.," *St. Louis Star-Times,* February 10, 1933, page 24.

694. Melissa McCanna and Fritz Dowling, *History of Saint John the Apostle and Evangelist Church: St. Louis, Missouri, 1847–1997* (St. Louis: The Church, 1998). "Old St. John's," *St. Louis Star-Times,* April 10, 1933, page 8.

695. Dana O. Jensen, "Historic St. Joseph's," Missouri Historical Society Bulletin 19 (1963): 273–276. "A Church Founded by the Jesuit Fathers," *St. Louis Star-Times,* November 18, 1935, page 11.

696. *St. Joseph's Church, Clayton, Missouri: Centennial Program* (Clayton: The Church, 1942).

697. *St. Jude's Catholic Church records, 1953–1993* (St. Louis: The Church, 1993).

698. "An Old Church the Irish Loved," *St. Louis Star-Times,* April 30, 1934, page 13.

699. "A Church Guided by Noted Priests," *St. Louis Star-Times,* March 4, 1935, page 4.

700. *St. Liborius Church 1856–1956* (St. Louis: The Church, 1956).

701. "Sentiment Has Revived St. Malachy's Church," *St. Louis Star-Times,* December 4, 1933, page 15.

702. *St. Mary of Victories Parish, St. Louis, Missouri, 1843–1943* (St. Louis: The Church, 1943).

ST. MATTHEW THE APOSTLE CATHOLIC, established in 1893 with an Irish focus, located at 2715 North Sarah Street.[703]

ST. MONICA CATHOLIC, established in 1872, located at 12136 Olive Boulevard in Creve Coeur.[704]

ST. PETER CATHOLIC, established in 1832, located at 243 West Argonne Avenue in Kirkwood, has served the Kirkwood community with a church, school, and cemetery. Originally located on Geyer Road next to the cemetery, after a fire, the church and school moved to the present location in 1875.[705]

ST. PIUS THE FIFTH CATHOLIC, established in 1905, located at 3310 South Grand Avenue.[706]

ST. ROCH'S CATHOLIC, established in 1911, located at 6052 Waterman Avenue at Rosedale Avenue, originally at 6008 Kingshighway Boulevard.[707]

ST. ROSE OF LIMA CATHOLIC, established in 1880, closed in 1992, formerly located at 1015 Goodfellow Boulevard at Maple Avenue.[708]

ST. TERESA OF AVILA CATHOLIC, established in 1865, closed in 2003, formerly located at 3636 North Market Street.[709]

ST. THOMAS OF AQUIN CATHOLIC, established in 1882, located at 3949 Iowa Avenue at Osage Street.[710]

ST. VINCENT DE PAUL CATHOLIC, established in 1841, located at 1408 South 9th Street at Park Avenue.[711]

STS. PETER AND PAUL CATHOLIC, established in 1849 to serve German families, located at 1919 South 7th Street.[712]

VISITATION CATHOLIC, established in 1882, merged to become Visitation–St. Ann's Shrine 1992, located at 4515 Evans Avenue at Taylor Avenue.[713]

---

703. "Father Shields, 41 Years Pastor of St. Matthew's," *St. Louis Star-Times,* January 21, 1935, page 9.

704. *St. Monica Parish 125th Anniversary Book* (Creve Coeur: St. Monica Parish, 1997). *Growing in Faith with Creve Coeur, 1872–1977* (Creve Coeur: St. Monica Parish, 1997).

705. Mary Broderick Chomeau, *One Hundred and Twenty-five Years: A History of Saint Peter's Parish, Kirkwood, Missouri 1832–1957* (Kirkwood, Missouri: St. Peter's Church, 1957).

706. *St. Pius 5th Parish, 1905–1980* (St. Louis: The Church, 1980).

707. Jean Fahey Eberle, *Saint Roch's: The Story of a Parish* (St. Louis: St. Roch's Catholic Church, 1967). "A Church That Grew in a Hurry," *St. Louis Star-Times,* October 27, 1932, page 2.

708. "Mgr. McGlynn and Parish in Golden Jubilee," *St. Louis Star-Times,* June 11, 1934, page 11.

709. *A History of St. Teresa's Parish, 1864–1899* (St. Louis: The Church, 1899). *St. Teresa Parish Diamond Jubilee, 1864–1940* (St. Louis: The Church, 1940).

710. "A Catholic Church Stressing Sociability," *St. Louis Star-Times,* January 29, 1934, page 5. *Golden Jubilee 1882–1932, St. Thomas of Aquin* (St. Louis: The Church, 1932).

711. "St. Vincent's—Landmark of Catholic Progress," *St. Louis Star-Times,* August 28, 1932, page 15.

712. *Sanctuary in Soulard: The First 150 Years, Sts. Peter and Paul Parish, 1849–1999* ([St. Louis]: The Church, 1999). *St. Peter & Paul, 1849–1921. Centennial Sts. Peter & Paul,* 1949. "SS Peter and Paul 86 Years Old," *St. Louis Star-Times,* June 17, 1935, page 9.

713. "Golden Jubilee at Visitation Church," *St. Louis Star-Times,* October 15, 1934, page 13.

CHRISTIAN CHURCH (DISCIPLES OF CHRIST)

The Christian Church, also known as the Disciples of Christ, was formed in St. Louis about 1837. For a while, the name of the church indicated its order of development. The First Church, the Second Church, the Third Church and so on. Today there are numerous Christian churches in the St. Louis area.[714]

COMPTON HEIGHTS CHRISTIAN, established in 1894, located at 2149 South Grand Avenue.[715]

DOVER PLACE CHRISTIAN, established in 1895, located at 701 Dover Place in Carondelet.[716]

FIRST CHRISTIAN CHURCH, established in 1837, formerly located at 6th Street and Franklin Avenue, 5th Street and Broadway, 17th and Olive Streets, Locust Street near Compton Avenue, and Delmar Boulevard at Pendleton Avenue.[717]

HAMILTON AVENUE CHRISTIAN, established in 1895, at Plymouth and Hamilton Avenues, currently located at 10545 Old Olive Boulevard in Creve Coeur.[718]

KINGSHIGHWAY CHRISTIAN, established in 1917, formerly located at Kingshighway Boulevard and Labadie Avenue. This church merged with Second Christian, thus forming Memorial Boulevard Christian.[719]

MEMORIAL BOULEVARD CHRISTIAN (see Kingshighway Christian).

UNION AVENUE CHRISTIAN, established in 1904 when Mt. Cabanne Church and Central Church merged, located at 733 Union Boulevard.[720]

CONGREGATIONAL

The Congregational denomination arrived in St. Louis in the 1850s. They had a strong presence in St. Louis until it merged with the Evangelical and Reform churches in 1957 forming the United Church of Christ denomination. The churches listed below use the same name as their publications.

BRENTWOOD CONGREGATIONAL, established in 1922, located at 2400 South Brentwood Boulevard in Brentwood, now part of the United Church of Christ denomination.[721]

COMPTON HILL CONGREGATIONAL, established in 1880, formerly located at Lafayette Avenue at Compton Avenue. Fifth Congregational Church was the first name for this congregation, but the name changed in 1887. It was also known as High Street Mission and the Fifth Congregational

---

714. *The Christian Church (Disciples of Christ) of Mid-America* (http://www.mid-americadisciples.org/churchphotos.htm).

715. "Compton Heights Church A Christian Center," *St. Louis Star-Times,* April 16, 1934.

716. "A Carondelet Center of Christian Faith," *St. Louis Star-Times,* July 3, 1934, page 5.

717. "First Christian Church Near Century Mark," *St. Louis Star-Times,* April 17, 1933, page 6.

718. *Hamilton Christian Church: The First Century, a Centennial History* (St. Louis: The Church, 1995). *Hamilton Avenue Christian Church, 1895–1945* (St. Louis: The Church, 1945).

719. "A Congregation Devoted to Primitive Christianity," *St. Louis Star-Times,* November 27, 1933, page 7.

720. "A Church That Thrived on Adversity," *St. Louis Star-Times,* November 21, 1932, page 3.

721. *The Brentwood Congregational Church, 1922–1972; Fifty Years of Fellowship and Service* (Brentwood: The Church, 1972).

Church. This church merged with Mount Hope Evangelical Congregational in 1955 and with St. Luke's UCC in 1962.[722]

FIRST CONGREGATIONAL CHURCH OF ST. LOUIS, established in 1852 as the First Trinitarian Congregational, located at 6501 Wydown Boulevard, formerly at 10th and Locust Streets, then at Grand Avenue and Delmar Boulevard.[723]

FIRST CONGREGATIONAL CHURCH OF WEBSTER GROVES, established in 1884, located at 10 West Lockwood Avenue in Webster Groves.[724]

FIRST TRINITARIAN CONGREGATIONAL, established in 1852, formerly located at 10th and Locust Streets, then Grand Avenue and Delmar Boulevard, and finally Wydown Boulevard, now called First Congregational UCC.[725]

FOUNTAIN PARK CONGREGATIONAL, established in 1867, formerly located at Aubert and Fountain Avenues.[726]

MAPLEWOOD CONGREGATIONAL, established in 1891, located at Sutton and Hazel Streets.[727]

MEMORIAL CONGREGATIONAL, established in 1882, closed 1997, 6234 Victoria Street known as Cheltenham Congregational.[728]

PILGRIM CONGREGATIONAL, established in 1866, located at 826 Union Boulevard, originally located at Garrison Avenue and Morgan Street.[729]

EPISCOPAL

The Episcopal Diocese of Missouri (1210 Locust Street, St. Louis 63103; phone 314-231-1220; http://www.diocesemo.org) provides online the history of the Episcopal denomination in St. Louis since 1819, a map of the Diocese, and links to the church websites.

---

722. "A South Side Center of Congregationalism," *St. Louis Star-Times,* July 17, 1933, page 18. Compton Hill Congregation Church records, 1881–1956; St. Louis County Library, microfilm, and Missouri State Archives film M84.

723. Ellis Walker Hay, *The First Congregational Church of Saint Louis: Centennial, 1852–1952* (St. Louis: The Church, 1952). Sylvia Stevens Schmid, *Centennial History of the First Congregational Church, Webster Groves, Missouri, (United Church of Christ), 1866–1966* (St. Louis: First Congregational Church, 1966). *First Congregational Church of St. Louis, United Church of Christ 1852–1977* (St. Louis: The Church, 1977). "A Mother Church of Congregationalism," *St. Louis Star-Times,* March 6, 1933, 11.

724. Ralph E. Davis, *Webster Groves Christian Church Disciples of Christ: 100 Years of Service and Witness, 1895–1995* (Webster Groves: Webster Groves Christian Church, 1995).

725. *First Trinitarian Congregational Church, Fiftieth Anniversary, 1852–1902* (St. Louis: The Church, 1902).

726. "Five Churches in One," *St. Louis Star-Times,* December 19, 1932, page 22.

727. "Maplewood's First Church—Its Rise," *St. Louis Star-Times,* April 22, 1935, page 22.

728. Memorial Congregational Church records available at St. Louis County Library.

729. *Fifty-fifth Year Book and Directory: Pilgrim Congregational Church, Saint Louis; Record of Work for 1921, List of Officers and Committees for 1922* ([St. Louis]: privately printed, 1922). *The Confession of Faith and Covenant of the Pilgrim Congregational Church in Saint Louis, Together with the Rules, a Catalogue of Members and a Historical Note* (St. Louis: Riverside Printing, 1884). *Manual of the Pilgrim Congregational Church in St. Louis, Missouri: Containing the History of the Church, Articles of Faith, Form of Admission, Covenant, Rules, List of Officers and Members, April 1892.* (St. Louis: J. A. Stanion, 1892). "A Cradle of Congregationalism," *St. Louis Star-Times,* November 7, 1932, page 13. Pilgrim Congregational church records, 1914–1939; St. Louis County Library, microfilm.

CHRIST CHURCH CATHEDRAL EPISCOPAL, established in 1819, located at 1210 Locust Street. Christ Episcopal Church was the first name for this congregation, which was the first Episcopal church in St. Louis.[730]

CHURCH OF THE HOLY APOSTLES EPISCOPAL, established in 1895, formerly located at Union Boulevard and Maple Avenue.[731]

CHURCH OF THE HOLY COMMUNION EPISCOPAL, established in 1869, located at 7401 Delmar Boulevard, previously located at 28th Street and Washington Avenue.[732]

CHURCH OF THE REDEEMER EPISCOPAL, established in the early 1890s, formerly located at Washington and Euclid Avenues. This congregation merged with St. James Episcopal in 1910.[733]

EMMANUEL EPISCOPAL, established in 1867, located at 9 South Bompart Avenue in Webster Groves.[734]

GRACE EPISCOPAL, established in 1846, located at 514 East Argonne Drive in Kirkwood.[735]

MOUNT CALVARY EPISCOPAL, established in 1870, formerly located at 3661 DeTonty Street.[736]

ST. GEORGE'S EPISCOPAL, established in 1845, formerly located at 7th and Locust Streets and 4301 Olive Boulevard, St. Louis. This church merged with St. Michael and St. George in 1928.[737]

ST. JAMES EPISCOPAL, established in 1868, formerly located at Goode and Cote Brilliante Avenues after a Whittier Street and North Market Street location. This church merged with Church of the Redeemer Episcopal.[738]

ST. JOHN EPISCOPAL, established in 1841, located at 3664 Arsenal Avenue by Tower Grove Park.[739]

ST. MICHAEL AND ST. GEORGE EPISCOPAL, established in 1928, located at 6345 Wydown Boulevard at Ellenwood Avenue in Clayton.[740]

---

730. *Christ Church Cathedral, Centennial Christ Church Cathedral, Saint Louis, 1819–1919* (St. Louis: The Church, 1919). Eugene Rodgers, *And Then a Cathedral: History of Christ Church Cathedral St. Louis, Missouri* (St. Louis: The Church, 1970).

731. "An Episcopal Church of English Village Design," *St. Louis Star-Times*, March 12, 1934, page 20.

732. *100 Years of Service, Church of the Holy Communion 1861–1961* (St. Louis: The Church, 1961). "A Church High in Ranks of Social Service," *St. Louis Star-Times*, April 24, 1933, page 13. *Church of Holy Communion, 1869–1919* (St. Louis: The Church, 1919).

733. "A Congregation Made Strong by Merger," *St. Louis Star-Times*, May 21, 1934, page 5.

734. Dorothy A. Rehkopf, *History of Emmanuel Episcopal Church, 1866–1966* (Webster Groves, Missouri: privately printed, 1966).

735. "A Church Dedicated to Social Service," *St. Louis Star-Times*, January 2, 1934, page 10.

736. "Mount Calvary Church Being Rehabilitated," *St. Louis Star-Times*, October 30, 1933, page 22.

737. St. George Episcopal Church records; St. Louis County Library, microfilm. Harriet A. Davidson, *Trilogy: A Story of the Three Parishes* (St. Louis: privately printed, 2006).

738. "A Congregation Made Strong by Merger," *St. Louis Star-Times*, May 21, 1934, page 5.

739. *100th Anniversary Celebration Program, November 2, 1941* (St. Louis: The Church, 1941). "St. John's Episcopal a Pioneer Church," *St. Louis Star-Times*, February 13, 1933, page 16.

740. *Susan Mount Guild of the Church Service League, Church of St. Michael and St. George, 6345 Wydown, Clayton, Missouri, 1969–1970* (Clayton: The Church, 1970). Harriet A. Davidson, Trilogy: A Story of the Three Parishes (St. Louis: Privately printed, 2006). "Two Churches Find Strength in Merger," *St. Louis Star-Times*, November 28, 1932.

ST. PAUL EPISCOPAL, established in 1866, located in Carondelet at 6518 Michigan Avenue.[741]

ST. PETER EPISCOPAL, established in 1872, located at 110 North Warson Road in Ladue.[742]

ST. STEPHEN EPISCOPAL, established in 1886, formerly located at 6th and Rutger Streets.[743]

TRINITY CHURCH EPISCOPAL, established in 1855, located at 600 North Euclid Avenue.[744]

EVANGELICAL

For information about the Evangelical Synod of North America and the German Evangelical Synod of North American churches turn to the United Church of Christ.

JEWISH

Early Jewish immigrants lived on the near south side of St. Louis in the early years. Built at Sixth Street and Cerre Avenue about 1855, the first synagogue was on property that is just south of Busch Stadium today. The earliest of St. Louis's Jewish immigrants were German. They were followed by a large influx of Eastern European Jews at the turn of the twentieth century. Two publications by Walter Erhlich, *Zion in the Valley, the Jewish Community of St. Louis*, and *Zion in the Valley, the Jewish Community of St. Louis, the Twentieth Century*, provide an overview of Jewish history in this city.[745] The St. Louis Genealogical Society website offers a list congregations in addition to those listed here.[746]

B'NAI AMOONA SYNAGOGUE, established in 1918, located at 324 South Mason Road in Town and Country, formerly at Academy Street and Vernon Avenue.[747]

B'NAI EL TEMPLE, established in 1852, located at 11411 North 40 Drive in Frontenac. Previous locations were 1) 6th and Cerre Streets, 2) 11th Street and Chouteau Avenue, 3) Spring Avenue and Flad Street, and 4) Clara Street and Delmar Boulevard.[748]

---

741. *St. Paul Episcopal, 1866–1966* (St. Louis: The Church, 1967).

742. *Seventieth Anniversary of the Founding of Saint Peter's Episcopal Church, 1868–1938* (St. Louis: The Church, 1938). *Past and Present of St. Peter's Episcopal Church, St. Louis, Missouri* ([St. Louis]: The Church, 1898). "A Church That Stays Young," *St. Louis Star-Times,* January 9, 1933, page 12.

743. "A Church Carrying on Against Great Odds," *St. Louis Star-Times,* August 27, 1934, page 5. St. Stephen's Episcopal manuscript collection, Missouri Historical Society.

744. *Trinity Church Episcopal, 1855–1955* (St. Louis: The Church, 1955). "Leading Anglo-Catholic Church in St. Louis," *St. Louis Star-Times,* December 3, 1934, page 15.

745. Walter Ehrlich, *Zion in the Valley, the Jewish Community of St. Louis, 1807–1907* (Columbia: University of Missouri Press, 1997). Also, Walter Ehrlich, *Zion in the Valley, the Jewish Community of St. Louis, the Twentieth Century* (Columbia: University of Missouri Press, 2002).

746. *St. Louis Genealogical Society* (http://www.stlgs.org/DBreligionsJewishTemples.htm).

747. Rosalind Mael Bronsen, *B'nai Amoona for All Generations* (St. Louis: Congregation B'nai Amoona, 1982). "B'nai Amoona—50 Years Stronghold of Judaism," *St. Louis Star-Times,* March 27, 1933, page 4.

748. "B'nai El—The Heart of St. Louis Jewry," *St. Louis Star-Times,* May 22, 1933, page 18.

BRITH SHOLOM SYNAGOGUE, established in 1908, located at 1107 East Linden Street in Richmond Heights, Previous locations were 1) 1020 Franklin Street, 2) Glasgow and Dayton Streets, and 3) 6169 Washington Avenue.[749]

SHAARE EMETH TEMPLE, established in 1866, located at 11645 Ladue at Ballas Roads in Creve Coeur.[750]

TEMPLE EMANUAL, established in the 1956, located at 12166 Conway Road in Creve Coeur.[751]

TEMPLE ISRAEL, established in 1886, located 1 Rabbi Alvan D. Rubin Drive, Creve Coeur. This facility had several prior locations 1) Leffingwell Avenue and Pine Street, 2) Kingshighway Boulevard and Washington Avenue in 1908, and 3) to Creve Coeur in 1962.[752]

UNITED HEBREW TEMPLE, established in 1837 as the oldest Jewish congregation west of the Mississippi River, it is located at 13788 Conway Road at Woods Mill Road in Chesterfield. It was originally located at 1) 3rd and Locust Streets, 2) 5th Street and Washington Avenue, 3) 6th Street between Locust Street and St. Charles Avenue, 4) 21st and Olive Streets, 5) Kingshighway Boulevard and Enright Avenue in 1903, and 6) before 1925 to Skinker Boulevard.[753]

LUTHERAN

Early Germans migrated to St. Louis before 1839 bringing the Lutheran faith with them; thus, old Lutheran records are in German and English.[754] Concordia Historical Institute, previously mentioned, retains the historical records for Lutheran Church–Missouri Synod churches. St. Louis also has Lutheran churches belonging to the Evangelical Lutheran Church in America.

Some records are available on microfilm at St. Louis County Library others are available in the original format at the Concordia Institute. The *Lutheran Church Guide of St. Louis* published in 1916 provides detailed information about Lutheran churches of that era.[755]

BETHANY LUTHERAN, established in 1870, located at 407 Fairview Avenue in Webster Groves, formerly at Natural Bridge Road and Clay Street.[756]

BETHEL LUTHERAN, established in 1913, located at 7001 Big Bend Road at Forsyth Boulevard in Clayton.[757]

---

749. "A West End Center of Orthodox Jewry," *St. Louis Star-Times,* August 21, 1933, page 4.

750. "The Gates of Truth," *St. Louis Star-Times,* January 5, 1933, page 4.

751. Estelle Shamski, *History of Temple Emanuel* (St. Louis: Temple Emanuel, 1972).

752. *Temple Israel, 70th Anniversary* (St. Louis: Temple Israel, 1956). Samuel Rosenkranz, editor, *A Centennial of the History Congregation of Temple Israel, 1886–1986* (St. Louis: Temple Israel, 1986). "A Center of Jewish Life in St. Louis," *St. Louis Star-Times,* November 14, 1932, page 3.

753. "City's Oldest Jewish Congregation," *St. Louis Star-Times,* February 16, 1933, page 13.

754. Walter O. Forster, *Zion on the Mississippi: The Settlement of the Saxon Lutherans in Missouri, 1839–1841* (St. Louis: Concordia Publishing, 1953).

755. Concordia Seminary, *Lutheran Church Guide St. Louis, 1916* (St. Louis: Lutheran Church Guide Association, 1916).

756. "Bethany Lutheran Church Celebrates 60th Birthday," *St. Louis Star-Times*, July 23, 1934, page 7.

757. "Bethel Lutheran Church a Leader in U. City," *St. Louis Star-Times,* December 10, 1934, page 15.

BETHLEHEM EVANGELICAL LUTHERAN, established in 1849 by the German immigrants in an area of North St. Louis City, then called New Bremen, located at 2135 Salisbury Street. Burial for many church members and area residents occurred at the church associated Bethlehem Cemetery.[758]

CHRIST LUTHERAN, established in 1868, located at 3504 Caroline Street at Theresa Street.[759]

CHRIST LUTHERAN CHURCH OF WEBSTER GROVES, established in 1897, located at 1 Selma Avenue at Lockwood Avenue in Webster Groves.[760]

CONCORDIA LUTHERAN, established in 1874, located at 505 South Kirkwood Road at West Madison Avenue in Kirkwood.[761]

EMMAUS LUTHERAN, established in 1894, located at 2241 Jefferson Avenue at Armand Place.[762]

EVANGELICAL LUTHERAN CHURCH OF OUR REDEEMER, established in 1892, located at 2817 Utah Place at Oregon Avenue, situated in South St. Louis. This was the second Lutheran church to provide the sermon in English.[763]

FAITH UNITED LUTHERAN, established in 1925, formerly located at Kingshighway Boulevard and Terry Street.[764]

GRACE EVANGELICAL LUTHERAN, established in 1889, located at 10015 Lana Street in Bellefontaine Neighbors, in North St. Louis. The church, originally located at St. Louis Avenue and Garrison Avenue, was called English Evangelical Grace Chapel, as it was the first Lutheran church to give the service in English.[765]

HOLY CROSS EVANGELICAL LUTHERAN, established in 1867, located at 2650 Miami Street at Ohio Avenue.[766]

---

758. *125th Anniversary: Bethlehem Lutheran Church* (Florissant: The Church, 1974). *One Hundredth Anniversary: Bethlehem Evangelical Lutheran Church, St. Louis, Missouri, 1849–1949* (St. Louis: The Church, 1949). "A Beacon of Spiritual Light in St. Louis," *St. Louis Star-Times,* February 27, 1933, page 20. Bethlehem Lutheran Church records; St. Louis County Library, microfilm.

759. Hubert May, *90th Anniversary of Christ: Christ Lutheran Church* (St. Louis: The Church, 1973). "Christ Lutheran Church Approaches 67th Year," *St. Louis Star-Times,* October 1, 1934, page 5.

760. Christ Lutheran Church records; St. Louis County Library, microfilm. "A Growing Church in Webster Groves," *St. Louis Star-Times,* April 15, 1935, page 10.

761. "Lutheranism 61 Years in Kirkwood," *St. Louis Star-Times,* August 5, 1935, page 9. *Concordia Lutheran Church 50th Anniversary, 1891–1941* (St. Louis: The Church, 1941).

762. "Emmaus Lutheran Church Strong and Sturdy," *St. Louis Star-Times,* November 5, 1934, page 13.

763. "A Pioneer English Lutheran Church," *St. Louis Star-Times,* June 25, 1934, page 4.

764. "A Church That Grew Up in 8 Brief Years," *St. Louis Star-Times,* December 11, 1933, page 15.

765. *Fortieth Anniversary, Grace Evangelical Lutheran Church, 1889–1929* (St. Louis: The Church, 1929). "Lutheran Church That Blazed New Trail," *St. Louis Star-Times,* January 16, 1933, page 16. Grace Chapel Lutheran Church records; St. Louis County Library, microfilm.

766. Norman H. Schneider, *Holy Cross Evangelical Lutheran Church: Anniversary Issue, 1983* ([St. Louis]: The Church, 1983). Paul William Jabker, *Holy Cross Lutheran Church, 1850–1975: A Typical Lutheran Church in the Growth of St. Louis* (St. Louis: The Church, 1975). *One Hundredth Anniversary, Holy Cross Lutheran* (St. Louis: The Church, 1958). "A Lutheran Church at 75th Milestone," *St. Louis Star-Times,* August 7, 1933, page 5. Holy Cross Lutheran Church records; St. Louis County Library, microfilm; Missouri State Archives film M56.

HOPE LUTHERAN, established in 1930, located at 5218 Neosho Street at Brannon Street.[767]

IMMANUEL LUTHERAN, established in 1847, located at 3540 Marcus Avenue, and is the second oldest Lutheran church in St. Louis. This church, originally located at 11th Street and Franklin Avenue, and then at 16th and Morgan Streets, moved to the current location in 1919.[768]

IMMANUEL LUTHERAN, established in 1844, located at 9733 Olive Boulevard in Creve Coeur.[769]

LUTHERAN CHURCH OF OUR REDEEMER, established in 1908, located at 2817 Utah Place.[770]

LUTHERAN CHURCH OF OUR SAVIOR, established in 1916, located at St. Louis Avenue and Abner Place.[771]

LUTHERAN CHURCH OF THE RESURRECTION, established in 1956, located at 9907 Sappington Road in Crestwood.[772]

MARKUS CONGREGATION LUTHERAN, established in 1904, formerly located at 22nd and Angelica Street.[773]

MESSIAH LUTHERAN, established in 1908, located at Grand Avenue and Pestalozzi Street.[774]

PILGRIM EVANGELICAL LUTHERAN, established in 1912, located at 4112 West Florissant Avenue.[775]

SALEM LUTHERAN, established in 1849, located at 5180 Parker Road in Black Jack.[776]

---

767. "Hope Lutheran Church Young and Growing," *St. Louis Star-Times,* December 24, 1934, page 2.

768. *Immanuel Lutheran Church, A Century of Grace, 1847–1947 (*St. Louis: The Church, 1947). *Eightieth Anniversary: Immanuel Evangelical Lutheran Church, St. Louis, Missouri, 1847–1928* (St. Louis: The Church, 1928). "A Pioneer Sanctuary of Lutheranism," *St. Louis Star-Times,* May 29, 1933, page 13. Immanuel Lutheran Church records; St. Louis County Library, 1848–1919, microfilm; FHL film 1,479,677–1,479,678.

769. *Immanuel Lutheran Church Olivette, 125th Anniversary, 1844–1869* (St. Louis: The Church, 1969).

770. Donald A. Prahlow, *The Lutheran Church of Our Redeemer: 100th Anniversary, 1894–1994* (St. Louis: The Church, 1994).

771. "A Young and Thriving Lutheran Church," *St. Louis Star-Times,* January 28, 1935, page 11.

772. *Declare His Glory: Twenty-fifth Anniversary, 1981: Lutheran Church of the Resurrection* (St. Louis: The Church, 1981). Lutheran Church of the Resurrection records; St. Louis County Library, microfilm.

773. "A Growing North Side Lutheran Church," *St. Louis Star-Times,* January 14, 1935, page 13.

774. *Messiah Lutheran Church, Saint Louis, Missouri: Grand Boulevard at Pestalozzi Street* (St. Louis: The Church, 1958). "Messiah Lutheran Church Young and Progressive," *St. Louis Star-Times,* January 15, 1934, page 6.

775. Alfred Doerffler, *Pilgrim Evangelical Lutheran Church* (St. Louis: The Church, 1927). Also, *Pilgrim Evangelical Lutheran, 1907–1957 50th Anniversary* (St. Louis: The Church, 1957).

776. *Salem Lutheran Church, 125, 1849–1974: Anniversary Pictorial Directory* (Hazelwood: Yearbook Directory Service, 1974). Margaret Ware and Vertrees Hood, *Salem Lutheran Church, Black Jack, Mo., 1850–1965* (St. Louis: M. Ware, 1998). *Salem Evangelical Lutheran Church (Missouri Synod), Black Jack, Missouri 1849–1949* (St. Louis: Salem Lutheran Church, 1949). Margaret Ware and Vertrees Hood, *Salem Lutheran Church, Black Jack, Missouri: Births and Baptisms, Confirmations, Marriages, Deaths and Burials: Vital Records 1850–1964* (St. Louis: Ware and Hood, 1964). "Black Jack, Mo., Church Celebrates 85th Year," *St. Louis Star-Times,* November 12, 1934, page 13. Salem Lutheran records; St. Louis County Library, microfilm.

SALEM LUTHERAN, established in 1909, located on Lakewood Street in Affton.[777]

ST. JACOBI LUTHERAN, established in 1906, located at 8646 Jennings Station Road in Jennings.[778]

ST. JOHN EVANGELICAL LUTHERAN, established in 1865, located at 3738 Morganford Road at Chippewa Street.[779]

ST. JOHN LUTHERAN, established in 1851, located at 15808 Manchester Road in Ellisville.[780]

ST. LUCAS EVANGELICAL LUTHERAN, established in 1905 as the first Slovak church in St. Louis, located at 7100 Morganford Road, formerly located at 13th Street and Allen Avenue in Soulard.[781]

ST. LUKE LUTHERAN, established in 1893, located 3415 Taft Avenue, originally at Compton Avenue and Itaska Street then moved to Alaska and Neosho Streets.[782]

ST. MARK EVANGELICAL LUTHERAN, established in 1867, located at 6337 Clayton Road.[783]

ST. MATTHEWS LUTHERAN, established 1901, located at Wren Avenue and Thekla Street in Walnut Park, formerly at Gilmore and Harney Streets.[784]

ST. PAUL EVANGELICAL LUTHERAN, established in 1883, located at 955 Highway 109 in Grover. Prior to 1883, many church members attended St. John's Lutheran in Ellisville or St. Paul's Lutheran in Des Peres.[785]

ST. PAUL LUTHERAN, established in 1862, located at 2137 East John Street.[786]

ST. PAUL LUTHERAN CHURCH OF DES PERES, established in 1838 as the German Evangelical Congregation of Des Peres, located at 1300 North Ballas Road in Des Peres. St. Paul Cemetery on Ballas Road is associated with this church.[787]

---

777. "A Growing Church in Gardenville," *St. Louis Star-Times,* August 26, 1935, page 9.

778. "Jennings Lutherans to Celebrate Progress," *St. Louis Star-Times,* November 25, 1935, page 22.

779. *125th Anniversary, 1865–1990, St. John's Lutheran Church, St. Louis, Missouri* (St. Louis: The Church, 1990). Lanette Russell, *Church Records from St. John's Lutheran Church: Marriages, Baptisms and Death Records, 1865–1900* (St. Louis: The Church, no date). "A Pastor Served This Church 55 Years," *St. Louis Star-Times,* February 19, 1934, page 7.

780. *St. John's Lutheran Church, Ellisville, Missouri, 1851–1976* (Ellisville: The Church, 1976). *A Century of Grace, 1851–1951: St. John's Lutheran Church, Ellisville, Missouri* (Ellisville: The Church, 1951). St. John's Lutheran Church records; St. Louis County Library microfilm.

781. "A Pioneer Slovak Lutheran Church," *St. Louis Star-Times,* February 4, 1935, page 5.

782. "Mount Pleasants' Mission Now a Sturdy Church," *St. Louis Star-Times,* August 21, 1934, page 4.

783. *St. Mark's Evangelical Lutheran, 1867–1967* (St. Louis: The Church, 1967).

784. *St. Matthews Lutheran Church, St. Louis: Golden Jubilee, 1901–1951* (St. Louis: The Church, 1951).

785. St. Paul Lutheran church records; St. Louis County Library microfilm.

786. Milton L. Rudnick, *Saint Paul Lutheran Church, 1863–1963: A Historical Review* (St. Louis: The Church, 1863). St. Paul Lutheran Church records; St. Louis County Library microfilm.

787. *St. Paul's Lutheran Church of Des Peres: 150 Years, Christ Our Foundation, Faith, and Future, 1849–1999* (Des Peres: The Church, 1999). St. Paul Lutheran Church records; St. Louis County Library, microfilm. "St. Paul Cemetery Index," *St. Louis Genealogical Society Quarterly,* volume 37, no. 2 (Summer 2004), 63–77.

ST. PETERS LUTHERAN, established in 1894, located at 1126 South Kingshighway Boulevard at Wichita Avenue. The first church was located at Vista Street and Newstead Avenue, then moved to Swan Street and Newstead Avenue, and then in 1925 to the Kingshighway location.[788]

ST. STEPHEN LUTHERAN, established in 1930, located at 515 Pendleton Avenue at Olive Boulevard.[789]

ST. TRINITY LUTHERAN, established in 1860, located at 7404 Vermont Avenue in Carondelet. This is the third oldest Lutheran church in St. Louis.[790]

TIMOTHY LUTHERAN, established 1927, formerly at Fyler and Ivanhoe Avenues.[791]

TRINITY GERMAN EVANGELICAL LUTHERAN, established in 1839, located at 8th Street at Lafayette Avenue. Trinity is the oldest Lutheran church in St. Louis established in 1839.[792]

ZION LUTHERAN, established in 1860, originally located at 1426 Warren Street and Blair Avenue until 1895 when it moved to 2500 North 21st Street.[793]

METHODIST

Methodist churches were divided into various groups including, but not limited to, the Methodist Episcopal Church, Methodist Episcopal Church South, and Methodist Protestant Church, before merging to form the United Methodist Church.

---

788. *1895 A New Congregation Founded by Faith* (St. Louis: The Church, 1895). "St. Peter's Lutheran to Observe 40th Year," *St. Louis Star-Times,* February 25, 1935, page 5. St. Peter's Lutheran Church records; St. Louis County Library, microfilm.

789. "A Church That Won Against Heavy Odds," *St. Louis Star-Times,* May 14, 1934, page 5.

790. Rev. J. J. Bernthal, *A History of Evangelical Lutheran St. Trinity Church of St. Louis, Missouri, From the Year 1859 to Year 1909 On the Occasion of the 50th Anniversary,* translated by Hans Mueller (St. Louis: The Church, 1909). *St. Trinity Lutheran Confirmations, 1861–1960* (St. Louis: The Church, no date). Rev. E. H. Bechman, *St. Trinity Lutheran Church, St. Louis, Missouri, History and Souvenir, 1859–1934* (St. Louis: Concordia Publishing House, 1934). *A Century of Blessings: St. Trinity Lutheran Church, Vermont at Koeln Avenues, St. Louis, Missouri* (St. Louis: The Church, 1959). "St. Trinity Lutheran Nears Its 75th Birthday," *St. Louis Star-Times,* May 28, 1934, page 5.

791. *Timothy Lutheran Church: Celebrating 50 Years of Service to the Glory of God* (St. Louis: The Church, 1977).

792. Dennis R. Rathert, *A History of Trinity Lutheran Church and School, 150th Anniversary* (St. Louis: The Church, 1989). *Old Trinity* (St. Louis: The Church, 1954). *Trinity Lutheran Church, One Hundredth Anniversary of Old Trinity Lutheran Church, Eighth and Soulard Streets, 1839–1939* (St. Louis: The Church, 1939). Walter O. Umbach, *Founded Upon Christ: A Brief Historical Summary of Trinity Lutheran Church of St. Louis, Missouri* (St. Louis: W. O. Umbach, 1966). Walter O. Umbach, *125th Anniversary, 1839–1964, Trinity Lutheran Church* (St. Louis: W. O. Umbach, 1964). "A Mother Church of Lutheransim," *St. Louis Star-Times,* April 2, 1934, page 18. Trinity Lutheran church records; St. Louis County Library microfilm, and Missouri State Archives, film M63–64.

793. *Diamond Jubilee Zion Lutheran, 1860–1935* (St. Louis: The Church, 1935). *A Short History of Zion Evangelical Lutheran Church St. Louis, Missouri, on the Occasion of its Golden Jubilee May 23, 1860–1910* (St. Louis: The Church, 1910). *100th Anniversary: Zion Lutheran Church, Twenty-first and Benton Street, St. Louis, Missouri* (St. Louis: The Church, 1960). "A Lutheran Church of Gothic Beauty," *St. Louis Star-Times,* October 31, 1932, page 2. Zion Lutheran Church records; St. Louis County Library microfilm.

Several books aid Methodist researchers. The *History of the United Methodist Churches in Missouri* provides an overview of the denomination.[794] *Methodist Saint Louis: The Official Directory...a Complete Roster of the Officers and Members of the Churches* provides a list of the members as of 1902.[795] An index provides a list of the obituaries for Methodist church members printed in the *St Louis Christian Advocate* newspaper dating from 1851 to 1882.[796]

The *Manual of the Methodist Episcopal Church of St. Louis and Suburbs* lists all Methodist churches in St. Louis ca 1906. It provides a photo of the church and the minister and a list of the members with their home addresses.[797]

BELLFONTAINE UNITED METHODIST, established in 1855, located at 10600 Bellefontaine Road in Bellefontaine Neighbors.[798]

BETHEL METHODIST, established in 1858, located at 17500 Manchester Road in Pond.[799]

BOWMAN METHODIST, established in 1879, located originally at 19th Street and Grand Avenue; then it moved to Carter and Grand Avenues.[800]

CABANNE METHODIST, established in 1896, located at 5760 Bartmer Avenue at Goodfellow Boulevard.[801]

CENTENARY UNITED METHODIST, established in 1839, located at 55 Plaza Square, formerly called 16th Street and Pine Street.[802]

CHOUTEAU AVENUE METHODIST, established in 1848, formerly located at 8th Street at Chouteau Avenue. This church later became Lafayette Park Methodist.[803]

---

794. Richard A. Seaton, editor, *History of the United Methodist Churches in Missouri* (St. Louis: Missouri Methodist Historical Society, 1984).

795. *Methodist Saint Louis: The Official Directory and Year Book of the Methodist Episcopal Churches, English and German, in St. Louis and Vicinity; a Complete Roster of the Officers and Members of the Churches* (St. Louis: Robert Newton, 1902).

796. Mrs. Howard W. Woodruff, *State-wide Missouri Obituaries: From* The St. Louis Christian Advocate, *1851–1882* (No place: The Author, 1986).

797. Robert Jessup Newton, *Manuel of the Methodist Episcopal Church of St. Louis and Suburbs* (St. Louis: The Author, 1905).

798. Bellefontaine United Methodist, *A Brief History of Bellefontaine United Methodist Church: A Historic Church, Alive in the Present, Looking Forward to an Exciting Future* (St. Louis: The Church, 1985). *The Centennial of Bellefontaine Methodist Church* (St. Louis: The Church, 1955).

799. John O. Gooch, *"God is in This Place": A History of Bethel United Methodist Church, 1858–1975* (Pond: The Church, 1975).

800. "A North St. Louis Methodist Center," *St. Louis Star-Times,* April 30, 1934, page 5.

801. "Cabanne M. E. Church Nears 38th Year," *St. Louis Star-Times,* October 2, 1933, page 4.

802. Francis Emmet Williams, *Centenary Methodist Church of St. Louis, the First Hundred Years, 1839–1939: Compiled for the Centenary Methodist Church in St. Louis, Missouri, in Commemoration of the Inception of its Organization One Hundred Years Ago, and in Honor of the Beginning of Methodism in England Two Hundred Years Ago* (St. Louis: Mound City Press, 1939). *The Story of Centenary Church, Saint Louis: Yesterday, Today, Tomorrow* (St. Louis: Shelly Printing, 1923). "Old Centenary Carries On," *St. Louis Star-Times,* December 29, 1932, page 13.

803. *The Appeal of Chouteau Avenue Church: Bishop McTyeire's Decision* (St. Louis: Charles E. Ware, 1876).

CHRISTY MEMORIAL UNITED METHODIST, established in 1892, located at 4601 Morganford Road.[804]

CUPPLES MEMORIAL METHODIST EPISCOPAL, established in 1913, formerly located at 1) 6624 Delmar Boulevard in 1915, and 2) 6901 Washington Avenue in 1920.[805]

EDEN METHODIST EPISCOPAL, established in 1848, formerly located at 19th and Warren Streets.[806]

ELMBANK METHODIST, established in 1885, formerly located at 4435 Elmbank Street. This church merged with Salem Methodist in 1937.[807]

EPWORTH METHODIST, established in 1865, formerly located at Warne and Maffitt Avenues.[808]

FERGUSON UNITED METHODIST, established in 1886, located at 33 South Florissant Road in Ferguson.[809]

FIRST METHODIST EPISCOPAL SOUTH, established 1850s, formerly located at 8th Street and Washington Avenue.[810]

FIRST UNITED METHODIST CHURCH OF WEBSTER GROVES, established in 1895, located at 600 North Bompart Avenue, Webster Groves.[811]

GRACE METHODIST, established in 1913, located at 6199 Waterman Avenue at Skinker Boulevard. The founding members previously attended Union Methodist Episcopal Church.[812]

HAVEN STREET METHODIST, established in 1856, formerly located at Virginia and Haven Streets.[813]

IMMANUEL METHODIST, established in 1888, located at 2105 McCausland Avenue in Maplewood.[814]

KINGSHIGHWAY METHODIST, established in 1877, located at 900 Bellerive Boulevard.[815]

---

804. *The History of the Christy Memorial United Methodist Church: A Celebration of 100 Years, 1894–1994* (St. Louis: The Church, 1994). "A Church That Proved Faith of Benefactor," *St. Louis Star-Times,* August 12, 1935, page 20.

805. *Cupples Memorial Methodist Episcopal: South* (St. Louis: The Church, 1913).

806. *Fiftieth Anniversary, 1848–1898, May 22–29, 1898* [Eden Methodist Episcopal] (St. Louis: Woodward and Tiernan Printing, 1898).

807. "Elmbank Methodist Church Observes Golden Jubilee," *St. Louis Star-Times,* October 7, 1935, page 13.

808. "Epworth M.E. Church a North Side Center," *St. Louis Star-Times,* May 21, 1934, page 5.

809. Lola Slater, *Ferguson United Methodist Church, 1886–1986: A Lighthearted History* (Ferguson: The Church, 1986). Wilbur Morse Shankland, *Zion in the Valley: Origin and Building of the Methodist Church in Ferguson, St. Louis County, Missouri* (St. Louis: W. M. Shankland, 1972).

810. J. E. Godbey, *History of the First Methodist Episcopal Church, South, St. Louis, Missouri* (St. Louis: The Church, 1879).

811. Ralph H. Lewis, *An Historical Sketch of the First Methodist Church of Webster Groves* (Webster Groves, The Church, 1945). Jerri Stroud, *First United Methodist Church of Webster Groves Celebrates its First 100 Years, 1895–1995* (Webster Groves: The Church, 1995). J. Wendell Davis, *100 Years in Webster Groves: The Centennial of the First United Methodist Church, 1895–1995* (Webster Groves, The Church, 1995).

812. *Grace Methodist Church: Historical Interpretations, its Gifts and Memorials* (St. Louis: The Church, 1943).

813. "Haven Street Methodist "the Friendly Church," *St. Louis Star-Times,* June 18, 1934, page 20.

814. *Immanuel United Methodist Church Centennial Celebration, 1888–1988* (St. Louis: The Church, 1988).

815. *A Brief History of the Kingshighway United Methodist Church, 900 Bellerive Boulevard, St. Louis, Missouri* (St. Louis: The Church, 1977).

KIRKWOOD METHODIST, established in 1868, located at 201 West Adams Avenue in Kirkwood.[816]

LAFAYETTE PARK METHODIST EPISCOPAL, established in 1843, located at 2300 Lafayette Avenue, formerly on Paul Street.[817]

LINDELL AVENUE METHODIST EPISCOPAL, established in 1892, located on Lindell Boulevard. In 1913, this church changed its name to Grace Methodist Church. (See Grace Methodist)

MAPLE AVENUE METHODIST EPISCOPAL, established in 1892, located at Maple and Belt Avenues.[818]

MELLOW METHODIST, established in 1941, located at 6701 Virginia Street.[819]

MEMORIAL METHODIST, established in 1852, located at 2157 South Jefferson Avenue at Accomac Street.[820]

MOUNT AUBURN METHODIST, established in 1847, formerly located at Hodiamont Avenue and Wabada Street.[821]

MT. ZION UNITED METHODIST, established in 1870, located at 1485 Craig Road in Creve Coeur, formerly on Olive Boulevard at Old Ballas Road.[822]

NORMANDY METHODIST, established in 1943, located at 8000 Natural Bridge Road in Normandy.[823]

OLIVE CHAPEL IN KIRKWOOD, established in 1867, located at Harrison Avenue and Monroe Street in Kirkwood, originally located at 330 West Washington Avenue from 1867 to 1923.[824]

SALEM METHODIST EPISCOPAL, established in 1841, located at 1200 South Lindbergh Boulevard in Ladue. Previous locations include 1) 7th and Carr Streets, 2) Wash and 11th Streets, and 3) Kingshighway Boulevard and Cote Brilliante Avenue.[825]

ST. JOHN METHODIST EPISCOPAL, established in 1868, located at 5000 Washington Avenue, at South Kingshighway Boulevard. [826]

---

816. "Kirkwood Methodists Look Back 67 Years," *St. Louis Star-Times,* April 29, 1935, page 30. Kirkwood Methodist Church records, 1869–1970; St. Louis County Library, microfilm, and Missouri State Archives film M62.

817. "A Pioneer Church of South St. Louis," *St. Louis Star-Times,* May 1, 1933, page 5. *Lafayette Park Methodist Church: 115th Anniversary, 1839–1954* (St. Louis: The Church, 1954).

818. "A Church Founded in Gay Nineties," *St. Louis Star-Times,* February 5, 1934, page 5.

819. *84th Anniversary 1857–1941* (St. Louis: The Church, 1941).

820. "Ninety-Four Years at Memorial M.E. Church," *St. Louis Star-Times,* July 29, 1935, page 5.

821. *Golden Anniversary Programme, Sept 20 and 21, 1902* (St. Louis: Mount Auburn Methodist Episcopal South, 1902). "Mt. Auburn Church Nears 90th Year," *St. Louis Star-Times,* February 18, 1935, page 7.

822. Helen Hampton Ruhrwien, *A History of Mt. Zion United Methodist Church and Creve Coeur Methodism* (Creve Coeur: H. H. Ruhrwien, 1984).

823. *Normandy Methodist Church: 10th Anniversary, 1943–1953* (Bel-Nor: The Church, 1953).

824. Fredrick McKissack, *Come This Far by Faith: The Story of the Olive Chapel African Methodist Episcopal Church of Kirkwood, Missouri* (Kirkwood: Olive Chapel, 2004).

825. Robert S. Appel, *Salem–The Congregations of the Faithful: A History of Salem Methodist Church, 1841–1991* (St. Louis: Salem-in-Ladue Methodist, 1991). "Salem M. E. Church Passes 95th Year," *St. Louis Star-Times,* June 3, 1935, page 15.

826. *The Centennial of St. John Methodist 1868–1968* (St. Louis: The Church, 1968). "Civic Leaders Built This Church," *St. Louis Star-Times,* November 3, 1932, page 2. *St. John's Methodist 75th Anniversary* (St. Louis: The Church, 1943).

ST. PAUL METHODIST EPISCOPAL, established in 1841, formerly located at 1927 St. Louis Avenue.[827]

SCRUGGS UNITED METHODIST, established in 1905, formerly located at Grand and Connecticut Avenues.[828]

SHAW AVENUE METHODIST EPISCOPAL, established in 1897, formerly located at Tower Grove and Shaw Avenues.[829]

STEPHAN MEMORIAL METHODIST, established in 1908, located at 2730 Walton Road in Overland.[830]

TRINITY METHODIST EPISCOPAL, established in 1856, located at 13th and Tyler Streets.[831]

UNION MEMORIAL METHODIST, established in 1862, located at 3543 Watson Road, formerly at 1141 Belt Avenue.[832]

UNIVERSITY METHODIST, established in 1909, located at 6901 Washington Avenue at Trinity Street, formerly at Garrison and Lucas Avenues.[833]

VINITA PARK METHODIST, established in 1911, located at 8145 Page Boulevard in Vinita Park.[834]

WAGONER MEMORIAL METHODIST EPISCOPAL, established in 1876, formerly located at Taylor and Gibson Avenues.[835]

WAGONER PLACE METHODIST EPISCOPAL, established in 1894, formerly located at Wagoner Place and Aldine Avenue.[836]

---

827. *Ninety-eighth Anniversary, 1841–1939* (St. Louis: The Church, 1939). "Descendant of Historic Mound Mission," *St. Louis Star-Times,* September 18, 1933, page 2.

828. Leah Albright, *History of the Scruggs United Methodist Church* (St. Louis: The Church, 1972).

829. "Philanthropy Made This Church Possible," *St. Louis Star-Times,* March 19, 1934, page 10.

830. Mrs. Arthur A. Hoech, *Stephan Memorial Methodist Church: Building a Christian Community, 1908–1958* (St. Louis: The Church, 1958). *Stephan Memorial United Methodist Church, St. Louis, Missouri, 1974, 1980, 1983, 1984* (St. Louis: The Church, 1974–1984).

831. *Golden Jubilee Book, 1856–1906, January 7–14, 1906* (St. Louis: Lambert-Deacon-Hull Company, 1906). "Oldest M. E. Church in St. Louis," *St. Louis Star-Times,* January 30, 1933, page 13.

832. *Golden Anniversary, Union Methodist Episcopal Church: Corner of Lucas and Garrison Avenues, Saint Louis, Missouri, 1862–1912* (St. Louis: The Church, 1912). "A Church Born of the Civil War," *St. Louis Star-Times,* May 15, 1933, page 4. *Union Memorial Methodist Church* (St. Louis: The Church, 1996). *Pictorial Review of Union Methodist Church and Souvenir Program of the Annual Conference, April 5th to 10th, 1916* (St. Louis: Press of C. K. Robinson Printing, 1916). *Dedication and 53rd Anniversary, March 7 to March 14, 1915* (St. Louis: Union Methodist Episcopal Church, 1915). *Golden Anniversary, Union Methodist Episcopal Church: Corner of Lucas and Garrison Avenues, Saint Louis, Missouri: 1862–1912* (St. Louis: The Church, 1912).

833 Ivan Lee Holt, *Now and Then: The Faith of 50 Years Golden Anniversary Sermon, Sunday, January 10, 1960 at University Methodist Church* (St. Louis: The Church, 1960). "A Center of Southern Methodism," *St. Louis Star-Times,* December 18, 1933, page 13.

834. *Vinita Park United Methodist Church: Your Place* (St. Louis: The Church, 1994). Lovelle Felt and Jeffery Carr, *History of Vinita Park Methodist Church, 1910–1985* (Vinita Park: The Church, 1985).

835. "A Church Prominent in Religious Education," *St. Louis Star-Times,* December 17, 1934, page 7.

836. "M. E. Epworth League Was Born in This Church," *St. Louis Star-Times,* September 24, 1934, page 5.

WEBSTER HILLS METHODIST EVANGELICAL, established in 1930, located on 698 Lockwood Avenue and Berry Road in Webster Groves.[837]

PRESBYTERIAN

The Presbyterian denomination came to St. Louis about 1817. The Presbyterian Church split over the slavery issue in 1861. One denomination was called the Presbyterian Church of the U.S.A., and another the Presbyterian Church in the U.S. The Associate Presbyterian Church and the Associate Reformed Presbyterian Church were also represented in St. Louis, merging to form the United Presbyterian Church in North America. All of these groups merged forming the Presbyterian Church (USA). The Presbyterian Church in America is another group with representation in St. Louis.

The Presbyterian Church of America Historical Center (12330 Conway Road, Creve Coeur; phone 314-469-9077; http://www.pcahistory.org/collections.html) may provide help for some researchers. In addition, the *Saint Louis Presbyterian Blue Book* provides details about Presbyterian churches in the St. Louis area in 1902.[838] The *Missouri Presbytery, 1816–1937* provides the history of the denomination.[839] The 1991 publication *Celebration of Beginnings: The Presbytery of Giddings–Lovejoy* provides a short history of this denomination in St. Louis and an overview of open Presbyterian churches in the metropolitan area, including photos of the building.[840]

BONHOMME PRESBYTERIAN, established in 1816, located at 14820 Conway Road in Chesterfield, formerly located at the Old Bonhomme Church on Conway and White Roads. The new facility opened in 1959.[841]

CARONDELET MARKHAM MEMORIAL PRESBYTERIAN, established in 1850, located at 6116 Michigan Avenue.[842] Markham Memorial Presbyterian merged with Carondelet in 1958.

CENTRAL PRESBYTERIAN, established in 1844, located at 7700 Davis Street at Hanley Road in Clayton.[843]

---

837. "A Young Church With Some New Ideas," *St. Louis Star-Times,* August 14, 1933, page 4.

838. *Saint Louis Presbyterian Blue Book: The Official Manual of all Presbyterian Churches in St. Louis and Vicinity* (St. Louis: George Harkness, 1902).

839. Joseph M. Garrison, *Missouri Presbytery, 1816–1937* (Columbia: The Presbytery, 1937).

840. Joan Furlong Huisinga, editor, *Celebration of Beginnings: The Presbytery of Giddings–Lovejoy* (St. Louis: Committee on History of Presbytery of Gidding–Lovejoy, 1991).

841. Frances Hurd Stadler, *A History of Bonhomme Presbyterian Church: The Church of Pioneers* (St. Louis: Eden Publishing, 1976). Bonhomme Presbyterian church record, 1841–1868; Missouri Historical Society microfilm.

842. *Over Ninety Years in Carondelet* (St. Louis: The Church, 1941). R. J. Sims, "The Founding of the Carondelet Presbyterian Church," *Carondelet Historical Society Newsletter* 7 (March 1975): 4, 8. "Carondelet's Oldest Protestant Church," *St. Louis Star-Times,* March 4, 1935, page 4.

843. Marilyn McCarthy, *Stones of Remembrance: A History of Central Presbyterian Church, 1844–1994* (St. Louis: The Church, 1994). "A Church That Grew with the City," *St. Louis Star-Times,* July 31, 1933, page 13.

COTE BRILLIANTE PRESBYTERIAN, established in 1885, located at 4681 Labadie Avenue at Marcus Avenue.[844]

CURBY MEMORIAL PRESBYTERIAN, established in 1873, located at 2621 Utah Place, formerly at 18th and Pestalozzi Streets.[845]

DES PERES PRESBYTERIAN, established in 1832, located at 11155 Clayton Road; prior to 1959 it was located on Geyer Road at the bend in the road next to the cemetery all in Frontenac.[846]

EAST GRAND BOULEVARD PRESBYTERIAN, established in 1876, formerly at 19th Street and East Grand Avenue. This was formerly the Second German Presbyterian Church.[847]

FIRST PRESBYTERIAN CHURCH OF KIRKWOOD, established in 1854, located at 100 East Adams Avenue in Kirkwood.[848]

FIRST PRESBYTERIAN CHURCH OF ST. LOUIS, established in 1817, located at 7200 Delmar Boulevard.[849] Previous locations include 1) 4th Street and Washington Avenue, 2) 14th and Locust Streets, and 3) Sarah Street and Washington Avenue.

FIRST UNITED PRESBYTERIAN, established 1839, eventually located at Kingsland and Washington Avenues in University City.[850]

GRACE PRESBYTERIAN, established in 1890, located at 5574 Delmar Boulevard, formerly located at Clara and Ridge Avenues.[851]

GRAND AVENUE PRESBYTERIAN, established in 1853, formerly located on Grand Avenue, this church is now called Westminister Presbyterian.[852]

GREELEY PRESBYTERIAN, established in 1865, formerly located at 23rd Street and St. Louis Avenue.[853]

KINGSHIGHWAY PRESBYTERIAN, established in 1908, formerly located at Kingshighway Boulevard and Cabanne Avenue.[854]

---

844. Jamie R. Graham, *Cote Brilliante Presbyterian Church, 1885–1977* (St. Louis: J. R. Graham, 1977). "Cote Brilliante Church," *St. Louis Star-Times,* September 30, 1935, page 13.

845. "Church Perpetuating a Member's Name," *St. Louis Star-Times,* April 8, 1935, page 11.

846. "A Short History of Des Peres Church," *Faith-Des Peres Presbyterian Church* (http://www.faithdesperes.org/meetinghouse.htm).

847. "A Church That Began with Six Members," *St. Louis Star-Times,* November 11, 1935, page 13.

848. *First Presbyterian Church of Kirkwood, 1854–1979* (Kirkwood: privately printed, 1979).

849. R. Calvin Dobson, *The Romance of a Pioneer Church: The First Presbyterian Church of Saint Louis, Missouri* (St. Louis: The Church, 1960). *Seventy-fifth Anniversary, 1817–1892, First Presbyterian Church* (St. Louis: The Church, 1892).

850. "Presbyterian Church Near Century Mark," *St. Louis Star-Times,* January 19, 1933, page 18.

851. "Grace Presbyterian Church Looks Back 45 Years," *St. Louis Star-Times,* October 28, 1935, page 15.

852. *Fiftieth Anniversary of the Grand Avenue Presbyterian Church, St. Louis, Missouri* (St. Louis: Robertson Print Company, 1903). John F. Cannon, *Yearbook of the Grand Avenue Presbyterian Church: Grand and Washington Avenues, St. Louis, Mo.* (St. Louis: Commercial Printing Company, [1895]).

853. "A Church Dedicated to Community Service," *St. Louis Star-Times,* November 26, 1934, page 13.

854. "A Church Noted for Its Able Leaders," *St. Louis Star-Times,* April 3, 1933, page 20.

LADUE CHAPEL PRESBYTERIAN, established in 1943, located at 9450 Clayton Road in Ladue.[855]

LAFAYETTE PARK PRESBYTERIAN, established 1878, formerly located at Missouri Avenue and Albion Place.[856] This church merged into Tyler Place Presbyterian in 1946.

MEMORIAL PRESBYTERIAN, established 1864, located at 201 Skinker Boulevard at Alexander Street.[857]

NORTH PRESBYTERIAN, established 1845, formerly located at St. Louis and Warne Avenues.[858]

OAK HILL PRESBYTERIAN, established in 1895, located at 4111 Connecticut Street.[859]

PETERS MEMORIAL PRESBYTERIAN, established in 1847, formerly located at 3100 Sidney Street and Minnesota Avenue.[860]

ROCK HILL PRESBYTERIAN, established in 1845, located at 9407 Manchester Road in Rock Hill.[861]

SECOND PRESBYTERIAN, established in 1838, located at 4501 Westminister Place, formerly at 1) 5th and Walnut Streets, and 2) 18th Street and Lucas Avenue.[862]

SOUTHAMPTON PRESBYTERIAN, established 1919, located 4716 Mackland Avenue.[863]

SUTTER AVENUE PRESBYTERIAN, established in 1898, formerly located at Sutter and Bartmer Avenues in University City.[864]

THIRD UNITED PRESBYTERIAN, established in 1892, formerly located at 1) Wagoner Place and North Market Street, and 2) 2426 Union Boulevard and Highland Street. This church was previously called Wagoner Place United Presbyterian.[865]

---

855. *Celebrating Our Past, Building for the Future: Ladue Chapel, 1943–1993* (Franklin, Tennessee: Providence House Publishers, 1993).

856. "Lafayette Park Church, A Presbyterian Center," *St. Louis Star-Times,* June 4, 1934, page 13.

857. "A Center of Conservative Presbyterianism," *St. Louis Star-Times,* September 25, 1933, page 20.

858. *Catalog of the Names and Residences of the Members of the North Presbyterian Church of St. Louis, January 1870* (St. Louis: A. C. Clayton, 1870). "Old North Church Reaches 90th Year," *St. Louis Star-Times,* April 9, 1934, page 5.

859. *90 Years of Faith and Service, 1895–1985: A Celebration, October 13, 16, 20, 1985* (St. Louis: The Church, 1985).

860. "Peters Memorial a Growing Church," *St. Louis Star-Times,* December 10, 1934, page 15.

861. *The One Hundredth Anniversary of the Organization of Rock Hill Presbyterian Church, 9407 Manchester Road, Rock Hill, Missouri* (St. Louis: The Church, 1945). Alena Chance Jablonsky, *Vital Statistics of Rock Hill Presbyterian Church, Rock Hill, St. Louis County, Missouri, 1845–1956* (St. Louis: DAR, Cornelia Green Chapter, 1973). "Old Rock Hill Church Passes 90th Year," *St. Louis Star-Times,* March 11, 1935, page 13.

862. Mary C. Bard, *A History of Second Presbyterian Church, St. Louis, Missouri, 1838–1988* (St. Louis: Second Presbyterian Church, 1987). *70th Anniversary, 1838–1908, Second Presbyterian Church* (St. Louis: The Church, 1908). "Thrift Built This Church and Kept It Going," *St. Louis Star-Times,* October 23, 1933, page 7.

863. *The Southampton Story, 1919–1969* (St. Louis: The Church, 1969).

864. "Sutter Avenue Church Pioneer in U. City," *St. Louis Star-Times,* October 29, 1934, page 10.

865. "Third United Church Ends 42nd Year," *St. Louis Star-Times,* May 13, 1935, page 7.

TYLER PLACE PRESBYTERIAN, established in 1896, located at 2109 South Spring Avenue, merged with Lafayette Park Presbyterian in 1946.[866]

WEBSTER GROVES PRESBYTERIAN, established in 1866, 45 West Lockwood Avenue in Webster Groves.[867]

WESTMINSTER PRESBYTERIAN, established in 1853, formerly located at 1853 Pine Street. The name of this facility changed from Pine Street Church to Grand Avenue Church to the present name. Many of the members moved to Curby Memorial Presbyterian.[868]

WEST PRESBYTERIAN, established in 1888, located at 5872 Maple Avenue at Maryville Avenue.[869]

WINNEBAGO PRESBYTERIAN, established in 1894, formerly located at Winnebago Avenue and Tennessee Avenue.[870]

UNITED CHURCH OF CHRIST

The United Church of Christ was formed in 1957 by a merger of the Congregational Christian Churches and the Evangelical and Reformed Church. The uniting denominations were themselves the products of previous mergers. The Congregational Church merged with the Christian Connection in 1931 to form the Congregational Christian Churches. The German Evangelical Synod of North America and the Reformed Church in the United States merged in 1934 to form the Evangelical and Reformed Church. Scott Holl's publication, *Stones Cry Out,* provides a list of the Evangelical churches, their ministers, and drawings or photos of the facilities.[871]

The Archives at Eden Theological Seminary (475 Lockwood Avenue, Webster Groves 63119; phone 314-252-3140; http://www.eden.edu/index.php/archives) holds many original records for St. Louis area United Church of Christ congregations. Most church records of interest to family historians are available on microfilm at the St. Louis County Library. Most early records are in German.

The Archives maintains a guide to St. Louis United Church of Christ churches and cemeteries on its websites. The Archives also has an alphabetical card file for pastors ordained before 1934. The card includes the pastor's name and a listing of the churches he served, when and where ordained and educated, marriage information, and death data.

---

866. Ellen Nini Harris, *The First Century of Tyler Place Presbyterian Church: At the Heart of the Shaw Neighborhood* (St. Louis: The Church, 1996). "A Leading Congregation of South St. Louis," *St. Louis Star-Times,* January 22, 1934, page 20.

867. *The Webster Groves Presbyterian Church: Beginning a Second Century of Christian Witness, 1866–1966* (Webster Groves: The Church, 1966). *Webster Groves Presbyterian Church, 75th Anniversary, March 30, 1941* (St. Louis: The Church, 1941).

868. William Witherspoon, *The History of Westminster Presbyterian Church, 1853–1978* (St. Louis: The Church, 1978). "Stormy History Marks Rise of This Church," *St. Louis Star-Times,* November 17, 1932, page 2. St. Louis County Library microfilm.

869. *West Presbyterian Church, 100 years of Serving Christ: 1888–1988* (St. Louis: The Church, 1988). "West Church—A Power in Presbyterianism," *St. Louis Star-Times,* June 26, 1933, page 5.

870. "German Presbyterians Founded This Church," *St. Louis Star-Times,* September 17, 1934, page 6.

871. Scott Holl, *The Stones Cry Out: Congregations of the Evangelical Synod of North America in the City of St. Louis, 1834–2005* (St. Louis: Archives of the Evangelical Synod of North America, Eden Theological Seminary, 2005).

BETHANY EVANGELICAL, established in 1867, merged with Peace UCC in 1970, located at 11952 Bellefontaine Road in Bellefontaine Neighbors. Bethany formerly located at 1) 22nd Street and Franklin Avenue, 2) 23rd Street and Wash Avenue, 3) Red Bud and Rosalie Streets.[872]

BETHEL EVANGELICAL, established in 1901, located at 14700 New Halls Ferry Road in Florissant, formerly at Garrison and Greer Avenues.[873]

CARONDELET EVANGELICAL, established in 1869, located at 7423 Michigan Avenue.[874]

CHRIST THE KING, established in 1856 as Independent German Evangelical Protestant, now located at 11370 Old Halls Ferry Road in Florissant, formerly at 1) 8th and Mound Streets, 2) 13th and Tyler Streets, and 3) Fair Avenue and Margaretta Street.[875]

EBENEZER EVANGELICAL, established in 1886, closed 1964, formerly located at 2911 McNair Avenue. This congregation merged with St. Andrew Church and formed Epiphany UCC in 1964.[876]

EDEN–IMMANUEL, established in 1919 when Eden Church, established 1894, merged with Immanuel, founded 1889, closed 1971, formerly located at 5630 Page Avenue at Temple Avenue.[877]

EPIPHANY, established in 1964 with the merger of St. Andrew and Ebenezer, formerly located at 2911 McNair Avenue.[878]

EVANGELICAL CHURCH OF THE REDEEMER, established in 1910, located at 6450 South Kingshighway Boulevard.[879]

EVANGELICAL PROTESTANT CHURCH OF HOLY GHOST, "Holy Ghost" established in 1834, closed 2007, located at 4916 Mardel Avenue at Kingshighway Boulevard.[880]

---

872. "Bethany Evangelical a Growing Church," *St. Louis Star-Times*, August 6, 1934, page 5. Bethanie German Evangelical Church Burial Receipts, 1870–1953; Bethanie German Evangelical Burial, Baptisms, Marriages, Deaths, Confirmed, 1870–1960; Bethany Evangelical church records, 1859–1991; St. Louis County Library microfilm, Missouri State Archives M181–182.

873. *Bethel Evangelical and Reformed Church: Fiftieth Anniversary, 1901–1951* (St. Louis: The Church, 1951). "An Eminent Though Youthful Church," *St. Louis Star-Times*, January 23, 1933, page 15.

874. Carondelet United Church of Christ, *Carondelet United Church of Christ, One Hundredth Anniversary, 1869–1969* (St. Louis: The Church, 1969). *85th Anniversary, Carondelet Evangelical and Reformed Church, St. Louis, 1869–1954 (*St. Louis: The Church, 1954). Carondelet Evangelical church records; St. Louis County Library microfilm.

875. Christ the King Church records (formerly known as Independent Evangelical Protestant); St. Louis County Library microfilm.

876. Ebenezer Evangelical, 1886–1964; St. Louis County Library, microfilm; Missouri State Archives film M74.

877. Eden–Immanuel Church Records, 1892–1966; St. Louis County Library microfilm, Missouri State Archives film M76.

878. Refer to the Ebenezer Evangelical records.

879. "A Church Founded in Hay and Feed Store," *St. Louis Star-Times,* February 26, 1934. Evangelical Church of the Redeemer, 1911–1977; St. Louis County Library microfilm, Missouri State Archives film.

880. "A Century Passes for Holy Ghost Church," *St. Louis Star-Times,* October 22, 1934, page 11. Holy Ghost Evangelical Church records, 1833–1961; St. Louis County Library microfilm, Missouri State Archives films, M50–M55.

FRIEDENS EVANGELICAL, established in 1857, located at 1908 Newhouse Street.[881]

HOLY GHOST, see Evangelical Protestant Church of Holy Ghost.

INDEPENDENT EVANGELICAL PROTESTANT, established in 1856, located at 11370 Old Halls Ferry Road in Florissant. This church was located at 1) 8th and Mound Streets, 2) 13th and Tyler Streets, and 3) Fair Avenue and Margaretta Street.[882] See Christ the King Church.

JESUS EVANGELICAL, established in 1894, closed in 2000, formerly located at 12th and Victor Streets.[883]

NAZARETH EVANGELICAL, established in 1903, closed in 1994, formerly located at Morganford Road and Tholozan Avenue.[884]

PARKWAY UNITED CHURCH OF CHRIST, established in 1838 as the Zion German Evangelical Church, located at 2840 Ballas Road in Town and Country. Some family records are available online thanks to volunteer indexer Robert Buecher.[885]

ST. JAMES EVANGELICAL, established in 1869, closed in 1979, formerly located at Blair and College Avenues.[886]

ST. JOHN EVANGELICAL, established in 1852, located 4136 Grand Boulevard near Lee Avenue, formerly at 14th and Madison Streets.[887] The affiliated cemetery is on St. Cyr Road.

ST. JOHN EVANGELICAL, established in 1850, located at 332 Old Sulphur Springs Road in Manchester.[888]

ST. JOHN EVANGELICAL, established in 1838, located at 11333 St. John's Church Road in Mehlville.[889]

---

881. "Carrying on Lofty Church Traditions," *St. Louis Star-Times,* December 1, 1932, page 2. "Friedens Church Here to Observe 75th Anniversary," *St. Louis Star-Times,* October 21, 1932, page 19. Friedens Church records, 1858–1942; St. Louis County Library microfilm.

882. "A St. Louis Church With Liberal Views," *St. Louis Star-Times,* October 8, 1934, page 13. Independent Evangelical church records, 1856–1965; St. Louis County Library microfilm.

883. "Jesus Evangelical a Sturdy Church," *St. Louis Star-Times,* March 18, 1935, page 5. Jesus Evangelical church records, 1883–1963; St. Louis County Library microfilm.

884. "A Church That Grew in a Crowded Field," *St. Louis Star-Times,* February 11, 1935, page 6.

885. "Parkway United Church of Christ," Archives of Eden Seminary (http://library.webster .edu/luhr_library/guides/stl_guide_records_links.html).

886. *75th Anniversary, 1869–1939, St. James Evangelical Church, St. Louis, Missouri* (St. Louis: The Church, 1939). "A Church Distinguished for Its Athletics," *St. Louis Star-Times,* March 13, 1933, page 11. St. James Evangelical church records 1886–1982; St. Louis County Library, microfilm. St. James Church Collection, Missouri Historical Society.

887. "Pioneer Germans Built This Church," *St. Louis Star-Times,* September 11, 1933, page 17. *A Century of Faith: St. John Evangelical and Reformed* (St. Louis: The Church, 1952). St. John Evangelical church records, 1853–1981; St. Louis County Library microfilm.

888. *St. John United Church of Christ, Manchester, Missouri* (Manchester: History Committee of St. John, 1994). Betty (Krueger) Sandsted, *St. John UCC, 1863–1989* (Manchester: The Church, 1989). "Manchester, Mo., Church Celebrates 75th Year," *St. Louis Star-Times,* September 2, 1935, page 5. St. John UCC Church records 1860–1994; St. Louis County Library microfilm.

889. *St. John United Church of Christ, Mehlville, Missouri, 1838–1988* (St. Louis: The Church, 1988). St. John Evangelical church records; St. Louis County Library microfilm.

ST. JOHN UNITED CHURCH OF CHRIST, established in 1892, located at 15370 Olive Boulevard in Chesterfield.[890]

ST. LUCAS UNITED CHURCH OF CHRIST, established in 1880, located at 11735 Denny Road in Sappington. This church has an affiliated cemetery.[891]

ST. LUKE EVANGELICAL, established in 1870, located at 2336 Tennessee Avenue.[892]

ST. MARCUS EVANGELICAL, established 1843, located at 2102A Russell Avenue. This church has an affiliated cemetery.[893]

ST. MATTHEWS EVANGELICAL, established in 1875, located at 2613 Potomac Street.[894] The affiliated cemetery is located at 4360 Bates Street.

ST. PAUL'S EVANGELICAL, established 1854, located at 9801 Warson Road, Creve Coeur. Thanks to indexer Linda Reichert, some records are available online at Rootsweb, accessible via a link through the Archives at Eden Seminary.[895]

ST. PAUL UNITED CHURCH OF CHRIST, established in 1844, located at 5508 Telegraph Road in Oakville.[896]

ST. PAUL UNITED CHURCH OF CHRIST, established 1848, located at 3510 Giles Avenue at Potomac Avenue.[897]

---

890. St. John's Historical Book Committee, *St. John's United Church of Christ, Chesterfield, Missouri, 1892–1992: 100th anniversary* (Chesterfield: The Church, 1992).

891. Linda Borgstede, *A History of St. Lucas United Church of Christ, 1880–1980* (St. Louis: The Church, 1980). St. Lucas Evangelical records, 1880–1947; St. Louis County Library microfilm.

892. "St. Luke's Evangelical Approaches 65th Year," *St. Louis Star-Times,* December 31, 1934, page 4. St. Luke's Evangelical church records; 1870–1976; St. Louis County Library microfilm and Missouri State Archives film M83.

893. *St. Marcus Evangelical and Reformed Church, St. Louis, Mo., Erich E. Leibner, Pastor: Souvenir Published to Commemorate the Celebration of the One Hundredth Anniversary of the Founding of the Congregation, July 16, 1843* (St. Louis: St. Louis County Library, Special Collections Department, 2004). "St. Marcus United Church of Christ," Eden Seminary Archives. "St. Marcus Church Has a Birthday—Its 90th," *St. Louis Star-Times,* June 12, 1933, page 15.

894. "St. Matthews Nears Its 60th Birthday," *St. Louis Star-Times,* April 23, 1934, page 20. St. Matthews Evangelical church records, 1875–1977; St. Louis County Library microfilm and Missouri State Archives film M65–66.

895. *Dedication by the Grace of God and to His Glory: St. Paul's Evangelical Church (United Church of Christ), Creve Coeur, Missouri, October 1961* (Creve Coeur: The Church, 1961). "St. Paul's Evangelical Church, Creve Coeur," *Eden Seminary Archives* (http://freepages.genealogy.rootsweb .com/~lindainmo/st_pauls/webimages/index.html).

896. *One Hundredth Anniversary, 1844–1944: St. Paul's Evangelical and Reformed Church* (Lemay: The Church, 1944). St. Paul Evangelical church records 1844–1971; St. Louis County Library microfilm, and Missouri State Archives film M75.

897. St. Paul UCC church records; St. Louis County Library microfilm.

ST. PETER EVANGELICAL, established in 1843 as the German Evangelical Congregation in St. Louis, located at 6905 St. Louis Avenue in Ferguson, originally located at 15th and Carr Streets, then moved to Warne and St. Louis Avenues and now in Ferguson. This church founded St. Peter's Cemetery on Lucas and Hunt Road in St. Louis County.[898]

ST. STEPHEN EVANGELICAL, established in 1896, located at 8500 Hall's Ferry Road in Baden.[899]

SALVATOR EVANGELICAL, established in 1906, closed in 1979, formerly located at Plover Avenue and Thekla Street in the Walnut Park area of St. Louis.[900]

TRINITY EVANGELICAL, established in 1893, located at 4708 South Grand Avenue at Itaska Street, formerly called German Evangelical Trinity Church of St. Louis.[901]

ZION EVANGELICAL, established in 1838, now named Parkway UCC, located on 2840 North Ballas Road in Town and Country.[902]

ZION UNITED CHURCH OF CHRIST, established in 1868, located at 5710 North Highway 67 in Florissant, originally located at 25th Street and Benton Street in the City. The church operates Zion Cemetery located on St. Charles Rock Road.[903]

OTHER RELIGIOUS CONGREGATIONS

CHURCH OF THE MESSIAH UNITARIAN, established in 1853, formerly located on Pine Street.[904]

CHURCH OF THE UNITY, established in 1868, formerly located at Park and Armstrong Drives.[905]

FIRST CHURCH, CHRIST SCIENTIST, established in 1894, formerly located at 28th and Pine Streets.[906]

---

898. *One Hundredth Anniversary of St. Peter's Evangelical Church, 1843–1943* (St. Louis: The Church, 1943). St. Peter's United Church of Christ records; Eden Seminary Archives (http://library .webster.edu/ luhr_library/guides/stl_guide_records_links.html). "St. Peter's Evangelical Passes 90th Milestone," *St. Louis Star-Times,* November 6, 1933, page 18. Also, St. Peter's Evangelical, church records, 1843–1980; St. Louis County Library microfilm and Missouri Archives microfilm.

899. "St. Stephen's Evangelical, Baden's Growing Church," *St. Louis Star-Times,* May 27, 1935, page 22. St. Louis County Library microfilm.

900. "A Church Founded by German Women," *St. Louis Star-Times,* June 10, 1935, page 9. Salvator Evangelical Church records, 1907–1980; St. Louis County Library microfilm.

901. Trinity Church records 1894–1991; St. Louis County Library, microfilm "Trinity Evangelical Nears 42nd Milestone," *St. Louis Star-Times,* October 21, 1935, page 11.

902. "A Church That Outgrew Three Log Cabins," *St. Louis Star-Times,* April 1, 1935, page 7. Zion Evangelical Church records, 1838–1968; St. Louis County Library microfilm.

903. *One Hundredth Anniversary of the Founding of Zion United Church of Christ: 25th and Benton Streets, St Louis, Missouri, 1868–1968* (St. Louis: St. Louis County Library, Special Collections, 2006). German Evangelical Zion Church records; St. Louis County Library microfilm.

904. Walter Samuel Swisher, *A History of the Church of the Messiah, 1834–1934* (St. Louis: The Church, 1934). "A Church That Sowed Intellectual Seeds," *St. Louis Star-Times,* January 26, 1933, page 21.

905. Church of the Unity, *Church of the Unity [Unitarian], Waterman Avenue and Kingshighway, Saint Louis* (St. Louis, The Church, no date). "A Center of Unitarian Culture Here," *St. Louis Star-Times,* December 5, 1932, page 6.

906. "Progress of Christian Science Here Rapid," *St. Louis Star-Times,* December 12, 1932, page 4.

FIRST CHURCH, CHRIST SCIENTIST IN UNIVERSITY CITY, established in 1921, formerly located at 6670 Delmar Boulevard in University City.[907]

FIRST CHURCH OF GOD, established in 1890, formerly located at Newstead Avenue and Penrose Street.[908]

FIRST CHURCH OF NAZARENE, established in 1918, formerly located at Delmar Boulevard and Pendleton Avenue.[909]

FIRST CHURCH OF THE NEW JERUSALEM, established in 1842, formerly located at 6th and St. Charles Streets.[910]

ST. MICHAEL THE ARCHANGEL RUSSIAN ORTHODOX, established in 1927, located at 1901 Ann Avenue at Gravois Road. Archangel Michael's Russian Orthodox Greek and Catholic Church was the original name for this church.[911]

ST. NICOLAS GREEK ORTHODOX, established in 1917, located at 4967 Forest Park Avenue.[912]

STS. CYRIL AND METHODIUS, established in 1907, located at 11th and Chambers Streets. This Polish congregation left St. Casimir's Catholic Church and the Catholic Church, forming this independent church.[913]

---

907. "Christian Science Church Flourishes in U. City," *St. Louis Star-Times,* January 12, 1933, page 18.

908. "Church of God Shows Growth in St. Louis," *St. Louis Star-Times,* September 16, 1935, page 8.

909. "A Nazarene Congregation That Grew Rapidly," *St. Louis Star-Times,* August 13, 1934, page 11.

910. "A Church Composed of Swedenborgians," *St. Louis Star-Times,* June 19, 1933, page 18.

911. *65th Anniversary, 1909–1974: St. Michael the Archangel Russian Orthodox Church* (St. Louis: The Church, 1974). "Religion of Old Russia Lives in St. Louis," *St. Louis Star-Times,* December 8, 1932, page 2.

912. *Seventy-fifth Anniversary Album 1917–1992: Saint Nicholas Greek Orthodox Church, 4967 Forest Park Boulevard, Saint Louis, Missouri* (St. Louis: The Church, 1992).

913. *50th Anniversary, 1907–1957, St. Cyril and Methodius Polish Catholic Church* (St. Louis: The Church, 1957). "Polish National Church Has Its Silver Jubilee," *St. Louis Star-Times,* November 4, 1935, page 13.

Wills and Probate Records

Wills and probate records often contain proof of kinship to the deceased's individual spouse, children, and sometimes grandchildren; location of current and previous residence; and the value of the estate, often with a list of the household goods. The estate inventory may provide clues to the occupation or social status of the family. Was there a book collection or did he have carpenter tools? Did he have farmer's equipment that helped him till the soil, harvest the crops, and feed the livestock? Is the will written in the hand of the ancestor, perhaps just days or maybe years before he died? Or, perhaps a scribe penned the document with the ancestor signing with his mark. Wills and probate records can open new avenues of research for most family historians.

Our ancestors recorded wills at the courthouse. The court clerk transcribed the information in the will book, thus making it a derivative source, not the original. The transcription may be the only version that has survived. The probate packet may or may not contain the original will along with other documents. Probate packages may be full of important documents and receipts or just contain a few loose documents. The purpose of the probate action is to distribute the estate of the deceased. In order to do that, the names and sometimes the addresses of the heirs are included in the packet. If a person died without a spouse, child, or grandchildren, the distribution extended to the collateral family. The court had to locate all siblings or maybe even cousins, possibly with a chart showing the relationship. The file most likely contains the names and addresses of the heirs as of the distribution date. By putting all of these clues together, you will probably find new information.

WILLS

St. Louis County — Before 1877

When the City-County separation occurred, the City retained the original St. Louis County will books dating from 1816 to 1876. The will books are available on microfilm at several repositories.[914]

---

914. "St. Louis Probate Court Digitization Project: 1802–1900," *Missouri State Archives* (http://www .sos.mo.gov/archives/stlprobate/default.asp). St. Louis City Will Books (Probate Court); Missouri State Archives microfilm dating from 1900–1967.

St. Louis Genealogical Society published the *St. Louis Probate Records, 1804–1876*; however, this four-volume publication actually provides abstracts and an index of the will books from 1804 to 1876. The publication also includes probate information for the St. Louis Spanish Archives, 1766–1804.[915]

St. Louis County — After 1876

ST. LOUIS COUNTY WILL BOOKS

The newly-formed government of St. Louis County started retaining wills and other documents in 1877. The County microfilmed the will books and records dating from 1877 to 1969, which are available at St. Louis County Library, Special Collections. The old will books are stored off site; therefore, microfilm is usually the only option even visiting the St. Louis County Government Center.

St. Louis County Wills Index, 1878–1976 (Probate Court) consists of four volumes of indexes on two rolls of microfilm. In 1951, the DAR indexed *Will Book 1, 1875–1889,* which is available in book form. All of this information is available at St. Louis County Library, Special Collections.[916] The indexes will expedite your search.

To search for a will, locate the name of the deceased in the index, which is alphabetical by the first letter of the surname, then arranged by date of filing. As an example, search for Samuel James, who died on 15 July 1898. By knowing the date or approximate year of death, it provides a guideline for the chronological search. The name Samuel James is listed in index volume 1 under "J" and then search chronologically to August 1898. The will index states that Samuel's will was filed on 8 August 1898 and recorded in book 3, page 174.

St. Louis County Library, Special Collections has County will books 1 to 46 (1877–1969) available on microfilm. Each will book has its own index in the front of the book and should match the overall index information. Using Samuel James again as an example, book 3, page 174 reveals the beginning of Samuel James' will. It is four pages and lists his wife and children by name. The will provides the married name of his daughters and his sons-in-law. It lists the acreage, section, township, and range with a diagram for all of the property left to his heirs. Wills are often worth the search. However, the signatures of the heirs and witnesses in the will books are those of the recorder, not the ancestors.

St. Louis City — After 1876

ST. LOUIS CITY WILL BOOKS

The original will books are housed in the Probate Court office in the Civil Courts Building. St. Louis City wills are available from 1877 to 1976. The Family History Library has City will books, 1917–1967, which include an index in the front of each book.[917] These records are typed for easy reading; however, be aware that errors occur any time records are transcribed. The film is available at St. Louis Public Library and St. Louis County Library Special Collections.

---

915.   St. Louis Genealogical Society, *St. Louis and St. Louis County, Missouri, Probate Records,* 4 volumes (St. Louis: The Society, 1989).

916.   Daughters of the American Revolution, St. Louis Chapter, *Will Book 1, St. Louis County, Missouri, 1875–1889* (St. Louis: DAR, 1951).

917.   St. Louis City Will Books, 1917–1967; FHL beginning 466,098.

PROBATE RECORDS

St. Louis County — Before 1877

ST. LOUIS COUNTY PROBATE

Missouri State Archives has digitized all probate packets for the County from 1802 to 1876 and City packets from 1877 to 1900. The Archives has microfilmed many beyond that date. A scanned image of the documents from 1802 to 1900 appears online making a probate search for that time period very easy. Researchers can save or print the images. The index lists only the name of the deceased, not the heirs, executors, administrators, or witnesses.[918]

St. Louis City — After 1876

ST. LOUIS CITY PROBATE

St. Louis City Probate Office (Civil Courts Building, 10 North Tucker Boulevard, St. Louis, 63103; phone 314-622-4301; http://stlcin.missouri.org/FAQs/displaytopiclist.cfm) is located on the tenth floor. Many of the records are available at the Missouri State Archives in Jefferson City, or at its St. Louis branch. As the microfilming progresses, the original records are archived. A phone call to the Probate office will help you determine the location of your record(s) of interest.

A card file maintained at the Probate office downtown has the name of the deceased, the date of the transaction, and the probate file number as seen in Figure 48. Missouri State Archives microfilmed this card file and it is available at the Archives and at St. Louis County Library, Special Collections. The probate information listed on the cards divides the records into one of four categories:

1. Estates of Deceased Persons before 1890 and Guardianships Before 1890

2. Estates of Deceased Persons After 1890

3. Guardianships After 1890

4. Letters of Refusal, Wills Proved, No Letters Granted, Unproved/Rejected Wills

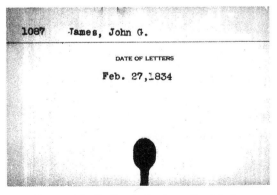

Figure 48: St. Louis Probate Card Index

---

918. "St. Louis Probate Court Digitization Project: 1802–1900," *Missouri State Archives* (http://www.sos.mo.gov/archives/stlprobate/default.asp).

St. Louis County — After 1876

ST. LOUIS COUNTY PROBATE

St. Louis County Probate Index to Closed Estates, 1877–2006 on microfiche offers a quick overview of the probate packets available in the County after the separation. The index is alphabetical by the first letter of the surname, then chronological.

As an example, the index provides the researcher the probate record number for Samuel James, file 1522, with the letters filed on 8 August 1898, and the final settlement on 26 November 1900 with Virginia James and Alphonso James serving as the executors. The entire probate record is on microfilm; therefore, it is possible to print, review, and analyze each page of the record looking for names, dates, and places.

The Probate Court also handles wards of the court. These records, dated 1877–1973, arranged alphabetically by the first letter of the surname, then chronologically, provide the name of the ward of the court, the date of the appointment, guardian or curator's name, amount of the bond, settlement date, and disposition of the estate.[919]

The Missouri State Archives and St. Louis County Library have microfilm of the probate and will indexes, registers, and records for St. Louis County.[920]

The St. Louis County Register of the Deceased is a computer-generated file arranged by estate file number. It gives the name of the deceased, executor, and bills paid, which include the name of the person or organization, the amount of the payment, and date.[921]

Probate Vocabulary

Administrator = a male appointed by the court to manage the estate of a decedent

Administratrix = a female appointed by the court to manage the estate of a decedent

Dower = women received one third of the property value upon the death of the husband

Estate = the assets and liabilities of a decedent

Executor = person named in a will to manage the estate of a decedent

Intestate = to die without a will

Probate = the process of administering the estate of a decedent

Testate = to die leaving a will

---

919.   St. Louis County Index to Wards, 1877–1973; Missouri State Archives film C16376.
920.   St. Louis County Probate Index, 1877–1977; Missouri State Archives film beginning C14823. St. Louis County Probate Registers (arranged by estate number); Missouri State Archives film C13487.
921.   St. Louis County Register of Deceased; Missouri State Archives film C13160.

Current Location of Records

DOWNTOWN
Location for all St. Louis records filed
before 1877 and City records after 1876.

RECORDER OF DEEDS OFFICE — City Hall
Marriage Records
- 1804–present
  - 1804–1876 StLGS printed index
  - 1804–1883 marriage records available at SLCL, SLPL
  - 1883–1965 marriage indexes at SLCL, SLPL
  - 1804–1965 marriages FHL

Deed Records
- 1804–present
  - 1804–1900 index SLCL, SLPL, FHL
  - 1900–present, indexes at City Hall

CIRCUIT COURT — Civil Courts Building
Probate Records (Missouri Archives is microfilming
these records; therefore, the location of the original
records may vary based on the filming schedule.)
- 1804–present
  - 1804–1900 digitized and available online at MoArchives website.
  - 1900–1930 in process at Missouri Archives (may be located at Archives St. Louis branch)
  - 1931–present at Probate Office

Divorce Records (Request document by mail,
providing name of parties and approximate date or date
range.)
- 1804–present

Naturalization Records (Most post-September 1906
records are federal records)
- Pre-September 1906 index online StLGS, MoArchives websites
- Pre-September 1906 microfilm at SLCL, SLPL, FHL

Civil & Criminal Court Cases (Some records and a
database available online at MoArchives)
- 1804–present (request by mail only)

CORONERS' OFFICE — Clark Street
Coroners' Records
- 1800s–1900 index online MoArchives
- 1800s–1900 microfilm SLCL, SLPL
- 1900–present (request by phone or mail)

CLAYTON
All St. Louis County records after 1876.

RECORDER OF DEEDS OFFICE — Government
Center
Marriage Records (request by phone or mail)
- 1877–present
  - 1877–1980 marriages at SLCL, FHL
  - 1877–1980 marriage index microfilm SLCL

Deed Records
- 1877–present
  - 1877–1931 microfilm at SLCL
  - 1877–1886 microfilm at FHL

Probate Records
- 1877–present (order records by mail)
  - 1877–1980 index on microfiche SLCL, SLPL, StLGS

CIRCUIT COURT — Courts Building
Probate Records
- 1876– present at Probate office
  - 1876–July 2006 microfiche available SLCL

Divorce Records (Request documents by mail,
providing name of parties and approximate date or
date range if known.)
- 1877–present

Naturalization Records
- 1877–1906 index online at SLCL
(Federal post-Sept. 1906 index online at SLCL)

Civil and Criminal Court Cases (request by mail)
- 1877–present

CORONERS' OFFICE — St. Louis County
Coroners' Records (request by mail only.)
- 1944–present

ABBREVIATIONS:
Family History Library = FHL
Missouri State Archives = MoArchives
St. Louis County Library = SLCL
St. Louis Genealogical Society = StLGS
St. Louis Public Library = SLPL

Appendix B

Alphabetical Contact List

ARCHDIOCESE OF ST. LOUIS ARCHIVES
20 Archbishop May Drive
Webster Groves, Missouri 63119
314-792-7020
(http://www.archstl.org/archives)

ARCHIVES AT EDEN SEMINARY
Luhr Library
475 E. Lockwood Avenue
Webster Groves, Missouri 63119
314-252-3140
(http://www.eden.edu/index.php/archives)

BELLEFONTAINE CEMETERY
4947 West Florissant Boulevard
St. Louis, Missouri 63115
314-381-0750

BRODSKY JEWISH COMMUNITY LIBRARY
12 Millstone Campus Drive
St. Louis, Missouri 63146
314-442-3720
(http://brodskylibrary.org/aboutus.php)

CALVARY CEMETERY
5239 West Florissant Boulevard
St. Louis, Missouri 63115
314-381-1313

CARONDELET HISTORICAL SOCIETY
6303 Michigan Avenue
St. Louis, Missouri 63111
314-481-6303

CATHOLIC CEMETERIES OF THE ARCHDIOCESE
(http://www.stlcathcem.com/iSearch.aspx)

CONCORDIA HISTORICAL INSTITUTE
804 Seminary Place
Clayton, Missouri 63105
314-505-7935
(http://chi.lcms.org)

EPISCOPAL DIOCESE OF MISSOURI
1210 Locust Street
St. Louis, Missouri 63103
314-231-1220
(http://www.diocesemo.org)

FAMILY HISTORY CENTER, FRONTENAC
10445 Clayton Road
Frontenac, Missouri 63131
314-993-2328

FAMILY HISTORY CENTER, HAZELWOOD
6386 Howdershell Road
Hazelwood, Missouri 63042
314-731-5373

FAMILY HISTORY LIBRARY
35 North West Temple Street
Salt Lake City, Utah 84150
(http://www.familysearch.org)

FAMILY HISTORY LIBRARY CATALOG
(http://www.familysearch.org)

JEFFERSON BARRACKS NATIONAL CEMETERY
101 Memorial Drive
St. Louis, Missouri 63125
314-263-8691
(http://www.cem.va.gov/CEM/cems/nchp/
jeffersonbarracks.asp#hi)

JEFFERSON COUNTY HISTORICAL SOCIETY
c/o DeSoto Public Library
71 Main Street
DeSoto, Missouri 63020
(http://www.rootsweb.com/~mojchs/about.html)

LAW LIBRARY ASSOCIATION OF ST. LOUIS
Civil Court Building
10 North Tucker Street
St. Louis, Missouri 63101
314-622-4386
(http://tlc.library.net/lla/default.asp)

MADISON COUNTY GENEALOGICAL SOCIETY
Post Office Box 631
Edwardsville, Illinois 62025
(http://www.rootsweb.com/~ilmadcgs)

MERCANTILE LIBRARY
University of Missouri—St. Louis
Thomas Jefferson Library
One University Boulevard
St. Louis, Missouri 63121
314-516-7240
(http://www.umsl.edu/mercantile)

MISSOURI DEPARTMENT OF HEALTH AND SENIOR
SERVICES
930 Wildwood Street
Post Office Box 570
Jefferson City, Missouri 65102
573-751-6378
(http://www.dhss.mo.gov/index.html)

MISSOURI HISTORICAL SOCIETY RESEARCH LIBRARY
225 South Skinker Boulevard
Clayton, Missouri 63105
314-746-4500
(http://www.mohistory.org)

MISSOURI STATE ARCHIVES
600 West Main Street
Post Office Box 1747
Jefferson City, Missouri 65102
573-751-3280
(http://www.sos.mo.gov/archives)

MISSOURI STATE ARCHIVES–ST. LOUIS BRANCH
Globe Democrat Building
710 North Tucker Street
St. Louis, Missouri 63101
314-588-1746
(http://www.sos.mo.gov/archives)

MONROE COUNTY GENEALOGICAL SOCIETY
Post Office Box 381
Columbia, Illinois 62236
(http://www.rootsweb.com/~ilmcghs)

NATIONAL ARCHIVES–CENTRAL PLAINS REGION
2312 East Bannister Road
Kansas City, Missouri 64131
816-268-8000
(http://www.archives.gov/central-plains/kansas-city)

NATIONAL PARK SERVICE, OLD COURTHOUSE
Jefferson National Expansion Memorial
Old Courthouse
11 North Fourth Street
St. Louis, Missouri 63102
314-655-1700
(http://www.nps.gov/jeff)

NATIONAL PARK SERVICE, WHITE HAVEN
Visitor's Center
7400 Grant Road
St. Louis, Missouri 63123
314-842-3298
(http://www.nps.gov/ulsg)

NARA CIVILIAN PERSONNEL RECORDS CENTER
111 Winnebago Street
St. Louis, Missouri 63118
314-801-9250
(http://www.archives.gov/st-louis/civilian-personnel/index.html)

NARA MILITARY PERSONNEL RECORDS CENTER
9700 Page Avenue
St. Louis, Missouri 63132
314-801-0800
(http://www.archives.gov/st-louis/military-personnel/public/archival-programs.html)

PRESBYTERIAN CHURCH OF AMERICA HISTORICAL
CENTER
12330 Conway Road
Creve Coeur, Missouri 63141
314-469-9077
(http://www.pcahistory.org/collections.html)

ST. CHARLES COUNTY HISTORICAL SOCIETY
101 South Main Street
St. Charles, Missouri 63301-2802
636-946-9828
(http://www.youranswerplace.org/other/historical_society)

ST. CLAIR COUNTY GENEALOGICAL SOCIETY
Post Office Box 431
Belleville, Illinois 62222
(http://www.stclair-ilgs.org/stchome.htm)

ST. LOUIS ARGUS OBITUARIES
(http://previous.slpl.org.libsrc/argusobit.htm)

ST. LOUIS CITY ASSESSOR'S OFFICE
St. Louis City Hall
1200 Market Street, Room 114
St. Louis, Missouri 63103
314-622-3212

ST. LOUIS CITY CIRCUIT COURT OFFICE
Civil Courts Building
10 North Tucker Street, 1st Floor
St. Louis, Missouri 63101
314-622-4405

ST. LOUIS CITY COMPTROLLER'S ARCHIVES
St. Louis City Hall
1200 Market Street, Room 1
St. Louis, Missouri 63103
314-622-4274

ST. LOUIS CITY MEDICAL EXAMINER'S OFFICE
1300 Clark Street
St. Louis, Missouri 63101
314-622-4971
(http://stlouis.missouri.org/government/medex
.html)

ST LOUIS CITY PROBATE COURT OFFICE
Civil Courts Building
10 North Tucker Street, 10th Floor
St. Louis, Missouri 63101
314-622-4301

ST. LOUIS CITY RECORDER OF DEEDS OFFICE
St. Louis City Hall
1200 Market Street, Room 127
St. Louis, Missouri 63103
314-622-4610
(http://stlouis.missouri.org/citygov/recorder)

ST. LOUIS COUNTY COURTS BUILDING
7900 Carondelet Avenue
Clayton, Missouri 63105
314-615-5000 [General Information]
(http://www.co.st-louis.mo.us)

ST. LOUIS COUNTY GOVERNMENT CENTER
41 South Central Avenue
Clayton, Missouri 63105
314-615-5000 [General Information]
(http://www.co.st-louis.mo.us)

ST. LOUIS COUNTY LAW LIBRARY
7900 Carondelet Avenue, 5th Floor
Clayton, Missouri 63105
314-615-4726

ST. LOUIS COUNTY LIBRARY
Special Collections Department
1640 South Lindbergh Boulevard
St. Louis, Missouri 63131
314-994-3300
(http://www.slcl.org)

ST. LOUIS COUNTY MEDICAL EXAMINER'S OFFICE
6039 Helen Avenue
St. Louis, Missouri 63134
314-522-3262
(http://www.stlouisco.com/doh/medexam/medexam.html)

ST. LOUIS COUNTY PROBATE OFFICE
Courts Building
7900 Carondelet Avenue
Clayton, Missouri 63105
314-615-2629
(http://www.stlouisco.com/circuit
court/probate.html)

ST. LOUIS COUNTY RECORDER OF DEEDS OFFICE
Administration Building
41 South Central Avenue
Clayton, Missouri 63105
314-615-3747
(http://revenue.stlouisco.com/RecorderOfDeeds)

ST. LOUIS COUNTY VITAL RECORDS
Birth and Death Certificates
111 South Meramec Avenue
Clayton, Missouri 63105
314-615-0376
(http://www.stlouisco.com/doh/vitals/vitals.html)

ST. LOUIS GENEALOGICAL SOCIETY
4 Sunnen Drive, Suite 140
St. Louis, Missouri 63143
314-647-8547
(http://www.stlgs.org)

ST. LOUIS POST-DISPATCH OBITUARIES
(http://www.slpl.lib.mo.us/lkibsrc/obit.htm)

ST. LOUIS PUBLIC LIBRARY
1301 Olive Boulevard
St. Louis, Missouri 63103
314-241-2288
(http://www.slpl.org)

ST. LOUIS PUBLIC SCHOOL DISTRICT
Student Record Room
801 North 11th Street
St. Louis, Missouri 63101
314-231-3720
(http://www.slps.org/slps_history/index.htm)

ST. LOUIS UNIVERSITY PIUS XII MEMORIAL LIBRARY
3650 Lindell Boulevard
St. Louis, Missouri 63108
314-977-3580
(http://www.slu.edulibraries/pius)

STATE HISTORICAL SOCIETY OF MISSOURI
1020 Lowry Street
Columbia, Missouri 65201
573-882-7083
(http://www.umsystem.edu/shs)

THOMAS JEFFERSON LIBRARY
University of Missouri–St. Louis Campus
One University Boulevard
St. Louis, Missouri 63121
314-516-5060
(http://www.umsl.edu/services/tjl)

WASHINGTON HISTORICAL SOCIETY
(FRANKLIN COUNTY)
4th and Market Streets
Washington, Missouri 63090
636-239-0280
(http://www.washmohistorical.org/index.htm)

WASHINGTON UNIVERSITY OLIN LIBRARY
One Brookings Drive
St. Louis, Missouri 63130
314-935-5444
(http://www.library.wustl.edu/unitsspec/archives)

WASHINGTON UNIVERSITY WEST CAMPUS LIBRARY
7425 Forsyth Boulevard, Lower Level
Clayton, Missouri 63105
314-935-9889
(http://library.wust.edu/unitswestcampus)

WESTERN HISTORICAL MANUSCRIPT COLLECTION
Thomas Jefferson Library
University of Missouri–St. Louis Campus
One University Boulevard
St. Louis, Missouri 63121
314-516-5143
(http://www.umsl.edu/~whmc)

Index

This index includes names, locations, and subjects. Excluded from this index are St. Louis City and St. Louis County locations since they appear on virtually every page. Cemetery and newspaper names provided in the alphabetical lists are not included in the index.

—G—